ECOLOGICAL
THINKING

Studies in Feminist Philosophy is designed to showcase cutting-edge monographs and collections that display the full range of feminist approaches to philosophy, that push feminist thought in important new directions, and that display the outstanding quality of feminist philosophical thought.

STUDIES IN FEMINIST PHILOSOPHY
Cheshire Calhoun, *Series Editor*

Published in the series:
Abortion and Social Responsibility: Depolarizing the Debate
Lauri Shrage

Gender in the Mirror: Confounding Imagery
Diana Tietjens Meyers

Autonomy, Gender, Politics
Marilyn Friedman

Setting the Moral Compass: Essays by Women Philosophers
Edited by Cheshire Calhoun

Burdened Virtues: Virtue Ethics for Liberatory Struggles
Lisa Tessman

On Female Body Experience: "Throwing Like a Girl" and Other Essays
Iris Marion Young

Visible Identities: Race, Gender, and the Self
Linda Martín Alcoff

Women and Citizenship
Edited by Marilyn Friedman

Ecological Thinking: The Politics of Epistemic Location
Lorraine Code

ECOLOGICAL

THINKING:

THE POLITICS OF

EPISTEMIC

LOCATION

Lorraine Code

OXFORD
UNIVERSITY PRESS

2006

OXFORD
UNIVERSITY PRESS

Oxford University Press, Inc., publishes works that further
Oxford University's objective of excellence
in research, scholarship, and education.

Oxford   New York
Auckland   Cape Town   Dar es Salaam   Hong Kong   Karachi
Kuala Lumpur   Madrid   Melbourne   Mexico City   Nairobi
New Delhi   Shanghai   Taipei   Toronto

With offices in
Argentina   Austria   Brazil   Chile   Czech Republic   France   Greece
Guatemala   Hungary   Italy   Japan   Poland   Portugal   Singapore
South Korea   Switzerland   Thailand   Turkey   Ukraine   Vietnam

Copyright © 2006 by Oxford University Press, Inc.

Published by Oxford University Press, Inc.
198 Madison Avenue, New York, New York 10016

www.oup.com

Oxford is a registered trademark of Oxford University Press

Library of Congress Cataloging-in-Publication Data
Code, Lorraine.
   Ecological thinking : the politics of epistemic location / Lorraine Code.
      p.   cm.
   Includes bibliographical references.
   ISBN-13 978-0-19-515944-8

   1. Knowledge, Sociology of.   2. Ecofeminism.   I. Title.

BD175.C56 2006
306.4'2—dc22   2005050875

Printed in the United States of America

This one is for Murray, for all the years

assumptions about isolated, abstract, formal knowledge claims advanced and evaluated in isolation from their circumstances of their making and the concrete conditions of their possibility and from their consequent situational effects. My thesis is that even the punctiform "*S*-knows-that-*p*" knowledge claims of exemplary status in orthodox Anglo-American epistemology can be articulated, heard, and enacted only by knowers inculcated into a form of life—a habitus and ethos—where conditions for their articulation and acknowledgment are already in place. More elaborated expressions or bodies of knowledge build on the same social, communal, situational conditions. Thus, as I show throughout this book, my position distances itself from the atomistic individualism according to which solitary individuals, extracted from the particularities of situation and place, can claim knowledge on the basis of their "own" unmediated observations. It distances itself, also, from theories for which knowledge is reliable insofar as it derives from an epistemic self-sufficiency that refuses epistemic interdependence, thus maintaining a principled distrust of testimony, from its simplest to its most elaborated forms.

On the view I elaborate in the 1987 book and uphold here, revised, reconfigured, and refined, people singly and collectively—indeed, singly *because* collectively—are *responsible* for what and how they know, on an understanding of responsibility that is as epistemological as it is ethical and political. In public and in more "private" knowledge alike, honoring such responsibilities is crucial to generating and maintaining trust. The position incorporates a healthy skepticism as a persistent backdrop against which trusting occurs: a skepticism of cautious circumspection, whose consequences are by no means nihilistic. Granting centrality to responsibility in this ecological framework affirms a pivotal role for consultative, deliberative, negotiated decisions in constructing, contesting, claiming, and circulating knowledge. Think, for example, of the choices—explicit or tacit—apparent in acknowledging or discounting gendered or racial implications of an episode of whistle-blowing, of environmental harms, or of workplace health issues. In the view I develop in this book, such choices are neither random, unconstrained, nor whimsical, for they are framed within a critical "normative realism," according to which knowledge construction is enabled and/or circumscribed by, but also responsible to, the evidence. Yet evidence is rarely self-announcing: establishing its status *as* evidence commonly requires careful deliberation, intricate negotiation, while honoring responsibilities can contribute to grounding knowledge reasonably well, if not as securely as epistemological foundationalists have hoped. Responsible, thoughtful practice mitigates against an epistemic chaos where trust could never be rational and where acknowledgment could rarely be justly claimed or conferred.

Preface

In my 1987 book, *Epistemic Responsibility*, I argue that a well-functioning epistemic community counts among its defining features an assumption that most of its members, most of the time and as a matter of course, can draw—if cautiously—upon a reservoir of beliefs about the soundness, the everyday reliability of other people's knowledge, in matters from the mundane to the esoteric. Intricate networks of *trust*, I suggest, are constitutive of the very possibility of viable epistemic lives and respectful coexistence. I name honoring such trust as integral to epistemic responsibility.

Yet *Epistemic Responsibility* relies on an excessively benign conception of community, imagined without contest to provide space for and uniform access to open debate, for deliberations neither cluttered by hidden agendas nor thwarted by searing disputes or tyrannical oppressions—thus imagined to enable a relatively smooth journey toward knowledge. While professing wariness of epistemic conformity and cautioning against beliefs in the capacity of consensus to produce truth, I represent communities and forms of life as more coherent than they could plausibly be, more like-minded in the place they accord to knowledge. Disagreements about knowledge production and evaluation appear more polite, more readily resolved, and with less at stake than the politics of knowledge I advance in this present book could allow. In short, I assume the matter-of-course, openly cooperative, constructively critical epistemic practice whose scarcity my discussion here deplores.

While its would-be knowers are as responsible *for* promoting and sustaining habitable epistemic community as they are *to* the evidence, the knowers who populate the pages of *Epistemic Responsibility* are caught within an ethos of the very liberal individualism I would eschew were I to rewrite the book. These are generic knowers, ethologically undifferentiated by their diverse "capacities for affecting and being affected" (in Gilles Deleuze's phrase) or by their positioning in a social order whose radical divisions along lines drawn by gender, race, class, materiality, ethnicity, sexual difference, and the myriad other asymmetries of epistemic situation are constitutive of the politics of knowledge. Implicitly, in the 1987 book, I assume their unmediated access to the "stuff" of which knowledge is made, imagining a self-transparency and epistemic-doxastic voluntarism, together with a faceless interchangeability of knowing subjects, firmly lodged within the social-ecological imaginary of a liberal society where cognitive autonomy is a universal possibility, and the acknowledgment upon which knowledge depends is unfettered by constraints consequent upon asymmetrical distributions of power and privilege.

Revisiting *Epistemic Responsibility* for its contribution to thinking about knowledge and public trust, I conclude, nonetheless, that its central regulative ideals are *right*, even though its imagined "individual" and community bring its conceptual apparatus up against its own limits. The examples I adduce in this new book combine to show how that apparatus needs to be reconfigured so as to incorporate awareness of the effects of geographical-ecological-material locations and of hierarchical social orders that enable, structure, and/or thwart practices of establishing, contesting, verifying, and justifying knowledge claims, whether scientific or secular, and of the constitutive effects of those practices for knowers, locations, and social orders. These reciprocal effects produce conditions within which epistemic responsibilities have to be negotiated, much more arduously than I had assumed, and where such responsibilities open out into concerns about how ecologically sensitive trust-promoting, democratic epistemic practices might be established to counter the excesses of demonstrably unjust social-political-epistemic orders.

The picture I now present is of an epistemic subjectivity and agency socially-culturally learned and practiced, for which community, ecologically conceived, is a condition sine qua non for the production, circulation, and acknowledgment of claims to know. Its articulation in the language of ecology, as I explain more fully in the chapters that follow, is intended to unsettle

Acknowledgments

This book, in its quest for conceptions of knowledge and subjectivity capable of informing transformative, responsible, and responsive epistemic practices, has been a long time in the making. It could not have emerged in its present form were it not for the people who, in their conversation, their work, and their critical-constructive engagement have helped me to develop the ideas I present here. Any list of such colleagues and friends will, inevitably, be incomplete, but I owe special thanks for their belief in the project and my capacity to bring it to fruition, and for encouragement along the way, to Linda Alcoff, Ayotunde Bewaji, Peta Bowden, Bettina Bradbury, Vincent Colapietro, Kathy Davis, Susan Ehrlich, Marilyn Frye, Joan Gibson, Heidi Grasswick, Genevieve (Jenny) Lloyd, Lynn Hankinson Nelson, Phyllis Rooney, Richard Schmitt, Kristin Shrader-Frechette, Rusty Shteir, and Nancy Tuana.

I have benefited enormously from opportunities to discuss these ideas-in-the-making at conferences and with university audiences too numerous to list in full. Outstanding among them are two sessions as guest lecturer (in 1996 and 2003) at NEH Summer Seminars on Feminist Epistemology, both organized by Nancy Tuana and in 2003 with Shannon Sullivan; a sabbatical year in

1995–96 as visiting scholar at the University of New South Wales in Sydney, Australia, at the invitation of Genevieve Lloyd (which included a six-week visiting fellowship at Marcquarie University at the invitation of Catriona Mackenzie), and a visiting lectureship at Rhodes University in South Africa in 2003, at the invitation of Tom Martin, Ward Jones, and Marius Vermaak.

Work on this book was launched with the support of a Walter Gordon Research Fellowship from York University in 1997–98 and much of the work that went into making it possible was supported by a Research Fellowship from the Canada Council Killam Foundation, which I held from 1999–2000. I extend my heartfelt thanks both to the Foundation, and to Carol Bream. I am grateful also for a YUFA sabbatical fellowship which allowed me to present work in progress at conferences and other meetings during my 2002–03 sabbatical leave. The contribution of all of these grants has been invaluable in providing the time and the means for concentrating on the development of the ideas I have articulated in these pages.

Early versions of the material presented in some of the chapters have been published elsewhere. Parts of chapter two appeared as "What Is Natural About Epistemology Naturalized?" *American Philosophical Quarterly*, vol. 33, no. 1, January 1996, 1–22, and reprinted in Lynn Hankinson Nelson and Jack Nelson, eds., *Feminist and Other Contemporary Interpretations of Quine*. University Park, PA: Penn State Press, 2003. An early version of chapter three appeared as "Statements of Fact: Whose? Where? When?" in Richmond Campbell and Bruce Hunter, eds., *Moral Epistemology Naturalized. Canadian Journal of Philosophy*, supp. vol. 26. Calgary: University of Calgary Press, 2001, 175–208; a preliminary version of chapter four is published as "Naming, Naturalizing, Normalizing: The Child as Fact and Artifact," in Patricia Miller and Ellin Scholnik, eds., *Toward a Feminist Developmental Psychology*. New York: Routledge, 2000; several sections of chapter five initially appeared as parts of "The Perversion of Autonomy and the Subjection of Women: Discourses of Social Advocacy at Century's End." In Catriona Mackenzie and Natalie Stoljar, eds., *Relational Autonomy*. New York: Oxford University Press, 2000; and an early version of chapter six is published as "Rational Imaginings, Responsible Knowings: How Far Can You See from Here?" in Nancy Tuana and Sandra Morgen, eds., *Engendering Rationalities*. Albany: State University of New York Press, 2001.

Cheshire Calhoun, in her capacity as editor of the Studies in Feminist Philosophy series, offered thoughtful, perceptive comments on the entire manuscript; Peter Ohlin at Oxford University Press has been an engaged and helpful editor since the inception of this project; Jessica Ryan and Lara Zoble have given excellent editorial support; and David Aiken was a fine copy editor. Once again, my thanks to Nicholas Humez for his splendid work in preparing the index. And special thanks to Ilya Parkins, who was an exceptionally good research assistant throughout the last stages of the project, providing invaluable assistance in many aspects of its production. I am grateful also to an anonymous reader for Oxford University Press.

My heartfelt thanks, as always, to Murray Code for his interest in this project and his technological and moral support in enabling me to bring it to completion.

My adult children, and now my amazing grandchildren, confirm in their lives and their hopes how important it is, and must be, to think ecologically. This book is dedicated also to them.

Contents

**ECOLOGICAL
THINKING**

And God said, Let us make man in our image, after our likeness: and let

them have dominion over the fish of the sea, and over the fowl of the air, and over

the cattle, and over all the earth, and over every creeping thing that creepeth

upon the earth.

—Genesis 1:26, Authorized Version

INTRODUCTION

In this book, I propose that *ecological thinking* can effect a revolution in philosophy comparable to Kant's Copernican revolution, which radically reconfigured western thought by moving "man" to the center of the philosophical-conceptual universe. Its effects were constitutive of the humanistic, post-Enlightenment world that members of present-day affluent western societies have known. Yet Kantian philosophy was parochial in the conception of "man" on which it turned: a recognition central to feminist, socialist, postcolonial, and critical race theory, among other theoretical stances that underpin and inform the "new social movements" of the late twentieth and early twenty-first centuries. In placing *man* at the center of the universe it tacitly promoted a picture of a world, both physical and human, that privileged and was subservient to a small class and race of people whose sex required no mention because it was presumptively male and in any case irrelevant and who were uniformly capable of achieving a narrowly conceived standard of rationality, citizenship, and morality.

Much as humanism unsettled the rhetorical and social authority of theism in seventeenth- and eighteenth-century European thought, so at the beginning of the twenty-first century ecological thinking interrogates and endeavors to unsettle the self-certainties of western capitalism and the epistemologies of mastery it underwrites. Yet ecological thinking is not unilinear as humanism claimed to be, for it emerges from and addresses so many interwoven and sometimes contradictory issues—feminist, classist, environmental, post-colonial, racist, sexist—that its implications require multifaceted chartings. Thus I am contending that despite the profusion of ecological discourses across the academic and social-political landscapes of the early-twenty-first-century western world, where the words are on "everyone's" lips and the rhetoric enlisted to serve diverse, even antiecological purposes; and despite contesta-tions in the politics of ecology, the creative possibilities of ecological thinking for interrupting and restructuring the dominant social and philosophical imaginary have yet to be adequately explored.

Ecology talk has an immediate appeal in an era when "right thinking" (= left-leaning) people are appalled by the destruction of natural and social environments and repelled by an escalating imperialism—at once local and worldwide—that accompanies and/or promotes it. The protective, nurturant aspects of ecology seem to promise a better way. Yet that very appeal is often counteracted by a romantic rhetoric of narcissistic closeness to nature and forced identifications of women or erstwhile "noble savages" with nature, while human-centered conceptions of an "environment" that must be pre-served in order to serve the interests of the human beings it surrounds reenact the spirit of the Genesis promise that "man" should have dominion over all the earth. Nonetheless, I am proposing, ecological thinking can generate an emi-nently responsible remapping of the epistemic and social-political terrains, animated by an informed attentiveness to local and more wide-ranging di-versity and by a commitment to responsible ideals of citizenship and preser-vation of the public trust, all of which concerns are notably absent from putatively universal, a priori theories of knowledge and action. As I will show in the following chapters, it proposes a way of engaging—if not all at once—with the implications of patterns, places, and the interconnections of lives and events in and across the human and nonhuman world, in scientific and secular projects of inquiry, where the dividing line between the traditional *Natur-wissenschaften* (natural sciences) and *Geisteswissenschaften* (human sciences) is often blurred and where epistemic and ethical-political concerns are recipro-cally informative.

Guiding the development of the position I will articulate in this book is a conviction that theories of knowledge are neither self-contained within phi-losophy nor isolated from people's lives in the societies where their ideals and standards prevail. Theories of knowledge shape and are shaped by dominant

social-political imaginaries. In their constitutive effects in institutions of
knowledge production and in ordinary, everyday epistemic lives, assumptions
that emanate from these theories participate in the structural ordering of
societies, large and small, according to uneven distributions of authority and
expertise, power and privilege. Yet ecological thinking is not simply thinking
about ecology or *about* "the environment," although these figure as catalysts
among its issues. It is a revisioned mode of engagement with knowledge,
subjectivity, politics, ethics, science, citizenship, and agency that pervades and
reconfigures theory and practice. It does not reduce to a set of rules or
methods; it may play out differently from location to location; but it is sufficiently coherent to be interpreted and enacted across widely diverse situations.

My epistemic and moral-political hypothesis is that the transformative
potential of ecological thinking can be realized by participants engaged in
producing a viable habitat and ethos, prepared to take on the burdens and
blessings of place, identity, materiality, and history, and to work within the
locational possibilities and limitations, found and made, of human cognitive-
corporeal lives. Thus the ecological subject who is the protagonist in this tale I tell
is but a distant relative of the abstract, interchangeable, autonomous individual
of liberal moral-political theory. He/she is self-critically cognizant of being part
of and specifically located within a social-physical world that constrains and
enables human practices, where knowing and acting always generate consequences. For this subject, internal interdependence within communities and
their external dependence on one another are given—neither to be repudiated in
illusory gestures of self-sufficiency nor elaborated in a nostalgic immersion of
self in nature or in Others. Acknowledging the partiality of their knowings and
self-knowings, and cultivating an awareness of the effects of that knowing
(however small, however local), ecological subjects are well placed, collectively
and singly, to own and take responsibility for their epistemic-moral-political
activity. Ecological thinking thus distances itself from quests for a priori or
transcendent principles and truths; but neither is the language of "context" and
"contextualization" adequate to explain it. The implication that text and context are separable—that text is best explained when it is inserted into or returned
to context, but the two are distinct—bypasses their reciprocally constitutive
effects.

Assuming no such separations, ecological thinking relocates inquiry
"down on the ground" where knowledge is made, negotiated, circulated; and
where the nature and conditions of the particular "ground," the situations
and circumstances of specific knowers, their interdependence and their negotiations, have claims to critical epistemic scrutiny equivalent to those of

allegedly isolated, discrete propositional knowledge claims. In its approach to knowledge, it works with affinities, analogies from location to location, imaginatively and interpretively discerned. Yet the practice-dependent, communicative, deliberative processes of negotiation from which knowledge, on this model, is made and remade, its critical reflexivity, and its grounding in the "givenness" of the physical, historical, corporeal *Lebenswelt,* guard against the subjectivism and/or relativism that have deterred philosophers from granting epistemic significance to place, particularity, imagination, and interpretation.

All of this having been said, certain caveats must be stated to expose the scope and limits of this proposal. The ecology that—literally and metaphorically—generates its core is no innocent place from which to derive pure, benign "alternatives" to the epistemologies of mastery. Ecology is as politically contested as any of the positions this project interrogates, as prone to self-serving articulations and to excesses of narcissistic aestheticism as any of the dominant theories on the philosophical landscape. Nor can it represent itself as either static or innocently benign, promise an unimpeded epistemic and moral flourishing, or claim to emanate from a pure, unreconstructed and unequivocally "good" nature concealed beneath the accretions of the exploitative Enlightenment-colonial-humanist practices it contests. Ecological thinking will yield no "poet's utopia," such as Richard Rorty's free-play of the ironic liberal imagination promises.[1] Ecosystems—both metaphorical and literal—are as cruel as they are kind, as unpredictable and overwhelming as they are orderly and nurturant, as unsentimentally destructive of their less viable members as they are cooperative and mutually sustaining; and ecological thinking is as available for feeding self-serving romantic fantasies as for inspiring socially responsible transformations. So if it is to avoid replicating the oppressions endemic to orthodox epistemologies and ethical theories, ecological thinking requires principled adjudication of incompatible claims, effective deliberative practices for enacting them, and the vigilant monitoring on which most revisionary social movements depend to promote and preserve their fragile gains while countering threats of renewed oppressions. Such issues are central to the chapters that follow.

An epistemological position whose starting point is in the ecological situations and interconnections of knowers and knowings—be they benign, malign, or merely equivocal—departs radically from inquiry directed toward analyzing discrete, disparate beings, events, and items in the world, only subsequently to propose connections among them or to insert them into

---

1. The phrase is Ferrell's in "Richard Rorty and the Poet's Utopia."

"contexts" conceived as separately given. The multiply contested character of ecology itself—its *instability*, in Penelope Deutscher's rich sense of the term—attests to the dynamic, live aspect of knowing ecologically, as it nudges out the punctiform, frozen epistemic moment, disconnected from what people care about and want to know.[2] Why, then, do I call the project ecological; and how is it epistemological?

A principal aim of this project is to understand the metaphorics, images, symbolisms woven into dominant social-political imaginaries: to examine how they work to shape and govern possibilities of being, thinking, acting; how they legitimate or preclude certain epistemic and other human relations, to one another and to the physical/natural/conceptual world; how philosophical systems reflect and reinforce these imaginaries. Of compelling interest in this regard are the effects of imagery and imaginaries commonly discounted as mere embellishments and hence not recognized for their constitutive effects. Thus, I will explain how the ethos of mastery that permeates the affluent western world condones multiple intolerable exploitations, while (borrowing a phrase from Verena Conley) ecological thinking offers a better "*way of inhabiting the world.*"[3] In the conceptual frame that ecological thinking makes possible, "inhabiting" is an active, thoughtful practice, socially, affectively, and responsibly engaged. But ecological thinking is not a matter of substituting one unified and unifying discourse for another. Ecological discourse is, as I have noted, both conflicted and unstable, but these very aspects, perhaps paradoxically, count among its strengths. It is capable of infiltrating gaps in the discourses of mastery, infusing the interstices with lines of thought that cause them to widen, shift, make way for the multiple and multiply suppressed issues at work just below their surface; of demonstrating how those discourses sit in the wider world; and thus of opening space for examining the character and the effects of these situations.

The proposal I develop in this book is epistemological, then, in the reconstructions of "the epistemological project" it requires. It is more interpretive-inductive than confirmationist-deductive: verification often gives way to interpretation, and Truth *simpliciter* to a textured, responsive conception of "truth to," as knowing moves transversely across geographical and social landscapes, following along the ground the trajectories of diverse habitat-constitutive or obstructive lines of evidence: mapping their paths and

2. The productive aspects of "instability" form a central thread in Deutscher, *Yielding Gender.*

3. Conley, *Ecopolitics,* 114 (emphasis original).

surrounds; showing how they can generate interpretive/coherent understandings that may bear analogously on other features of the habitat. Likewise, it aims to understand whether certain practices make ethological sense for the circumstances of people's lives, for preserving or for changing them. Physical, social, or other location, then, functions neither as backdrop nor context, but as constitutive of the *Lebenswelt*, and the *Leben* within it, shaping possibilities of knowing, and demanding, themselves, to be known. The proposal requires stretching the limits of imagination toward responsive and responsible local sensitivity: interpretively, a hermeneutic of suspicion wary of universalizing judgments and premature closure, while cognizant of the explanatory potential of comparative, analogically interpretive analyses, counts among its most active ingredients. Suspicion is directed, principally, at the excesses of scientism, reductionism, and the instrumental-utilitarian moral and political theories that sustain an ethos of dominance and mastery, where a dislocated knower-as-spectator seeks to predict, manipulate, and control the behavior of the material world and of other "less enlightened" people. The imperialism of overdeveloped countries imposing their knowledge, social orderings, customs, economics, and other values, with scant concern for local sensitivities of land or of people, is one of the most visible wide-ranging—antiecological—products of such thinking. More locally, the individualistic rhetoric of self-reliance in knowledge and action, derived from the circumstances of a privileged few to rationalize dismantling social welfare and to justify persistent patterns of hierarchy and inequality, requires analogous critical intervention. Some of these ideas are around and healthy in feminist epistemology: in Linda Alcoff's "new versions of coherence theory"; my own conceptions of "epistemic responsibility" and "rhetorical spaces"; Donna Haraway's "situated knowledges"; Sandra Harding's "strong objectivity"; and Lynn Nelson's feminist readings of "epistemology naturalized."[4] Reframing these ideas ecologically, I am suggesting, will reconfigure their interconnections so as to radicalize their effects for women and other erstwhile Others in socially and politically transformative ways.

My overriding thesis is that the dominant model of knowledge and epistemology in Anglo-American philosophy produces an *epistemological monoculture* both in the academy and in everyday life, whose consequences are to suppress and choke out ways of knowing that depart from the stringent

---

4. Alcoff, *Real Knowing*; Code, *Epistemic Responsibility*; idem, *Rhetorical Spaces*; Haraway, *Simians, Cyborgs, and Women*, 183–201; Harding, "Rethinking Standpoint Epistemology"; and Nelson, *Who Knows*.

dictates of an exaggerated ideal of scientific knowledge making. Developed out of a reading of the Enlightenment legacy that emphasizes "the calculability of the world" as what makes knowledge-as-mastery possible, and reinforced by the undeniable successes of physical and psychological science, this model demarcates the epistemic domain so as to exclude from knowledge properly so called "whatever does not conform to the rule of computation and utility."[5] By contrast, I will propose that specifically located, multifaceted analyses of knowledge production and circulation in diverse biographical, historical, demographic, and geographic locations generate more responsible knowings than the reductionism endemic in the positivist post-Enlightenment legacy can single-handedly allow.[6]

Cautionary Tales

In a beautifully illustrated children's book, *The Story of Rosy Dock*, Jeannie Baker tells of a settler in the Finke River district in Australia who "brought seeds with her from the other side of the world and planted a garden." Among the seeds she scattered were those of a plant called "rosy dock," which she "loved for its beautiful red seed pods." These seeds remained dormant during the long dry years until, after a period of torrential rains, "the desert suddenly blossomed," and "rosy dock, the plant with beautiful seedpods, is spreading like a great red blanket farther than the eye can see." The illustration where we see it blanketing the earth is lovely to behold. But in a modestly didactic ecological afterword, the author reminds us: "Throughout the world, often with the best of intentions, people introduce plants and animals into a new environment with enormous unforeseen consequences. Without their normal predators, some non-native plants and animals multiply so quickly they change whole landscapes and push many native plants and animals to extinction."[7] From dealing with feral rabbits,

---

5. I borrow these turns of phrase from Horkheimer and Adorno, "Concept of Enlightenment," 46. For a compelling history of the rise in authority of the numerically based fact, see Poovey, *History of the Modern Fact*.

6. Levins and Lewontin's definition of reductionism is broadly useful for my arguments throughout this book: "In ecology, reductionism takes the form of regarding each species as a separate element existing in an environment that consists of the physical world and of other species. The interaction of the species and its environment is unidirectional: the species experiences, reacts to, and evolves in response to its environment. The reciprocal phenomenon, the reaction and evolution of the environment in response to the species, is put aside" ("Dialectics and Reductionism in Ecology," 219).

7. Baker, *Story of Rosy Dock*.

cats, dogs, camels, horses, and other imported creatures who prey on indigenous animals and trample or destroy indigenous plants, much as "feral" plants
such as rosy dock choke out indigenous species, Australians know such phenomena well. These practices run alongside the less frequently broached issue
of the settlers themselves, in Australia, as also in Canada, New Zealand, South
Africa, and other erstwhile colonies, whose lives trample and destroy indigenous
human lives, whose thriving eradicates the thriving prospects of indigenous
people.

Feminist environmentalist Vandana Shiva, in an analysis consonant with
the rosy dock story, details how eucalyptus trees, introduced into India, spread
to render vast tracts of agricultural land infertile for indigenous food crops.
Addressing the effects of "development" more generally for Indian agriculture,
Shiva takes issue with the pivotal assumption of western-style *monocultural*
agriculture, for which land is most productive when it is cultivated to produce
a single, homogeneous crop. In the rhetoric of development, she observes,
"natural forests remain unproductive till they are developed into monoculture
plantations of commercial species."[8] Yet genealogical chartings of the inter-
weavings of farming practices, ideologies, population distributions, political
power structures, and land management expose monoculture's reductive, coercive effects in depleting the land's resources and its inhabitants' self-reliance
together. Monocultural agriculture, specializing in crops such as wheat and rice
and dependent on pesticides and herbicides to achieve maximum yield, has
transformed local Indian edible plants into "weeds" and destroyed the fish
culture long associated with rice-growing in Asia. In consequence, populations
reduced to producing a single crop find themselves reliant on other monocultural populations, often located at nearly unmanageable distances, for many
of their nutritional needs. Sounding a cautiously optimistic note, however,
Shiva suggests that some women's cultures in India have been subverting the
would-be hegemony of monocultural practices by engaging in local projects
designed to reproduce a biodiversity that could promote a renewal of self-
sustaining communities.[9] Analogously, detailing some more positive ecological
effects of Mexican and Chinese "integrated" agricultural practices, Henry Gee
commends such farming practices, which use "all the hi-tech appurtenances
of conventional farming" while, nonetheless, taking "a cue from studies on
natural ecosystems that show how diverse plots" have been able successfully
to resist "external perturbations such as drought or disease." He reports a

8. Shiva, *Staying Alive*, 4.
9. See also Shiva, "Biotechnological Development," 202.

massive study of rice-growing in China, whose results showed that "plots mixed with varieties of rice were significantly more resistant to fungal disease than rice monocultures."[10] Drawing on evidence such as this, Shiva advocates a shift in models of knowledge "from a reductionist to a relational approach [as] . . . necessary for the protection of both biological diversity and cultural diversity."[11] Her interest is in how reductionist epistemological methods suppress indigenous and traditional agricultural systems when they are enacted without taking time to understand their local viability or to consider alternatives that serve local populations and circumstances well. The general point, then, is not about preserving the status quo at all costs, but about how innovation has to be ecologically sensitive in its conception and application.

In my view, the effects of reductionism, which are indeed writ large in the suppressions Shiva details, extend much further across an epistemic terrain marked by an excessive veneration of the mastery, efficiency, and control modern science is imagined to provide. These effects were apparent in classical empiricist projects of reducing objects of knowledge to putatively basic units, often in the form of "observational simples" abstracted from their surroundings, and of representing knowledge, then, in discrete, isolated propositions, commonly in the rubric "*S-knows-that-p.*" The formal propositional structure implies uniformity among knowing subjects and among objects of knowledge, once they are extracted from the messiness of situation and circumstance, whose specificities claim no epistemological significance. In present-day variations on such commitments, in order to avoid contamination by interests and affect, properly objective knowledge is disconnected from what people care about and want to know. Hence a plea for rethinking reductionism is at the same time a plea for reconsidering hegemonic conceptions of knowledge and subjectivity, all the way down.

These ecological cautionary tales recall Friedrich Engels's contrast between animals' *unwitting* destruction of a locality's soil and vegetation and "man's" equivalently destructive, but *purposive* activities of sowing field crops, planting trees and vines cultivated for maximum yield, and transferring plants and animals from one country to another, thus altering the flora and fauna of whole continents. Engels notes that although animals merely *use* nature, "man by his changes makes it serve his ends, *masters* it."[12] The purposiveness of such human activity, like that of the settler who planted rosy dock, needs to be

---

10. Gee, "Force of Nature."
11. Shiva, *Tomorrow's Biodiversity*, 129.
12. Engels, *Dialectics of Nature*, 41 (emphasis original).

evaluated with care, for the condemnation these activities and projects invite when they are told in the language of "destruction" rests on assumptions about human purposes and prescience that are as contestable as they are plausible. Undoubtedly, many of these practices, from scattering "alien" seeds, to clearing forests to create arable land or build cities, to damming streams and rivers to produce reservoirs, alter nature radically and irrevocably. Yet it is implausible to think of them, uniformly, as produced from an intent to destroy or driven by such malicious purposes as the language of destruction implies. As William Leiss suggests, the most common goal of mastery over nature is "the security of life—and its enhancement—alike for individuals and the species."[13] Criticism thus has to take seriously the limits of human prescience and the (indistinct) line separating it from greed, unthinking exploitation, carelessness, or failure to investigate far enough. It has to be mindful of the urgency of securing the basic elements of human survival, in places, societies, economic classes, and social and political circumstances where information about short- or long-term effects may be less readily available than beneficiaries of a flourishing "knowledge economy" routinely expect it to be, or where the sheer desperation of present necessity blocks any thoughts of planning for an uncertain future.

Nonetheless, Engels cautions his readers, each human conquest over nature "takes its revenge on us": each may "have the consequences on which we counted," but it also "has quite different, unforeseen effects which only too often cancel out the first."[14] Ecologically uninformed policies of mastery commonly filter evaluations of multiple forms of "damage" through utilitarian assumptions about the end (= greater productivity, efficiency, and human comfort or safety) justifying the means (= the conquest of nature), none of which may be intrinsically wrong, but all of which require further assessment. Critical-constructive analysis thus needs to be directed at the entitlements and presumptions endorsed by governing conceptions of security and enhancement, at the evaluative ordering of species built into patterns of justifying these purposes, and at the overarching picture of the world—the dominant *social imaginary*—that holds this conceptual apparatus in place. Hence with respect to the tacit knowledge of nature and human nature that informs practices such

13. Leiss, "Domination of Nature," 63.
14. Engels notes, for example, that people, both ancient and more modern, who "destroyed the forests to obtain cultivatable land, never dreamed that they were laying the basis for the present devastated condition of those countries, by removing along with the forests the collecting centres and reservoirs of moisture" (*Dialectics of Nature*, 41).

as these, suppressing other possible ways of knowing, questions about the scope and limits of individual and collective *epistemic responsibility* need also to be posed. Those questions are central to my position in this book.

Shifting from a literal to a metaphorical ecological focus exposes social-justice analogies to the thinking engendered by monocultural agricultural practices. Consider the tired but not defunct idea that "allowing" women into the work force unjustly thwarts men's unfettered prospering; that too-liberal immigration policies threaten the jobs and living spaces of those who— allegedly—were there first; that blacks and indigenous people fare better when they are confined to a reserve, a ghetto, a designated neighborhood, a geographical region where they can "enjoy the company of their kind." And consider a counterpart to these practices detailed in Charles Mills's analysis of the *racing* of space, where "white space is patrolled for dark intruders, whose very presence, independently of what they may or may not do, is a blot on the reassuring civilized whiteness of the home space."[15] Talk of contamination, of pristine innocence despoiled, feeds into this rhetoric of damage and destruction, promoting a protective, conservative ethos of attention to the interests of a few at the expense of the many and animated by profoundly unjust assumptions about which members of "the species" count and which do not.

Skeptics might dismiss such localized examples and transparently political claims as romantic yearnings for an impracticable stasis: for practices and states of affairs no longer viable in twenty-first-century mass societies when hitherto unimaginable numbers of people need food, work, clothing, and shelter. Although I believe there are no good grounds for such a dismissal, I defer contesting it to a later place in this book. I cite these preliminary examples as an introduction to my intention to appeal to ecology, metaphorically and literally, as a route to developing a conception of knowledge capable of loosening the hold of a single-minded drive toward mastery by any means.

Feminism and the Politics of Ecology

This engagement with ecological thinking grows out of my work in feminist epistemology and the politics of knowledge and pivots on modes of analysis and explanation pertinent to feminist inquiry. Implicitly or explicitly, it evaluates modalities of ecological thinking for their feminist or counterfeminist effects. Yet the discussion's salience—like that of most early-twenty-first-century

15. Mills, *Racial Contract*, 41, 48.

feminist theory and practice—extends well beyond female-feminist concerns, to engage with wide-ranging social-justice and politics-of-knowledge issues of dominance and oppression born out of the new social movements of the 1960s.

In chapter one I enter the main subject matter of this book through a close reading of Rachel Carson's ecological practice. Although she claimed no feminist allegiance, and hers is neither a unified epistemological standpoint nor one that has achieved the eminence it deserves in late-twentieth- or early-twenty-first-century ecological inquiry, I read Carson as an accomplished scientist and activist who practiced a way of knowing nature and human nature consonant in many respects with the position I advocate. To locate her projects in this way, and to convey a sense of the range and heterogeneity of positions that inform ecological discourse, politics, and practices, I begin with a sampling of diverse conceptions of ecology that are as often mutually incompatible if not outrightly opposed one to another as they are reciprocally informative.

As I will show, Carson's ecological work, like that of other early (mid-twentieth-century) environmentalists, contrasts with activities in the environmental-ecological movements of the final decades of the twentieth century, particularly with respect to the extent and manner of its political engagement. Many, if not most, of the more recent movements in the United Kingdom, the United States, Canada, Australia, New Zealand, and western Europe are overtly political and activist in linking environmental degradation and preservation to political exploitation, militarism, colonialism, diverse forms of local and more wide-ranging oppression, and activist projects of resistance and reform.[16] None of these developments diminish Carson's own political commitment, evident in her tireless—often effective—lobbying for public action in response to the warnings of ecological disaster she issued, especially in *Silent Spring*,[17] but they allow her readers, retrospectively, to reevaluate her activism. She is one of the most eminent precursors and catalysts of the new social movements fueled by the 1960s civil rights and women's movements in North America and in the aftermath of the events of 1968 in France and elsewhere in Europe—movements energetic in their opposition to multiple, mutually enforcing injustices. Civil rights, antiracist, and women's movements; environmental, peace, and antimilitarist movements; anti-imperialism, postcolonial,

16. For a detailed history of environmental movements in the United States since the early 1980s, see Sturgeon, *Ecofeminist Natures*. Sturgeon makes reference throughout the book to environmental-ecological activism elsewhere in the world, but her focus is primarily American.

17. According to Sturgeon, Carson is "an ecofeminist foremother because of her book, *Silent Spring*, which arguably initiated the first nonconservationist environmental movement in America" (*Ecofeminist Natures*, 200 n. 4).

and radical challenges to intellectual-academic authority and the hegemony of Enlightenment rationality in post-1968 Europe figure prominently among projects whose effects, separately and together, have been subversive of entrenched power structures and tenacious beliefs in the "natural" (pre-1960s) order of things, both human and nonhuman, a subversiveness prefigured, if sometimes tacitly, in Carson's work.

The common political themes that link these movements confirm the appropriateness of Carolyn Merchant's having foregrounded "domination" in the introduction to her *Ecology* volume (in the series Key Concepts in Critical Theory)—a peculiarly useful concept, in her view, for coming to understand "human-human and human-nature relationships."[18] Like the "mastery" in Val Plumwood's *Feminism and the Mastery of Nature*,[19] invoked in my references to the language and practices of mastery, this emphasis on domination signals that, for Merchant, ecology is as thoroughly political as it can be responsibly scientific in its capacity to expose the often-covert implications and agendas of pre- or antiecological theories and practices. Nor, in her own work, does Merchant endorse artificially separating science and politics.[20] In relation to nature, she argues, natural science inevitably takes up a political-epistemological stance within an imaginary infused by specific conceptions of "man's" place in and in relation to nature, whether in according "him" a position apart from nature to know it from a distance and exploit it as he will or in attributing an apolitical purity to scientific inquiry as such and to inquiry into nature in particular. It is a commonplace that even putatively apolitical claims can be political in character, content, and effect: in environmental thinking, the truth at the core of this notion is clearly evident.

In the white affluent west, I have noted, ecology talk (when it is not dismissed as lefty fringe fanaticism) conjures up a protective, nurturant image of human relationships to or with(in) nature. But twentieth-century ecological science and environmental thought stretch across a range of hetereogeneous, conceptually multifaceted, and politically incompatible theoretical-philosophical orientations with their own, often bitter, conflicts and disagreements. To sample the flavor of these disputes as a prelude to fuller discussion in chapter one, recall how the environmentalism revitalized in the United States in the aftermath of World War II, with Rachel Carson's warnings about the risks of DDT to birds and other wildlife, was dismissed as trivial in the 1960s

18. Merchant, *Ecology*, 1.
19. Plumwood, *Feminism and the Mastery of Nature*.
20. See especially Merchant, *Death of Nature*.

by "man-centered" antipollution reformers who had little patience with "nature-lovers." Their issue was the threat to *human* health posed by industrial pollution and other toxic substances.[21] Proposing a different set of challenges to man-centered thinking, Verena Conley reads the events of 1968 in France as a turning point in ecological awareness, claiming: "The decentering of the subject, gained by the labors of structuralism and poststructuralism, leveled hierarchies and shifted a vertical vision of the world toward a more horizontal one, so important for feminism, that places on the same surface both multi-culturalism *and* ecology."[22] Yet this very "decentering" has drawn biting critique from Luc Ferry and, to a lesser degree, Jean Baudrillard: Ferry decries post-1968 ecological movements as fascist threats to humanism, democracy, and the legacy of the Enlightenment, targeting deep ecology and ecofeminism in particular; whereas for Baudrillard, in the world of hypertechnology and simulacra the real world—and hence nature—is no longer real.[23] The trajectory of the deep ecology movement from a holistic to an individualist and sometime hypermasculinist stance traces another set of disagreements and conflicts;[24] as does Deane Curtin's critical reading of social ecology as rehearsing an "old ploy of colonialism" in which "traditional people are first identified with nature and then patronized for their pre-rational, folkish identification with nature."[25] Equally contentious are divisions in ecofeminism around questions of essentialism: essentializing "nature" as benign, and essentializing "woman" as close to, at one with, immersed in nature, and therefore also inherently good, caring.[26] None of these disagreements has been resolved; yet the (productive) tensions they continually generate attest to the ongoing urgency and vitality of matters ecological.

In the last three decades of the twentieth century, ecology and feminism intersected most visibly and vocally in theories and practices gathered under the label *ecofeminism*. Although it has found its principal articulators in the English-speaking world, and primarily in the United States, the term *ecofeminism* itself originates with French feminist Françoise d'Eaubonne in her 1974 book *Le féminisme ou la mort*,[27] whose section referring to "the launching of

21. I owe this formulation to Zimmerman, *Contesting Earth's Future*, 30.

22. Conley, *Ecopolitics*, 26 (emphasis original).

23. See Ferry, *New Ecological Order*, esp. chap. 5: "Nazi Ecology"; and Baudrillard, *Simulations*.

24. See, e.g., Mathews, "Deep Ecology"; and idem, "Ecofeminism and Deep Ecology."

25. Curtin, *Chinnagounder's Challenge*, 147–48.

26. See Sturgeon, *Ecofeminist Natures*, esp. chap. 6.

27. D'Eaubonne, *Le féminisme ou la mort*.

a new action: *ecofeminism*" appeared in English translation only in 1994.[28] D'Eaubonne represents ecofeminism as a way of addressing an urgent need "to remake the planet around a totally new model,"[29] a remark consonant with my claim for ecological thinking's capacity to effect a Copernican revolution in philosophy. Characterizing ecology as "the science that studies the relations of living beings among themselves and the physical environment in which they are evolving," she emphasizes its attentiveness to "the relations between the sexes and the ensuing birthrate...the exhaustion of resources and the destruction of the environment."[30]

My project in this book is not to develop an ecofeminist epistemology, but it is often contiguous to and in conversation with ecological feminism, itself a diverse and multiply contested area of inquiry.[31] Despite differences I have mentioned around matters pertaining to essentialism, "woman-nature" identifications, and spirituality, a revolutionary impulse—a commitment to changing the world—animates most ecological feminism, shaping its intellectual-political allegiances and alliances with other ecological positionings. Feminists who look to other ecological theories are usually as committed to social-material transformation and to practices conducive to viable citizenship as they are to analyzing individual experiences of nature and/or preservation and aesthetics.

Ecological thinking and feminism frequently make good allies: epistemologically, neither can be responsively accountable to the specificities of its subject matters while subscribing to reductionism or to a unity-of-science/unity-of-knowledge credo that assimilates differences under a rubric of sameness. Neither in their ethical nor their epistemic moments can they deal adequately with problems and events in isolation from their myriad connections, both synchronic and diachronic. In their commitment to honoring complexity, ecofeminism and ecological thinking require sensitivity to detail, to

28. D'Eaubonne, "Time for Ecofeminism." Two excerpts from this essay, translated by Betty Schmitz, appear in Marks and de Courtivron, *New French Feminisms*, but the term *ecofeminism* occurs only in the version in the Merchant volume.

29. D'Eaubonne, "Time for Ecofeminism," 176. D'Eaubonne counts among the recipients of Ferry's scorn; see *New Ecological Order*, 116.

30. D'Eaubonne, "Time for Ecofeminism," 178 (quoted from the *New York Times*). For Cuomo, more than twenty years later, ecological feminism—feminist environmentalism—focuses on "similarities and connections between forms and instances of human oppression, including the oppression of women, and the degradation of nature." She maintains: "Our strategies—both theoretical and practical—for resisting oppressions...[have to] attend to these connections" (*Feminism and Ecological Communities*, 1).

31. See Warren, *Ecological Feminism*; and idem, *Ecofeminist Philosophy*.

minutiae, to what precisely—however apparently small—distinguishes this woman, this contestable practice, this social intervention, this place, this problem of knowledge, this injustice, this locality from that—just as biologically based ecologists distinguish this plant, this species, this rock pool from that one. Both examine meanings of differences for how they promote or thwart living well. Both resist superimposing a ready-made cognitive grid upon events and situations, tucking in the bits that spill over, letting aberrations fall through the cracks. And both have often to combine empirical attention to observational evidence with examining local crises, specific harms, social issues, problems within wider patterns of power and privilege, oppression and victimization.

Sometimes ecofeminism appears to be *the* locus of intersection and cooperation between feminism and ecological thinking; but for the ecological thinking I advocate, so close an alliance, whether with ecofeminism or with deep ecology or the Green movement, has little to recommend it. Problematically, as I have noted, the practice in some ecofeminist writings of identifying an essential "woman" with an equally essential "Nature" reconfirms the biological determinism that has long kept women "in their place."[32] Likewise, some ecofeminist attempts to naturalize women's traditional caregiving, expanded to include taking care of nature, accord scant attention to how hierarchal social structures posit, and thence exploit, women's "natural" caring capacities, thereby perpetuating their subjection. The rehearsals of hypermasculinity enacted in romantic quests for a "return to nature," often as a place for male self-discovery; the spiritualism of some facets of environmentalism; and the tendency Plumwood detects in deep ecology "to focus exclusively on identification, interconnectedness, sameness and the overcoming of separation, treating nature as a dimension of self"[33]—all invite feminist wariness for their capacity to perpetuate oppressive states of affairs. Donna Haraway's injunction—"we must find another relationship to nature besides reification, possession, appropriation, and nostalgia"[34]—indicates that reworking the currently hegemonic relationship is vital to human survival; ecological thinking sets out to determine how such reworkings might proceed.

32. See, e.g., Griffin, *Woman and Nature*; Merchant, *Death of Nature*; Plant, *Healing the Wounds*; Diamond and Orenstein, *Reweaving the World*; and Biehl, *Rethinking Ecofeminist Politics*.

33. Plumwood, *Feminism and the Mastery of Nature*, 174. For discussions of deep ecology, see Devall, "Deep Ecology Movement"; and Naess, "Deep Ecological Movement."

34. Haraway, "Otherworldly Conversations," 70.

Practicing a methodological pluralism that stems from a respect for particularity, both ecological thinking and the feminisms of the late twentieth and
the early twenty-first century draw, often similarly, on studies of (linked)
oppressions, to generate multiple coalitions and forms of activism.[35] Their task
is to develop liberatory strategies to counter the myriad, mutually reinforcing
oppressions endemic to white patriarchal capitalist societies. In contrast to
single-issue defined and enacted theories and activism, ecological feminism
yields multi-issue theories and practices: it engages with multiple oppressions.
Ecological thinking thus redirects theoretical analyses toward situated knowledges, situated ethico-politics, where situation is *constitutive of*, not just the
context for, the backdrop to, enactments of subjectivity. Haraway comments:
"I have a body and mind as much constructed by the post–Second World War
arms race and cold war as by the women's movements."[36] This is not, then, a
merely contextualized subjectivity.

Ethical self-mastery, political mastery over unruly and aberrant Others,
and epistemic mastery over the "external" world pose as the still-attainable
goals of the Enlightenment legacy. Yet I have observed how these discourses of
mastery derive from and underwrite a reductive imaginary in which epistemic
and moral agents are represented as isolated units on an indifferent landscape,
to which their relation, too, is one of disengaged indifference. These discourses
enlist ready-made, easily applied categories to contain the personal, social, and
physical-natural world within a neatly manageable array of "kinds," obliter-
ating differences in a desire to assemble the confusion of the world into
maximally homogeneous units. In contradistinction to these hegemonic discourses of mastery and domination, *ecological* thinking becomes a frame for
reconfiguring knowledge, sociality, and subjectivity and for reexamining the
potential of epistemic and ethico-political practices to produce habitats where
people can live well together[37] and respectfully with and within the physical/
natural world. Often, it yields to and modifies its conclusions by tracing analogies and disanalogies from situation to situation—"transversally," as Conley
puts it, "making a link between ecosystems that international capitalism seeks

35. Sturgeon, in *Ecofeminist Natures*, traces a history of such coalition movements and
forms of activism in the United States, especially in the last three decades of the twentieth
century.

36. Haraway, *Simians, Cyborgs, and Women*, 173.

37. The term *ethico-political* is from Bar On and Ferguson, *Daring to Be Good*. They pose
"the central ethico-political question of feminism" thus: "*What is wrong with our current state,
government, economy from a feminist perspective, and what ethical and political alternative values,
visions, and strategies should feminists stand for and engage in?*" (xiii, emphasis original).

to polarize and ecological issues that pertain to local cultures."[38] Being-in-the-world informed by ecological thinking differs radically from the masterful way of autonomous man, whose assumption of mastery over all he surveys allows surveying to substitute for engaged participation and mastery to suppress diversity for the sake of instrumental simplicity.

The challenge in mapping such projects is to craft a conceptual apparatus sufficiently sensitive and powerful to carry them forward, thinking of Gilles Deleuze and Felix Guattari's deceptively simple definition of philosophy as "the art of forming, inventing, and fabricating concepts"; "the discipline that involves *creating* concepts."[39] In so defining it, Deleuze and Guattari are not returning philosophy to the conceptual analysis of mid-twentieth-century analytic philosophy. They are showing how transformative philosophical projects can put into circulation a critical-constructive conceptual apparatus rich and complex enough to generate innovative ways of inhabiting, engaging with, contemplating, the physical and human world. Feminist, postcolonial, and critical race theory—among other "new" social theories—are sustained, sometimes overlapping, projects of critiquing and displacing the conceptual structures that hold oppressive social orders in place. So these are not "just" verbal matters: revisionary conceptual frames are practically-materially efficacious. Ecological thinking, then, is about putting into circulation a radically innovative conceptual apparatus, enabling it to infiltrate the social order where it can expand to undermine the intransigent hierarchical arrangements that hold it in place.

Catriona Sandilands aptly contends: "Environmentalism, by virtue of its inclusion in other political struggles, contains the potential to redirect them toward a more progressive articulation, one which focuses on radical democracy as an ecological necessity, one which necessarily includes a variety of struggles in transcendence of fundamentally limiting notions of the subject."[40] Consonantly, ecological thinking works with a conception of materially constituted and situated subjectivity for which place, embodied locatedness, and discursive interdependence are conditions for the very possibility of knowledge and action. It ushers in a renewed conception of responsible deliberative-negotiative citizenship, as responsible in its knowing as in its doing. Epistemologically, the "situated knowledges" of Haraway's "modest witness" serve as provocative examples of such citizenship. This modest witness "insists on its situatedness,

38. Conley, *Ecopolitics*, 110.
39. Deleuze and Guattari, *What Is Philosophy?* 2, 5.
40. Sandilands, "From Natural Identity to Radical Democracy," 90.

where location is itself always a complex construction as well as inheritance, and . . . casts its lot with the projects and needs of those who could not or would not inhabit the subject positions of the self-invisible and the discursive sites, the 'laboratories,' of the credible, civil man of science."[41] If it can establish a firm enough footing, ecological thinking—like feminism at its best—will reconceive human and natural locations and relations all the way down.

Ecological thinking thus naturalizes feminist epistemology's guiding question—"whose knowledge are we talking about?"—and situates it in places whose intersections with other locations and their occupants, whose multiple structures of power and privilege and distributions of epistemic authority, all reveal their epistemological significance. My intention in this book is to show why an ecologically reconfigured epistemology recommends itself to feminist and other postcolonial thinkers engaged in building successor epistemologies. It offers a conceptual frame within which to construct a responsive-responsible theory of knowledge and subjectivity: responsive to singularity, diversity, and community; responsibly committed to knowing well so as to counteract the oppressions that the epistemologies of mastery sustain; and sensitive to the multiple responsibilities invoked in claiming a place within naturalistic inquiry. The proposal is naturalist, environmentalist, and democratic in the transformative inspiration of its enactment of thoughtful epistemic practice and in its belief in the salience of theories of knowledge to emancipatory social movements.

About This Book

As I argue in the chapters that follow, *ecological thinking* points toward ways of developing a conceptual framework for a theory of knowledge—an epistemology—sensitive to human and historical-geographical diversity and well equipped to interrogate and unsettle the instrumental rationality, abstract individualism, reductionism, and exploitation of people and places that the epistemologies of mastery have helped to legitimate. Ecological mappings, tracing the interests, power structures, and sedimented assumptions about "nature" and "human nature" enlisted and enacted in postpositivist epistemological orthodoxy, expose the contingency—the historical-cultural specificity— of those assumptions and the imaginary that generates and sustains them, showing that these are not the only ways of knowing well.

41. Haraway, *Modest_Witness*, 270.

With their capacity to inform feminist, multicultural, and other post-colonial revisionary practices, the understandings derived from ecological remappings open conceptual-deliberative spaces for developing nuanced appraisals of the myriad human and (other) environmental constraints on, and implications of, knowledge gathering, and thence for generating reconfigured regulative principles, responsive and responsible to the specificities of knowledge making in the natural and social world, both found and made. These remappings extend from a rejection of an individualism for which citizenship is merely incidental and perhaps instrumental, all the way to matters of globalization and ways of living with/in/as part of nature. They reconsider how to think about naturalistic epistemology, about science, about the politics of factuality, about subjectivity, autonomy, and knowing other people—the rights and wrongs of it—addressed in relation to matters of knowledge and public trust, offering multiply interpretable ways of linking the subject matters of the next seven chapters.

The sequence of chapters is as follows: In chapters one and two, I delineate the conceptual apparatus with which I analyze the examples and studies that inform the discussion in subsequent chapters. Beginning with an examination of how entrenched *social imaginaries* work to hold certain conceptual frames in place, thereby maintaining the legitimacy of hegemonic interpretations of experience and the world, while discrediting others, I argue that ecological thinking initiates a renewal at the level of an *instituted imaginary* that has long claimed pride of place in the western world. To demonstrate what this renewal involves, I offer a reading of how the focus of Rachel Carson's thinking shifted in the early 1950s from geographical to ecological; and I extrapolate an epistemological position from her work to illustrate the literal sense of ecology I am invoking, charting it against a more metaphorical sense enacted in the work of biologist Karen Messing. The analysis moves back and forth between specific examples of situated knowings and conceptions of ecology that depart from the ethos of mastery central to postpositivist epistemology. Chapter two starts with a critical evaluation of the promise and the problems of Quinean naturalized epistemology for feminist and other postcolonial theories of knowledge, to prepare the way for characterizing my position as "ecological naturalism." Whereas Quinean naturalism takes laboratory-based cognitive science as the place to study how human beings "naturally" know, ecological naturalism derives its conception of the natural and of natural knowledge making in large part from the science of ecology and also from studying everyday epistemic practices. Showing how the science of ecology counts as a "weak" science by orthodox positivist standards (drawing on Kristin Shrader-Frechette's and Sharon Kingsland's arguments) I show how this so-called weakness can become a strength in the enhanced capacity it offers to know interpretively, non-reductively, and responsibly.

With its title "Negotiating Empiricism," chapter three announces its political agenda. Oxymoronic though it may seem to be, *negotiated empiricism* is an empirically based, evidence-respecting position that takes empirical evidence seriously while contending that evidence rarely speaks for itself either in its claims to count *as* evidence or in its meanings and implications. Picking up a discussion of interconnections between empirical and "anecdotal" evidence that begins in chapter one, and illustrating my claims with "statements of fact" drawn from medicine and law, I show how experiential, testimonial reports claim an enhanced, if not uncontested, credibility and authority in this approach to knowledge.

Chapter four begins to develop the conception of subjectivity on which my argument relies, taking issue with the model of developmental psychology developed by Jean Piaget and central to Lawrence Kohlberg's stage theory, for its reliance on assumptions about achieved rational mastery as the mark of moral and cognitive maturity. Taking my point of critical departure from Valerie Walkerdine's reading of Piaget in *The Mastery of Reason*, I argue for an approach to developmentality that is socially-ecologically aware in its conception of subjectivity, sociality, and citizenship and in its view of knowledge as a power-saturated social institution. This chapter prepares the way for arguments in the next three chapters, which are variously situated within examples of epistemic practice designed to show how a knower's or social group's status within social structures of epistemic authority, together with the credibility of her, his, or their testimony, are socially-politically produced, if not determined.

Chapters five and six are concerned with showing how advocacy figures as a practice directed toward claiming credibility for the knowledge of hitherto marginalised or disadvantaged knowers. The focus of chapter five is on the covert capacity of autonomy—the celebrated goal of moral-political life in liberal-democratic societies—to oppress women and Others who do not fulfill its requirements. With reference to the collapse of the welfare state, the analysis suggests how an ecological model of citizenship and collective responsibility could begin to reconfigure the inequalities and injustices enacted under the umbrella of a too-rigorous veneration of autonomy. The chapter's most contentious claim is that advocacy often makes knowledge possible: indeed, that without advocacy certain kinds of knowing are impossible, in a strong sense. That line of argument extends into chapter six where, despite having argued both in chapter one and elsewhere in my work, that knowing other people affords better exemplars of the complexity of knowing than knowing medium-sized physical objects can offer, I consider the scope and limits of such knowledge. Taking a cautionary stance, I address some difficulties of knowing well enough to think responsibly, beyond one's own situation, and extend the analysis to ask whether or how it could ever be possible to "think globally" or, more accurately, how knowledge derived from and shaped by quite specific circumstances could claim wider pertinence, albeit less world-encompassing than the term "global," often misleadingly, implies. I ask who could plausibly claim to be in a position to do so. Finally, drawing on an example of the suppression of research findings by a pharmaceutical company with a vested interest in keeping them from the public eye, chapter seven reads the—ambiguous—gendered implications of the positioning of a female scientist and doctor as the principal player in the story, where questions about credibility, answerability, academic freedom, and public trust figure centrally. The analysis shows how ecological thinking fosters the development of a productive ideal of responsibility, rooted neither in individualism nor in an implausible voluntarism, yet attentive to the climatic conditions in which much scientific and other research in the twenty-first century takes place.

The brief conclusion draws together the interpretive dimensions of ecological thinking, linking the lines of inquiry I have followed to show how an ecological remapping of the epistemic terrain such as I promise at the end of my 1991 book, *What Can She Know?*, can initiate transformations in the social order capable of destabilizing the epistemologies of mastery and unsettling their hegemony. It reaffirms a wariness of premature closure, reductionism, and master narratives, while insisting that the promise of ecological thinking is as constructive as it is critical, for it opens new deliberative spaces for democratic dialogue. Ecological thinking may indeed appear to restrict the range of justifiable, definitive knowledge claims, yet it maintains vigilance for irresponsible, careless, too-swift knowings that fail to do justice to their objects of study.

As I have observed, ecological thinking is not simply thinking *about* ecology or *about* the environment: it generates revisioned modes of engagement with knowledge, subjectivity, politics, ethics, science, citizenship, and agency, which pervade and reconfigure theory and practice alike. First and foremost a thoughtful practice, thinking ecologically carries with it a large measure of responsibility—to know somehow more *carefully* than single surface readings can allow. It might seem difficult to imagine how it could translate into wider issues of citizenship and politics, but the answer, at once simple and profound, is that ecological thinking is about imagining, crafting, articulating, endeavoring to enact principles of ideal cohabitation.[42] This idea runs as a thematic thread through this book.

---

42. I am grateful to Vincent Colapietro for this elegant suggestion.

Starting at real-life events, at radical subjectivity, her experience as a species treated

as a minority, separated, reified, looked at, a woman of my generation discovers

that her "little problem," her "secondary question," this so-minute detail of the

subversive front, indeed, her "fragmentary struggle," is no longer content to link with

but identifies directly with the number one question, with the original problem; the

basis, even, of the indispensable need to change the world, not just to improve it, but

so that there can still be a world.

—Françoise d'Eaubonne, "The Time for Ecofeminism" (emphasis in original)

I

ECOLOGICAL THINKING:

Subversions and

Transformations

Social Imaginaries

The working definition of *ecology* that informs my conception of ecological thinking is something of an amalgam, pieced together from diverse sources. Broadly speaking, it is a study of habitats both physical and social where people endeavor to live well together; of ways of knowing that foster or thwart such living; and thus of the ethos and habitus enacted in the knowledge and actions, customs, social structures, and creative-regulative principles by which people strive or fail to achieve this multiply realizable end. It draws one of its dominant threads from Rachel Carson's work on her "Conservation in Action" booklets to which her biographer, Linda Lear, traces the entry of the term *ecology* into everyday English, commenting: "She approached each [site]...from a perspective that can only be described as ecological, even though that word had little common currency in wildlife science in the late 1940s."[1] Carson's approach meshes well with Sharon Kingsland's conception of ecology as "the study of patterns in nature, of how these patterns came to be, how they change in space in time, why some are more fragile than others"; while population ecology, whose history Kingsland charts, studies "how populations interact with the environment and how these interactions give rise to the larger patterns of communities and ecosystems ... [of] how ... organisms interact, through food webs, in competition, and in cooperation."[2] Like Lear, Raymond Williams traces the term's entry into everyday English to the mid-twentieth century ("though its scientific use ... dates from the 1870s"). Significantly for my purposes, he notes ecology's evolution into "the study of the relations of plants and animals with each other and with their habitat," understood as "a characteristic living place," and observes that post-1960s ecology extends to reinterpret economics, politics, and social theory "from a central concern with human relations to the physical world as the necessary basis for social and economic policy."[3] In such reinterpretations, which I read both literally and metaphorically, the politics of knowledge claims a central place.

Adding another layer to this working definition, according to Verena Conley, in post-1968 France "ecology takes on the double meaning of being at once a social and natural concern aimed at measuring habitability."[4] Still more germane to my purposes here, for Gilles Deleuze (with respect to ethos), *ethology* refers to "the capacities for affecting and being affected that characterize each thing"; it studies "the compositions of relations or capacities between different things. ... It is ... a matter of sociabilities and communities."[5] Ethology as it figures—albeit only occasionally—in Deleuze's work, gestures toward ways of mapping human beings' relations to one another, to physicality, sociality, place, cultural institutions, materiality, corporeality, to name just some of the possibilities for charting its effects.[6]

1. Lear, *Rachel Carson*, 132.
2. Kingsland, *Modeling Nature*, 1.
3. Williams, *Keywords*, 111. Kingsland notes that "one of the early Darwinians, Ernst Haeckel, defined a new science of *ökologie* in 1866. The word means the study of households; Haeckel intended it to stand for the science of the relations of the organism to the environment, including the study of all the conditions of existence, both organic and inorganic" (*Modeling Nature*, 11).
4. Conley, *Ecopolitics*, 110.
5. Deleuze, *Spinoza*, 125–26.
6. In addition to the discussion in Deleuze's *Spinoza*, see Deleuze and Guattari, *Thousand Plateaus*, 336, for a more specifically biologically based definition of ethology than the one I enlist here. For an excellent feminist reading of Deleuzian ethology where the language of "social cartography" and "mapping" is effectively used, see Gatens, "Through a Spinozist Lens," 168–70. For a reading that accords ethology a central place in Deleuze's thought, see Pearson, "Viroid Life."

Its social-political-ethical potential is both remarkable and subtle. Deleuze asks, for example, "How can a being take another being into its world, but while preserving or respecting the other's own relations and world?"[7] He resists simplistic taxonomies that issue in reductive, mechanistic understandings of individual capacities and powers; a body, he says, "can be anything... it can be a linguistic corpus, a social body, a collectivity."[8] Understanding practices through which such possibilities could be realized is a principal concern of ecological thinking.

Indebted to Lucretius, as well as to Spinoza, as Patrick Hayden persuasively suggests,[9] Deleuze is in fact proposing a naturalistic, ecologically oriented way of thinking that "seeks to eliminate the traditional dichotomy separating humanity (as subject) and nature (as object)," as a route to understanding diverse, complex, multiply interconnected *milieux*. According to Hayden, a milieu encompasses multiple dimensions of the interactions "between elements, compounds, energy sources, and organisms from the molecular to the molar levels" (recalling the links I claim between ecology and habitat).[10] A milieu is "the site, habitat, or medium of ecological interaction and encounter," where ecology aims to understand the "interrelationships of living things and their environments." This emphasis on the continuities of human and nonhuman life acknowledges the complexity of interrelationships in any milieu, while positing connections among "the physical, biological and chemical and the social, ethical and political"[11] and, most significantly, seeking to determine which "*concepts*, practices, and values best promote the collective life and interests of the diverse modes of existence inhabiting the planet,"[12] where so many already-instituted concepts, practices, and values are saturated with contempt for the earth and the well-being of its inhabitants. It recognizes the profundity of Deleuze and Guattari's so simple remark, which I cite in the introduction: "Philosophy is the art of forming, inventing, and fabricating concepts":[13] a task apparently so modest until one considers how much, for lack of a viable conceptual frame, is unknowable, undiscussable, unavailable to animate thought and action.

7. Deleuze, *Spinoza*, 126.
8. Ibid., 127.
9. Hayden, "Gilles Deleuze and Naturalism."
10. Deleuze and Guattari write: "Every territory, every habitat, joins up not only its spatiotemporal but its qualitative planes or sections: a posture and a song for example, a song and a color, percepts and affects" (*What Is Philosophy?* 185).
11. Ibid., 192, 194.
12. Ibid., 196 (emphasis added).
13. Ibid., 2.

Politically-epistemologically, Deleuze's emphasis on micro- and macro-politics is responsive in its micropolitical aspects to the problems and specificities of the habitats and inhabitants of local bioregions, in its macropolitical aspects to intersections of smaller local practices and conditions, themselves "affected by the influences and activities of macropolitical institutions." All of these stances require a just measure of knowledge of ecological conditions, if they are to produce responsibly informed and "effective ecopolitical interventions," whether locally or further afield: interventions grounded in "current situations, knowledge, and experiences" and intended to achieve "modes of existence that exemplify appropriate, sustainable, and beneficial relationships between human and nonhuman beings and their environments."[14] Reread through an epistemological lens, this formulation captures the commitment implicit in ecological thinking to imagining, crafting, articulating, working to enact principles of ideal cohabitation.

Although it makes for a somewhat uneasy theoretical juxtaposition, I am thinking about ethos as it figures in Deleuze's ethology together with habitus in Pierre Bourdieu's sense. Habitus captures the notion of an "embodied history, internalized as a second nature and so forgotten as history"; yet it is also an "active presence" evident in lived "systems of durable, transposable dispositions . . . which generate and organize practices that can be objectively adapted to their outcomes without presupposing a conscious aiming at ends or an express mastery of the operations necessary . . . to attain them."[15] It has to do with having a sense of one's place, with the cumulative totality of sedimented cultural and personal experiences a human being carries as he or she moves about in a social space and in relation to the power structures that shape such places. Yet it is a system of "generative schemes" that neither denies nor obstructs agency: its limits are "set by the historically and socially situated conditions of its production" although, perhaps paradoxically, Bourdieu conceives it as "an infinite capacity for generating . . . thoughts, perceptions, expressions and actions."[16] Ethos and habitus thus contribute to a conceptual frame for the modalities of ecological thinking and for shaping a conception of ecological subjectivity.

My brief for ecological thinking conceives of it as infusing, shaping, and circulating throughout the social-material-intellectual-affective atmosphere(s), like the air we breathe. Ecological knowings are enacted and ecological principles

14. The phrases are from Hayden, "Gilles Deleuze and Naturalism," 197–98.
15. Bourdieu, *Logic of Practice*, 56, 53.
16. Ibid., 55.

derived within a transformative, interrogating, and renewing *imaginary*—a loosely integrated system of images, metaphors, tacit assumptions, ways of thinking—a guiding metaphorics that departs radically from the imaginary through and within which epistemologies of mastery are derived and enacted. As I have noted, my larger purpose is to interrupt and unsettle the instituted social-political-epistemological imaginary of the affluent western world that generates and sustains hegemonic practices of mastery with a web of assumptions, of tacit agreements that are everyone's and no one's, about "nature" and "human nature," and how best to know them singly and in their interrelations.

A social imaginary as I adduce it here bears a distant resemblance to a Kuhnian paradigm or a Foucauldian episteme; but its scope is not restricted to regulative assumptions within normal science, nor is it principally about how knowable items in successive historical periods are spread out before *the* observant knower. It is as productive in locating and evaluating practices of scientific inquiry as in generating and sustaining images, metaphors, and operative idea(l)s that underwrite patterns of legitimacy and credibility and their opposites. It is about often-implicit but nonetheless effective systems of images, meanings, metaphors, and interlocking explanations-expectations within which people, in specific time periods and geographical-cultural climates, enact their knowledge and subjectivities and craft their self-understandings. Imaginaries are self-reinforcing rather as self-fulfilling prophesies are. Ongoing "successes" within them consolidate their sense of rightness. Yet in one structural feature, they resemble both paradigms and epistemes: pressures, destabilizations, ruptures, breaks—from above, within, or below—repeated explanatory stress, can become so insistent that the imaginary, ultimately, cannot sustain its status as a seamlessly enveloping story: the center cannot hold. And this—particularly in epistemology—despite the tenacity of beliefs that the center *must* hold, which continue to inform the replicability and universalizability requirements and to sustain the regulative normativity integral to the theoretical positions that the orthodox epistemic subject silently inhabits.

A shift to a reconfigured imaginary is not precisely like a paradigm shift or a (Foucauldian) rupture, for disruptions and transformations may not render an imaginary redundant; it may be implausible or impossible to trace a history of successive, hegemonic imaginaries, superseded just as Kuhnian paradigms become obsolete and/or Foucauldian epistemes disappear into the past. "Paradigm" talk carries the connotation of a relatively closed system with a governing assumption or set of assumptions, put into play by a breakthrough event whose effects are to reconfigure subsequent inquiry. It plays a normalizing

role in determining the legitimacy or otherwise of problems and lines of investigation, thus requiring researchers to toe the line it puts in place. Thinking
through imaginaries is different in this regard. The positivistic, scientistic post-
Enlightenment epistemology of mastery may indeed not be rendered false in all
its detail and commitments by ecological thinking, but its limitations are exposed, its pretensions to tell—and be—the one true story are challenged, its
hegemonic status cast in question. Thus contesting, infiltrating this entrenched
imaginary is a reflexive process of requiring it to submit its assumptions of
universal rightness to scrutiny, its residual and totalizing unity-of-science assumptions, and its governing beliefs about the nature of nature, knowledge,
and knowledgeable subjectivity. The process is of necessity gradual, and by no
means linear. It introduces and plays on certain incongruities and tensions:
productive tensions that unsettle taken-for-granted authoritarian assumptions
of self-certainty, yet resist efforts to return to a more comfortable stasis.

In contrasting an ecological imaginary to an established imaginary of
mastery, I am indebted to the work of Cornelius Castoriadis on the *instituted
social imaginary*. He writes:

> The socialization of individuals—itself an instituted process, and in
> each case a different one—opens up these individuals, giving them
> access to a *world* of social imaginary significations whose instauration
> as well as incredible *coherence* goes unimaginably beyond everything
> that "one or many individuals" could ever produce. These signifi-
> cations owe their actual (social-historical) existence to the fact that
> they are *instituted*.[17]

The instituted imaginary thus conceived carries within it the normative social meanings, customs, expectations, assumptions, values, prohibitions, and
permissions—the habitus and ethos—into which human beings are nurtured
from childhood and which they internalize, affirm, challenge, or contest as they
make sense of their place, options, responsibilities within a world, both social
and physical, whose "nature" and meaning are also instituted in these imaginary significations. A social imaginary is social in the broadest sense: it is not
merely about principles of conduct, although it is about those too; but it is
about how such principles claim and maintain salience; about the scope and
limits of human knowledge and the place of knowledge in the world; about the
structural ordering of institutions of knowledge production; about intellectual
and moral character ideals, subjectivity, and agency; about the kinds of habitat

17. Castoriadis, *Philosophy, Politics, Autonomy*, 62 (emphasis in original).

and living conditions that are within reach and/or worth striving for; about
social-political-economic organization and just distributions of goods, privileges, power, and authority. In this complex sense, the social imaginary of
mastery extends across the ethos and expectations of the affluent white western
world that sees no limits to human possibilities of mastering and controlling the
world's resources—animal (both human and nonhuman), vegetable, and
mineral—no reason to contest the rightness of "man's" claims to dominion
over all the earth, and no reason to take issue with the generic concept "man's"
exclusionary referential scope.

To the instituted imaginary, Castoriadis opposes the *instituting* imaginary:
the critical-creative activity of a society that exhibits its autonomy in its capacity to put itself in question,[18] in the ability of (some of) its members to act
from a (collective for some collectivity) recognition that the society is incongruous with itself, with scant reason for self-satisfaction. Imaginatively initiated
counterpossibilities interrogate the social structure to destabilize its pretensions to naturalness and wholeness, to initiate a new making (a *poiesis*—
Castoriadis claims an abiding debt to Aristotle).

Castoriadis's work carries no presumption in favor of a single, hard-edged
hegemonic imaginary (no counterpart, then, of Kuhnian paradigm talk). His
interest is in the imaginary of late capitalism that holds social hierarchies and
unjust distributions of power and privilege in place, perpetuates a mythology
of the instrumental innocence and neutral expertise of scientific knowledge,
and generates illusions of benign equations between power and knowledge. It
works from assumptions about relations between and among people, between
citizens and society, and between human beings and the natural world that
legitimate the exploitations and oppressions known to every reader of feminist,
postcolonial, antiracist, and critical ecological theory. His is in many respects
a familiar Marxist critique, but its innovative dimension, whose effects he
intends to be far-reaching, is its concept of *the imaginary*, whose positive
inspiration comes from Freud, Marx, and Kant's *Critique of Judgement* and
whose negative inspiration from an overblown post-Enlightenment individually owned reason posing as the legitimator of knowledge of physical nature
and human nature alike, which carves out and defends its domain by relegating
imagination to the merely fanciful, unable to make contact with reality and
thus powerless as a producer of or contributor to knowledge.

Epistemologically, the instituted social imaginary of the early-twenty-first-
century affluent white western world holds in place a view of the appropriate

18. See Castoriadis, "Radical Imagination."

human relation to the natural world as one of a spectator consciousness standing outside and apart from that world. Its epistemic purpose is to master the ruly and unruly aspects of nature, both physical-geographical and human, and to know the world well enough to be able to manipulate, predict, and control it to serve human ends. This imaginary upholds a complex of inter-locking assumptions according to which Enlightenment reason can "lay the world out before itself as a set of objects for [the] contemplation and dis-passionate investigation"[19] of a transcendent and dispassionate knowing subject, an indifferent observer of an inert, indifferent world.

In ecological thinking, knowers are repositioned as self-consciously part of nature, while anthropocentric projects of mastery are superseded by projects of displacing Enlightenment "man" from the center of the universe and devel-oping radical critiques of the single-minded mastery claimed for "human reason." Ecological thinking works against the imaginary of God-given human dominion over all the earth and, more precisely, of dominion arrogated to certain chosen members of the human race, not just over the earth but over human Others as well. Yet its purpose is not to substitute pure, disinterested contemplation for mastery. It aims to reenlist the successes of empirical science together with other kinds of knowledge, reflexively and critically, in projects committed to understanding the implications and effects of such ways of knowing and acting, regardless of short-term costs to "efficiency," and capable of seeing nature and human nature as reciprocally engaged, intra-active. Thus it conceives of human interventions throughout the world, both physical and social, as requiring sensitivity to, and responsibility in relation to, specificities of diversity and detail, placing respect above mastery, preservation before control, understanding for what is and has been before predictions of what might be. The point is not to eschew mastery *simpliciter* or to resist control outright, but to develop ways of articulating and enacting both, so as to shift the emphasis away from presumptions of entitlement and toward assuming the responsibilities and precautionary policies integral to democratically negoti-ated power and authority. Thus, with regard to the universalizability that orthodox epistemologies require, although ecological thinking may manifest itself quite differently in response to the specificities of particular organisms, situations, habitus, or ethos, it works from an overarching commitment to shaping epistemological standpoints in ways fundamentally different from the ways of thinking—the imaginary—put together around and animated by unquestioned assumptions about the overriding value of mastery for its own

19. The words are from Kruks, *Retrieving Experience*, 117.

sake. Just how these shapings play out in epistemological and social-political practices is the subject of the examples I present in subsequent chapters of this book. Its demonstrations of the shortcomings of the instituted social imaginary, and the creative reconfigurations that its twist of the epistemic kaleidoscope makes possible, most strongly recommend ecological thinking.

Provocatively, Castoriadis argues that the ecological movement has cast in question "the whole conception, the total position and relation between humanity and the world and, finally, the central and eternal question: what is human life? What are we living for?"[20] He advances no naive proposal that ecology can provide a single or total solution to the problems of the modern world but, he contends, only such an imaginatively conceived and politically savvy *instituting imaginary* can effectively interrogate an already instituted imaginary. Nor is it a matter merely of opposing one imaginary to another for the sake of showing one to be right and the other wrong, but of variously, and through diverse practices, complicating sedimented assumptions and exposing undesirable, unjust, inequitable, less-than-adequate effects, where criteria of adequacy, too, have to be ecologically deliberated, negotiated. It is a matter of opening up other possibilities, marking what has to be questioned, "making strange" what passes for natural in epistemic practice, in the people, events, and phenomena it studies and in the practices it informs. The *instituting* imaginary is a vehicle of radical social critique: it requires thinking and acting away from received conceptions of knowledge, subjectivity, responsibility, and agency, from positions located squarely within the power-infused rhetorical spaces where knowledge making and knowledge circulating occur; determining how reconfigurations might be proposed, innovative hypotheses articulated and tested in and for that climate, that place, positioned as it is in relation to other places and climates.

The instituted imaginary is never seamless or static in a nontotalitarian society: it is always in motion, whether in maintaining itself or in critical interrogations within and around it. Its gaps, its motility open up spaces for the work of the instituting imaginary. Epistemologically, local imaginative critique such as Castoriadis's ecology essay offers prepares the way for a regenerative imaginary—a cluster of subversive and productive practices, metaphors, images—capable, with persistent effort, of shaking epistemology free from the monocultural/monological hold of the imaginary that has kept standard theories of knowledge isolated from the very knowledge they have sought to explicate. Offering an analysis that links ecology and autonomy within an ethical-epistemological-political frame,

20. Castoriadis, "From Ecology to Autonomy," 14.

Castoriadis's ecology essay is multiply pertinent to these issues as they bear on dominant ways of conceiving—*knowing*—nature and human nature. He observes how representations of scientific knowledge as disinterestedly, apolitically neutral shape "the dominant social imaginary (*imaginaire social*) of our epoch," for which "the central aim of social life is the unlimited expansion of rational mastery."[21] This imaginary claims the assent of the social majority by sustained processes of nurturing citizens throughout their lives to ingest an unquestioned relationship to an "ensemble of needs" whose satisfaction becomes a lifelong project, even though Castoriadis affirms, unequivocally and provocatively (for the western world), "there are no natural needs"—only the needs capitalism creates, that it alone can satisfy.[22] His remark must be interpreted with caution: presumably he is not contesting such basic needs as those for food, water, shelter, community, safety, affection, or freedom from oppression and disease: his target is the excessive material indulgence of the affluent, capitalist world and the putative needs it generates. Nonetheless, the point is plausible in the extent to which the discourse of needs naturalizes its referents, obscures their artifactuality.

The ecology movement thus engages with human existence at a fundamental level: that of its "needs." Taking *electricity* as a regulative, society-governing commodity, Castoriadis argues that an overwhelming impulse to produce the energy required to satisfy this need has played a dominant part in generating a relationship to nature of mastery and possession, stretching well beyond attitudes to wilderness, animals, and romanticized conceptions of "our" participation in nature. This relationship underpins patterns of domination whose effects are, ultimately, to enslave the society: "It implies the totality of production, and at the same time, it involves the totality of social organisation."[23] For Castoriadis, genealogies of the *creation* of the "individual," complete with her or his needs, within this imaginary, expose the contingency of the process and the interests it tacitly serves, thus making it possible to utilize that same scientific, technological, and social-psychological knowledge to begin thinking about how to reconstruct human relations to the social and natural world. He cautions: "The transformation of present technology . . . will have to seize part of what exists at present as technology and utilize it to create another technology."[24] A plausible example of the power of such a countertechnology to disturb the presumed self-evident

21. Ibid., 8.

22. Ibid., 12.

23. Ibid., 16. Instructive in this connection is Glendenning's novel *Electricity* for its historical reconstruction of the coming of electric light, in the 1880s, to an English country house.

24. Castoriadis, "From Ecology to Autonomy," 20. Recall Gee's comments ("Force of Nature") about the use of high-tech in integrated agriculture, which I cite in the introduction.

rightness of reliance on electricity is renewable energy, such as solar and wind power or small-scale hydrogen and fuel cells, all of which transform energy-producing technology as they redirect its knowledge base to create other technologies: processes that could counter the kind of energy-addiction Castioriadis condemns were government subsidies and tax incentives transferred to these initiatives and away from fossil-fuel industries. "Alternative" energies open ways of transforming the technologies an energy-addicted society has created, so that they cease to enslave their creators, thereby enabling "the producers as individuals and groups . . . [to be] truly masters of their productive processes."[25] Following this transformative line with analogous examples and practices, the ecological movement can function as a resource for addressing many of the "political problems of the reconstruction of autonomous society" that, Castoriadis suggests, have posed as many problems for the women's movement and the youth movement, as for the workers' movement. It offers a creatively inspired, emancipatory conceptual apparatus within which to refuse ongoing colonization by an imaginary that requires relations of dominance and submission to sustain it, relies on concealed linkages between power and knowledge, and promotes the individual autonomy of a few through the heteronomy of the many.

I have observed how the dominant epistemologies of post–Industrial Revolution affluent societies are (often tacitly) complicit in perpetuating the rhetoric of mastery and possession: knowledge acquired for manipulation, prediction, and control over nature and human nature; knowledge as a prized commodity legitimating its possessors' authoritative occupancy (and sometime abuse) of positions of power and recasting "the natural world" as a resource for human gratification. The ecology movement's critical skepticism toward the pretensions of an energy-fetishized society challenges the capacity of an unreconstructed physical science to provide the best epistemological route toward knowing that resource, responsibly and well. In the process, it becomes a site of revisionary social-political praxis.

An ecologically modeled conception of knowledge and subjectivity thus initiates an *instituting* epistemic-moral-political imaginary in which these three conjoined modes of inquiry work reciprocally, intra-actively together. Taking its point of departure from the—natural—interdependence of knowledge-making activities and the constitutive effects of sociality and location in their practice, it *situates* the negotiations a renewing epistemology requires and refuses the unimaginative, dislocated levelings-off that the epistemologies of mastery have too often performed. Because its effectiveness requires responsible intermappings

25. Castoriadis, "From Ecology to Autonomy," 20.

(from region to region), as well as internal mappings, *negotiating differences* is a prominent item on its agenda. Such negotiating is reliant upon activities of initiating public, democratic conversations—debates—which aim, interpretively, imaginatively, and critically, to know differences of subjectivity and agency, habitus and ethos, circumstance and history; honoring them where practical wisdom (*phronēsis*) and deliberation show them worthy of preservation; interrogating and contesting them where necessary; yet neither in stasis nor in isolation.

In my view, social-epistemological commitments such as these can be traced throughout Rachel Carson's scientific practice, in investigations that, as I indicate at the beginning of this chapter, were the source of "ecology's" entry into everyday parlance in the English-speaking world, in work that was indisputably ecological before the term achieved common currency either in everyday English or in professional scientific circles. It is from her epistemic practice that my more detailed mappings of the literal and metaphorical understandings of ecology in the rest of this book take their point of departure. As it has evolved—albeit contentiously—to inform late-twentieth-century ecological science and environmental activism, her practice is impressive in its potential to unsettle the sedimented assumptions of the Anglo-American epistemological orthodoxy that shapes and sustains the hegemony of the instituted social imaginary of mastery and control, of which Castoriadis is so critical. A commitment to democratic conversation and negotiation figures centrally in her manner of weaving scientific and extrascientific evidence together and of circulating her findings to a skeptical public. Thus her work enters the public arena with the power to interrupt the complacency and hubris of "man's" presumptive dominion over all the earth. To readers who know Carson as a pathbreaking practitioner of twentieth-century ecological thinking and practice, these claims will not be startling. But it is worth recalling that it is possible, then as now, to work as a naturalist, even as an environmentalist or a wildlife scientist, without thinking ecologically. What, then, makes Carson's work distinctively ecological?

Rachel Carson's Epistemological Practice

According to Linda Lear, it was when she was gathering material for *The Edge of the Sea* in the early 1950s that Carson's thinking shifted from geographical to explicitly ecological: to a reconceived process of producing a "biographical sketch" to explain the "special features of each environment to which creatures...[had] to adapt," to studying their "life cycles and physical habitats," identifying "ways in which they had adapted to various and often continuously changing conditions."[26] From this refined and refining ecological stance, Carson began to write about different types of shore—rock, sand, and coral—about "each geological area as a living ecological community rather than about individual organisms."[27] As her commitment to ecological thinking consolidated, Carson came to characterize the scope of biology as "the history of the earth and all its life—the past, the present, and the future," adding the specifically ecological claim: "Neither man [sic] nor any other living creature may be studied or comprehended apart from the world in which he lives,"[28] thus echoing a point from her acceptance speech for the National Book Award: "It is impossible to understand man without understanding his environment and the forces that have molded him physically and environmentally."[29] This, briefly, is her ecological credo.[30] It would overstate the case to represent such factors as *determining* knowledge production or the substance of the knowledge produced, but understate it to gloss over their constitutive effects. Likewise, it would distort Carson's position to read it as tracing discrete, unilinear causal relationships to explain the "forces that have molded" nature and human nature, but give it less than its due to gloss over the multiple connections she exposes.

This focus on habitat as a place to know is central to ecological thinking, as I conceive it, although in its more metaphorical applications, social-political, cultural, and psychological elements figure alongside physical and (other) environmental contributors to the "nature" of a habitat and its inhabitants, at any historical moment.[31] In its epistemological mode, social-moral-political analyses of the geographical, institutional, and material circumstances, historical events, and climatological shifts that foster or constrain scientific/epistemic practice are integral to ecological thinking. With these thoughts in mind, from pieces of her own writings and the story her biographer tells I am assembling a picture of Carson as epistemologist, whose epistemic-scientific imaginary, rhetorical strategies, and practices of inquiry contrast productively with those of a (perhaps caricatured)

26. Lear, *Rachel Carson*, 229.
27. Ibid., 243.
28. Carson, "Biological Sciences," quoted in Lear, *Rachel Carson*, 278.
29. Speech given by Carson at the National Book Award on 29 January 1952; in the Rachel Carson Papers, Yale University Collection of American Literature, Beinecke Rare Book and Manuscript Library, Yale University, New Haven, CT, cited in Lear, *Rachel Carson*, 219.
30. Deleuze remarks: "So an animal, a thing, is never separable from its relations with the world" (*Spinoza*, 125).
31. In its emphasis on habitat and place, my position is in some respects consonant with the position Preston develops in his *Grounding Knowledge*.

postpositivist faith in the power of an idealized, monolithic science to explain everything worthy of explanation. The point must be developed with care, for the strength of Carson's position, especially in *Silent Spring* but also in her earlier books, is in her informed, judicious respect for empirical, observational evidence: her scientific credentials are firmly in place; nor is she a naive antiscience crusader. Indeed, Sandilands proposes that in consequence of Carson's meticulous work in assembling "a complex body of data for lay readers" in *Silent Spring* "a discourse of environmentalism based on scientific proof (as opposed to earlier versions based on preservation and aesthetics) became the standard."[32] Yet as I will show, for Carson, proof was not confined to the laboratory, nor could scientific and ethical issues be separated from one another.[33]

Why, then, am I representing Carson's approach, with its solid grounding in empirical science, as subversive of scientific orthodoxy on issues of mastery, precisely because of its ecological commitments; and why am I presenting it as exemplary for ecological knowing? One of my overriding interests in this project is to show how the discourse of autonomy and individualism, integral to epistemologies of mastery, comes into tension—*productive* tension—with the rhetorical and practical challenges ecological thinking poses to the self-certainties of western capitalism. Of Carson, therefore, I am suggesting that, even though as a scientist she was as vilified as she was acclaimed (especially, again, for *Silent Spring*), her research practice counts as scientifically-epistemically exacting, and responsible, by many of the criteria of mid-twentieth-century "normal science." Yet in cutting "against the grain of materialism, scientism, and the technologically engineered control of nature" it also subverts some of the most basic assumptions of instituted scientific practice, thereby generating a healthy skepticism about how reductive, mechanistic scientific research isolates parts of nature so as to obscure the constitutive functions of multiple and complex interconnections in producing the phenomena it studies. Hence, Gary Kroll describes *Silent Spring* as "an essay in ecological radicalism that attempted to wake up a populace quiescent to the techno-scientific control of the world," heralding Carson as one of the first scientists to bring ecological debate into the public sphere.[34] This point can be illustrated with reference to questions of evidence and to the scope and limits of scientific inquiry: to its place in the

32. Sandilands, "Environmental Science," 167.
33. See, e.g., Cafaro, "Rachel Carson's Environmental Ethics."
34. Kroll, "Ecology as a Subversive Subject." Strong also elaborates ecology's potential to subvert environmentally destructive practices and ways of life (advocating engaged, disclosive discourse over "a strictly scientific account"); see "Disclosive Discourse," 89–90.

habitat-enhancing or habitat-endangering aims of an ecological stance such as hers. I address these issues briefly here, to prepare the ground for a more detailed discussion of what I call "ecological naturalism" in chapter two.

Despite its careful attention to empirical-observational evidence and its commitment in *Silent Spring* to blocking—thus indeed to controlling, to achieving mastery over—the vast and unforeseen environmental degradation consequent upon excessive use of pesticides and other chemicals, Carson's is no epistemology of mastery, nor is its knower a disinterested spectator of the objects of knowledge. Starting from a conviction born of wide-ranging evaluations, *both scientific and secular*, of practices of controlling "pests" with chemical pesticides and herbicides, Carson insists that not even scientifically sanctioned observational evidence speaks for itself either in its claims to count as evidence or in its meanings, whether instantaneous or long-term, for lives and habitats. She urges an intellectual-moral humility in scientific inquiry and scientifically informed practice to displace the hubris driving indiscriminate eradication programs and to contest the arrogance of human aspirations— indiscriminately—to achieve "control of nature." Deploring a "vogue for poisons" that, without humility, ignores "the extraordinary capacities of life," Carson writes: "It is our alarming misfortune that so primitive a science has armed itself with the most modern and terrible weapons, and that in turning them against the insects it has also turned them against the earth."[35] From a position deeply critical of chemical and biological interventions that are insufficiently grounded in knowledge of their implications for specific living beings and their habitats, Carson is urging a shift toward taking respectful and detailed account of the creatures, both human and nonhuman, whose lives and habitats they alter, for better or worse. Implicit in her work is a principled opposition to risk-assessment approaches to environmental decision-making, to estimating damages likely to follow from certain actions, when they are articulated within a conceptual frame constructed around convictions that damage is inevitable: the only pertinent question is how much is, or can be represented as, acceptable. Carson cites numerous examples where harm is declared inevitable, yet where alternative, much less damaging, more environmentally respectful solutions are available if people take the time and make the political and financial commitments required to know them well enough to act otherwise.

Analogously, claiming that despite the undoubted promise of science and technology in the new space age she was coming to know, "man" must

35. Carson, *Silent Spring*, 297.

approach the "'new heaven and the new earth'...with humility rather than arrogance,"[36] Carson argues consistently for reading evidence—say, for the power of DDT and other pesticides—together with careful investigations of implications for human and other lives of profligate usage. The mappings that such inquiries demand are themselves ecological, for they require charting, bringing together, and moving back and forth between/among quite different subject areas: studying not just discrete natural organic kinds, but wind and water patterns, food chains, longitudinal patterns of soil drainage and rock formations, human, animal, and plant susceptibilities: various kinds of knowledge with widely differing histories, methods, and assumptions, in whose complex interactions a quite different picture emerges from one that concentrates solely, for example, on the damage wrought by a single species such as the spruce budworm, seeking to eradicate it quickly and efficiently. As committed to achieving—perhaps interim—coherence, both synchronic and diachronic, as to accumulating discrete items of information, Carson maps patterns, tracing lines of interconnection and disjunction, regularities and irregularities, histories and influences, effects and meanings across meticulously detailed habitats, drawing analogies when appropriate, reading disanalogies to puzzle out their significance. She does not favor simply abandoning projects designed to bring an end to environmental "harms" but, crucially, she studies less invasive ways of achieving control than such practices as mass spraying had achieved: taking more sensitive account of the attendant situation-specific damages and benefits and investigating methods committed to respecting and utilizing nature's frequently ignored capacity to offer less ecologically devastating solutions.

Nor—and this is no small point—does Carson conduct her research only in controlled observation conditions, even though she is guided by and returns to laboratory findings, from the field where she studies living things in their habitat, studying the habitat itself just as systematically, in its detail and interactions with its inhabitants. In a language Donna Haraway has made available, this is situated knowledge,[37] elaborated to show that "situation" is not just a place *from which to know*, as the language of "perspectives" might imply, indifferently available to anyone who chooses to stand there. Situation is itself *a place to know* whose intricacies have to be examined for how they shape both knowing subjects and the objects of knowledge; how they legitimate and/ or disqualify knowledge projects; how they are constituted by and constitutive of entrenched social imaginaries, together with the rhetoric that holds them in

36. Carson's February 1958 letter to Dorothy Freeman, cited in Lear, *Rachel Carson*, 311.
37. See Haraway, *Simians, Cyborgs, and Women.*

place. It is an achieved epistemic stance, knowledgeably chosen as a place that can be mapped to facilitate responsible knowing.

Carson's epistemic practice thus approaches knowledge making quite differently from an epistemology conceived as an a priori project of discerning necessary and sufficient conditions for knowledge in general; of producing normative, universally valid justificatory principles; and of silencing the skeptic for whom, because knowledge in the most precise sense of the term is impossible, human beings must confess—and accept—their ignorance.[38] Working from an idealized picture of scientific inquiry performed in the laboratory as a standard-setting cognitive achievement, such an epistemology deploys a model of knowledge derived from discrete, replicable observations, equally available to any (interchangeable) observer. Knowledge claims lend themselves readily to propositional formulation in an "S-knows-that-p" rubric ("Carson knows that this bird is a heron") or multiples and elaborations thereof and to verification by revisiting the observational evidence. In such spectator epistemologies, the self-reliant individual knower, who is in fact not individuated, stands as a shadow figure invisibly and indifferently apart from discrete objects of knowledge. Objects remain inert in and unaffected by the knowing process, which is directed toward achieving knowledge of how to manipulate, predict, and control their behavioral patterns. Knowers bring no affective, personal-historical, or idiosyncratic baggage to "the epistemological project," imagined as value free and theory neutral in its distanced objectivity—neither deriving from nor serving particular interests or motivations nor allowing enthusiasms or aversions to divert its rational course. The centrality of such assumptions for epistemological orthodoxy makes it difficult to *see* ecological issues as epistemologically significant: difficult to map their specificity and evaluate their relevance. With their veneration of the punctiform yet paradigmatic objective fact, such assumptions generate a sense that more textured, ambiguous ecological issues are—and should be—of scant epistemological import.

Its conviction that objects of knowledge are best known in ideal observation conditions, of which controlled laboratory experiments are the clearest example, marks one of the most striking contrasts between orthodox epistemology and ecological thinking. When objects, cells, organisms, people are thus abstracted from their natural surrounds, the belief is that observation can confront empirical evidence directly, with the naked eye or with microscopic, telescopic, or other more sophisticated technological enhancements—that objects, isolated and protected from extraneous interference, whether natural

38. A locus classicus for such an argument is Unger, *Ignorance.*

or coincidental, are maximally available to observation.[39] It follows that if they are to be known well, individual items, entities must be extracted from the cluttered messiness of their ordinary situation; yet also, paradoxically, that knowledge thus achieved translates readily into the circumstances where its objects ordinarily live or occur. Such are the operative ideals of knowledge and knowledge seekers shaping the epistemic imaginary of the scientific world in which Carson moved and against whose excesses her work protests: a world for which divisions between science and literature, laboratory and nature, affect and intellect, fact and anecdote, and thus between truth and narrative were precise and sharp.

Patterns in Nature

How, then, is Carson's work distinctively ecological? Referring to the science of ecology, which, she maintains, "cannot provide precise, fundamental, testable, scientific laws," Kristin Shrader-Frechette distinguishes quantitative, deductive "hard" ecology from qualitative "soft" ecology. Because of its limited predictive powers, she observes, even hard ecology can only ever be a "weak" science; and soft ecology's "inspirational" goals of preserving ecosystem integrity are unclear and vague. In short, hard ecology's theories are underdetermined, and soft ecology's are untestable. This rhetoric, with its gendered inflections, will be familiar to feminist readers of successor epistemology projects. Yet these observations, for Shrader-Frechette, are descriptive rather than evaluative, in the sense that they are not meant to disqualify ecological science from claiming scientific status, but to delineate its scope and limits. Thus, she proposes, "the ecology necessary to undergird sound environmental philosophy requires that people avoid the extremes of using either soft or hard ecology alone and instead use a 'practical ecology' based primarily on case studies, natural history, and rules of thumb."[40] Putting this thought together with Kingsland's bare-bones definition of ecology that also frames Shrader-Frechette's discussion—"the study of patterns in nature, of how those patterns came to be, how they change in space and time, why some are more fragile than others"[41]—I am situating

---

39. Horkheimer and Adorno contend that "abstraction, the tool of enlightenment, treats its objects as did fate, the notion of which it rejects: it liquidates them." The authors point to "the leveling domination of abstraction (which makes everything in nature repeatable), and industry (for which abstraction ordains repetition)" ("Concept of Enlightenment," 47).
40. Shrader-Frechette, "Ecology," 304–5.
41. Shrader-Frechette, ibid., 304, cites Kingsland's *Modeling Nature*.

Carson on a middle path—as a practitioner of a practical ecology reliant on "*empirical* generalizations," yet also dependent on "*narrow* and *precise* local hypotheses,"[42] to amplify my working conception of ecological thinking. In short, I see her as living the tension I have mentioned, working back and forth between an instituted, rhetorically monitored scientific orthodoxy and an attentive respect for particularity that is subversive of many of the fundamental assumptions of scientific orthodoxy. In the public and often in the scientific imagination, orthodox science is hard science: governed, in its epistemic imaginary, by an allegiance to a deductive-nomological model whose purpose is to deduce monolithic, reliably predictive laws. The moving back and forth that makes Carson's ecological practice possible, together with the contributions her craft and training as a writer have made to her work, take that tension into an ironic register, for the fact of her directing her work, throughout her life, to a general rather than merely to a specialized audience softens it, further unsettling the rhetoric and subverting the aura of esotericism surrounding modern science and orthodox epistemology, whose power to confer or withhold the acknowledgment on which legitimacy depends derives from a founding gesture in which, as Lynette Hunter observes,

> neutral logic and pure language replaced "rhetoric." . . . [And science assumed] a rhetorical stance which denied that the rhetoric of social persuasion in historical context was needed, even denied that it existed. . . . Built upon the concept of the "universal autonomous man," able to communicate infinitely replicable experience [and isolated] from the social world, which might contaminate the purity or challenge the totality of explanation. . . . *Its rhetoric claims that there is no need for rhetoric.*[43]

A writer such as Carson who self-consciously and proudly writes for the general public, in a language that often leaves the rhetoric of "normal science" behind, forfeits a certain professional stature. Yet the result, for those who are prepared to go some of the distance with her, is to promote a more participatory, democratic epistemology than the uncontaminated purity of the discourse of mastery can allow. The place she holds open for experiential—testimonial—evidence, to which I turn shortly, consolidates this claim, while both exacerbating the tension and enhancing its productive import. Following Shrader-Frechette's lead, I will illustrate my reasons for locating Carson's practice as I do

42. Ibid., 311 (emphasis in original).
43. Hunter, *Critiques of Knowing*, 30–31 (emphasis added).

by appealing to the epistemology implicit (on my reading) in the case studies she elaborates in *Silent Spring*.

There, Carson displays ecological thinking at work, across diverse modes of knowledge, domains of inquiry, subject matters; bringing together scientific and experiential evidence to produce conclusions sufficiently particular to address the distinctive character of precisely individuated local phenomena; sufficiently cognizant of wider patterns in nature to generate hypotheses for knowing other, relevantly analogous phenomena; and sufficiently informed and coherent to engage with the agendas of policy-makers, the doubts of disbelievers, and the bewilderment of a public caught between expert scientific assurances and experiential incongruities. The very complexity of each separate subject matter requires a knower to be multilingual and multiply literate: to speak the language of laboratory science, wildlife organizations, government agencies, chemical-producing companies, secular nature lovers, and many others; to understand the detail of scientific documents and the force of experiential reports; to work back and forth between variations on the imagery of mastery and of ecology—sometimes, all for the sake of understanding something so very small as a beetle.

Carson's accounts of massive insect-control spraying programs nicely exemplify the interplay between precise local hypotheses and empirical generalizations. To cite but a small sampling, she documents control of the Japanese beetle near Detroit in 1959 (aerial dusting of suburbs with pellets of aldrin); Dutch elm disease in Michigan, Ohio, and New York State in the mid-1950s (spraying with DDT);[44] spruce budworm about the same time in British Columbia, eastern Canada, and Maine (spraying of millions of acres of forests with DDT);[45] and the fire ant in southern U.S. states and the gypsy moth in northern states also in the late 1950s (spraying nearly a million acres with DDT-in-fuel-oil).[46] Germane to the ecological implications of these examples are the contrasts Carson draws between the environmental destruction consequent upon massive spraying and the success of natural methods in achieving equivalent or often better regulation and control with markedly less environmental damage and monetary cost. Equally germane for the social-political-epistemological implications of ecological thinking are stark contrasts between the enormous sums of money made available for spraying operations and the minuscule budgetary provisions for research into wildlife damage and natural methods of insect or

44. Carson, *Silent Spring*, 112–17.
45. Ibid., 130.
46. Ibid., 158.

disease control; between minimal levels of consultation with fish, game, and other wildlife departments and bland assurances from the U.S. Department of Agriculture that such consultation is, in fact, a matter of course; between a near-fanatical resistance to knowing about the "almost unparalleled wildlife destruction"[47] that drives the eradication programs forward and Carson's claim, based on widespread testimony, that citizens often "show a keener understanding of the dangers and inconsistencies of spraying than do the officials who order it done."[48] All of these contrasts, Carson notes, "raise a question that is not only scientific but moral. . . . Whether any civilization can wage relentless war on life without destroying itself, and without losing the right to be called civilized."[49] She is proposing both the detail and the larger imaginative frame of a more civilized approach—a renewing imaginary—that seeks to know more carefully and cautiously, monitoring its alleged knowings as it goes: an epistemically responsible approach.

Viewed vertically, from a top-down observation position from which linear causal connections are drawn from chemical applications to the destruction of a targeted pest, the power of the then-new post–World War II chemicals to free the environment quickly and efficiently of such diseases and insects is indeed remarkable. Yet viewed horizontally, taking a longer temporal and spatial view, across terrains and time frames where their effects become manifest more slowly, the chemicals do not obliterate only a predetermined target species. With Japanese beetle spraying, Carson documents the destruction and/or sterilization of insect-eating birds, ground squirrels, muskrats, rabbits, and domestic cats, sheep, and cattle: destruction that often does not follow the spraying instantaneously (as in the next hour, day, or week), so the causal connections are not immediately obvious to people neither informed—nor prepared—to look ecologically. It is so easy to discount or ignore causal hypotheses that extend temporally and geographically away from an actual chemical application, requiring time, imagination, conjecture, and patience for confirmation or falsification. Still more persuasive is Carson's account of natural controls against the spread of the beetle in the eastern United States, developed before massive spraying had begun, in a program of importing parasitic insects from the Orient that had held it in check in its native habitat (again, consider how much local empirical evidence had to be collected to make such a hypothesis plausible). Not only had the process brought the beetle under reasonable—and not otherwise harmful—control before the

47. Ibid., 92.
48. Ibid., 113.
49. Ibid., 99.

panic-driven Illinois spraying started, but natural protection persisted in the east at a fraction of the monetary and environmental cost of spraying that, regardless of the attendant damage, has constantly to be repeated. Analogously, Carson documents the control of Dutch elm disease in New York State not by spraying, but by "isolation": removing and destroying diseased, infected wood. This discouragingly slow process seemed unlikely to succeed until a further hypothesis was (slowly) confirmed, that cut wood was also a breeding ground. For effective control, it, too, had to be destroyed. In consequence, Dutch elm disease was controlled more reliably (i.e., without recurrence) and economically than by chemical saturation. By analogy and with variations, these examples recall Castoriadis's observation about seizing part of existent technology/knowledge and utilizing it to create another technology: pieces of the observational knowledge indicating where spraying should be directed are enlisted toward other, ecologically more sensitive ways of achieving a comparable end.

Carson clearly understands the allure of mastery and the need for control: but the practices she proposes for achieving it demand following up narrow and precise local hypotheses—different for each of the Japanese beetle, the gypsy moth, Dutch elm disease—hypotheses that guide inquiry whose empirical generalizations stand up well against any of the quick and dirty solutions proposed by the chemical industry and its champions. Catching a central contrast between an ethos of mastery and an ecological ethos, she remarks on a stubborn corporate resistance to taking a longer view (to waiting "an extra season or two")[50] when a quick (chemical) fix is ready to hand.

In deploring the massive destruction of birds and other wildlife produced by spraying for Dutch elm disease, Carson makes a larger ecological point that in the early twenty-first century would be couched in the language of biodiversity, also invoking reasons at once respectful of, and going beyond, preservation and aesthetics. One of the strengths of her approach in both its scientific and its discursive dimensions is in how it takes scientific evidence and preservation-aesthetics seriously, thereby requiring her to perform a difficult balancing act but ensuring that her work reaches experts and "ordinary folk" alike. Thus—the biodiversity point—writing of "the critical role of birds in insect control in various situations," Carson observes how insect populations commonly increase dramatically following chemical applications, yet when the same chemicals destroy the birds, they will not be there to keep insect numbers naturally in check.[51] Further spraying follows, setting in motion an endless

50. Ibid., 98.
51. Ibid., 112–13.

cycle. (Likewise Vandana Shiva writes in the year 2000, in the now-available language of biodiversity, "during the past forty years, crop loss to insects alone has nearly doubled, despite a tenfold increase in the amount of pesticides applied.")[52] Documenting the feeding patterns of birds, grubs, raccoons, and other species allows Carson to trace patterns of chemical damage and natural fragility-vulnerability across a range of interrelated ecosystems and to understand species-interdependence in sustaining a natural balance that may in fact require minimal chemical intervention.

My purpose in recounting these examples in detail is to indicate the pertinence—and power—of ecological thinking beyond the already-wide purview of naturalism, environmentalism, and the science of ecology, as a prelude to showing in the remainder of this book how this epistemological imaginary is translatable, with refinements and variations of substance and detail, across other parts of the epistemic terrain, other lives and situations. But my aim is not to propose an *alternative* epistemology—a simple either/or choice—that legitimates itself by the entrenched criteria, standards, and values of current orthodoxy. Ecological thinking reconfigures relationships all the way down: epistemological, ethical, scientific, political, rational, and other relationships between and among living beings and the inanimate parts of the world. Thus an ecologically derived epistemology is differently sensitive to the detail and larger patternings of human and "natural" diversity than the epistemologies of mastery have been: it invokes criteria and standards of knowing well that do in fact seek and respect empirical evidence, while urging another, arguably better, way of imagining knowledge and its place in social-political, geographic structures. It is better able to animate feminist, multicultural, and other postcolonial transformative politics and practices, whose effectiveness requires bracketing and reevaluating ossified assumptions, attending to specificities hitherto taken for granted or falling below the threshold of imagined salience. With its realist commitment to reading observational evidence respectfully, while recognizing that evidence cannot speak for itself, but achieves its status *as* evidence out of human-nature encounters, Carson's epistemic practice has marked affinities with Karen Barad's *agential realism*, especially as she presents it in her aptly titled "Meeting the Universe Half Way."[53] For Barad, events, materialities, bodies, are phenomena realized in, disclosed through "intra-actions" between objects and agents of observation "who are themselves specific local parts of the world's

52. Shiva, *Tomorrow's Biodiversity*, 16.
53. Barad, "Meeting the Universe Halfway."

ongoing configuring"[54] and thus bear a certain responsibility for how and why they intervene in the world, how they effect its reconfiguring to and for the conceptual apparatus they enact.

Recall how well Carson has to know the Japanese beetle—or the gypsy moth or Dutch elm disease—in a sense of "know" both thicker and broader (on an analogy with notions of "semantic depth") than those with which epistemology has tended to work: deeper than standard "knowing that" or claims formulated in the "S-knows-that-p" rubric. She has to meet it in its habits, habitat, susceptibilities, thrivings, history—know it in ways remote from and even inaccessible to the more straightforward observational-empirical knowings that lead to mastery along a narrow path of linear connections from what the beetle does, to how it poses a threat, to what can destroy it. She may have to know these things, too, but to know ecologically she has also to encounter it on something like "its own terms," both synchronic and dia-chronic, so as to be able to understand (in language distantly related to the language of empathy) how to meet with it halfway—not in order to "com-mune" with it but to nurture, protect, control, or destroy it.

As I have argued elsewhere,[55] such knowings occupy a larger place on the epistemic terrain, both "private" and "public," than positivist-empiricist epistemologies allow. Thus, I have proposed, theorists of knowledge com-mitted to centering their analyses around exemplars of "good knowing" might benefit from examining some of the structural modalities of knowing other people in "everyday lives," as contenders as worthy of exemplary status as perceptual knowledge of medium-sized material objects. Thinking of how infants learn to respond, cognitively and emotionally, to other people even before they can recognize the simplest physical objects, of how their induction into language generates a framework of presuppositions and expectations—of habitus and ethos—through which they construct and are shaped by their social and physical environments according to the substance and quality (positive or negative) of their affective, interactive locations, attests to the centrality of such knowing. Knowing other people "well enough" to do well by them, locally or more distantly, and to confer or withhold trust and respect wisely is an ongoing, always demanding practice, whose contrast with the imag-ined immediacy of direct sense perception so easily masks sense perception's

---

54. Barad, "Posthumanist Performativity," 829. For an excellent reading of Barad's position, see Rouse, "Barad's Feminist Naturalism."

55. See my What Can She Know? esp. chap. 2; and idem, Rhetorical Spaces, esp. chaps. 3, 4, and 6.

reliance on sedimented habit, expectation, cultural-social ethos and place. Such knowledge is not primarily propositional; and even though empirical "facts" are integral to it, it does not reduce to "*S*-knows-that-*p*" propositions. Even (*per impossibile*) knowing all such facts about another person might not warrant claiming to know her. If such limitations of empirical knowledge were taken seriously, the challenge posed by the many-faceted, textured character of knowing other people to the stark, stripped-down abstractness of standard empirical examples would be clear, as would the challenge posed by Carson's epistemic practices, in her multiply sensitive studies of the particularities of living things. Neither "knowing how" nor "knowing that," together or separately, can begin to tell an adequate story.

Structurally, knowing other people has as good a claim to exemplary status in an ecologically modeled epistemology as it does in interpretive social sciences.[56] Thus, as I shall argue in chapter two, epistemologists who require a scientific model of knowledge could find in ecological science a better resource than in "normal" laboratory science—or physics. Anglo-American epistemology evinces a certain confidence that physical objects are knowable, but people never really are: a conviction that whereas carefully controlled observational knowledge can claim unequivocal, universal validity, knowing other people in any but a superficial, behavioral sense can only ever be a pale approximation. Why this standard, which governs so minuscule a part of the epistemic lives even of the privileged class, race, and gender, should regulate the scope of knowledge per se remains a puzzle. Contesting the hegemony of such assumptions—as Shrader-Frechette does—in complex analyses where knowledge claims can be provisional and approximate and where case studies are accorded legitimacy as sources of evidence makes room to suppose that knowing other people is indeed less unmanageably aberrant. In fact, the skills required for constructing good case studies are closely akin to the interpretive skills exercised in responsibly knowledgeable human relationships. Although the analogy, admittedly, is less than perfect, the translations need not be flat-footedly literal. Nor is it more preposterous to urge people to approach "nature," physical objects, or complex social-political arrangements and events in the nuanced way they know their friends than to advocate knowing people in the unsubtle way they often claim to know physical objects. Carson's knowing the Japanese beetle shows as much. In ecological knowing, practices of verification and falsification are more gradual than in classical empiricism, but putting hypotheses into play, tracing them back and forth across fields of

56. See Rabinow and Sullivan, *Interpretive Social Science.*

inquiry, is not new, even though such detailed horizontal mappings as those knowing ecologically requires have rarely been part of the stuff of which epistemology is made.

Classifying and constructing taxonomies generate related considerations. Carson observes: "To understand the shore, it is not enough to catalogue its life" or "pick up an empty shell and say 'this is a murex' or 'That is an angel wing.'"[57] Producing ever more complete taxonomies was once the primary goal of the kind of natural science Carson practiced. Yet entities, organisms, and events do not fall naturally into categories and kinds; and classifications are multiply contestable. Nor, because it yields no understanding of interrelations among (classifiable) organisms, geography, climates, and/or human beings, can taxonomy be an end in itself or pinpoint an incontestable given. Too many classificatory projects fail even by traditional empirical ideals, because they rely on minimal information about the habitats, patterns, or processes in which seemingly distinct organisms and entities interact; nor do they consider how such processes are constitutive of an organism's "nature" or of its effects upon the "nature" of its environment. These issues translate, by analogy, into practices of classifying people, by race, gender, physical ability, age, and so on, with comparable tendencies to reify, solidify into stereotyped identities. In the epistemologies of mastery, taxonomies thus often achieve, create, or impose a certain order: ecological thinking does not discredit this achievement, but it maps it differently, is vigilant for its ambiguities and lacunae.

For Carson, then, as for the ecological thinking I advocate, responsible knowing is about more than knowing the surface characteristics and internal specificities of organisms: it requires understanding how those specificities work together, reading them as responses, adaptations, resistances to places and circumstances whose local detail and connections with other locations contribute to how organisms, whether human or other, can be. Out of the explanatory power of an attentive concentration on local particulars, specificities, it seeks to generate responsible remappings across wider, heterogeneous epistemic terrains.

In summary, then, noting how the shift from geographical to ecological reconfigured Carson's scientific practice, I am proposing that ecological thinking can reconfigure epistemology, piece by piece in detailed specifically situated inquiries whose effects are often widely pertinent. Because it is so finely tuned an approach, it has the potential in its micropractices to capture

---

57. Carson, *Edge of the Sea*, vii, cited in Lear, *Rachel Carson*, 275.

detail and nuance that slip through larger evidence-sifting grids and precast templates and thus to achieve linkages from location to location that could begin to close a gap that has held theories of knowledge at a distance from the experiences and practices they have sought to explicate. In its macropractices, it engages critically with more widespread implications of discourses and practices of mastery and constructively with the transformative potential of ecological reconfigurations. Ecology (literally), then, looks to state-of-the-art ecological science to supply some of the substance of its deliberations; yet it does not assume science has a direct line to "the truth" or merits uncontested license to intervene where it pleases. Ecology (metaphorically) draws the conclusions of situated inquiries together, maps their interrelations, consonances, and contrasts, their impoverishing or mutually sustaining consequences, from a commitment to generating a creatively interrogative, instituting social imaginary to denaturalize the instituted imaginary of mastery that represents itself as "the [only] natural way" of being and knowing.[58]

Questions of Evidence: Karen Messing's Respect for Testimony

As I have remarked, Carson's scientific world was structured by hierarchical divisions between fact and anecdote, truth and narrative, with the first item in each pair claiming greater credibility, authority, and epistemological accreditation than the second. Her respect for experiential-testimonial evidence of the everyday, down-on-the-ground variety, often dismissed as merely *anecdotal*, shows how Carson's epistemic practice complicates such distinctions.

The methodological and politics-of-knowledge issues prompting denigrations of testimony as a source of evidence derive from the (lowly) status of experience in putatively experience-based epistemologies, which accord minimal evidential import to individuated, "concrete," first-person, experiential narratives as they contrast with a controlled, formal experience that is everyone's and no one's. Feminist and other postcolonial theorists of knowledge, ever cognizant of the social-environmental hierarchies of power and privilege whose effects are to valorize *some* people's experiential claims—their testimony—and to denigrate others', have to contend with persistent, vexed questions about how experience can stand as evidence and about whose experiences count and why, on an epistemic terrain where credibility is unevenly distributed and testimony often discounted or denigrated on the basis of whose it is. Understandably, given

58. See in this connection Castoriadis, "Radical Imagination."

the apolitical epistemic climate of her time, Carson is less explicitly interested in the "identity" or social-political positioning of a testifier than in the substance of the testimony. But the issue is currently alive and urgent in feminist, anti-racist, and other postcolonial theories of knowledge. I revisit it to frame another example, at a microlevel, of how ecological thinking repositions and revalorizes experiential evidence, drawing structural analogies between Carson's ecological practice and Canadian biologist Karen Messing's avowedly feminist-informed research on women's occupational health.

As Carson the wildlife scientist maps the minutiae of bioregional life in studying different types of shore—rock, sand, coral—so Messing the work-life scientist maps the minutiae of different types of workplace lives and jobs—of poultry processors, waitresses, bank tellers, telephone operators, and others.[59] As Carson, in *Silent Spring*, relies on scientific-observational evidence and "*anecdotal evidence*... from nonexperts—suburbanites and ornithologists upset by the dead and dying birds they found on their lawns... campers poisoned by DDT"[60] ("her conclusions were based not only on the work of scientists on the cutting edge of their fields but on the case histories that filled her file cabinets," Lear notes),[61] so Messing and her colleagues rely on scientific-observational evidence and experiential evidence culled from interview upon interview with workers, union members, and other "ordinary folk," investigating how "women workers and scientists can be brought together to make occupational health studies more accurate and effective in improving working conditions."[62] The purpose of the inquiry—like Carson's—is to discern patterns, relationships between "living things and their abiotic or non-living environments" (in Shrader-Frechette's words), in studies where it is extremely difficult "to achieve unifying and successful laws and predictions."[63] Symptoms are often so specific to tiny groups of workers with reasonably similar physical and other characteristics, in meticulously detailed and differentiated work environments, that they afford insufficient (statistical) *certainty* either to establish the reality of

59. Messing observes that her team's work since 1978, in collaboration with women workers, is not "entirely driven by women's questions" since it attempts to achieve a compromise "between the needs of women and other workers and the requirements of academia, granting agencies, employers, and unions." Nonetheless, she continues, "if we define feminist research as research that responds to questions asked by women and advances the status of women in society, we have been engaged in feminist research for more than 15 years" (Messing, *One-Eyed Science*, 188).

60. Raglon, "Rachel Carson and Her Legacy," 206 (emphasis added).

61. Lear, *Rachel Carson*, 357.

62. Messing, *One-Eyed Science*, xvi.

63. Shrader-Frechette, "Ecology," 304.

suffering or to support workers' compensation claims. Yet Messing—in an approach I read as (metaphorically) ecological—concentrates on showing how minutely individuated complaints manifest and play themselves out for specific people (usually, in her studies, women) in the particularities of workplaces, habitats governed by an ethos of profit and efficiency. Messing, too, is a practicing scientist whose credentials are firmly in place, yet her epistemological practice is as subversive as it is respectful of the norms of empirical scientific inquiry, especially with regard to the place she accords particularity and testimony in the production of knowledge. She urges reading statistical evidence against the intransigence of specific problems and symptoms to inclusion under general, putatively lawlike descriptions, moving between the laboratory and the workplace floor, much as Carson moves between the laboratory and the field or the ocean floor. Messing's work, too, is marked by an interplay between local hypotheses and empirical generalizations, where analogies traced can move the inquiry forward, disanalogies can initiate productive rethinking.

Frustrated by difficult negotiations required to convince unions, employers, and workers themselves of the significance—indeed, the *factuality*—of correlations between women's health problems and specific workplace conditions, Messing points to a vicious circle in which "researchers do not think of looking for an occupational cause..., such causes are not demonstrated, so the problems are attributed to women's biological or psychological 'nature.' "[64] Through minutely detailed studies of "interactions among social, biological, and political factors in the historical context of particular factories and services," she aims to achieve ways of understanding gendered divisions of labor and workplace health that can undermine such careless, stereotype-reliant naturalizing: to develop "a model for biology-job interactions that should supersede the notion of fitness and center on the promotion of health in the workplace."[65] Arguing that women's workplace health has less to do with "facts" about a generic female incapacity, singly or collectively, to perform certain jobs and more with standards of fitness produced out of preconceived ideas about jobs, equipment, work environments, and attitudes derived from what is imagined typical for men, Messing claims that "even when a biological characteristic has an important genetic component, it can be changed by altering the environment."[66] Although statistics representing the occupational fatality rate for men at twelve times the rate for women are commonly read to

64. Messing, *One-Eyed Science*, 19.
65. Ibid., 25.
66. Ibid., 26.

demonstrate the greater safety of women's jobs, supporting a paternalistic contention that "job segregation has kept women out of dangerous jobs,... protected their health," Messing's thesis, designed and evidentially supported to subvert such readings, is that "women have fewer compensated injuries and illnesses because the compensation system has been set up in response to problems in jobs traditionally held by men."[67] Hence she distrusts comparisons of accident rates between the sexes when they fail to address the different positions women and men occupy in the workplace, noting: "It is easier to relate an injury to the workplace (as when a chemical worker is injured in an explosion) than an illness (such as cancer developing over many years)."[68] She studies how work stations, tools, and equipment designed for the "average man" place many women and some men at a disadvantage, whose effects in pain, stress, and discomfort are rarely discernible except in the language of failing to meet an abstract, one-size-fits-all criterion of fitness. (Thus women blue-collar workers reported "too-large boots and gloves, too-big shovels, and clippers with too-wide intervals between the handles.")[69] Many of the consequences are nothing short of bizarre: women eliminated from a Canadian study of exposure to agricultural chemicals because, in most provincial records, "only the husband of the [presumptively heterosexual] farm family was identified as a farmer";[70] a doctor informing the International Ergonomics Association that "it had been scientifically proved that *all* carpal tunnel symptoms among older women were due to the menopause";[71] and a study of train cleaners, where chrome polishing—an easy task, performed standing up—was assigned to men nearing retirement who were no longer required to drive the water truck or carry bags of refuse, while women both younger and older, who cleaned up to 150 toilets a day, were threatened with disciplinary action even when doctors corroborated reports of their symptoms: "The extreme strength and endurance requirements of this job were invisible, so the workers' back problems were not relieved."[72]

The politics are complex. When workers engage in activist projects to improve their circumstances, their activities tend to corroborate a suspicion that "they will fake symptoms to gain their point... even when the patterns of physiological change are so specific to the toxic effect that the worker would

67. Ibid., 13.
68. Ibid., 15.
69. Ibid., 35.
70. Ibid., 58.
71. Ibid., 97 (emphasis in original).
72. Ibid., 163.

have to be a specialist...to produce them";[73] a mail sorter who reported extreme arm, shoulder, and elbow pain lost a compensation claim because an expert witness "quoted from the scientific literature purporting to show that repeated movements could not produce injury below a specific weight manipulated...[and] described his own laboratory tests, which...showed that this type of work was not dangerous."[74] No one examined the mail sorter's specific situation;[75] yet without the acknowledgment that only so careful an examination could provide, these experiential tales claim dubious validity. Such events generated one of the principal questions animating Messing's work: "*How do scientists decide whom and what to study in the occupational health field?*"[76]—a question that, as I read it, can find (interim) answers only by studying people, work and workplaces, and health together—ecologically— analyzing the detail of their intra-actions and diverse situatedness, from a research stance at once informed and vigilant to detect specific, often minuscule, operations of the politics of knowledge (gendered, raced, classed, aged, ableist, and other) and the profit-driven vested interests that produce patterns of invisibility and insignificance, credulity and incredulity, across populations and occupations.

Even when such social-political-environmental "forces" are taken into account, neither Carson's nor Messing's inquiries are apt to yield causal laws or terminate in a single, monolithic truth. In fact, the expanded and reconfigured conception of causality that informs ecological thinking can rarely deliver the unilinear, uniform, universal, and immediate causal accounts that, in the public imagination, are the hallmark of scientific inquiry. Philosophers are aware of the vexed history of the issue of causality in western thought, from Aristotle through Hume to Collingwood, Mill, and Russell, to mention only the most frequently cited figures. They are also aware that a commitment to tracing causes, and a belief in the ease of so doing, governs the secular and scientific social-epistemic imaginary of the affluent western world, in politics, law and jurisprudence, applied science, business, public health, medicine, policy deliberations, and social planning, where causes of unwanted events can be traced and eliminated and causes of improvement discovered and initiated. The operative conception of causality in such places is quasi-mechanistic, reliant on law-governed regularities and on a certain temporal and spatial

73. Ibid., 69.
74. Ibid., xv.
75. Ibid., xvi.
76. Ibid., xvi (emphasis in original).

proximity between cause and effect—factors on which the plausibility of much causal explanation relies.

Yet recall my caution against reading Carson as tracing discrete, unilinear causal relationships to explain and understand the "forces that have molded" nature and human nature and Shrader-Frechette's warning about the difficulty, in ecological science, of achieving "unifying... laws and predictions."[77] Messing notes a contrast between "fuzzy definitions of diseases and possible causes... [and] easily recognized accidents"[78] to explain problems in drawing neat causal connections across symptoms and workplace health problems, where causes may be so temporally and/or spatially remote from alleged effects as to appear, or be discounted as, irrelevant. Carson observes that, with respect to the human body, "cause and effect are seldom simple and easily demonstrated relationships";[79] and Messing points to a difference between infectious diseases "where a single causal agent (germ) can be sometimes be isolated" and such contributors to work-related musculoskeletal disorders (MSDs) as repeated movements and postures that "are not easy to analyze."[80] Succinctly summarizing these problems, Carson writes:

> We are accustomed to look for the gross and immediate effect and to ignore all else. Unless this appears promptly and in such obvious form that it cannot be ignored, we deny the existence of hazard.... "But," someone will object, "I have used dieldrin sprays on the lawn many times but I have never had convulsions...." It is not that simple. Despite the absence of sudden and dramatic symptoms, one who handles such materials is unquestionably storing up toxic materials in his body.[81]

Detailing the effects on the human liver of chlorinated hydrocarbon insecticides in an account both empirically documented and detailed and accessible to lay readers, Carson records a sharp rise in hepatitis, starting in the 1950s as applications of such chemicals proliferated, and she cites rumors of an increase in cirrhosis. Addressing epistemic complexities such as those I have been discussing, she writes: "While it is admittedly difficult, in dealing with human beings rather than laboratory animals, to 'prove' that cause A produces effect B, plain common sense

---

77. Shrader-Frechette, "Ecology," 304.
78. Messing, *One-Eyed Science*, 90.
79. Carson, *Silent Spring*, 189.
80. Messing, *One-Eyed Science*, 89.
81. Carson, *Silent Spring*, 190.

suggests that the relation between a soaring rate of liver disease and the prevalence of liver poisons in the environment is no coincidence."[82] Although she takes such reports very seriously and, as I have noted, apolitically, this is no naive "experientialism" for which experience is inviolate, unchallengeable. Testimony becomes both evidence and a catalyst for ongoing investigation: she affirms its contestability and its interpretability, while advocating its value.

What, in these situations, is the problem about experience? Why are its deliverances so readily denigrated as "merely anecdotal"? The short answer, within the imaginary that holds a residual positivism in place, is that even under the elevated label *testimony*, experiential evidence derived from first-person tellings is assumed inevitably to compromise objectivity: a problem that mitigates against the public credibility of research for which testimonial reports comprise part of "the evidence." Historically, incredulity in the face of testimony is scarcely surprising, given a long lineage of distrust in the putative chaos, naivety, and unsubstantiated muddle of everyday experiences, especially of people situated on the bottom rung on Plato's hierarchy of would-be knowers, and the complex patterns of corroboration required—if inconsistently throughout western history[83]—to elevate them to the status of a (negotiated) credibility. But the problem, as feminists and other Others have amply shown, is in the presumed contrast, no longer, perhaps, to the highest level of knowledge achieved in contemplating the Forms, but to Scientificity, allegedly cleansed of distortions, subjective elements, and vested interests: a contrast that feminists and other unmaskers of the situatedness and background assumptions of scientific inquiry, and of its complicity with larger social-political-economic agendas, have shown to be bogus. Nonetheless, Carson's insistence on placing secular, testimonial evidence alongside more "respectable" scientific evidence, together with her narrative presentation, especially in the earlier works, and her having attained neither a doctorate nor an official position in institutional science, figure among factors invoked to discredit her work. Industries marketing DDT and other pesticides were among her most audible opponents: an advisor warned her: "You are going to be subjected to ridicule and condemnation.... Facts will not stand in the way of some confirmed pest control workers and those who are receiving substantial subsidies from pesticides manufacturers."[84] All of which leaves aside the egregiously sexist, insinuatingly

82. Ibid., 192.

83. Shapiro details interesting historical exceptions to these presumptions of distrust in her *Culture of Fact*, esp. chaps. 3–4.

84. Letter from Clarence Cottam to Carson, February 1962, quoted in Lear, *Rachel Carson*, 401.

homophobic, and blatantly *ad feminam* dismissals that both Lear and Rebecca Raglon detail, including a former U.S. Agriculture Secretary who wondered why a spinster was so worried about genetics, critics who dismissed her as a "hysterical female," and others, differently motivated, for whom she must surely be a communist.[85]

As for Carson, so, too, for Messing, testimony is problematic. Fellow scientists, workplace employers, and granting agencies see a research team's reliance on evidence gathered from interviews with workers as an uncontrollable source of bias. A rhetorical contrast to the scientific rigor of statistical mappings, impersonal data, or laboratory experiments figures in charges that workers "may have an ax to grind" or "will overreport exposure to whatever they think may have caused it";[86] and scientists doing participatory work are "*less* scientific"[87] than those positioned at a distance. The nonquantifiable character of workers' stories of their symptoms casts them as too particular, too variable in their detail to yield appropriately credible results, the charge runs. Messing contends: "For the same researcher, grant proposals were more likely to be accepted if the project involved nonhumans or human cells in culture rather than live humans."[88] Thus referees vetoed funding a proposed study of cell mutations in radiology technicians that was designed to examine cells from the workers themselves, because it did *not* plan to study Chinese hamster ovary cells, prompting Messing to observe: "Chinese hamster ovary cells are unlikely to furnish the answers to all our questions about the effects of working conditions on workers."[89] Her point is not to condemn studies of hamster cells, but to expose the leap of faith required to translate studies of those cells in controlled isolation into conclusions about the health of specific people in real employment situations. Hence the value of the situated study in revealing the possibilities and pitfalls of translation. Analogously, a study of warts—an industrial disease of poultry workers—was refused funding because workers were to count their own warts, while the granting committee insisted a medical practitioner should do it "even though workers, with up to a hundred warts on their hands, were quite familiar with [their] appearance."[90] Again, the potentially enhanced accuracy of scientific observation is not in question, but the imagined irrelevance of experiential evidence is. Both Messing and Carson

85. Lear, "Rachel Carson's Silent Spring," 5.
86. Messing, *One-Eyed Science*, 67.
87. Ibid., 177.
88. Ibid., 47.
89. Ibid., 63.
90. Ibid., 61.

demonstrate their reciprocal epistemic value. Commenting on the working conditions of part-time bank tellers, Messing observes: "We would not have been able to interpret this . . . [situation] had we not spent hours observing the tellers at work. We know researchers who have never been inside the factories whose data they analyze, and interpretation of data can be a problem for them."[91] Echoes of Carson's insistence that no living creature can be understood apart from an understanding of the world in which it lives and of Deleuze's that an animal, or a thing, is never separable from its relations with the world are audible in these examples.

The larger epistemological issue is about the relative positioning of expert and testimonial evidence: how they work appropriately together, bypassing entrenched beliefs that, when both are available, expert evidence, just naturally, claims greater credibility, supersedes everyday testimony to render it redundant, automatically claims ascendancy. In Carson's and Messing's work, testimony often sets inquiry in motion and functions as an ongoing corrective: it generates very precise local hypotheses, confirms or contests interim findings. Practices of moving back and forth between testimony and science make these (interim) empirical generalizations possible. So Carson recommends *both* looking "at some of the major control programs and learn[ing] from observers familiar with the ways of wildlife, and unbiased in favor of chemicals, just what has happened in the wake of a rain of poison falling from the skies";[92] and Messing explains her reasons for studying human cells. Collecting such evidence is never as straightforward as accumulating observation-based evidence in controlled laboratory experiments is imagined to be. It is untidy, oblique, slower, and less direct, constantly needing to evaluate the credibility of both expert and secular witnesses in ways masked in orthodox epistemologies' formal models of instantaneous verification and falsification.

Bioregional narratives, as Jim Cheney conceives of them, speak to the import of Carson's and Messing's studies, disrupt the instituted social-epistemic imaginary of top-down mastery and control, and are intriguingly continuous with Shiva's critique of "monoculture." For Cheney, "narrative grounded in geography rather than in a linear, essentialized narrative self"[93] is vital to developing an ethics—and, in my view, an epistemology—of accountability. As I understand the idea, bioregional narratives map local ecological relations to discern conditions for mutually sustaining lives within a specific locality—be it

91. Ibid., 91.
92. Carson, *Silent Spring*, 86.
93. Cheney, "Postmodern Environmental Ethics," 126.

an institution of knowledge production, an urban setting, a workplace, a geographical region, a community, society, state, or the interrelations among them. Shiva's story of the impact on rural Indian agriculture of western-style "development," which I mention in the introduction, counts as such a narrative, as do Carson's narratives of the sea and the pesticide-saturated land and Messing's of the workplace. The strength of such narratives is in the detail of their situational sensitivity, their genealogical (= power-focused) exposure of local knowledge-making and knowledge-circulating conditions. Their potential weakness is in the risk of achieving only a local pertinence, of imagining the bioregion whose story they tell as closed, harmonized, static and also as representative and thus able to function as a surrogate for any other region. Hence they have to be evaluated both for their internal detail and for their interconnections with the power-saturated systems of the wider world. Christopher Preston aptly observes that places "draw together the natural, the social, and the intellectual...they give us a location from which to understand the...complexity of our relationships to what lies around us."[94] Yet they are neither wholly natural, nor do they offer deterministic, causal explanations.

Bioregional narratives map knowledge-enhancing and knowledge-impeding possibilities, critically, to derive normative conclusions that can—deliberatively and negotiably—translate from one region to another, not without remainder, but as instructively in the disanalogies they expose as in the analogies they establish. Michel Foucault's analyses of "local knowledges" qualify in some respects.[95] Patricia Williams's interconnected mappings of the effects of systemic racism produce another powerful such narrative: grounded in the particularities of the (regional) life of an urban professional black woman in the United States, yet translatable by analogy to racism and democratic accountability as they play out in wider, or contrasting, circles of relevance.[96] And Bruno Latour speaks in favor of such narratives (using an ecological metaphor from Michel Serres): "The only way to respect the heterogeneity and the locality is...to do *a lot* of philosophy. But philosophy is not unifying factors.... [It] is a *protection* against the hegemony of the present sciences."[97] In well-

94. Preston, *Grounding Knowledge*, 107.
95. See Foucault, *Power/Knowledge*, esp. chap. 5.
96. See Williams, *Alchemy of Race and Rights*; idem, *Rooster's Egg*; and idem, *Seeing a Color-Blind Future*.
97. Latour, "Irreduction," 218. In the conversation cited here, Callebaut is Latour's interlocutor, and it is he who describes the metaphor as ecological.

conceived bioregional narratives, epistemic issues intersect with questions about responsibility and agency, with the uneven distribution of cognitive resources in twenty-first-century societies, and with the moral-political effects of institutional knowledge production. They refuse the reductionism of totalizing theory, to engage in analyses of specific, local epistemic resources. Ecological thinking, I have noted, focuses as closely on the exemplary possibilities of knowing other people—in everyday and social scientific contexts—as on those traditionally derived from knowing "facts" about the world. It interrogates social structures of expertise and authority together with patterns of consultation and negotiation that assume—indeed, often presume—to know (an)other person(s). Such structures are primary sites of empowerment and disempowerment in patriarchal, racist, and otherwise hierarchically ordered societies. As the examples I discuss in subsequent chapters will confirm, the quality of the putative knowledge with which, and from which, such authoritative assumptions work is often concealed behind stereotyped social identities posing as knowledge of human natural kinds.

Implications

With the stories that Carson and Messing tell—one literally ecological and thus overdetermined to make my point; one metaphorically ecological, thus showing how the overriding conceptions and underlying effects of ecological thinking translate across other knowings—I am suggesting that the precepts, principles, practices, and ideologies of orthodox epistemology are not merely reconfigured but reimagined, rethought all the way through, when they are thought ecologically. It is not that some pieces of an epistemological system are rejigged, some castoffs reclaimed, and some rejects recycled from a misremembered romantic and symbiotic earlier era, but that a whole way of thinking about the diverse positionings and responsibilities of knowing subjects, the "nature" of knowledge and its place in the social-political-natural world, are differently thought. Hence my suggestion that ecological thinking can generate a revolution comparable to Kant's Copernican revolution.

But what can it achieve that orthodox epistemologies and philosophies of science cannot? What can it contribute to environmental projects, literally conceived, and projects of inquiry more widely construed? Here I offer but a brief answer, as a prelude to the examples I adduce in the chapters to follow. First, although its working conception of empirical inquiry departs radically from classically conceived empiricism, ecological thinking is distantly related to a radicalized rereading of the "strong objectivity" associated with standpoint epistemology.[98] Its *strength* derives not from cleansing inquiry of interests, materialities, presuppositions, or the constitutive effects of situation and place, but from analyzing these as fully as it analyzes traditionally conceived "objects of knowledge" and from its self-reflexive commitment constantly to monitor its processes of inquiry. Second, I take Shrader-Frechette's point that the science of ecology, and by extension, ecological thinking, cannot promise the deductive, predictive certainty that the hard sciences claim to deliver. This point no doubt pertains to varying degrees across the relevant domains of inquiry; and such hesitations may, for some, point to its down side. But the up side, which for me signals a greater achievement, is captured in two ideas from Shrader-Frechette and a thought of my own. For Shrader-Frechette, some of the best "ecological applications arise when (and because) scientists have a great deal of knowledge about the natural history of organisms investigated in a particular case study":[99] hence the aptness of reading Carson and Messing in this way and at such length. She has high praise for the explanatory insights ecological science can achieve, working inductively, bottom-up (the reverse of the vertical process of superimposing a grid), and for the lawlike character of many of its explanations. My own thought, referring to her claim that natural history can generate *ethical* guidelines for policy formation, is to propose— more broadly—that such inquiry reopens a space for democratic, deliberative, negotiative practices of epistemic responsibility,[100] approaches to knowing meticulous in their attention to evidence, yet cognizant of the extent to which evidence is multiply interpretable, with wide-ranging human and ecological consequences as it goes. For me, one of the principal virtues of thinking ecologically about knowing is the renewed engagement with issues of epistemic responsibility it invites: this, too, will be a recurrent theme in this book.

98. See Harding, "Rethinking Standpoint Epistemology."
99. Shrader-Frechette, "Ecology," 313.
100. See Code, *Epistemic Responsibility*.

Once we have exited from the great political diorama of "nature in general," we

are left only with the banality of multiple associations of human and nonhumans

waiting for their unity to be provided by work carried out by the collective, which

has to be specified through the use of the resources, concepts, and institutions of all

peoples who may be called upon to live in common on an earth that might become,

through a long work of collection, the same earth for all.

—Bruno Latour, The Politics of Nature

2

ECOLOGICAL NATURALISM

Naturalistic Promise, Emancipatory Hopes

The epistemological lens through which I have been reading Rachel Carson's work is *naturalistic* in a quasi-literal, root sense of the term. Intentionally mobilizing equivocations on the language of "the natural," I read Carson as gathering knowledge naturalistically; Linda Lear's biography as developing a naturalistic account of Carson's epistemic-scientific practice; and the knowledge Carson gathers as natural knowledge. Yet I have noted that, surprisingly in view of her experience, expertise, and meticulous scientific practice, Carson's work does not stand high on the ladder of scientificity. The hegemony of an epistemic imaginary for which this kind of inquiry counts merely as "nature study" and, in consequence, is easily discounted as unscientific, random, contributes to the minimal institutional esteem accorded her. Equally salient in the work's reception, in my view, is Carson's practice of deriving evidence, data, piecemeal from investigations in the field and/or from first-person narratives, and presenting it in popularly accessible form, thus seeming, unprofessionally, to ignore the rules of "normal" scientific practice. Here I will consider how the equivocal status of ecology as a putative science also contributes to this reception.

What then is this science of ecology whose status I characterize as equivocal? Kristin Shrader-Frechette (whom I introduce in chapter one) and E. D. McCoy conceive of it as an inquiry designed to solve practical environmental problems, as "more a science of case studies and statistical regularities than a science of exceptionless general laws," contending that "insofar as ecology is an applied endeavor, it is more a science that moves from singular to theoretical explanation than one that proceeds from theoretical to singular explanation."[1] Likewise for Sharon Kingsland, whom I also cite in chapter one, ecological science is a historical inquiry, concerned to understand "short-term ecological changes and long-term evolutionary changes." It thus contrasts with "the mathematical way of thinking," which, in its use of ahistorical models to construct plausible scenarios, is at odds with "the way of thinking familiar to most ecologists."[2] Ahistorical approaches governed, for example, by a physics-derived theory of equilibrium, impose a regulative universal model, thereby aggregating events and entities, with the consequence that it can be difficult to understand their uniqueness or to perceive apparently erratic fluctuations in populations. Such approaches are implausibly reductive, Kingsland argues. Her picture of ecology, like Shrader-Frechette and McCoy's, is of a science obliged to resist temptations to search for the kinds of causal law that an essentialized conception of physics promises, in favor of developing "more sophisticated techniques of analysis,"[3] so as to study nature in a particular time and place, focus on singular, specific phenomena, and pull events together into larger, more complex, if less controlled, explanations. The language of "temptation" is instructive, for on these views, ecological science cannot produce its best efforts if it is constrained to gauge its success by deductive-nomological standards. Thus it promises less by way of calculability and precision than positivistically accredited sciences can achieve. Conceived as a science of case studies, its attempts to develop general laws are fraught, for no two cases will be exactly alike in all significant respects; hence its reliance on inductive inference is greater, its predictive power slighter than people might hope from a theory intended to guide environmental policies and programs. Moreover, its interpretive tasks are larger than those deemed appropriate for more "exact"

---

1. Shrader-Frechette and McCoy, *Method in Ecology*, 1.
2. Kingsland, *Modeling Nature*, 5.
3. Ibid., 3.

sciences, with their practitioners' ingrained distrust of interpretation's allegedly subjective character.[4]

Nonetheless, ecology's heuristic power is impressive: according to Shrader-
Frechette and McCoy, it does well at proposing informed (if not definitive)
policy and practical guidelines for solving environmental problems, less well at
offering specific conservation strategies, given "the epistemological point that
different conservation strategies are based on different ecological concepts."[5]
("Community" and "stability" are two such concepts, for whose characteristics
there is no "universally applicable specification...no set of necessary and
sufficient conditions.")[6] Thus for their detractors, the theoretical pluralism to
which ecologists, more often than not, are committed tells against their projects'
scientific respectability; whereas for their champions, it tells in favor of their
capacity to yield conclusions *truer to* circumstance, situation, and place than
dislocated analyses can yield.

A still more significant contributor to the contested scientific status
of ecological science, Shrader-Frechette and McCoy show, is its explicitly value-
laden character: indeed, the cases they study "involve evaluative methodological
conflicts over ecological evidence for appropriate environmental policy," for
which ecology alone cannot provide adequate grounding. "We need epistemological and ethical analyses as well,"[7] they conclude, thus affirming the
pertinence of epistemic responsibility as a regulative principle for a well-
articulated, politically engaged, ecological naturalism. For Shrader-Frechette
and McCoy, values play a larger part in science than is commonly imagined:[8]
taking island biogeography as an exemplary case, they contend that "although
all science is empirically underdetermined, the magnitude of ecological un-
derdetermination"[9] is especially troubling to more orthodox scientists. To offer
a small sampling, their list of contributors to methodological value judgments
in island biogeography includes the need to decide whether ethical and conservation priorities require protecting an individual species, an ecosystem, or

4. Thus Abram, for example, advocates a "sensual and participatory ecology...a relat-
edness or reciprocity between the self and the biosphere," criticizing ecological science for
"objectif[ying] life on Earth," viewing it "from the outside" (*Spell of the Sensuous*, cited in
Kirkman, "Why Ecology Cannot Be All Things," 376).

5. Shrader-Frechette and McCoy, *Method in Ecology*, 54.

6. Ibid., 57–58.

7. Ibid., 86.

8. In their analysis of value-laden science (ibid., 82), Shrader-Frechette and McCoy appeal
to feminist empiricist Longino's *Science as Social Knowledge*.

9. Shrader-Frechette and McCoy, *Method in Ecology*, 88.

biodiversity; the need to choose between maximizing present and future bio-diversity; the need to determine how to evaluate the worth of a general theory when specific knowledge of taxa and their habitats fail to fit; the need to make subjective evaluations of nontestable predictions; and the need to make a subjective assessment of the value of different reserve shapes. Because islands, they maintain, are significantly disanalogous, value judgments will, of necessity, be invoked about their representative status and their importance.[10] Yet different value judgments clearly generate different policies: if scientists work from an "account of the balance of nature that presupposes causal regularities,"[11] their support for diverse, locally specific, sometimes even whimsical methods of pest management will be less situationally sensitive than it might otherwise be. Of particular note, and consonant with Carson's views I have cited, the authors imply that presupposing causal regularities is neither the only plausible nor even the best approach to a viable ecological science, whose heuristic power can be demonstrated in elaborated, worked-through case studies that display the theory in action.[12] Nor, *ex hypothesi*, could it be otherwise.

This having been said, the lack of consensus among environmentalists and ecological thinkers about how to conceive the place and practice of ecological science is remarkable,[13] with the consequence that "ecology" emerges as a concept almost as contested as "natural" will turn out to be, in my analysis that follows. Kingsland, for example, addresses the difficulty of reconciling an ahistorical, "mathematical way of thinking" common to the physical sciences with an ecological science often reliant on mathematical modeling, yet many of whose questions have to be approached historically.[14] She examines the complex relationships between popular environmental movements and ecological science: uneasy partnerships animated by mutual interests, yet often at odds because of a tendency for popular movements to "take on a distinctly antiscientific cast" and for ecology to "be conducted in ways that had little bearing on environmental problems."[15] Shrader-Frechette and McCoy maintain both that "ecologists are the gurus of the environmental movement" *and*

10. Ibid., 88–89.
11. Ibid., 95.
12. Shrader-Frechette's *Environmental Justice* presents richly elaborated examples of such case studies.
13. For an instructive analysis of this lack, see Keller and Golley, *Philosophy of Ecology*, 15, who observe, for example, that "the public looks to ecologists to provide a description of the inner workings of the biosphere, yet ecologists are far from arriving at any consensus."
14. Kingsland, *Modeling Nature*, 4–5.
15. Ibid., 216.

that ecology, for all its many successes, "has provided neither a largely de-scriptive general theory capable of yielding precise, conservation-related pre-dictions nor a normative foundation for specific environmental problems."[16] But such conclusions, tensions, and conundrums clearly have not been per-mitted to paralyze inquiry or to deny its vital significance: on the contrary, these contestations generate the impetus for ongoing investigation and delib-eration.

Although this ongoing investigation involves thinking within large frame-works—within places, situations, structures, few of which are hard-edged, many of which overlap with and are conceptually and spatially contiguous to others—it would be a mistake to read the ecology I am drawing on as holistic, either implicitly or explicitly. Nor does the ecological thinking I derive from it have holistic aspirations. Its emphasis on the detailed specificity of cases studied, the wariness of assuming overarching causal regularities, the diverse conservation strategies that figure in these analyses, recommend a principled agnosticism on the matter of whether the soft-edged, permeable conglomerates with which ecology deals could ever map/fit together like the pieces of a giant jigsaw. They are too disparate, too malleable by "natural" events and human purposes to be amenable, separately or together, to unified explanation rem-iniscent of the old unity-of-science model. Moreover, ecological thinking at its best is marked by a wariness of too-swiftly aggregating events and phenomena, thereby eclipsing salient specificities: a wariness that, in my view, nourishes its commitment to being "true to" its subjects and objects of study while guarding against attributions of holism.

From the Science of Ecology to Ecological Naturalism

Ecological naturalism, as I name the position I am developing, locates domains or regions of epistemic inquiry analogically, within specific practices and in-stitutions where people produce knowledge and from which they enact its effects. It makes no before-the-fact assumptions about "knowledge in gen-eral," yet it is committed to drawing (interim) conclusions that can map from region to region, location to location, to inform and enable larger emancipatory projects, while recognizing that the meaning of emancipation varies with regional and demographic diversity, and working to understand and address those variations. It is wary of the power-infused tendencies of

16. Shrader-Frechette and McCoy, *Method in Ecology*, 2–3.

racial-gender-class and other stereotypes and of essentialized conceptions of science and nature, to take on self-fulfilling, self-perpetuating qualities that foster illusions of sameness.[17]

Ecological naturalism neither turns its back on empirical knowledge-gathering processes nor eschews standard scientific practices of observation, justification, and evaluation. But it reassesses them in their specificity, relocates them to consider how they can function productively together with other ways of achieving knowledge, reevaluates them for their sensitivity to the detail of geographical and human specificity, of habitat and ethos. It looks to natural and social scientific evidence in its projects of crafting and enacting principles of ideal cohabitation; yet, denying that observational evidence can speak un-equivocally, for itself; acknowledging its artifactual status, it rejects empirical science's claims to occupy the position of master metanarrative. It derives its evidence in self-critical reflexivity where locally, environmentally informed studies and their interdisciplinary relations generate ongoing skeptical suspicions of presumptions to theoretical hegemony.

Standard theories of knowledge, with the gap they maintain between knowledge made and applied, work with residues of a (positivistic) unity-of-knowledge/unity-of-science assumption, whose guiding principle is that a narrowly idealized physical science offers the best, if not the only, valid method for acquiring and adjudicating knowledge. In consequence, disciplines, "branches" of science, domains of inquiry, are formally assimilated one to an-other, homogenized, from a belief that knowledge must be methodologically-epistemologically uniform from one domain to another in the conditions of its possibility and its methods of verification, if it is to count, legitimately, as knowledge. At the same time, areas of inquiry are commonly kept separate by a cluster of border-patrolling practices which determine, for example, that empirical science alone can yield meaningful—that is, properly verifiable or falsifiable—knowledge claims, whereas ethics, politics, or aesthetics cannot.[18] Ecological thinking refuses any unity-of-knowledge assumption as a before-the-fact constitutive principle. It maps locations of knowledge production and the demographics of knowledge producers separately and comparatively, considers the specificities of the habitat conditions and of the inhabitants within and surrounding each such location, discerning where analogies can

---

17. The concept *ecological naturalism* is not entirely my own; Hayden uses it to charac-terize aspects of Deleuze's work, in "Gilles Deleuze and Naturalism," 204.

18. This is the classical positivistic distinction, set out, e.g., by Ayer in *Language, Truth, and Logic*.

reasonably be drawn, and where disanalogies demand acknowledgment and/or rethinking. It examines the ethico-political implications of knowing as fully as its formal structures. Thus in its critical engagement with natural science, ecological naturalism concerns itself (in Conley's words) "with active inter-relations among... [species] and between them and their habitat in its most diverse biochemical and geophysical properties,"[19] to learn, analogically and literally, from ecological science.

In knowing other people, ecological thinking is guided, in part, by Castoriadis's cautionary remark: "It is never the *logos* that you are listening to but always *someone*, such as he is, speaking from the place where he is at his own risk, but at yours too."[20] For its conception of embodied, materially and socially-affectively situated subjectivity, temporal, physical, social location and interdependence are integral to the possibility of being, knowing and doing: ecological human subjects are shaped by and shape their relations, in reciprocity with other subjects and with their (multiple, diverse) environments.[21] Yet as I have noted in the introduction, this model is not self-evidently benign, for ecosystems are as competitive and unsentimentally destructive of their less viable members as they are cooperative and mutually sustaining. So, for work within it to avoid replicating the exclusions and suppressions endemic to traditional epistemologies, its adherents require moral-political guidelines for regulating and adjudicating claims to epistemic authority and will thus refuse artificial separations between epistemic, ethical, and political inquiry.[22] Here again, matters of epistemic responsibility come into the frame.

Quinean Naturalism

In presenting ecological thinking as a revisioned *naturalism*, I am at once in-debted to and critical of the naturalized epistemology born out of the work of W. V. O. Quine, which claims pride of place in North American philosophy. My

19. Conley, *Ecopolitics*, 42.
20. Castoriadis, *Imaginary Institution of Society*, 4 (emphasis in original).
21. For Conley ecological subjectivity requires relating "consciousness of the self to that of being attached to and separated from the world" (*Ecopolitics*, 10).
22. Bohm, for example, contends that inquiry, be it scientific or secular, is inseparable from "a kind of intrinsic morality... [in which] truth and virtue would not be kept apart as they currently are in science" ("Postmodern Science," 343). And consider Scheman: "It is precisely as a social practice, naturalistically understood, that science needs to be evaluated.... The normativity that characterizes epistemology can be found not in ahistorical canons of rationality but in the normativity of politics" ("Epistemology Resuscitated," 44).

critical stance, as I note in the previous section, is based in a recognition of the extent to which, even for self-proclaimed naturalized epistemologists, "natural" is a contestable concept. Thus, for example, at an impasse in a colloquium exchange about the promise of naturalized epistemology for feminism, I asked a not-too-friendly interlocutor, in some exasperation, "What exactly do you mean by 'natural' "? His reply—"Oh, it's what scientists do in the laboratory"— prompted me to wonder, in a 1996 essay, "What Is Natural about Epistemology Naturalized?"[23] This exchange and the puzzlement it generates form part of the backdrop against which I elaborate this conception of ecological thinking. For despite the skepticism of my "what is natural?" question, the thesis I have been developing is that an ecologically revisioned naturalism offers an impressive range of resources and possibilities to participants in successor epistemology projects. Yet in introducing a critical reading of Quinean naturalized episte-mology into the discussion, my intention is to expose and cautiously deplore the tenacity of physical-science-derived conceptions of knowledge and sub-jectivity in even so pathbreaking a departure from the formalisms of reductive abstraction and transcendental analysis as naturalized epistemology promises, and to some extent achieves.

Shifting the focus of inquiry onto questions about the nature and scope of real knowing, Quinean naturalized epistemology appears to offer a way of undoing many of the exclusions that have held orthodox Anglo-American epistemology aloof from the very knowledge it aims to explicate. Constrained neither to analyzing what ideal knowers ought to do nor to silencing the skeptic, naturalists assume that knowledge is possible and set out to explicate its real-world ("natural") conditions. Hence some feminist and other post-colonial theorists, disenchanted with orthodox epistemology's incapacity to engage with "situated knowledges" in all their situatedness, have thought to make common cause with them. According to Sabina Lovibond, there are good feminist reasons to participate in a naturalistic revival, for feminist theory, as she sees it, is

> indebted to the efforts of philosophy over the last century and more
> to "naturalize" epistemology ... to represent the activity we call
> "enquiry" as part of the natural history of human beings. For
> naturalist or materialist analyses of the institutions of knowledge-
> production—schools, universities, the wider "republic of letters"—
> have made it possible to expose the unequal part played by different

---

23. Code, "What Is Natural?" I draw on this essay in parts of this chapter.

social groups in determining standards of judgement. . . . They have
revealed the ideological character of value-systems which have passed
as objective or universally valid.[24]

These theorists have shown how epistemic agendas and social-political
commitments are intertwined and mutually constitutive; how orthodox
epistemologies—often tacitly—sustain a status quo and perpetuate entrenched
structures of power and privilege. Recalling my chapter one discussion of
Castoriadis and the instituted social imaginary, interrupting taken-for-granted
presuppositions and occlusions is central to the emancipatory aims of successor
epistemologies, which complicate sedimented assumptions to expose their
unjust and oppressive effects and "make strange" what passes for natural in
epistemic practices and in the people, places, events, social arrangements, and
phenomena they study.

Epistemology's emancipatory potential has not figured prominently in
Anglo-American projects of determining necessary and sufficient conditions
for knowledge in general, although historically, it claimed a more central place.
Plato's quest for principles of certain knowledge was meant to ensure the
capacity of the Guardians in the Republic to exercise knowledgeable authority;
and Bacon believed that the new experimental science would contribute to
securing the best life for humanity.[25] Marxist emancipatory epistemology set
out to shatter the naturalistic illusions of the capitalist social order;[26] and for
early positivists, scientific knowledge offered enhanced standards of "clarity
and responsibility"[27] capable of liberating humanity from thralldom to reli-
gious or metaphysical excesses. Naturalized epistemology could succeed in
reanimating such interests.

A well-conceived (natural historical) naturalism such as Lovibond recommends is timely when the formal, universalist aspirations of "the activity
we call 'enquiry'" are under strain from postpatriarchal, postmodern, postcolonial, and numerous other critiques. Yet for all its promise, the transformative potential of naturalism's most successful North American version, with
its originary debt to W. V. O. Quine, is circumscribed in ways that have

24. Lovibond, "Feminism and Postmodernism," 12–13.
25. As Tiles and Tiles argue, theoretical divisions between knowledge and social-political-
moral concerns have pertained only contingently, in specific historical periods; see *Introduction
to Historical Epistemology*.
26. For a now-classic view of the feminist potential of Marxist theory, see Hartsock,
"Feminist Standpoint."
27. Carnap, "Autobiography," 21, quoted in Sorell, *Scientism*, 8. Sorell discusses how this
interest in the beneficial character of science mutated into a less desirable scientism.

far-reaching implications for how knowledge figures in human lives. First, its veneration of an idealized physical science as the "institution of knowledge production" most worthy of analysis perpetuates a reductive scientism; second, Quinean naturalists' reliance on scientific psychology and cognitive science as straightforward routes to knowledge of human cognitive functioning begs the question about the epistemic status of psychology itself; and, third, Quinean naturalism works with contestable representations of physical and human "nature." Mindful of these limitations, my analysis is as critical of naturalized epistemology as it is indebted to it.

Here, I am interested in the naturalism that derives from Quine's now-landmark claim: "Epistemology, or something like it, simply falls into place as a chapter of psychology and hence of natural science. It studies a natural phenomenon, viz., a physical human subject."[28] In North America since the (1969) publication of this manifesto, Quinean naturalism has come to stand for naturalized epistemology as such. Yet in its reductive practices, it bears minimal resemblance to the naturalizing for which I—with Lovibond—have high hopes. Evidently assuming they are more or less in order as they stand, Quineans, for the most part, do not engage in analyses of *institutions* of knowledge production. They neither take account of the unequal contributions of different social groups to determining the status of evidence and the salient standards of judgment nor do they consider how allegedly objective value systems can themselves be ideological in character. Hence the promise of Quinean naturalism for such emancipatory projects has to be reevaluated.[29]

Hilary Kornblith states the naturalistic agenda thus: "We must now try to explain how creatures with the faculties cognitive science tells us we have could come to understand the kind of world which the sciences generally tell us that we inhabit."[30] Knowledge of the world is to derive from physics, chemistry, biology, and other laboratory sciences; knowledge about creatures like us, from a scientific psychology reliant on a rejuvenated doctrine of "natural kinds."[31] Naturalists seek to understand how "we" are adapted to the structure of the

28. Quine, "Epistemology Naturalized," 25.

29. Fricker discerns an intriguing parallel between Quinean naturalistic reductions of norms to causes and the reductive program of postmodernism: "The former reduce norms to causal operations in nature; the latter reduce them to operations of power in the social realm. Each has a problem fitting the normative into the world as they find it" ("Feminism in Epistemology," 164 n. 32).

30. Kornblith, "Naturalism," 43.

31. Quine observes: "For surely there is nothing more basic to thought and language than our sense of similarity; our sorting of things into kinds" ("Natural Kinds," 58).

world so that it is rational for us to rely on observational data and inductive inference. Their ontology may include mental states and processes, but it assumes that they are physically constituted and believes that the natural kinds to which "we" belong are not denatured in laboratory studies. In both psychological and physical science, Quinean naturalism relies on prediction, causal explanation, and technological application as knowledge-attesting processes.[32]

To cite just some examples, naturalists study laboratory experiments designed to show how people justify beliefs, generalize to new conclusions, correct perceptual errors, conserve information in memory, assimilate testimony, and accommodate or resist novelty.[33] Such empirical investigations, the assumption is, will issue in normative requirements tailored to what/how people *can* know; thereby allowing epistemology to remain within the demonstrably possible, to eschew concentration on formal, idealized standard-setting. Yet the point is not to turn every "is" into an "ought," but to work toward more humanly manageable regulative principles than a priori theories of knowledge have required. Hence Alvin Goldman commends naturalism for maintaining contact with "epistemic folkways."[34] Because people's survival depends on their information-processing abilities, understanding real human capacities and limitations should yield a better epistemology than one committed to an ideal of epistemic perfection that no human knower could ever achieve: epistemological injunctions are hollow if they require people to perform cognitive tasks that their intellectual-perceptual capacities do not permit. Such, then, is Quine's physical human subject: a processor of knowledge as information whose experiential input is inadequate to account for the "torrential output" evident in its knowledge of "the three-dimensional external world and its history."[35]

Quine's influence in setting the stage for post-1969 naturalistic epistemology in North America has been considerable. It is evident in some of the most innovative work in feminist epistemology from the 1990s, which acknowledges its Quinean inspiration. Noteworthy are Lynn Hankinson Nelson's

32. Some versions of naturalism grant other sciences the privilege that Quineans accord to cognitive psychology. Evolutionary biology, neuroscience, cognitive sociology, genetic epistemology, and ethnomethodology are among the contenders. See Maffie, "Recent Work on Naturalized Epistemology," 290 n. 7.

33. See Kornblith, *Naturalizing Epistemology*; Goldman, *Epistemology and Cognition*; and Callebaut, *Taking the Naturalistic Turn*.

34. Goldman, "Epistemic Folkways."

35. Quine, "Epistemology Naturalized," 25.

and Richmond Campbell's subtle readings of Quine as a protofeminist, Jane Duran's presentation of naturalism as a resource for feminist epistemology, and several essays in the 1993 volume *Feminist Epistemologies* which claim a debt to naturalistic epistemology.[36] Yet these philosophers have tended to work in and out of Quinean naturalism, drawing on its resources, refining and expanding its conceptual frame while, variously, critiquing its reductive features: they have not adopted its aims and ideals uncontested and whole. In particular, several have challenged its scientistic excesses and its epistemic individualism, both of which demonstrably limit its promise for many feminist and other postcolonial projects.[37]

Nonetheless, Quineans cite an impressive array of scientific-technological achievement in support of their conviction that natural science offers the best available knowledge of the physical world and thus of their belief that scientific method is indeed in order as it stands. Hence, Kornblith asserts, philosophy "does not have the credentials . . . to dictate how science itself should be carried out."[38] Yet neither has science the credentials to dictate how philosophy—epistemology—should be done: a naturalism that ignores this cautionary point risks escalating into an uncritical scientism. Still, according to Arthur Danto, for naturalists there could exist no "entities or events which lie, in principle, beyond the scope of scientific explanation."[39] With its echoes of the unity-of-science credo, this observation indicates that although naturalism's focus on real cognitive activity counts as a radical departure from dislocated a prioricity, its claims for the scientificity of all knowledge install a new a priori capable of exerting an equivalently restrictive, reductive pressure. Moreover, the belief that scientific psychology can yield definitive explanations of natural human knowledge making is troubling in its circularity, for at issue is psychology's capacity to yield these very conclusions. It cannot, without begging the question,

36. Nelson, *Who Knows*, and idem, "Epistemological Communities"; Duran, *Toward a Feminist Epistemology*; idem, *Philosophies of Science/Feminist Theories*; and Nelson and Nelson, *Feminist Interpretations of W. V. O. Quine*. See also Potter, "Gender and Epistemic Negotiation"; Babbitt, "Feminism and Objective Interests"; Addelson, "Knowers/Doers and Their Moral Problems"; and Campbell, *Illusions of Paradox*.

37. Antony affirms the radical feminist import of Quinean naturalism, but she endorses a stark epistemological individualism and a scientism that separate her analysis from the others I list ("Quine as Feminist"; "Sisters, Please"; and "Naturalized Epistemology"). In "Naturalized Epistemology," 129, Antony gestures toward an "ecological model of human moral activity," but she does not develop the idea beyond indicating that it locates the norm of impartiality within the "circumstantial features of human life."

38. Kornblith, "Naturalism," 50.

39. Danto, "Naturalism," 448, cited in Callebaut, *Taking the Naturalistic Turn*, 1–2.

be enlisted whole to establish conclusions that contest its own warrant and hegemonic status. Even accurate accounts of how people display knowledge in laboratory experiments do not show that epistemology *reduces to* psychology or that human particularities naturally level out into sameness or replicability. There are too many leftovers.

Feminist and other postcolonial hopes are tempered, then, by the claims of Quinean naturalists and their progeny to recolonize the epistemic territory—to commandeer the best and the only reliable means of regulating or evaluating beliefs and knowledge claims. They are further tempered by denigrations of the "native" practices of the colony with the labels *folkways* and *folk psychology*— as Jerome Bruner observes, "*coined in derision* by the new cognitive scientists for its hospitality toward such intentional states as beliefs, desires, and meanings."[40] Locating natural knowledge making in the physical and cognitive sciences ignores and effectively denaturalizes (normatively and descriptively) extrascientific, nonmainstream, marginalized knowledge, practices, and wisdom, such as the myriad knowledgeable dimensions of *allgemeine Alltäglichkeit*; naturopathic, homeopathic, and indigenous medicine; women's traditional domestic arts; the much-maligned "folk psychology"; "nature study"; historical, cultural, legal, and anthropological knowledge; and the testimony, narrative knowledge, and meaning-making practices integral to human lives, yet unfettered by the stringent dictates of scientific-instrumental rationality. Withholding the (honorific) label *knowledge,* a priori, from the workable, often empirically effective deliverances of such practices sustains the hegemony of an essentialized science as the arbiter of knowledge and of its practitioners as paradigmatically authoritative knowers. Because such exclusions absolve scientific practitioners from the task of interrogating their own presuppositions and from engaging with knowledge-producing practices and institutions beyond a narrowly demarcated subset, they circumscribe the promise of a naturalistic revival. And because its imagining of "the natural" contests the credibility of knowledge made outside the laboratory, Quinean naturalism neither (in Lovibond's words) exposes "the unequal part played by different social groups in determining standards of judgement" nor engages with reason in "its historical and cultural particularity."[41] These omissions, in my view, limit its epistemological promise.

In confining their analyses to self-contained, isolated, one-on-one, observer-observed experiments, Quineans denature both knower and known.

40. Bruner, *Acts of Meaning,* 36 (emphasis added).
41. Lovibond, "Feminism and Postmodernism," 12–13; idem, "End of Morality?" 72.

For the known, they preserve the monocultural purity of a statistical formalism that glosses over differences and specificities within "natural kinds," while the knower, who can be everyone or anyone, is merely a neutral place holder, occupying a place abstracted from all "natural" knowledge-enhancing or knowledge-thwarting relationships and surrounds. Because "our" presumed homogeneity as members of a natural kind, apparent in Quine's contention that "the uniformity of people's quality spaces virtually assures that similar presentations will elicit similar verdicts,"[42] erases possibilities of factoring "historical and cultural particularity" into investigations of reason's natural operations, the naturalistic program, on closer examination, invites an interpretive wariness—a hermeneutic of suspicion—with respect to the extent of its contributions to a "natural history of human beings."

What Is Natural?

According, again, to Lovibond, some version of naturalism is "indispensable" to an epistemology working with

> a conception of reason that has been "irrevocably desublimated"...
> revealed...in all its historical and cultural particularity. Human
> reason is now understood not as the sign of our participation in
> something that goes *beyond* our merely natural existence...but as
> one expression of our identity as a natural species whose members are
> exposed to an enormous variety of environmental and social
> conditions.[43]

Yet rereading reason and knowledge production as expressions of our identity as a natural species must, inevitably, rely on decisions—albeit often tacit—about what counts as "our" natural identity and which of its myriad expressions are epistemologically significant. Producing a natural history of human knowing is hampered by a remarkable ignorance of what "we" naturally are: of where nature begins and cultural or other artificial accretions end; indeed of how the idea of a nature "in itself" or "as such" behind the accretions could be remotely plausible. Constrained by these imponderables, epistemology has, all along, been in the business of naturalizing as it goes. Theories of knowledge—like metaphysical and moral theories—have been assumed

42. Quine, "Natural Kinds," 65.
43. Lovibond, "End of Morality?" 72 (emphasis in original).

without question to derive from and pertain to human nature *tout court*, while their effects have been to naturalize the very attributes and actions they commend or condemn. Representations of female nature as more emotional than rational or less rational than (idealized) male nature have been enlisted to naturalize women's putative rational inferiority; while analogous presuppositions about some people's—blacks', women's, slaves', the workers'—incapacity for rational self-governance have been enlisted to naturalize hierarchical social arrangements (Aristotle, one of the first naturalists, is notorious in these respects).[44]

Quine-derived naturalized epistemology has a different agenda: because it claims a basis in the empirically-experimentally revealed nature of (putatively generic) human cognitive capacities, it will not resort to tacit naturalizing. Yet as feminist and nonwhite, nonaffluent philosophers have emphasized, the laboratory where knowledge, according to Quinean naturalists, is naturally made is itself an artifact of cultural-historical contingencies. It is designed and usually occupied by affluent white men, with women and other Others rarely gaining easy access. Coincidentally or otherwise, its accredited occupants are among the principal producers of the knowledge enlisted to naturalize women's irrationality and the cognitive inferiority, truncated credibility, and limited epistemic authority of other nonstandard knowers, many of whom may nonetheless appear in the laboratory as objects of experimental study. Even as some critics worry, then, about a naturalistic tendency to eschew normativity, the rhetoric of the natural claims a proximity to "the real" that exercises a different kind of normative pressure, dismissing the practices of its interrogators as unnatural, supernatural, unreal—as its patronizing references to "the folk" amply show. The language of "the natural" locates naturalistic projects in a rhetorical space whose initial appeal is strong, in a social-intellectual climate where "returns to nature" are figured as means of stripping away cultural, theoretical, and political baggage, thus returning to "the things themselves"—with the aid of the most sophisticated methods of inquiry that humankind has known: the exact and esoteric techniques of physical science and scientific psychology. Hence "the naturalistic turn" turns away from rarefied abstractions toward reestablishing putatively lost connections with things as they are; and the language of

44. Writing of an earlier naturalism, Poovey notes, provocatively: "When we examine the way knowledge is produced in the double-entry bookkeeping system ... we do not see nature speaking for itself, as the natural philosophers claimed the laboratory enabled it to do; we see fictions being installed as props to systematic meaning and coherence" (*History of the Modern Fact*, 11).

naturalism implies that no stipulating has occurred: philosophers are merely observing what naturally presents itself.

Yet, rather than returning to nature as its rhetoric implies, Quinean naturalism participates in constructing both its subject and its object.[45] Although any self-declared naturalism must *select* what it will count as natural—for nature is not self-announcing—such selections often amount merely to making explicit and continuing to enact the beliefs, images, metaphors, and rhetorical assumptions woven into the very fabric of the instituted social imaginary where the theory-making and its attendant stipulating occur. Such stipulations are rarely innocent, seldom neutral: they have to be exposed, interrogated, read against the grain to reveal the inclusions and exclusions on which they rely and the social-political effects they produce. Ironically, then, the very language of "naturalism" that inspires feminist enthusiasm for naturalized epistemology generates questions such as these.

Claiming to study a "natural phenomenon ... a physical human subject" whose informational output in the course of laboratory performances vastly exceeds its available input reveals sedimented—and contentious—assumptions about the kinds of knowledge best suited to show what this "natural phenomenon" can do, and thus about who or what it is. Why should *this* kind of knowledge, among all the options, count as the knowledge capable of revealing what human cognizers naturally are? Why should the belief prevail that human knowers are, naturally, information processors and problem-solvers whose epistemic practices reduce to multiples and/or elaborations of these activities? And why should the assumption prevail that information, evidence, and problems are themselves unmediated and thus self-announcing? All of these assumptions require sustained argument to establish their plausibility; and none are forthcoming. Continued human survival may indeed attest to the reliability of "our" perceptual-inferential processes;[46] but while survival varies so widely, qualitatively and quantitatively, across this putatively natural kind, and possibilities of claiming epistemic authority and achieving acknowledgment on the basis of information processed and inductions successfully performed are so narrowly determined and unevenly distributed, there is more to say about who "we" are. In according uncontested epistemic hegemony to knowledge of behaviors studied in the laboratory, naturalism fails to relinquish a prioricity, after all.

45. For a provocative analysis of such naturalizing, see Nye, "Saying What It Is."
46. I refer to Quine's pronouncement in "Natural Kinds," 66: "Creatures inveterately wrong in their inductions have a pathetic but praiseworthy tendency to die before reproducing their kind."

When naturalists imagine epistemic subjects as essentially solitary information processors, the contestability of their conception of "the natural" is still more striking. The abstract individual who figures as the (Quinean) knower is a faceless, dispassionate, infinitely replicable "individual" who *knows* only when he suppresses interdependence both situational and personal, along with affect, meaning and indeed all aspects of his sociality and individual*ity.*[47] Yet considering that in individual isolation, human survival would simply not be possible, it is surely neither ideology nor fancy that prompts natural historians (in Lovibond's richer sense) to emphasize human interdependence, but reasonably invariant features of the biology of human procreation and maturation, and of the ethology of human sociality. Hence individualism sits uneasily with naturalism, and justifiably so. Naturalists might represent human maturation as following a "natural" trajectory from interdependence to autonomy, self-sufficiency, and the fully realized individualism of the man of reason whose works comprise the western philosophical canon,[48] whose words, understandings, and deeds inform the character ideals accorded regulative status in moral, political, and epistemological theory. Yet feminists and other Others have charged individualists with glossing over the inescapable cognitive-affective-situational interdependence characteristic, and indeed constitutive, of human lives not just in infancy, but at every age, in the name of an illusory self-reliance, and thus of offering a deeply implausible view of human being.

For feminists and other Others, adequate successor epistemologies need to evaluate the epistemological significance of individual and local specificity, socially-culturally produced and situated.[49] Abstract individualism disallows this possibility, for it lacks the conceptual resources to account for how

47. Departures from individualism are evident in socialized naturalistic philosophy of science such as Downes, "Socializing Naturalized Philosophy"; Nelson, "Feminist Naturalized Philosophy"; Solomon, "Social Empiricism"; and Stump, "Naturalized Philosophy." My concern is with the individualism of most essays in Kornblith's *Naturalizing Epistemology* and with Goldman's claim that knowledge "is the property of individual minds" (*Epistemology and Cognition*, 1). Goldman intended this book to launch a project that would go on to socialize epistemology, but in assuming that individuality precedes sociality, he presupposes an implausible ontology of separate individuals who are only derivatively social.
48. The now-classic text on this subject is Lloyd, *Man of Reason.*
49. Alcoff and Potter observe: "The authors in this collection who agree that epistemology should be naturalized disagree with malestream naturalization programs in two important ways.... [They] reject the assumption of epistemological individualism that the individual is the primary epistemic agent of knowledge. It follows that the use of sciences such as neurophysiology to study individual human brains or evolutionary biology to study the evolution of human individuals puts the epistemological cart before the horse" (they also disagree with the reduction of epistemology to science; *Feminist Epistemologies*, 10–11).

"individual" options—cognitive or other—are constituted, thwarted, and/or enhanced within and by diverse, power-infused social-material situations. An individualist ontology thus underwrites a methodological solipsism for which knowers are, can, and should be separately self-reliant in gathering and corroborating evidence.[50] Individualists assume evidence to be equally available to any (interchangeable) self-sufficient observer, postulate self-sufficiency as an epistemic duty, and condemn as epistemically culpable any observer who fails, all on her or his own, to know how things are. In none of these aspects does individualism serve successor epistemology projects well. It sustains and is sustained by an epistemic imaginary whose (perhaps unintended) effects emerge as sexist, racist, and otherwise obstructive of the very self-realization that individualists advocate. Himself a product of the discourse that relies upon and upholds values of mastery and control, the "individual" of individualism is called upon to enact those same values both in moral-political activities aimed to ensure self-mastery and in experiments designed to demonstrate cognitive self-sufficiency and self-reliance.[51]

There is a curious tension, then, in imagining human beings as *biological* creatures whose innate "spacing of qualities" or linguistic readiness demonstrate the universality of rational processes[52] when, in epistemological analyses informed by the theory, "individuals" rarely figure as embodied or located in the world, except accidentally and inconveniently, while biology disappears from view in justificatory strategies meant to legitimate universal conclusions that transcend bodily, and other, specificities. Paradoxically, then, individualistically conceived psychology fails, indeed refuses to individuate: it reduces and assimilates "natural" and social-political-ecological differences under its universality and objectivity requirements, denaturing the very natural kinds to

50. As Maffie notes, both Alvin Goldman and J. Angelo Corlett "favor an information-processing approach to human cognition which is solipsistic, i.e., which seeks to understand cognition without reference to states external to the mind-brain of the cognizer" ("What Is Social?" 106). Maffie argues convincingly that "the native vs. acquired distinction lacks both epistemic significance and conceptual precision" (101).

51. According to Fuller, "the institution of experiments in psychology...exaggerated the foregrounding effects of ordinary vision by physically isolating the organism in the artificially sparse setting of the laboratory" ("Epistemology Radically Naturalized," 436). Analytic epistemologists, he claims, "form a close-knit subculture who, through frequent written and oral rehearsals of the test cases for knowledge, prime each other's intuitions into mutual conformity" (441).

52. Quine refers to an "innate spacing of qualities" in "Natural Kinds," 64, 67, claiming that "a standard of similarity is in some sense innate" (63). Stich disagrees, arguing that it is "extremely plausible that there are substantial individual differences in cognitive competence" ("Could Man Be an Irrational Animal?" 353).

which its founding intuitions appeal. In this respect, too, Quinean naturalism is a limited resource for feminist and other postcolonial epistemologists.

How, then, might a naturalist imagine human kinds differently? Outlining a "naturalist view of persons," Annette Baier observes: "A naturalist . . . takes it as obvious that a person is, as Montaigne put it, 'marvellously corporeal' . . . and that a person's ability to think is affected by genetic inheritance from parents and is vitally dependent upon the sort of care received in childhood—for example in being introduced into a language community."[53] Throughout her work Baier shows by example how theories like (Quinean) naturalism *read past* the implications of social situation in establishing their conclusions.[54] Her position "emphasize[s] the interdependence of persons,"[55] pointing to the incongruity, for naturalists, of an individualist ontology whose way of imagining human nature sits uneasily with its own naturalistic thesis.

Yet in explicating the implications of her position, Baier need not turn her back on psychology as an "institution of knowledge production," for there are distinguished—if eccentric—voices in professional psychology that accord well with hers. To name just two as a prelude to developing this claim more fully in chapter four: Couze Venn protests against conceiving of psychology as the science of the individual, "the 'rational man' with no past," "the 'individual subject' minus everything that pins down its identity and its lived experience of social relations";[56] and Jerome Bruner maintains: "It is man's participation *in* culture and the realization of his mental powers *through* culture that make it impossible to construct a human psychology on the basis of the individual alone."[57] Studying how sociality contributes to making individuality possible opens up ways of addressing the unevenness of survival, for it is in radically diverse social-material-situational circumstances that such inequities are enacted. In Bruner's view, a revivified folk psychology located within an elaborated "cultural psychology" avoids many of the egregious denaturings consequent upon cognitive science's position as uncontested master narrative. For him, cultural psychology is "an interpretive psychology, in much the sense that history and anthropology and linguistics are interpretive disciplines. But that does

53. Baier, *Moral Prejudices*, 316.
54. See especially Baier, *Postures of the Mind*.
55. Baier, *Moral Prejudices*, 313.
56. Venn, "Subject of Psychology," 140–41. See also Hollway, *Subjectivity and Method in Psychology*.
57. Bruner, *Acts of Meaning*, 12 (emphasis in original). The extensive bibliographies in Bruner's text and in Henriques et al.'s *Changing the Subject* serve to dispel any thought that these are isolated voices contesting the hegemony of mainstream cognitive science.

not mean that it need be unprincipled or without methods, even hard-nosed ones. It seeks out the rules that human beings bring to bear in creating meanings in cultural contexts."[58] Like the testimonial-anecdotal evidence I discuss in chapter one, meaning-making practices, narratives, stories where people locate and explicate their experiences, are integral to adequately naturalized accounts of cognition: stories peopled as much by human actors as by medium-sized information-generating objects, locational specificities, and perceptual-memory stimulants. Aptly told narratives enhance possibilities for people, interactively, to understand and negotiate the circumstances that make laboratory experiments worth doing, to question the salience of those same experiments, to interpret their results and/or assess their significance. Narratives—like those Carson hears from nature lovers or Messing from female workers, or the bioregional narratives Cheney advocates—can function as catalysts, setting in motion the critical and self-critical deliberation on which knowledge making relies just as frequently as on artifactual conditions. As in the science of ecology in Shrader-Frechette and McCoy's account, inquiry moves from singular observations to theoretical explanation, relying heavily on induction.

Neither Bruner nor Venn frames the options as a forced choice between (hard, scientific) experimentation and (soft, folksy) narrative, nor do they advocate abandoning experiment to rely on narrative alone, any more than Carson or Messing would leave standard scientific evidence behind to dwell only on testimony or would assume that scientific data inevitably discredit testimonial accounts. The debate is, in part, between taking what happens in a laboratory as self-justifying—allowing its genesis in experimental psychology to supply its warrant—and finding in naturalism what Steve Fuller labels "a call to self-reflection, or reflexivity."[59] Reflexivity entails no simplistic refusal to acknowledge the power of experimentation, but it enlists genealogical, interpretive, and negotiative practices to evaluate experimental and narrative knowledge making and to expose the effects of power within them. As with Messing's hesitations about studying Chinese hamster ovary cells, the call to reflexivity functions as a reminder that the meaning and translatability of experimental findings beyond the confines of the laboratory are rarely self-announcing:[60] laboratory results are as much artifacts of the situation of their

---

58. Bruner, *Acts of Meaning*, 118.
59. Fuller, "Epistemology Radically Naturalized," 431.
60. Recall Maffie's claim that seeking "to understand cognition without reference to states external to the mind-brain of the cognizer" yields a solipsistic approach to human cognition ("What Is Social?" 48). Ecological thinking, *ex hypothesi*, contests the plausibility of such an approach.

provenance as they are indicative of how things "naturally" are. Likewise, even the most sincere, responsible narratives require critical scrutiny of the circumstances of their utterance, analysis of the structures of power and privilege that accord or withhold acknowledgment. Untangling such issues, I will argue, requires careful interpretation.

Feminist/postcolonial analyses of "desublimated" reason in action can forge viable alliances with naturalized epistemology, therefore, only by working past scientific psychology's complicity in the naturalizing that erases human differences even as it casts the objects of inquiry in its own image. Examples are too numerous to detail, but recalling some now-classic instances, the very title of Naomi Weisstein's "Psychology Constructs the Female" heralds her still-apt demonstration that natural (female) human "kinds" are as artifactual as they are factual;[61] Carol Gilligan engages critically with Lawrence Kohlberg's developmental psychology at the point where it naturalizes female moral immaturity through readings of women's lower-than-men's scores on the Kohlberg scale of moral maturity;[62] and the connections between genital and brain size that Philippe Rushton claims to *discover*, work in effect, to *produce* "natural" differences in black, oriental, and white intelligence as persuasively as they merely record them.[63] In these studies, "nature" is as much a product of experimental design as it is a given, suggesting that when in fact it sees them at all, psychology constructs—as frequently as it "finds"—the female, the black, the other Other, as natural kinds. More commonly, it overlooks them, for its "individual" subjects are gender-, class-, race-, and ethnicity-neutral, an odd way of imagining corporeal subjects so (naturally) diverse as members of the human species.

Biology (here somewhat cursorily homogenized), which is integral to many ecological investigations, has at least as strong a claim as cognitive psychology to recognition as a mode of inquiry that studies the physical human subject as a natural species, thereby contributing to a "natural history" of human beings. Yet, recalling Shrader-Frechette's insistence that the science of ecology "cannot provide precise, fundamental, testable, scientific laws," Richard Lewontin, speaking in a similar vein, maintains there are almost no causal laws in biology: every organism is the outcome—often unpredictable,

61. Weisstein, "Psychology Constructs the Female." For other accounts of these debates, see Crawford and Marecek, "Psychology Reconstructs the Female"; and Marecek, "Psychology and Feminism."
62. Gilligan, *In a Different Voice*.
63. See my discussion of this issue in *Rhetorical Spaces*, 38–44.

surprising—of networks of internal and external relations.[64] Such departures from linear, mechanistic causality do not disqualify the science in question—biology or ecology—from claiming scientific status, despite familiar debates about the scientificity of each. Biology, however, is no more innocent than psychology of constructing and thus denaturing the human subjects who become the objects of its inquiry.[65] Messing's biologically derived studies of women's occupational health, for example, uncover persistent (establishment) preferences for "controlled studies...in situations which bear little resemblance to real life."[66] She and her associates document patterns familiar to feminist and other postcolonial science critics: women's dizziness, nausea, and headaches after exposure to toxic solvents or pesticides represented as "mass psychogenic illness"; restrictive, "universal" definitions of occupational impacts on health that read past effects specific to female workers; statistical procedures designed to conceal class- or sex-biased assumptions that "increase the suffering of workers"; women eliminated from sampling procedures "to make samples uniform"; and investigative presuppositions and techniques that sustain representations of women as "physically, mentally and emotionally 'the weaker sex.' "[67]

In both her 1995 article and her 1998 book, Messing exposes the power of company interests to denigrate worker credibility, reinforced by an "image of workers as lazy malingerers coddled by their colluding physicians...[that] block[s] compensation to injured workers who stay out 'too long' "[68] and supported by refusals to accept self-reported workplace experiences (= testimony) as evidence. Such occurrences indicate yet again how (Quine's) innate "standard of similarity" can mask variations in natural kinds[69] while erasing the systemic, structural, social-institutional effects that ensure its own warrant. Attesting further to the need for interpretive-genealogical natural-historical analyses to evaluate the place—and the naturalness—of naturalism, these examples expose the denaturing that a self-proclaimed naturalism can accomplish.

64. Lewontin, "Interpenetration of Environment"; and idem, *Biology as Ideology*. Shrader-Frechette, "Ecology," 304–5.

65. A minimal sampling of now-classic feminist critiques includes Hubbard, Henifin, and Fried, *Biological Woman*; Sayers, *Biological Politics*; Birke, *Women, Feminism, and Biology*; idem, *Feminism and the Biological Body*; Birke and Hubbard, *Reinventing Biology*; Fausto-Sterling, *Myths of Gender*; Hubbard, *Politics of Women's Biology*; and Haraway, *Primate Visions*.

66. Messing, "Don't Use a Wrench," 219.

67. Ibid., 230, 233.

68. Ibid., 242.

69. Recall Quine: "A standard of similarity is in some sense innate. This point is not against empiricism; it is a commonplace of behavioral psychology" ("Natural Kinds," 63).

In a cultural climate where reason is "irrevocably desublimated," it is puzzling that "the naturalistic turn" and "the interpretive turn"[70] are so often cast as turnings away from one another, often in antagonism. Collaboratively, combining their resources, each contesting the other's excesses and drawing on the other's strengths, they might issue in impressively reskilled, resensitized approaches to knowledge. Science-located naturalists have little time for cultural narrative and interpretive methods, however, whose failure to produce causal-predictive explanations exposes them to charges of generating merely subjective, soft conclusions. Naturalists' disdain for interpretation is particularly puzzling, since interpreting is as evidence-reliant a practice as the activities Quinean naturalists study and as essential to survival, even though it may treat evidence differently—less literally—than more orthodox evidence-reading practices do. Nor is causality so unequivocally automatic (on-off) as linear models suggest.[71] People's ineluctable "locatedness," and the consequent impossibility of achieving perfect understanding or producing a view from nowhere, makes of every inquiry, scientific or secular, a reading "from somewhere" whose circumstances, which variously shape its presuppositions and conclusions, require interpretation and deliberation. The interpretations invoked to naturalize the practices of laboratory life have to be as closely interrogated as those whose power-generated effects are to limit the populations of laboratories to a chosen few. Hence my suggestion in chapter one that the skills required for constructing good case studies, such as Shrader-Frechette recommends, are closely akin to the interpretive skills exercised in responsibly knowledgeable human interactions. Interpretation can expose the contingency of the commonly enacted power structures, prejudgments, motivations, and extrascientific beliefs so tightly woven into experimental design and narrative structures as often to disappear into an unquestioned picture of how things naturally are.[72] Thus its value for naturalistic inquiry need not be discounted.

70. I refer here to the title of Hiley, Bohman, and Shusterman's *Interpretive Turn.*

71. Curiously, Tanesini reads the outline of ecological naturalism in my 1996 "What Is Natural?" essay as endorsing a conception of reason that "like all 'natural' occurrences . . . is to be explained scientifically in purely causal terms," maintaining that the ecological model I propose "is committed to a causal account of knowledge" (*Introduction to Feminist Epistemologies*, 117–18). It is not easy to see where she finds support for such a reading, given my discussion of reason as desublimated, my criticisms of the artifactual character of Quinean conceptions of "the natural" and its scientism, and my analyses of the multiple contributions of situation to knowledge and rationality.

72. The genealogically informed interpretation that I advocate has one of its sources in the work of Foucault; see especially his "Nietzsche, Genealogy, History."

In short, a *scientistic* naturalistic turn and an interpretive turn would indeed be seriously at odds with one another: this point is pivotal to my critique of scientistic naturalism. But the debt to ecology I have claimed presents ecological naturalism as an epistemological approach that is as interpretive in its methods as it is committed to negotiating the pertinence and import of empirical evidence and causal hypotheses. Ecological thinking entails no naive dismissals of science; yet neither does it subscribe to a unity-of-science credo on whose terms any science—or social science—indebted to causal explanations must conceive of these explanations mechanistically and accord them absolute force. There is a difference between taking natural science very seriously and imagining it to be capable of explaining everything, mechanistically and without remainder.[73] Scientific knowledge, like all products of human cognitive endeavor, rarely speaks for itself in the contexts either of discovery or justification; nor is it a morally neutral product of simple or innocent manipulations of "nature," whether for good or evil. Contingent practices operate at every stage: choices, judgments of relevance and meaning, issues of credibility, expertise and authority, power and privilege, and of epistemic responsibility. A scientistic conception of science fails to distinguish among the sciences in respect to the extent and manner of their reliance on (uni)linear, mechanistic causal explanation. But unless a scientist can show that mechanistic accounts are *sufficient* and can thus condemn interpretive practices for granting them no, or too little, credence, or unless she believes naturalism is interpretation free, it is not easy to understand a conviction that interpretation and naturalism are mutually antithetical.

In endorsing Lovibond's contention that feminism and other postcolonial inquiry requires desublimated conceptions of reason and knowledge, capable of representing both as practices in and of this world, I am working with reason conceived as neither transcendent nor fully realized in particular case studies or singular epistemic events. The structures, metaphors, images, and symbolisms through which "we" develop a natural history of reason (hence also of knowledge and justification) are themselves woven into a social-epistemic imaginary with whose workings a natural-historical ecological naturalism needs to engage. Reason's manifestations are thus, in significant ways, historically, locationally, culturally variable. But addressing reason's situatedness and its intrications with emotion, affect, and wisdom as I have done, while preserving space for reflexivity and immanent critique;

---

73. Such imagining, presumably, characterizes what La Caze aptly dubs "the scientism of the analytic imaginary" in *Analytic Imaginary*, 81.

weighing and evaluating reason's instrumental, critical, practical (*phronēsis*), and interpretive aspects; reconceiving science and causality so as to do justice to their substantive ontological and methodological variations across sciences and theories of science; and working with divergences between/among theories of causality—all this is tantamount neither to endorsing a mechanistically causal account of knowledge[74] nor to eschewing objectivity, as some critics of interpretation contend. I have shown that interpretive folk psychology and narrative are sites of natural knowing at least as valid as the data of cognitive science. Their exclusion from orthodox epistemology shows why *ecological*, social-moral-political analyses of institutional and material forces that foster or constrain scientific-epistemic practice are vital to a well-conceived naturalized epistemology, for natural epistemic activities and projects cannot plausibly be imagined as confined to laboratories either in their praxis or in the conditions that make knowledge possible. Nor does endorsing a sophisticated, nuanced conception of causality require a crudely mechanistic analysis, for as I show in chapter one, ecological thinking calls for a subtler, less automatic view of causality than mechanistic thinking commonly presupposes.

Even Hans-Georg Gadamer, to whom interpretive inquiry in its hermeneutic aspects owes so significant a debt,[75] sets up no stark either-science-or-interpretation divide. In his work on medicine, which is exemplary of the engagement evident in his later works with a science at once empirical and social, Gadamer speaks of a balance between science and art in medical knowledge,[76] thereby refusing to participate in a forced "science or art" choice. In his insistence that knowledge—all knowledge, if in varying degrees across subject matters and disciplinary boundaries—is achieved in cooperation between observation and interpretation, science and art, he is deeply critical of orthodox positivism. The reciprocity he highlights is integral to the epistemological approach ecological thinking fosters. Its repudiation of mechanistic thinking and its sensitivity to myriad interdependences, chaotic though they may often be, recommends ecological naturalism, literally and metaphorically.

74. Here again, I disagree with Tanesini's reading of my essay "What Is Natural?" in *Introduction to Feminist Epistemologies*, chap. 5, esp. p. 118.

75. See, e.g., Rabinow and Sullivan, *Interpretive Social Science*, which includes Gadamer's "Problem of Historical Consciousness"; and Hiley, Bohman, and Shusterman, *Interpretive Turn*, where Gadamer's influence is evident throughout.

76. Gadamer, *Enigma of Health*. See also my introduction to *Feminist Interpretations of Hans-Georg Gadamer*.

Nature Reclaimed: Ecology and Epistemology

Carolyn Merchant maintains that

> the postmodern, ecological world view, *unlike the modern mechanistic one*, is based on the impossibility of completely predicting the behavior of the natural world.... Most environmental and biological systems, such as weather, noise, population, and ecological patterns, cannot be described accurately by the linear equations of mechanistic science and may be governed by nonlinear chaotic relationships.[77]

In this chapter I have situated my position in the vicinity of Quinean naturalism, which I have evaluated as a resource for feminist and other successor epistemology projects. I have taken issue with its adherence to a scientistic conception of knowledge and methodology, with the unnaturalness of its conceptions of the natural and with its failure to prepare the way for social-political critique of the "institutions of knowledge production." *Ecological naturalism*, which captures what I intend this reconfigured approach to achieve, offers richer, less reductive possibilities for transformative, emancipatory epistemology. Working horizontally across the epistemic terrain while seeking to discern the knowledge-enhancing or knowledge-thwarting specificities of the terrain itself, eschewing practices of viewing evidence through top-down, superimposed theoretical frames, it aims to unsettle the hegemony of dislocated instrumental reason and thereby to dislodge the instituted epistemic imaginary of mastery and control. Indebted to the science of ecology, to environmentalism, and to the ethico-political impetus that inspired many of the new ecological and other social movements in the second half of the twentieth century, ecological naturalism offers more natural accounts of human epistemic practices and their products than formal epistemological analysis or Quinean naturalism can offer.

Looking to the knowledge base that ecological naturalism requires, my proposal respects the demonstrated successes of modern science in explaining and producing ways of "managing" the physical universe, and it acknowledges the power of empirical inquiry. But it takes issue with physical science's hegemony in the academy, the marketplace, and other institutions of knowledge production and with its trickle-down effects into people's daily lives, where it installs monolithic norms of epistemic practice. Physical science and technology are neither the only nor the only reliable, epistemologically significant

---

77. Merchant, *Ecology*, 19 (emphasis added).

forms of knowledge: physics-derived models and methods offer neither definitive nor appropriate exemplars for all scientific inquiry or for knowledge "in
general." Yet ecological naturalism looks to the science of ecology, to sciences
operative within and for ecology, and to ecological thinking as it circulates
literally (in its scientific modes) and metaphorically (in more secular modes)
within the epistemic imaginary, as a route toward thinking differently about
knowledge. Refusing to separate human knowers from the knowledge they/we
produce or knowledge production from its constitutive practices, places, and
circumstances or from the social-moral-political effects of its circulation,
it takes the peculiarities of subjectivity, cognitive agency, and geographical-
material-historical-cultural location seriously into account. Ecological science
serves such purposes well: its reliance on field studies where knowers are, by
definition, precisely situated as active participants in producing and testing
knowledge claims makes it implausible to imagine them isolated from the
knowledge they produce, even when they appeal to laboratory-derived experimental evidence for pieces of it. Rachel Carson's practice, again, illustrates this
process, working back and forth from field studies to scientific analyses, explanations, and experiments, specifically located experiential (anecdotal) evidence, and local (or larger) histories of the sites and species she studies.

Departing from the positivistic aspects of Anglo-American philosophy-of-
science—whose traces linger in Quinean naturalism—for which interchangeable observers leave their subjectivity and agency, interests and enthusiasms,
actions and interactions, prejudices and hopes, outside the laboratory door,
thereby isolating their disinterested practices of gathering and collating evidence from what Latour aptly calls "matters of concern," ecological naturalism
looks to the new (by comparison with physics, chemistry, geology, astronomy)
science of ecology.[78] It is a politically charged, engaged inquiry, accountable for
the knowledge it produces, often explicitly and unabashedly conducting its
inquiries in the service of values, commitments, agendas, and political programs that have themselves to be kept open to critical evaluation. Hence, if
science-derived models or exemplars of knowledge are required, ecological
science provides more diversified, less unnatural exemplars than those that
Quinean naturalists have invoked. It represents scientific knowing as continuous with modes of knowing that inform "everyday life" and are crucial to
developing and sustaining habitats and collectivities conducive to enabling
people to live well together.

---

78. See Latour, *Politics of Nature*. Latour asks: "When will we be able not to reduce
matters of concern . . . to matters of fact?" (51).

Interim Conclusions

I have connected my sketch of the methods and commitments of ecological science with an outline of ecological thinking in its social dimensions because, in the accounts of the practitioners I have cited, ecological science offers an instructive example of a science cognizant of its own epistemic peculiarities, of its social-geographical location and accountability. Avowedly driven by social-environmental concerns, it has no pretensions to be interest-free or value-neutral: its self-presentation is of a self-reflexive science, more so than most putatively value-neutral and impersonal scientific inquiry has been. The examples I have cited involve ways of knowing nature, human nature, materiality, and place in/with their interrelations. The ethico-politics they enjoin are informed by these knowings, as all ethico-political systems are, if not always so transparently.

In this revisioned naturalism, the guiding image of epistemic normativity is an ecological model of reciprocally informing and sustaining, critically interrogating practices of engaged inquiry. Relationships within and among institutions of knowledge production—their effects for social-political structures and the effects of social-political structures for them, their interworkings, their negotiated, deliberative character, and their social-environmental implications—have as meticulously to be analyzed as their putatively separate self-consistency and internal coherence.[79] No longer a science of the individual subject whose epistemic processes are flattened in a mechanical, input-output modeling, the ecological subject-as-inquirer is—like Baier's—"marvellously corporeal" and interdependent, active, resistant and reactive, accountable; created out of sociality and creative, in its turn, of the forms of sociality in which it participates, where sociality is the (mutable) frame in which seemingly isolated experiences *and* experimental performances contribute to the ongoing realization, suppression, deterioration, or other modalities of subjectivity.[80]

Ecological naturalism builds on the relations of organisms with one another and with their habitat, which comprises not just the physical habitat or the

---

79. Here I am again drawing on my "What Is Natural?" paper.

80. Ecology talk is not foreign to other versions of naturalism, though they accord it no regulative function. Giere notes that for Michael Gorman "a claim is *externally valid* if it generalizes well to other well-controlled, idealized conditions... *ecologically valid* if it generalizes well to natural settings, for example, to the reasoning of scientists in their laboratories" (*Cognitive Models of Science*, xxvi). Fuller poses ecological questions about how the "contrived situations" that analytic epistemologists study bear upon "conditions under which people try to make sense of the world" ("Epistemology Radically Naturalized," 442)—questions germane to the ecological thinking I advocate. Maffie's position in "Towards an Anthropology of Epistemology" has some affinities with my analysis.

present one, but the complex network of locations and relations, whether social, historical, material, geographical, cultural, racial, sexual, institutional, or other, where organisms—human or nonhuman—try to live well, singly and collectively. At any moment in its history an organism reveals how it has incorporated and/or accommodated to such relations; and not passively, for organisms participate in the making of habitat. Issues of agency and the developmental processes that foster or circumscribe it figure centrally in evaluations of epistemic practices. Ecological analyses work to understand the implications, for organisms, of living where and as they do while constructing strategies for knowing well that are exploitative neither of the habitat nor of other inhabitants. The ecological subject, then, is materially situated: embodied location and interdependence are integral to its possibilities for knowledge and action.

Ecological thinking is as interested in developmental studies of human cognition as in its adult manifestations. The persistent individualism of such natural-social projects as Goldman's acquires plausibility from its concentration on experiments with adult, hence seemingly well-individuated, human beings (presumptively male, and members of the dominant, "normal," social group).[81] As I shall show in chapter four, critical developmental analyses of how individuality is variously and unevenly fostered in such experiments and how it is thwarted, in the real world, from situation to situation are better cognizant of the interplay between independence and interdependence in fostering cognitive agency than one-size-fits-all studies conducted with "average" adult subjects in standardized laboratory conditions. Epistemologically, rather than treating knowledge as information gained in isolation and articulated in monologic statements, ecological naturalism starts from the— natural—dependence of knowledge production upon and within human and human-nonhuman interaction, in adult lives as in infancy and childhood.

It would be a mistake to conclude that ecological naturalism is antiscientific: it looks to ecological and social-scientific evidence to understand how survival can be ensured and enhanced, not by requiring epistemology to "fall into place as a chapter" of ecological science, but by learning—analogically— from ecology's projects and methods. It establishes its (contestable) conception of evidential reliability in self-critical reflexivity where locally informed studies of disciplines, subject matters, and interdisciplinary relations generate a healthy suspicion toward presumptions to theoretical hegemony. Although it counts state-of-the-art physical and cognitive sciences among its principal resources,

81. Noteworthy exceptions to concentration on adult behavior among Quinean naturalists are Markman, "Natural Kinds"; and Carey, "Origin and Evolution."

ecological naturalism rejects their claims to joint occupancy of the position of master metanarrative. Wary of the power-infused effects of racial/gender/class stereotypes and essentialized conceptions of science and nature, it is less sanguine than many Quineans about the before-the-fact reliability of "our" capacities to generalize the relevant features of natural kinds "against the background of the environments in which they operate."[82] Its normative possibilities are instrumental, but in a deflationary sense with scant resemblance to the instrumental rationality that figures as one of the villains in the story I have been telling. They derive from an imperative that epistemic activity be evaluated—in form and content—for its capacity to promote cohabitability in ecologically sustaining habitats and communities and to foster ecological viability in the "natural" world.[83] Projects of inquiry and appraisals of ecological goals proceed in concert, integrating epistemology and moral-political-historical-anthropological debate.[84]

Epistemology does not, however, reduce to a chapter of ecological science; and single "S-knows-that-p" claims may function as neutral components of an inquiry, with no immediate ecological import either way. Consider Ursula Franklin's "impact studies" in which she required engineering students, during their summer jobs, to keep a daily record of the impact in/on their surroundings of the work they were doing. The purpose of the studies was to teach them that whatever they did, however menial or nonscientific (house painting, child minding, table serving) would produce unexpected effects, or effects so embedded in their habitual conduct and social imaginary, so seemingly matter-of-course, as to escape their notice.[85] Learning to see the imperceptible,

82. In his "Naturalism" Kornblith notes the need to evaluate "our inductive inferential habits...against the background of the environments in which they operate...which are populated by natural kinds" (46).

83. According to Kornblith, epistemic norms that derive from a theory of epistemic virtue or responsibility (he cites my *Epistemic Responsibility*) require an instrumental account of epistemic value ("Epistemic Normativity," 375 n. 11). He is not "convinced that it is possible to give an account of epistemic norms which provides more than this" (359).

84. Writing of a balance that moral-epistemological debates must achieve between "reverence" and "suspicion," Lovibond observes: "The appropriate relation between these two attitudes will be a mutually correcting or 'dialectical' one; and the balance between them at any given moment will be the outcome of this continual process of mutual correction" ("End of Morality?" 75).

85. Franklin cited this example in conversation. Elsewhere, she sounds a cautionary note: "I feel that 'the environment' is now more often a term of befuddlement than a concept that is helpful in the search for clarity....It seems such an egocentric and technocentric approach to consider everything in the world with reference to ourselves. Environment essentially means what is around us, with the emphasis on *us*. It's *our* environment, not the environment or the habitat of fish, bird, or tree" (*Real World of Technology*, 84–85).

learning to let go of indifference so as to be appropriately sensitive to their surrounds in ways that extend beyond their first imaginings, was intended to cultivate an awareness, for these students, of how all knowledge, all knowledge-informed practices have consequences; none are immune before the fact to critical scrutiny.

Starting from the inherent sociality of human lives and knowledge construction, aware of the material, social, affective, and political forces that are productive of subjectivity, ecological thinking creates rhetorical/discursive spaces for engagement with social-global issues and epistemological questions together. But the question persists as to how any self-proclaimed naturalism can produce normative, and not merely descriptive conclusions. I have two interim responses that will guide my inquiry in subsequent chapters. First, even if, at the outset, it is primarily descriptive, it will not be *purely* descriptive, for descriptions are rarely pure. They are value-laden artifacts of location and choice: they begin (and end) within always-contestable theoretical presuppositions and background assumptions, even though they are often capable of determining nodal points where action is possible. Good descriptions are not easily achieved, and they are seldom definitive, final. Articulating good, plausible descriptions and circulating them well are among the most challenging epistemic-moral-political tasks; inserted into the public domain they become catalysts of ongoing deliberation, contestation, negotiation, and action. If epistemology has systematically misdescribed all but a select portion of human cognitive activity, as I believe it has, then better descriptions are vital, crucial to ongoing survival. Second, there is an ambiguity in the sense of description underlying worries that naturalism's "mere descriptiveness" encourages a violation of prohibitions against deriving *is* from *ought*. The working hypotheticals that naturalists extrapolate from consequential patterns in the natural (and human-natural) world—"if you want to succeed in doing X, then you [had] best do Y"[86]—need to be distinguished from mechanistic, linear, causal accounts. Furthermore, narrative descriptions tend always to be normative: it is impossible, as Bruner puts it, to "argue any of these interpretations without taking a moral stance and a rhetorical posture."[87] Ecological naturalism establishes such a moral stance at the core of its deliberations, insisting on obligations to answer for oneself/ ourselves, to maintain skepticism in the face of overweening authority, and to work toward ways of ensuring better, justice-honoring cohabitability.

86. I owe this formulation to Hull, who alludes to this ambiguity in "How to Get beyond the Purely Descriptive," 99.
87. Bruner, *Acts of Meaning*, 60.

Ecological thinking supplies a partial answer to the question "what is natural about epistemology naturalized?" Naturalistic projects contribute to emancipatory epistemological agendas when they are open to examining the constructed dimensions of nature and knowledge, to assessing the ecological effects of these constructs, and to engaging questions of historical, cultural, situated, gendered epistemological specificity as constitutive of "science as an institution or process in the world."[88] Naturalized epistemology is natural in its positioning as one episode—albeit a major one—in a natural history of human beings. Its provenance and effects are as significant as its explanatory powers: powers whose pretensions to global dominance need to be curbed in the interests of respectful human and natural coexistence.

88. Quine, "Epistemology Naturalized," 26.

In all that mass of authorities . . . there is no single mention of a reasonable

woman. It was ably insisted before us that such an omission . . . must be something

more than a coincidence; that . . . there might be expected at least some passing

reference to a reasonable person of the opposite sex; that no such reference is

found; and that therefore in this case the learned judge should have directed the jury

that, while there was evidence on which they might find that the defendant had not

come up to the standard required of a reasonable man, the conduct was only what

was to be expected of a woman, as such.

—A. P. Herbert, Uncommon Law *(emphasis added)*

3

NEGOTIATING EMPIRICISM

Statements of Fact: Whose? Where? When?

The phrase *statements of fact* has a clear, unequivocal ring.[1] It speaks of a stable place untouchable by contests either in epistemology or in more mundane places, around questions of constructivism, subjectivism, and the politics of knowledge. It seems to offer fixity, a locus of constancy in a shifting landscape where traditional certainties have ceased to hold, to maintain a vantage point outside the fray where knowledge seekers can go on believing in some degree of correspondence between items of knowledge and events in the world. Within the social institutions and practices where knowledge is an issue, it appears to designate a secure starting place for deliberation, a way of ensuring that processes of decision-making remain cognizant of the "realities" they have to address.

1. This chapter is revised and adapted from my "Statements of Fact."

In the institutions of knowledge production and knowledgeable practice that generate the examples I appeal to in this chapter—law and medicine—statements of fact appear to comprise an incontestable core around which interpretive strategies may indeed have to be enlisted, but which itself functions as something like an interpretation-exempt zone.[2] There are quite good epistemological and social-political reasons for preserving that status, for resisting the instabilities and sheer whimsicalities that would follow from dislodging it. If doctors could not rely on statements of fact about thermometer readings, lawyers or judges on statements of fact about fingerprint or DNA evidence, then bases for treatment or judgment would be so shaky as to destroy public confidence not only in the knowledge that purports to inform legal and medical agency, but in the social fabric of which these institutions comprise central threads. I have taken these examples, intentionally, from places where the most basic, old-style empirical observation yields the evidence on which knowledgeable practice is based. And indeed in scientific-technological societies, the reliability of such everyday empirical knowledge about the simple behaviors of people and things counts virtually as an "absolute presupposition,"[3] as one of the crosspieces holding the epistemic raft together, which could not be replaced while the raft is afloat without causing the entire structure to sink.[4] If the network of assumptions generated by such statements of empirical fact and their analogues could never hold fast, social chaos would presumably ensue. In short, statements of fact are the stuff of the deliberations, decisions, and designs that enable modern western societies to function: they sustain the institutions that comprise these societies and that the societies legitimate.

Factuality, however, is a hotly contested issue in the late-twentieth- and early-twenty-first-century affluent western world both within philosophy and without it, in feminist theory and in other postcolonial critical projects. On the one hand, information networks saturate the social domain with impersonal

2. This point recalls Wittgenstein: "It may be that *all enquiry on our part* is set so as to exempt certain propositions from doubt, if they are ever formulated. They lie apart from the route travelled by enquiry" (*On Certainty*, §88, emphasis original).

3. The term is Collingwood's, who writes, "*An absolute presupposition is one which stands, relatively to all questions to which it is related, as a presupposition, never as an answer*" (*Essay on Metaphysics*, 31, emphasis original).

4. The image of the raft comes from Otto Neurath, who represents human knowledge as a freely floating raft. Repairs (= revisions in a system of knowledge) have to be made while the raft is afloat. No part is immune from repair, but it is vital to be able to stand on some parts in order to replace or repair others: it would be impossible to dismantle the whole structure at one time.

statements of fact about what "surveys show" and "experts have proved": the quotidian deliverances of a faceless instrumental rationality mold and shape the dominant social-political-epistemic imaginary with a plethora of facts. Yet on the other hand, from the radical constructivism attributed to post-modernists in the second half of the twentieth century and articulated in the 1980s by such feminist theorists as Liz Stanley and Sue Wise[5] to Ruth Hubbard's now-classic declaration "every fact has a factor,"[6] statements of fact have taken on a less matter-of-fact, neutral, and innocent demeanor than they once quite naturally could claim. "Just the facts, ma'am" has, for more than one theorist, come to be ironically emblematic of a more naive time when it was (apolitically) reasonable to believe such a request could expect an adequate response.[7] Indeed, the pull between maintaining an interpretation-exempt factual zone of epistemic stability and addressing the imperialistic, power-infused practices that maintaining such a zone has legitimated in the post-Enlightenment politics of knowledge counts as one of the principal, and potentially most productive, tensions to have emerged in feminist and other postcolonial epistemologies of the 1990s.

Epistemologists, in consequence, need methods/methodologies capable of generating and adjudicating knowledge both about the factuality of the physical-material world and about a social order whose epistemic assumptions are complicit in sustaining its own negative and positive enactments. They need revisionary ways to engage knowledgeably, wisely with the palpable material-social interactions of "nature" and "human nature." Indeed, they even seem to need an empirical-realist foundation just when foundationalism counts—justifiably—as one of the villains of the Enlightenment story. They also need to be able to show how even the simplest material-observational knowledge claim is open to critical scrutiny in itself and in the circumstances of its making: none of these circumstances can be presumed innocent before the fact, and many are less innocent than they seem. Yet the imaginative creativity that this tension generates has the effect of making it more productive than *aporetic*: who could presume to propose closure?

As I observe in chapter one, the dominant epistemologies of late modernity—the epistemologies of mastery—are built around stylized examples of the very statements of fact whose status I am simultaneously affirming and interrogating: observationally derived propositional knowledge claims whose formulation in

5. Stanley and Wise, *Breaking Out*.
6. Hubbard, "Science, Facts, and Feminism," 5.
7. Consider, e.g., Scheppele, "Just the Facts Ma'am."

the "S-knows-that-p" rubric presents them for confirmation or falsification in controlled, universally replicable circumstances. In this exemplary mode, they function as pivotal points in the neoempiricist theories that have held pride of place in mainstream twentieth-century theories of knowledge, unifying communities of practitioners around an imaginary of direct, demonstrable access to reality. The apparent simplicity, political neutrality, and discrete atomicity of the facts these propositions state generate three striking assumptions germane to my argument in this book: first, that all simple, atomistic, observationally verifiable propositional knowledge claims are equally innocent, and the circumstances of their utterance are equivalently irrelevant to their evaluation; second, that more elaborated knowledge claims are mere multiples of such simple claims, with the same apolitical status; and, third, that the subjectivities of knowledge-claimants are as epistemologically inconsequential elsewhere as they are imagined to be in such stripped-down events as knowing the cup is on the table or the cat is on the mat.[8]

Post-Enlightenment critics of positivist empiricism and its offspring are at once drawn to and suspicious of these simple facts: drawn by the urgency of demonstrating the factuality of the material, historical, physical, social world—of its stubborn intransigence *and* its amenability to prediction and intervention—suspicious because of the injustices and harms rationalized, and *naturalized*, in appeals to facts about nature and human nature. Hence in her now-classic essay "Situated Knowledges," Donna Haraway names *radical constructivism* and *feminist critical empiricism* as the polarities of a powerful dichotomy that both tempts and traps feminist epistemologists.[9] A premature dissolution of this tension, Haraway shows, would force feminists to stop well short of the epistemological-political goal of producing "faithful accounts of a 'real' world" and critical analyses of the "radical historical contingency" of power-implicated knowledge and subjectivity. She therefore advocates a "feminist objectivity [of] limited location and situated knowledge," in which objectivity responds to the pull of empiricism, and location and situation respond to the pull of constructivism and diversely enacted subjectivities.[10]

Integral to the position I have been developing in this book is an assumption that statements of fact indeed acquire or fail to achieve factual status

---

8. Latour observes: "The tempting aspect of the distinction between facts and values lies in its seeming modesty, its innocence, even: scientists define facts, only facts: they leave to politicians and moralists the even more daunting task of defining values" (*Politics of Nature*, 95).

9. Haraway, "Situated Knowledges," in *Simians, Cyborgs, and Women*.

10. Ibid., 187, 190.

situationally, according to the patterns of authority and expertise constitutive of the institution(s) of knowledge production in whose discursive spaces they circulate and within whose praxes they are constituted and embedded: institutions neither so alike as to be amenable to universal, abstract, and interchangeable analyses nor so unlike and isolated as to require separate and radically distinct analyses. Critical-revisionary engagement with the presuppositions that sustain their status, while serving to legitimate "normal" epistemic practice within them, expose some of the complexities in the politics of knowledge that successor epistemologies have to address.

Here I take the goals Haraway articulates as a point of departure for analyzing two examples from specifically situated ("local" in Foucault's sense) regions of cognitive practice: law and medicine. I enter feminist legal inquiry through Regina Graycar's analyses of judicial knowledge,[11] and medicine through Kirsti Malterud's analyses of epistemological problems posed by women's "undefined" medical disorders.[12] I read these examples as salient epistemic moments within "natural" or "material" institutions of knowledge production (recalling Sabina Lovibond's words).[13] Yet my argument does not depend on finding in Haraway's situated knowledges a ready-made solution. Insightful and compelling as her arguments are, she accords vision a more exclusive epistemic primacy than I do and, at least in her 1991 essay, she does not show how theoretical space could be made for drawing connections across diverse politico-epistemic situations.[14]

In addressing these issues I draw together three lines of thought. On the issue of vision—and indebted to Sonia Kruks—I show how the project of developing an epistemological position for which praxes (hence specific practices) are primary sites of knowledge production, which I have illustrated with my analyses of Carson's and Messing's work, can travel also to these other sites. For connections that escalating affirmations of difference in the 1990s rendered increasingly tenuous, and recalling my plea for interpretation in chapter two, I examine certain interpretive practices that, I suggest, escape the

11. Graycar, "Gender of Judgments." The phrase *statements of fact* is pivotal to Graycar's discussion.

12. Malterud, "Women's Undefined Disorders"; Malterud and Hollnagel, "Magic Influence"; Malterud, "Art and Science."

13. Recall that for Lovibond, naturalizing epistemology represents "the activity we call 'enquiry' as part of the natural history of human beings," and "naturalist or materialist analyses of the institutions of knowledge-production . . . have made it possible to expose the unequal part played by different social groups in determining standards of judgement" ("Feminism and Postmodernism," 12–13).

14. Haraway begins to draw such connections in *Modest_Witness*.

subjectivist dangers of what Kruks calls "an epistemology of provenance," one of whose analogues I have called "experientialism."[15] And to demonstrate how such remappings of the epistemic terrain could be achieved, taking naturalistic practices within institutions of knowledge making as geographical markers, I locate these regions of cognitive practice within the conceptual frame and the range of responsibilities that ecological naturalism engenders, whose very possibility is dependent upon the engaged praxis of practitioners. Commonalities and differences across places, praxes, and practitioners have always to be evaluated for their significance to projects of promoting epistemic circumstances conducive to viable cohabitability, thus neither oppressive nor exploitative of the habitat and its inhabitants.

As I have observed in chapter one, crucial to this exercise in the debt it (partially) owes to Haraway is that situation becomes *a place to know* in two broad senses: as a place where epistemic activity occurs, and as a place that itself demands to be known in those of its aspects that facilitate or thwart knowing responsibly and well. The mappings integral to this analysis chart the structural intricacies of place; the materialities, ethologies, genealogies, commitments, and power relations that shape the knowledge and subjectivities enacted there; the intractable locational specificities that resist homogenization or suggest novel connections; the positionings available or closed to would-be knowers; the amenability or resistance of both human and nonhuman entities to being known. Situation, then, is not just a place *from which to know*, as the language of perspectives implies, indifferently available for occupancy by anyone who chooses to stand there.

Naturalized Epistemology Revisited

Methodologically, in departing from any conviction that empirical facts are self-announcing to the observant eye and that ambiguity or contestation inevitably destabilize their factuality, this ecological project requires a *negotiating empiricism*. Negotiations permeate its ongoing practices: they occur not merely at a commonsense level where scientists or secular knowers deliberate about which pieces of evidence to count and which to leave aside, although they occur there as well. But they are about how the going explicit or tacit commitments of *any*

---

15. See Kruks, *Retrieving Experience*, esp. chap. 4, "Identity Politics and Dialectical Reason: Beyond an Epistemology of Provenance." I am indebted to Kruks in thinking about Haraway's views.

inquiry generate questions about evidence and its relation to "facts"; about why some potential candidates for the status of evidence are suppressed, concealed, or never noticed; about how or why a statement of fact—a putatively factual claim—"goes through," carries weight, manages or fails to establish itself, where the answer is not always to be found in assertions of error, carelessness, replicability, or correspondence. Often the conceptual apparatus is simply not available for accommodating certain potential facts, for seeking acknowledgment for a specific set of claims (at one level) or for articulating an observationally derived theory (at another). Often the politics of knowledge intervene to block acknowledgment, so that innovative, eccentric, maverick readings of the evidence, or readings disruptive of the received story, fail to achieve a place "within the true." (Michel Foucault writes: "Mendel spoke the truth, but he was not *dans le vrai* [within the true] of contemporary biological discourse.")[16] So much, both visible and invisible, traceable and untraceable, has to happen for such landmark, reconfiguring claims, to attain a place, after all, "in the true."

For ecological naturalism, the most urgent epistemological questions are about negotiating anew the intricacies of claiming and evaluating knowledge. Goals of striving to be better empiricists, to do better at practicing empirical science, to discern and eschew bad science/bad epistemic practices, figure among its goals, but they do not begin to capture all of the complexities at issue. My discussion of the power of a hegemonic epistemic imaginary gestures toward the problems with posing a solution wholly within the framework of the epistemological edifice that has long occupied pride of place: with attempting to rebuild it from recycled materials, while leaving its basic structure intact.

Bruno Latour is helpful on this issue. In the opposition between matters of fact and matters of concern, thus in the word *fact* itself, he finds an entrenched obligation for philosophers to erase from epistemological consideration "the *work* required in order to establish the persistent, stubborn data." They are, thus, "to limit 'facts' to the final stage in a long process of elaboration."[17] The investigations, consultations, deliberations, negotiations, and, equally significantly, the values that collaborate in the production of knowledge disappear from view. The term *fact*, with its inbuilt finality, fixity, obliterates genealogical traces, erases marks of the interactive, often conflictual labor out of which (recalling Ruth Hubbard) "factors" successfully (if for now)

---

16. Foucault, "Discourse on Language," 224.
17. Latour, *Politics of Nature*, 95 (emphasis added).

promote some candidates to the status of factuality, suppressing others as they go. In a sense, the contrast is the old positivist one between contexts of discovery and justification, between facts and values; but in Latour's analysis it acquires a more complex and, in my view, more appropriately naturalistic cast, where the powers and the inquirers intra-actively at work in producing facts, values, and thus knowable-known materialities, and the historical-circumstantial particularities of the process have to be factored in to any epistemologically and politically cogent analysis. Consider, for example, how Messing's inquiries both discern and construct certain kinds of women's workplace suffering as knowable and treatable, yet how she struggles to achieve acknowledgment of the facts she proposes. So it is not just a matter of looking more carefully, being more objective, but of value-infused investigations that, for this very reason, involve learning how to see accurately, outside the rigidity of standard empiricist frames.

Within orthodox epistemology, the very idea of negotiation sits just as uneasily as does interpretation, for the epistemic imaginary of mastery, especially when it is enacted in concert with strict adherence to the dictates of formal logic, generates a confidence drawn from the impressive achievements attributable to logic itself. With that confidence comes a complacency that tends to lull inquirers into an ongoing faith in the powers of the knowing it venerates and normalizes. As Rachel Falmagne persuasively argues, when logic dominates legal and political debate, not only does it become an instrument of power (not always malign), but it precludes "any negotiation of ambiguities of meaning and of alternative forms of knowledge." Especially worth pondering for the position I am developing is her comment that "when valid arguments are formalized...the *content* of the argument is erased."[18] For ecological thinking, by contrast, content is a matter of primary concern. Hence, a negotiating empiricism urges "looking around" in a manner akin to circumspection, both in a literal looking-around sense, aimed at seeing how things— particular things—*are* and are situated, and in a more diffuse and diverse sense of looking and listening well. It is a deliberative process rooted, as Carson puts it, in a preparedness to wait "an extra season or two," where a season may be as short as an hour or a day, or much longer, and where looking is rarely solitary, but frequently communicative, consultative, and rarely inactive or passive.

18. Falmagne, "Positionality and Thought," 200 (emphasis added). Welch-Ross observes that for feminist theorists (referring to my work and Lynn Nelson's) "the meaning of experience is *negotiated* and constructed within the regular, everyday patterns of activity that are typical of a particular group" ("Feminist Perspective," 111, emphasis added).

Circumspection involves vigilance for clues perhaps not noticed, rather in the manner of a good detective story; a willingness to go halfway to encountering what needs to be seen, an open receptivity capable of granting interim plausibility to the prima facie implausible, an attentiveness to the surrounds just at the periphery of vision. Of course there are risks: inquirers may look around too long, fail to seize the day, bypass a crucial moment. So there is an Aristotelian flavor to such circumspection: a need to determine a mean, in processes that will necessarily vary from inquiry to inquiry (as the elaborated examples in Kristin Shrader-Frechette's *Environmental Justice* amply show) and will require considerable political savvy. For the appeal of mastery and control is as political as it is purely epistemic, and the temptation to produce the flashy, instant solution can seem irresistibly strong.

As I have shown in chapters one and two, this project enlists the resources of naturalized epistemology for feminist and other emancipatory ends, while locating the natural in places orthodox naturalists would scorn to acknowledge and showing how "natural" itself is a negotiable designation. It proposes that situated knowledges critically elaborated through analyses of institutional, material, and other specifically located praxes and naturalistic epistemology deflected from its scientistic course become cooperators in charting a way forward for successor epistemologies. The project maintains an allegiance to a critical empirical-realism in its accountable (= evidence-reliant) engagement with the natural and social worlds, both found and made. Yet this is no spectator epistemology emanating from a value-free position; nor is it reliant either on propositional atomicity or on an abstract epistemic agency whose monologic statements of fact could count as epistemological basics. Thus it is continuous, to an extent, with Helen Longino's contention that a philosophical theory of knowledge "requires a characterization of empirical subjects and of the situations in which they seek to produce (things that have the status of) knowledge."[19] Taking such a thought into an ecological register, with a conception of subjectivity that departs in some respects from Longino's, the aim of my project is also to develop principles and guidelines for negotiating situations in which knowledge and subjectivity are reciprocally implicated, variously enacted on complex, institutionally patterned, and diversely populated epistemic terrains. In this chapter I examine how certain kinds of statements of fact operate within this larger project.

19. Longino, *Fate of Knowledge*, 10. In chap. 4, "Pluralism and Local Epistemologies," Longino analyzes experiment and measurement in ecology, in ways that recall my analysis of Carson's practice.

In the late twentieth century, as I have shown in chapter two, naturalists made notable moves away from a dislocated epistemology preoccupied with analyzing what ideal knowers ought to do and/or with silencing the skeptic. Starting from an conviction that knowledge is indeed possible, they work to delineate its real-world (natural) conditions. Rather than seeking a priori, necessary, and sufficient conditions for "knowledge in general," they aim to study how people actually produce knowledge, variously, within the scope and limits of human cognitive powers as these powers are revealed in the same projects of inquiry. As I have also explained, naturalism's most successful North American version, with its originary debt to the work of W. V. O. Quine, looks to physical science as the institution of knowledge production most worthy of epistemic analysis because of its accumulated successes in revealing the nature of the world, and finds sources of exemplary knowledge of human cognitive functioning in scientific psychology and cognitive science.[20] While Quinean naturalists draw their normative conclusions from studies of knowledge production in the scientific practices they esteem, they consistently deny that their project could reduce to turning an "is" of epistemic practice into an "ought" of epistemological normativity. Hence although they shift from a purely formal toward a descriptive epistemic mode, their descriptions are meant to be no mere recordings of how people know in certain settings. Naturalism's reflexive turn commits its practitioners to a critical and self-critical examination of the practices in which they engage: critical both of the conduct of the practices themselves and of the values and commitments that animate them.[21] In my readings of naturalistic projects, this reflexive stance could create space for interpretive negotiation. And because, for naturalists, descriptive analyses of experimental findings yield more adequate normative and evaluative principles than a priori theories can provide, they should enable epistemic exhortations to be more directly pertinent to the capacities and projects of real knowers than experience-remote analyses of monologic knowledge claims ("S-knows-that-p") that are everyone's, and no one's, can provide.

20. For Kornblith, I have shown, naturalism's central questions are "What is the world that we may know it? And what are we that we may know the world?" Answers will be sought at the places where the best current theories of the nature of the world and the best current psychological theories dovetail. See also Kornblith, *Inductive Inference.*

21. According to Richard Campbell, naturalism's reflexive turn is one of its principal sources of value for feminist epistemology. The fact-value reciprocity and the meaning-value interconnections he elaborates are advanced to show that a committed political stance can promote objective knowledge of a real world (*Illusions of Paradox,* esp. chaps. 7–8 and p. 219).

These commitments notwithstanding, a tacit normative assumption, pivotal to the work of Quinean naturalists and their associates, sounds a cautionary note. It appears in the evaluative contrast I have mentioned, through which cognitive science arrogates to itself the power to denigrate the knowledge claims of folk psychology[22] in any setting other than folksy conversation, a move emblematic of the hierarchy persistently operating to elevate scientific above "other" knowledge, even for naturalists, thus allowing the still-experience-remote laboratory to retain its claim to be the natural knowledge-making setting. It sustains the assumptions, first, that it is legitimate to represent this constructed, artificial setting as "natural"; second, that the assumptions, methods, and evaluative techniques of cognitive science are in order as they stand, translatable without negotiation across knowledge-making situations and institutions; third, that naturalism fulfills its mandate by importing into diverse locations the relative valuations of scientific versus "other" knowledge, characteristic of the very mainstream naturalists contest and in whose eyes *their* projects are transgressive;[23] and, fourth, that the questions I pose in the title of the previous section—"whose? where? when?"—are epistemologically *hors de question* because any adequately trained and appropriately positioned knower would, almost by definition, produce the same statements of fact as any other, and when human subjects are the objects of study, any "typical" member of a sample would behave just like any other. The matter of epistemic negotiation thus does not and should not arise.

All of these assumptions are contestable; all come under scrutiny in feminist and other postcolonial epistemologies. As I argue in chapter two, nature is neither self-announcing, nor does it naturally distinguish itself from culture or artifact. The choice of physical science-cognitive science as *natural* preserves the science-dominant assumptions governing standard epistemic analyses, despite naturalism's critical stance toward more orthodox epistemology. Continuing to favor this source of "natural" knowledge, then, generates scientistic excesses whose effects are to widen rather than narrow the gap between a naturalism that promises to relocate itself "down on the ground" and the everyday epistemic practices and concerns that prompt many inquirers to seek revisioned strategies and methods for assessing the factuality of statements of fact.

22. Recall Bruner's charge that the term *folk psychology* was "*coined in derision* by the new cognitive scientists for its hospitality toward such intentional states as beliefs, desires, and meanings" (*Acts of Meaning*, 36, emphasis added).

23. For an interesting analysis of these relative valuations see Fuchs, "New Wars of Truth."

Situations, Legal and Medical

To make good my contention that scientific knowledge production is neither the
only nor the most natural focus of naturalistic analysis, I turn in this chapter to
law and medicine as candidates at least as worthy: situations where empirical
scientific findings are often integral to the knowledge that informs and is informed by practice, and where scientific method frequently governs "fact-finding";
yet where science neither yields the only knowledge worthy of the label nor
counts incontestably as the epistemic master narrative. In these two examples,
which I offer as variants on Cheney's bioregional narratives, situation is a place
to know whose governing imaginary is infused with the judgment of "the reasonable man" (in law), of whom a judge is the exemplar par excellence, and with
the remarkable successes of orthodox empirical science (in medicine), of whom
an objective, science-obedient diagnostician (also presumptively reasonable) is
the exemplar par excellence. Analyses of knowledge thus situated expose the
historical-material-ecological contingency—the *negotiability*—of the social-
political arrangements of authority and expertise enabled and enacted there.

Law

Having discerned markedly gendered subtexts in a range of statements of fact
that inform judicial pronouncements, Regina Graycar shows how the "doctrine
of judicial notice" sanctions appeals to highly contestable "commonsense"
knowledge that figures in their formulation—knowledge imagined to require
neither negotiation, corroboration, nor verification.[24] Judgments, she notes, are
often informed by tacit yet powerful beliefs about what "women in general"
want and are like, how domestic arrangements work, what the reasonable man
would think or do—or expect a woman to think or do—in allegedly typical
situations. Graycar urges feminists to "confront the epistemological processes
by which legal discourses construct reality and give authority to particular
versions of events, while at the same time entrenching and dangerously
widening...the 'perceptual fault lines' of understanding."[25] Many of the

---

24. The doctrine of judicial notice is "a construct whereby the law absolves the parties
from proving by evidence everything necessary to make out a case and allows the courts to take
judicial notice of certain things considered not to be contentious." Graycar notes that "courts
may use this doctrine to incorporate into their judgements common sense ideas about the
world, common assumptions or, indeed, widely held misconceptions" ("Gender of Judgements," 274–75).
25. Ibid., 281.

generalizations from experience out of which a judge produces small, seemingly innocent statements of fact that generate or give rhetorical force to the content of judgments (though not singly or without appeal to precedent and the letter of the law) plainly amount to extrapolations from *his or her own* experiences, shaped by the specificities of a privileged socioeconomic and frequently male-gendered position. Yet from this elevated, power-infused status the pronouncements claim an authority that far exceeds their evidential basis. They defy the most elementary principles of induction to yield statements of fact whose effects are to promote and sustain a social order whose contribution to women's oppression—and to classism, racism, ethnocentrism, xenophobia, homophobia—is well documented throughout feminist, postcolonial, and other critical literature. Nor are these judges especially notorious persons of evil intent. Yet stereotypes and fictions circulate out of control in their utterances: of women as naturally mendacious and untrustworthy, of rape as "not a serious form of harm," and of judges themselves as so (relevantly) experienced as to render their commonsense beliefs reliable on matters well beyond their experience.[26]

It is not surprising for a judge, whose endowments and credentials have secured her/his admission to so lofty a position, to manifest the prejudices or biases that these judgments bespeak. Yet—and this is the crucial point—the liberal-empiricist language of biases and prejudices, which "belong" to someone, of which a judge can purge him- or herself with a dose of appropriate counterevidence, is inadequate here. In the dominant imaginary of objective, professional knowledge lodged in the western world's most august institutions, law, together with science, occupies an impartial seat removed from the whimsicality and vested interests afflicting more ordinary pursuits, to stand as a repository of evenhanded decision making that has thrust such idiosyncrasies behind it. Graycar's reading, like other feminist and racially informed analyses, contests this imaginary absolutely,[27] exposing the secular face of law as situated—and implicated—knowledge akin to every other. Her reading shows why it takes more than an occasional counterexample to contest its status: why only systemic, social-structural

---

26. Ibid., 72. It is not my intention to imply that such biases in law are restricted to judges. Ross, for example, notes that when a juror invokes "any of . . . the most commonly held narratives about women, sex, and rape—then 'forcible compulsion' means guns and knives and strangers coming out of the darkness. . . . [It] does not mean the insistent demands, the pushing and shoving, of a former lover in the woman's apartment" (*Just Stories*, 9).

27. For comparable stories see Williams, *Alchemy of Race and Rights*; idem, *Rooster's Egg*; and idem, *Seeing a Color-Blind Future*. See also Morrison, *Race-ing Justice*; and my *Rhetorical Spaces*, esp. chap. 3.

negotiations around its purportedly empirical core can destabilize the "truths" it keeps in circulation.

Epistemologically, then, Graycar's argument is no mere insistence on the urgency of displacing the gender-inflected statements of fact that inform judicial decision-making with statements "more factual" and less oppressive to women. The struggle here is not for simple empirical ascendancy, to be won by the contestant armed with the most powerful facts, for a sexist judge is not contradicted simply by showing him (or her) some women who do not confirm the established definition, as an unnegotiated empiricism would claim. He or she already knows such women, and they do not make enough difference: evidence and counterevidence are of little avail. Thus, epistemologically, the issue is again less about devising a better empiricism than about acquired immunities to evidence that threatens to contradict the sedimented assumptions of an instituted social-epistemic imaginary: about how to negotiate around their territorial hegemony.

Although Graycar focuses her discussion on judicial statements, similar fault lines pervade legal discourse,[28] prompting Nicola Lacey to argue that "differently sexed legal subjects are *constituted by* and inserted within legal categories via the mediation of judicial, police, or lawyers' discourse."[29] Established legal discourse, Lacey suggests, works from a set of uncontested assumptions about "normal" human subjectivity and agency, whose effects are to legitimize certain ways of reading evidence and to thwart others. Here again, it is a matter of a sedimented imaginary that, paradoxically, is both intransigent and elastic. Its intransigence sloughs off such counterevidence as might seem to threaten its stability; its elasticity allows it to rationalize and thus accommodate counterevidence it cannot ignore. Thus certain forms of conduct (recalling the epigraph to this chapter) continue to be represented as "only what was to be expected of a woman, as such."

So, for example, the conception of consent operative in sexual-assault cases trades on a belief in autonomous freedom of choice, of which a rational *man* is by definition capable, while leaving "no space for the articulation of the affective and corporeal dimensions of *certain* violations of autonomy."[30] In presupposing only two possible modalities of agency in any assault case—an

28. See also Smart, *Feminism and the Power of Law*; and Cornell, *Beyond Accommodation*.
29. Lacey, *Unspeakable Subjects*, 10 (emphasis added).
30. Ibid., 117 (emphasis original). For a discursive analysis of the implications of entrenched yet malleable conceptions of consent operative especially in sexual-assault trials, see Ehrlich, *Representing Rape*, 123–28.

active, freely choosing assailant and a passive, subordinate victim, who either "consents" or "submits," but will be judged either way according to patterns of "normal" rational choice—the restrictively dichotomous conceptual apparatus available to and perpetuated in judging such cases recirculates stereotypes of active masculinity/passive femininity. Because none of the emotional-psychic damage such as "violation of trust, infliction of shame and humiliation, objectification and expectation"[31] that assault tends to incur finds expression in this model of the rational, autonomously choosing individual, there is no place for naming such damage in the statements of fact that allegedly generate morally-judicially adequate judgments of the harms inflicted by sexual assault. Thus many of the "facts" produced by heterosexist, patriarchal distributions of power disappear behind the screen of a normal, interchangeable human sameness, extricated from the locational-ecological regions that produce its putative normality. The practice of invoking "exonerating circumstances" in the law, to excuse what might and even should be inexcusable, situates arguments for the necessity of empirical negotiation on a terrain where they could easily be deflected. But as Graycar and others show, the prevailing patriarchal social imaginary is often a major contributor to such appeals to "the facts": it needs always to be addressed, for these taken-for-granted beliefs cannot be allowed just to count as background assumptions, and an innocent but inconsequential background at that.[32]

Neil Gotanda tells an analogous story of racial stereotypes—Asian American and African American—circulating out of control, in the Soon Ja Du trial of "a fifty-one-year-old Korean immigrant, mother, and store owner, [who] shot and killed . . . a fifteen-year-old African American girl in a dispute over a bottle of orange juice,"[33] and in the notorious O. J. Simpson trial. In each trial, albeit differently, the "model-minority" stereotype of the Asian American and the dangerous and out-of-control stereotype of the African American are mobilized to shape the facts that inform judicial behaviors and decisions. Asian Americans are represented as living just as nonwhite people should, in lives that

31. Lacey, Unspeakable Subjects, 106.

32. I am suggesting, therefore, that despite its pathbreaking contribution to feminist epistemology, Longino's Science as Social Knowledge, with its appeal to the constitutive part played by background assumptions in shaping scientific research, does not distance itself sufficiently from an old-style empiricism to be able to address such issues of sedimented power and exclusion as collaborators in producing the specificities of place and epistemic location. Her analysis in Fate of Knowledge moves toward taking power relations such as these more fully into account.

33. Gotanda, "Tales of Two Judges," 66.

display a suitable recognition of the privilege of living in white society; African Americans as troublemakers, bound to stir things up, and thus never able to be presumed truly innocent, whatever the empirical evidence. Because the stereotype of "gangness" is unquestioningly accepted as endemic in African American youth, facts about the dead girl's "respectable" family and school life that were striking enough to unsettle the stereotype fail to cross the threshold of admissible evidence. By contrast, the "model-minority" stereotype tells in favor of the shopkeeper's innocence, even as it blocks the possibility of weighing the specific facts of the situation to determine whether the black girl was so dangerous as to leave the shopkeeper with no choice but to shoot her. Similarly, in the Simpson case, Judge Ito's model-minority status allowed him to appear "color-blind and without 'values or history'... [as he remained] safely hidden within his judicial robes and [maintained] the invisibility of the black-white racial framework."[34] Gotanda reads these events to support his claim that in the prevailing racial climate in the United States, the law, like the media and the education systems, plays a constitutive part in the making of race: in naturalizing a persistent color-coding of certain behaviors, stances, and putative knowings. Thus a complex and pernicious ecology of race- and gender-relations marked by multilayered, sedimented stereotypes structures the places where judicial reasoning is enacted.

These stories, as I read them, tell of natural knowledge *making*, not just of *using, applying* ready-made knowledge, but the point may not be obvious. A residual and tenacious tabula rasa rhetoric of empirical knowledge making, both in the laboratory and in simpler observational moments, sustains a belief that "reality" writes itself upon a blank page when knowledge is properly *made*. Thus when a judge, a lawyer, or a juror appeals to commonsense "facts" already in circulation, and to law established, codified, it looks as though he or she is merely applying, using knowledge, not making it. On this derivative tabula rasa assumption the empirical moment is indeed not negotiable: it simply records facts that command assent, verification, consolidation. These assumptions thus mask the extent to which legal deliberations and judgments participate in continuously making and remaking knowledge, as the epigraph to this chapter insistently suggests. Neither laboratory experiments nor everyday observations amount to a knowing *ex nihilo*, nor are courtroom situations unlike these more common (to epistemologists) moments of knowing, although the pieces may be differently configured. Judicial robes fitting to her/his esteemed "station and its duties" clothe not merely a judge's

---

34. Ibid., 80. Recall Venn's comments in "Subject of Psychology," 140–41.

person but her or his epistemic practice and social-political location. She or he brings perceptual-observational habit and experience to the process of fact-finding, just as does everyone who observes that the cup is on the table, and every participant in a controlled experiment.[35] And each act of judging confirms, alters, embellishes, recirculates "the facts" that give substance to her/his statements. Judging, then, is no mere repetition of the same but a subtly accumulative, altering process where the fact at issue is sometimes consolidated, reconfirmed—if only because now there is more, sometimes loosened from its moorings, even dislodged, should the judge succeed in contesting the going wisdom. When interpretation and observation work critically together in negotiating empirical claims, no repetition is a mere reusing of the old: it is simultaneously a making of the new, reinforcing the dominant imaginary, reconfiguring or unsettling it.

On first reading, then, judicial pronouncements may seem to have the last word in a chain of processes inside and outside the courtroom, which coalesces in a judgment, informed by encoded law and by the common knowledge invisibly suffusing it. But a judgment is also the first word in larger intra-active processes (in Karen Barad's sense of "meeting the universe halfway") of critical, consultative, and corroborative material realizations, one word among many in patterns of orthodox and less orthodox judicial knowing. It is situated within affirmations capable of consolidating a judge's position and the status of the law within an instituted social imaginary and within the racial, gendered, economic structures of the social-political-moral order it sustains. But ongoing critical interrogations set in motion by the changing faces of the profession and its theorists and critics also play into the situation where judgments are made, as do the dissensions and deliberations that keep the law resistant to closure even as its rhetorical patterns and institutional structures pull toward conservation of the same comfortable yet contestable "facts."[36]

We then—we "situated" epistemologists committed to a negotiated empiricism—have to engage, genealogically, in exposing what judges, lawyers, and their challengers and supporters bring to and take from such knowledge making. Such an exercise is ecological, I am suggesting, in the care with which it has to chart the geographical, demographic, and political patternings that

35. My argument here resists the philosophical "myth of the given," if "given" means presented to the innocent and untutored eye. For a classic discussion, see Sellars, "Does Empirical Knowledge?"

36. For an analysis of debates over critique versus closure in legal theory, see Lacey, *Unspeakable Subjects*, chap. 6.

allow certain stereotypes and other feral notions to flourish unchecked, thereby poisoning the ecosystem in which justice is sought and dispensed. The making that issues in such statements of fact reverberates through and shapes the social-ecological order well beyond these relatively small events, subtly reinforcing, sometimes challenging the hegemony of the instituted imaginary, sometimes entrenching it more firmly. The challenge for epistemologists, then (recalling Haraway), is to produce "faithful accounts of the real world" by working through genealogical, power-, and situation-sensitive inquiry to destabilize the imaginaries that confer a critical immunity upon statements of fact whose historical-material contingency attests to their vulnerability to critique. It is a challenge that moves Rachel Carson's ecological practice into a domain of power relations missing from, and indeed alien to, even a self-proclaimed social empiricism.

Medicine

Comparable negotiations in medicine supply my second set of examples. Trained in a climate of virtually uncontested—and amply vindicated—respect for scientific medical knowledge, Kirsti Malterud learned that "the physician's task was to ask, the patient's task was to answer, and the answers were expected to fit into a universal pattern."[37] What, then, is a physician to do about women's "undefined disorders" for which there are no established eliciting questions or technologically diagnosable signs, even though the reality of women's physical suffering is incontestable? How is she to propose them as items for treatment? Two incompatible sets of statements of fact equally—hence impossibly—demand assent: empirical tests identify no symptoms; experiential testimony attests to painful, persistent symptoms. Recurring lack of fit between authorized objective knowledge and patients' allegedly unstable subjective knowledge, and an ongoing realization in practice that "identical diseases might present and proceed quite differently in different patients,"[38] prompt Malterud's challenge to the epistemologies that sustain *scientific* medicine as the nonnegotiable locus of overriding truth. Her work contests medical science's pretensions to universal applicability and—reminiscent of Messing's work with women's workplace health—claims validity (albeit a negotiated validity) for women's subjective knowledge. It is a validity for which she has also to

37. Malterud, "Strategies for Empowering Women's Voices," 366.
38. Malterud, "Legitimacy of Clinical Knowledge," 184. See also idem, "Symptoms as a Source"; and idem, "Women's Undefined Disorders."

advocate in the wider world where patterns of incredulity prevail, sustained by an epistemic imaginary for which scientific fact trumps all such interpretive-negotiative endeavors.

Malterud counts among women's undefined disorders fibromyalgic pain (chronic muscular pain) and a cardiac condition (syndrome X), both of whose symptoms have failed to find straightforward, causal confirmation in testing by even the most sophisticated, state-of-the-art scientific-medical procedures. Fibromyalgia presents no standard symptomology; and syndrome X tends to slip through the net of many of the most refined cardiac-screening procedures. Both conditions, coincidentally or otherwise, are more prevalent in women than men: both tend in orthodox consulting rooms to elicit dismissal as sufferings that are "all in her mind," reinforcing stereotypes of women as hysterical, overreactive, irrational complainers, whose complaints, again, merely confirm what is "to be expected of a woman." Their experiential narratives, read through these ready-made stereotypes, meet with an incredulity that blames the patient, often for wasting the doctor's time with fantasized symptoms that cannot claim factuality because there is none of the standard corroborating evidence. For Malterud, the issue is not just about practicing better science, but of working past the limits of established scientificity to give careful attention to concerns that commonly fall outside those limits. As Susan Wendell notes of her experiences with chronic fatigue syndrome (myalgic encephalomyelitis), "my subjective descriptions . . . need the confirmation of medical descriptions to be accepted as accurate and truthful."[39] Malterud is committed, where appropriate, to providing acknowledgment of the sort Wendell requires.

Malterud, then, is engaged in knowledge-making practices marked by respect for her patients' testimonial evidence and an openness to taking seriously the constitutive part played by their locational—ecological—situation in producing the conditions they present. Her research-in-practice seeks to show, empirically *and* critically/self-critically, that these women's experiential knowledge indeed counts as worthy of acknowledgment. There is no before-the-fact justification for dismissing it as folk conjecture waiting to be trumped by the doctor's accredited expertise. Yet neither does her practice simply contradict the findings of scientific medicine by assuming that every "I feel" utterance warrants uncontested corroboration. A commitment meeting her patients half way, to taking seriously—if not always literally—what a patient knows, permeates these negotiative diagnostic consultations. Doctor and patient construct meanings and treatments cooperatively, weighing the

39. Wendell, *Rejected Body*, 122.

evidence, interpreting it critically and creatively. Cognizant of how social-material-ecological mediations originating perhaps in domestic circumstances, perhaps in wider social-political or workplace conditions, can contribute to the etiology of such symptoms, the doctor is watchful for traces of their effects in phenomena that might seem remote, merely extraneous, irrelevant to the current concern. Thus Lucy Candib, analogously, observes of her own clinical practice: "I look hard for past experiences of abuse and victimization, knowing that women with these unexplained disorders are more likely to have suffered prior or ongoing physical and sexual abuse"; yet she also knows "that middle-aged women's neck pain could...be due to characteristic decay of muscle fibres...that can be treated with medications or physical therapy."[40] The point is not to frame the problem as only a "relational or social-cultural disorder," thus discounting scientific/biological diagnosis, but to work with the intricacies and intersections of medical and experiential knowledge, of situation and circumstance, of multiple explanations salient to the patient's situation and to her physiology. Malterud, similarly, observes: "I neither feel comfortable about developing causal explanations that refer exclusively to psychosocial conditions, nor about the opposite."[41] Both doctors are prepared to evaluate causal explanations for these symptoms that the patient herself might advance, with reference to parts of her body or aspects of her life seemingly remote from the site of pain: to treat them as hypotheses just as worthy of consideration as "the received view," despite their incongruity with established patterns of medical etiology and fact-finding diagnosis. And both are vigilant for traces of the power-infused politics of racist, classist, sexist societies that make it difficult for the most vulnerable to speak about even "their own" symptoms. As in Carson's and Messing's work, the conception of causality operative in these consultations is neither mechanistic nor does the doctor discount causes physically or temporally distant from the symptoms the patient presents. She proposes solutions for deliberation and negotiation with patients: she does not impose them.

In the discourse of an observation-based epistemology devoted to verifying or falsifying knowledge claims, these undefined disorders might seem to represent a triumph for an old-style empiricism. By the best standard tests, they yield pretty definitive statements of (negative) fact. Yet on a different reading they expose the limits—indeed the impotence—of an unnegotiated empiricism because of the inbuilt constraints and limitations on the range of

40. Candib, in Malterud, Candib, and Code, 16.
41. In Malterud, Candib, and Code, idem, 16.

potential evidence its theoretical commitments allow; because of its conceptual incapacity to seek or provide explanations adequate to the diverse, often chaotic specificities of the complaints; and because of the systemic structural problems within the institution of scientific medicine it is incapable of addressing. The causal connections these female patients narrate may elicit no established linear scientific correlations, yet treatment can often be successful if a doctor acknowledges a patient's capacity to "present plausible causal chains, sometimes [going] beyond the doctor's medical imagination."[42] When physician and patient work together with such unorthodox causal hypotheses and connections, the effects can contribute to reconfiguring some of the most stringent empirical requirements.

The issue is not merely that Malterud does not know all she might know in the initial interactions with these patients: that if she would just include more/learn more, then both she, and we, could know better. It is about the persistent ubiquity of a veneration of scientific knowledge to the point of blocking her methods/her knowings from extending, ecologically, beyond the confines of sanctioned medical facts, to what Latour would call "matters of concern." It need not prohibit these unorthodox knowings explicitly, purposefully, or even visibly yet its effects are to ensure that there will be no place for them within public knowledge of a sort that could make a broader difference, that might count as the first small steps toward an epistemic shift. What has to be factored in, then, to aspects of received medical knowledge in their patterns of thwarting these eccentric knowings is the force of the assumption (which is naturalistic in a truncated scientistic sense) that human beings are bodies, mechanically knowable and fixable, and empirical science alone can know what they "really" are. The mechanical model of the body, which governs decisions about what counts as evidence/facts, has to be dealt with on the same plane as the evidence accredited within it or discredited for falling outside its purview. Thus Malterud, Candib, and other like-minded doctors are caught in an imaginary in which they risk dismissal as quacks by a science-venerating public if they allow their interpretive and negotiative skills to play an appropriate part in shaping their diagnostic practice, yet they risk being unable to treat their patients well, in and because of the ecological regions those patients inhabit, if they block interpretive engagement.

Malterud's project is no naive antiscience crusade, any more than Rachel Carson's or Karen Messing's is. It neither dismisses science (essentialized) as the villain in the medical story nor accepts the patient's every word as a source

42. Malterud, "Women's Undefined Disorders," 301.

of indisputable truth: it negotiates through and away from these old tyrannies of *scientism* and *experientialism*. Nor does it seek new universals to displace the old, for it reworks claims to universality through analogy and disanalogy from specifically mapped locations. Nonetheless, knowledge is made in this negotiated consultation, not just for the patients but also for the doctor, with effects that disrupt institutional patterns and taken-for-granted power structures beyond the purview of locational specificity. Nor is a simple reversal of epistemic hierarchies the aim, a shift in the locus of knowledge from doctor to patient. The image of a twist of the kaleidoscope captures it better: knowledge made in the consulting room may translate to other practices, but the *art* of medicine that is as active as the science in its making will ensure that "fit" is a matter of creative interpretation, ongoing negotiation. Analogies may be only partial, but ecologically sensitive practitioners will be as skilled in recognizing and learning from disanalogies as in discerning repetitions.

Standard, seemingly unnegotiated empiricist principles could be read into both of these examples. A judge structures her/his judgments around statements of fact about which others "like her/him" in relevant respects could equally appeal to observational evidence, to reach the same conclusion. Years of accumulated observations (in settings arguably less controlled than a laboratory, but thus more "natural") and the rhetorically sustained wisdom of the judicial position confer an immediate presumption of credibility on what he or she says. On a Kuhnian reading, the occasional exception to the norm that informs this thinking is merely that: an aberration. And a naturalist plucked from the laboratory would have no trouble reading the event through observational lenses ground in a laboratory setting, to corroborate both process and product. With women's undefined disorders, empirically established diagnostic techniques used with meticulous precision, and repeated, as scientific method requires, yield no identifiable, diagnosable "facts." Since scientific diagnosis alone claims social-political-epistemic legitimacy as a producer or revealer of facts, these women's reports of their symptoms—even their identical or analogous experiences—fail to achieve recognition as knowledge either singly or cumulatively, because they fail by the very state-of-the-art fact-corroborating techniques to which these women have, in good faith, appealed.

These examples are intended to support the larger claim that although these power-infused public institutions are, in many ways, analogous one to another with respect to how knowledge functions within them, a "knowledge-in-general" presumption would gloss over salient *epistemological* differences. Thus in law, I point to the circulation—the sedimentation—of commonsense statements of fact in legal judgments, and thence to their constitutive function in judicial decision-making, despite their empirical contestability. In medicine, subjective, experiential knowledge—which nonetheless merits the label *knowl-edge* (this, too, is integral to the argument)—slips through the grid of scientific diagnostic procedures to remain invisible to all but the most maverick, eccentric clinician. Thus, as these examples show, *situated knowledge* does not just an-nounce "where it (or its articulator) is coming from" or situate itself merely by selecting examples from specific practices. Rather, it *engages critically in and with* the material and affective-political detail of situations, as natural sites of knowledge making inhabited by particular fallible, vulnerable human beings. Their epistemic practices are shaped by the instituted imaginary governing the institution of knowledge production within which they craft their knowledge, as that knowledge, in turn, establishes a claim for itself in a larger habitus and ethos whose viability its knowings affirm or contest. These sites of knowledge making may be analogically-ecologically implicated with others; but facts in-sensitive to their local specificities cannot just be applied whole and uncontested elsewhere, as though they counted as universal truths. Situated knowledge is ever cognizant of its own situatedness; willing to examine the specificities and implications of its positioning, to engage in self-scrutiny: Malterud and Candib are engaged in just such self-critical processes, as are Graycar and Lacey. Yet in consequence of its negotiated, deliberative dimension, such scrutiny reduces neither to monologic introspection nor an individualistic retreat into auto-biography. These examples show how even the most venerable of facts is vul-nerable to analysis that "puts it in its place," doubly, to evaluate it there, *in medias res*. Neither the judge's perceptual failures nor failures of scientific di-agnosis, then, are simple empirical errors, for at issue are the imperatives and limits of an *instituted* epistemic imaginary. Critique at the level of the imaginary itself, imaginatively institut*ing* critique is integral to critique of the would-be statements of fact that claim authority within it.

This inquiry is, thus, about the politics of knowledge: it shows how ques-tions about knowledge *making*, subjectivities, and power-saturated institutional structures have to be accorded centrality in epistemological inquiry, for the minutiae of agency, place, structure, and practice are as significant to the pro-duction of knowledge as are the statements of fact it yields. My allusion to the impotence of simple empirical strategies to dislodge and discredit patently erro-neous stereotypes and beliefs shows why epistemologists need to reconfigure their regulative beliefs. Once they eschew idealized propositional analyses of "S-knows-that-*p*" statements of fact, they have to engage critically and self-critically with epistemic practices situated at the intersections of vested interest, background beliefs, rhetorical assumptions, and the politics of social-political hierarchy, framed within imaginaries too elastic and elusive merely to be gainsaid, yet suf-ficiently complex to require and permit interrogative reexamination.

Haraway's "Situated Knowledges"

Donna Haraway's "Situated Knowledges," whose central insight I enlist in chapter one, is a pathbreaking contribution in transformative feminist science-knowledge projects. Most startling is the challenge it poses to a dominant imaginary according to which interchangeable knowers, spectators "from nowhere," produce universally valid observational knowledge that enables them to manipulate, predict, and control "the world and all that dwell therein." The pieces of this now-classic essay that bear most directly on my inquiry in this book are its demonstrations, first, of how the universal mastery that the discourses of the mainstream assume is incongruous in its presumption that knowledge coming from nowhere can be applicable and regulative everywhere; and, second, of how avowedly situated knowledge functions to break the spell of the "god-trick" that offers the pretense of dislocated transcendence.

The pretensions of the "god-trick" claim a special place in Haraway's reading of the implications of certain requirements central to the epistemology of modernity and indeed to a much more ancient legacy traceable to Plato's *Republic*. The central idea, variously articulated throughout the history of philosophical theories of knowledge, is that *knowledge* is an honorific label, reserved for those products of rational-intellectual endeavor that have left behind the messiness, confusion, and concerns of the everyday, to achieve a "view from nowhere," unsullied by the concrete particularities of place or circumstance and therefore imagined able to offer the purest possible objectivity. Such a positioning, moreover, makes it possible to survey all there is to be seen. Plato's Forms, Descartes's clear and distinct ideas, classical empiricism's ideal observation conditions count, across notable variations, among the best-known attempts to achieve such a goal. Haraway's provocative term *god-trick* signals an ironic reading of this quest: an insistence that only a god could claim such transcendence, which, by implication, is too remote to serve human epistemic purposes well, too grand in its claims to escape the partiality of all (human) seeing and knowing. Objectivity and talk about objective *reality*, Haraway insists, are possible only in situated knowledges, located down on the ground, answerable for their seeings, frankly and self-critically acknowledging the mediated, embodied, locational specificity of their knowings and the artifactual character of the knowledge they produce.

A renewed analysis of vision is central to Haraway's argument: a vision not found but made, because an untutored vision can see what is neither before nor behind its eyes. The seeing that informs an objectivity thus negotiated requires *learning* to see what is ordinarily invisible: to see from below, from the margins, and—self-critically—from the center. Haraway retains no brief for the (classical empiricist) vision that sees accurately, simply by virtue of its ocular endowments. Thus again, a reeducated vision explicitly cognizant of its partiality relinquishes any claim to see "everything from nowhere": it works from its "particularity and embodiment" and with the technological enhancements modern science and technology afford, toward a "usable, but not an innocent, doctrine of objectivity"[43] that participates in constituting both subject and object. The self-consciously situated epistemic subject, aware of the partiality of its location, is as fully immersed in politics and ethics as in the positionings that conspire to "ground struggles for the contests over what may count as rational knowledge."[44]

The rhetorical apparatus that carries Haraway's case forward is as eccentric to sedimented epistemological assumptions as is its visionary promise: its respect for ambiguity, radical interpretation, meaning-making; its recognition of the active agency of the nonhuman world (the surprises and ironies it throws up to antireductivist knowers); its heterogeneities that disappear into the homogenizing strategies of falsely self-satisfied universalism. Yet the mobile positioning Haraway advocates is neither careless nor antirealist: it is about refusing the abdications of responsibility the "god-trick" allows; the urgency of preventing "gross error and false knowledge"[45] from passing as knowledgeable instruments of mastery and domination. It is about *negotiating* empiricism. It is consonant with a revisioned naturalism, albeit variously across subjects and subject matters; with a turn toward hermeneutic-interpretive analysis; and with (Foucauldian) genealogical investigations of power-infused disciplinary societies where subjugated knowledges ironically and transgressively disrupt the self-satisfaction of the epistemic order and the panopticon is the "other self" to Haraway's mobile vision.

For Sonia Kruks, Haraway's analysis of vision is at once one of the most useful, and most troubling, aspects of her argument. I single out Kruks's analysis for discussion because it engages subtly with Haraway's argument just where it connects with my interests here. Many of the directions Kruks proposes for epistemology after "Situated Knowledges" run parallel to mine, and where they do not, the divergences are instructive. Kruks reminds her readers of the limitations of vision as a metaphor for knowing: despite Haraway's affirmation of "the embodied and situated nature of knowledge," it

43. Haraway, "Situated Knowledges," 189.
44. Ibid., 193.
45. Ibid., 198.

is hard to grant vision epistemic centrality without "implying that knowledge is rather passively received through the senses and will simply vary according to where we happen to be situated."[46] The point is well taken: by representing the senses—especially vision—as passive receptors of the world's messages, epistemologists reinforce the abstracted, "god-trick" assumptions to which Haraway and Kruks alike take exception. Yet Haraway is careful on this issue. Vision as she revisions it, particularly in her emphasis on *learning to see*, acknowledging its partiality, assuming responsibility for it (a meaningless requirement if the world imprints itself identically on every retina), is indeed more active than the rhetoric of epistemic passivity allows. Nonetheless, Kruks is worried by Haraway's failure to pursue investigations into how/why people are differently situated, with diverse "partial perspectives," about who makes the instruments of vision that are (unevenly) available to situated knowers, who has these instruments, who controls access. Haraway, as Kruks reads her, needs to engage more fully with the politics and practices where vision is physically and technologically implicated.[47] Nor are my legal and medical examples primarily about vision, except in an attenuated sense: they are about voice and listening, about positionings and repositionings of authoritative, expert practitioners interacting, negotiating evidence with often-disenfranchised Others. Feminist praxis works around the judge's utterances to negotiate counterinterpretations and expose sedimented presuppositions; in the consulting room it reconstructs the exchanges *away from* exclusive reliance on standard clinical readings of evidence to produce newly negotiated connections across a reconfigured epistemic terrain. Issues of seeing are involved: neither the orthodox sexist judge nor the orthodox scientistic physician has seen well enough. But the metaphor is too thin, detached where it needs to be implicated within the power-infused structures that enable or limit ways of seeing. All of these points hold, too, for the epistemic practices that Carson and Messing engage and for which they advocate by example.

For Kruks the issue is about connections across voices and practices, thus across *differences*. For all that it is politically compelling, she worries about the potential of the logic of situatedness to lead feminists and other emancipatory theorists into "an epistemology of provenance" for which "knowledge arises from

46. Kruks, *Retrieving Experience,* 114.
47. Haraway begins to do just this in *Modest_Witness.* Her position there is adumbrated both in "Situated Knowledges" and also in "Manifesto for Cyborgs" (both in *Simians, Cyborgs, and Women*), in the bleak metaphor of an anonymous technological making and control that is everywhere and impersonally nowhere, silently making us and our vision in the most sophisticated of molds, making "identities" ever more elusive.

an experiential basis that is so fundamentally group-specific that others, who are outside the group and who lack its immediate experiences, cannot share that knowledge."[48] In this essay, Haraway has not shown how situated knowledges can avoid terminating in the logical dead end of a subjectivism for which experiences are so radically distinct as to allow no speaking or acting across them. In consequence, she leaves unanswered the question of how to accord privileged status to "the claims to knowledge of particular identity groups, without thereby wholly denying the possibility that there is a more general basis for knowledge, or that more general visions and projects of emancipation are possible."[49] For Kruks, then, Haraway's analysis in "Situated Knowledges" does not, on its own, offer feminist epistemologists the conceptual resources necessary for accommodating the radical particularity of experiential knowledge while at the same time demonstrating its communicability and intelligibility to other people.

In *Modest_Witness*, Haraway moves in a direction that could address some of Kruks's justified concerns. Introducing the idea of *diffractions* as a way of moving beyond the reflexivity favored by some of the naturalists I discuss earlier in this chapter, she argues that reflexivity as a critical practice "only displaces the same elsewhere, setting up worries about copy and original and the search for the authentic and really real." Thus it can neither offer an escape from the false choice between realism and relativism, nor can it provide the critical tools needed for engaging with heterogeneity. Diffraction, by contrast, is an optical metaphor for "the effort to make a difference in the world"[50] and for "another kind of critical consciousness,"[51] in which "heterogeneous histories" unsettle preoccupations with preserving the same. The metaphor recalls my reference to the creative reconfigurations ecological thinking's twist of the epistemic kaleidoscope make possible.[52]

Kruks proposes a rather different way of moving forward from "Situated Knowledges," in an impressive reading of the radical potential of Jean-Paul Sartre's *Critique of Dialectical Reason*. While acknowledging some feminists' resistance to finding a theoretical resource in Sartre, she reads past the androcentrism and sexism of his philosophy to extract the outlines of a position "that would privilege differences while still exploring the possibility of a project of

48. Kruks, *Retrieving Experience*, 109.
49. Ibid., 111.
50. Haraway, *Modest_Witness*, 16.
51. Ibid., 273.
52. See in this regard K. Campbell's creatively critical reading of the promise and political limitations of Haraway's post–"situated knowledges" work in "Promise of Feminist Reflexivities."

world-wide human emancipation."[53] Sartre's beginning in situation, in the world of the embodied, "practically engaged" subject, and his examination of "the purposive and transformative human activity that he calls *praxis*" mark a conviction that theory must start from what people do in the world, but not merely as individuals face-to-face with, yet detached from, the world. He chooses an individualistic starting point heuristically "in order to be able to demonstrate that human action is in fact social through and through."[54] Sartre achieves this end well enough, Kruks believes, to establish the practical and situated character of human knowledge, while opening possibilities for reciprocity and mutual comprehension between subjects.

Individual praxis discovers its connections with the praxes of others, not a priori but as it goes—and never once and for all—through mediations of "the practical material field." It is intelligible across subjectivities because of its intentionality, its *project*, which becomes an entry point into *ontological* recognitions that other subjects are analogously, comparably engaged in projects and experiences like mine[55] and that projects—*praxes*—are constitutive of the world. Yet human reciprocity is no essential or enduring connectedness. It could as readily manifest itself in reciprocal antagonism as in solidarity; nor does it reductively aggregate the substance of diverse projects of transforming the "practical material field."[56]

Kruks is not claiming Sartre has solved the problems that Haraway and other standpoint theorists leave unaddressed. She takes from him, rather, a way of going on, showing some real-world effects of a position for which knowledge is both practical and situated, uncovering its implications for a global emancipatory politics sensitive—ecologically—to the capacity of specific praxes to coalesce as social ensembles and thence to shape practical material fields.[57] To take her interim conclusions in a somewhat different direction, I return to Haraway's "Situated Knowledges" essay to draw out another of its

53. Kruks, *Retrieving Experience*," 117. In "Simone de Beauvoir," Kruks suggests that in the *Critique*, and probably influenced by Beauvoir, Sartre reformulates his notion of the "absolute subject" to work with "an account of the subject as an agent of *praxis* who, in order to overcome organic need, transforms nature into those humanized forms of matter [he] calls the *practico-inert*" (92). Nonetheless, she observes, the *Critique* is "deeply flawed by sexism" (117).

54. Kruks, *Retrieving Experience*, 119.

55. I discuss such issues more fully in chap. six.

56. Kruks, *Retrieving Experience*, 120.

57. Ibid., 122. Kruks cites as an example individual decisions of U.S. women to enter the traditionally "caring" professions as contributors to an unanticipated "consolidation of a segmented labor market" in which women tend to be trapped in "low-status and poorly paid employment" (121).

central threads, reading it through the conceptual framework of Cornelius Castoriadis's also-Marx-indebted analysis, which I introduce in chapter one. Mixing the resources available from these three thinkers might advance the task of opening theoretical space for the mutual recognition that can make negotiating differences possible.

Especially transgressive in an epistemological heritage centered upon venerating a disembodied, dispassionate reason is Haraway's claim that "the imaginary and the rational—the visionary and objective vision—hover close together,"[58] to which I now turn. Throughout this book so far I have been speaking of "the imaginary" in a more substantive sense, referring to an instituted social-epistemic imaginary that holds in place complexes of socially informing beliefs, sustains the authority of institutions, knowledge, patterns of expertise, and perpetuates a hierarchically arranged social order. It manifests itself in a rhetoric of justifiably conferred and located power and privilege. Haraway's appeal to "the imaginary" as it contrasts with "the rational" meshes with aspects of Castoriadis's work that are germane to transformative social-political-epistemological critique, thus making it a principal contributor to instituting the ecological thinking I am advocating in this book and thereby destabilizing the epistemology of autonomy and ubiquitous—if dislocated, detached—individual mastery.

The complex of interlocking assumptions that allows Enlightenment reason—in Kruks's words—to "lay the world out before itself as a set of objects for [the] contemplation and dispassionate investigation"[59] of a transcendent knowing subject is held in place by what Castoriadis calls an *instituted social imaginary*, which I have discussed in some detail in chapter one. Recall his reference to "a *world* of social imaginary significations whose instauration as well as incredible *coherence* goes unimaginably beyond everything that 'one or many individuals' could ever produce."[60] To it he opposes the idea of an *instituting* imaginary, through which imaginatively initiated counter-possibilities interrogate the social structure radically enough to destabilize its pretensions to naturalness and wholeness, thereby initiating a new making. Castoriadis's interest is in how the imaginary of late capitalism produces and sustains unjust social hierarchies. It perpetuates a mythology of the instrumental innocence and neutral expertise of scientific knowledge and generates illusions of benign connections between power and knowledge. Its assumptions

---

58. Haraway, "Situated Knowledges," 192.
59. Kruks, *Retrieving Experience*, 117.
60. Castoriadis, *Philosophy, Politics, Autonomy*, 62 (emphasis in original).

about the relations between individual and society work to create and legitimate exploitation and domination. An *instituting* imaginary, by contrast, is a vehicle of radical social critique: it is about exposing and working to reconfigure the power-infused rhetorical spaces where knowledge making and knowledge circulating occur. The larger vision encompasses entire societies or social orders, but the activities—the praxes—will usually occur locally, as my legal and medical examples, and those drawn from the work of Messing and Carson, also suggest.

The conceptual apparatus Castoriadis proposes opens a way of enlisting the insights Kruks draws from Sartre so as to mobilize critical-emancipatory projects, of which praxis in a somewhat different sense is a vital component. Valuable in Kruks's account is its tracing of a movement from a (heuristically conceived) individualistic starting point to a conception of human action as "social through and through." Missing from that same part of the story is a sufficiently developed sense of the social as both *pregiven to* and the *frame of* practical action, of the social as it exceeds the sum of individual recognitions and makings, which alone could not suffice to produce the solidarity and/or antagonism essential to politically committed, transformative action. The point holds even though, as she shows, "the social" itself is produced out of the collective efforts of social actors. As Kruks is careful to observe, even a theory of knowledge represented as both practical and situated would not be capable of supplying the entire substance of a transformative politics. Thus, returning to my reading of Castoriadis, I am locating praxis and situation not just as originary moments in a process that issues, cumulatively, in social configurations, but as contributors to, productive of, formed by and within, sociality. I am positioning them—praxis and situation—*within* the social as "always already" given, constitutive of the world into which the knowing subject is "thrown" at birth and repeatedly throughout her or his life, where the sense of being thrown is of finding oneself in a world whose bare facticity may be a given, yet of which he/she has continually to make something, whether in acquiescence, enthusiasm, refusal, interrogation, rebellion.

A creative addressing-interrogating stance toward what is already there is missing from Sartrean praxis in Kruks's reading (even in her references to the practical-material field)—as perhaps it must be in enlisting an ontology that retains the flavor of a commitment to radical making and self-making. Her claim that the Sartre of the *Critique* has, in consequence of the events of World War II and its aftermath, moved to acknowledge *la force des choses* is persuasive; nor is she obliged to provide a complete politics where she promises only an element. But this palpable absence of a full sense of the instituted givenness (if only "for now") of the hegemonic imaginary, in Castoriadis's sense, leaves the connections Kruks is seeking to forge across differences less manageable than they might be, even within the limits she sketches. Sartre, as Kruks presents him, appears to remain with what "one or many" individuals could produce, despite the space he leaves open for moving from the individual to the social.

Yet because the instituted imaginary is never seamless nor static, sustained local imaginative critique can, ultimately, be effective in generating a renewed and renewing imaginary equipped to shake itself free from the patterns of domination that, for Castoriadis, ultimately enslave the society. My reading of his ecology essay is intended to show its doubled pertinence to these issues. Recall that he sees in the ecology movement the potential for transforming the technologies an energy-addicted society has created so that they cease to enslave their creators, so that "the producers as individuals and groups are truly masters of their productive processes."[61] The ecology movement's critical skepticism toward the pretensions of an energy-fetishized society challenges science's position as the dominant religion. Thus conceived, it becomes a transformative praxis in much the way that Kruks, via Sartre, might endorse.

As I have also observed in chapter one, the dominant epistemologies of post–Industrial Revolution societies participate in the same rhetoric of mastery and possession: knowledge acquired for manipulation, prediction, and control of nature and human nature; knowledge as a prized commodity legitimating its possessors' authoritative occupancy of positions of power and recasting "the natural world" as a human resource. The "god-trick" of the dislocated knowers Haraway takes to task is about mastery and possession, as are the self-certainties of judicial common sense and the intransigence of scientific medicine in the face of challenges to its mastery over all the medical facts worthy of the name. Aggregating, amalgamating differences is also about mastery—over the wayward, the unfamiliar, the strange—in the problems that engage Kruks, about acknowledging differences while not representing them as individual possessions, discrete identities.

Conclusion

As I have indicated, ecological naturalism is intended to yield a reconfigured epistemic-moral-political imaginary where these three conjoined modes of inquiry—epistemological, moral, political—work reciprocally and interactively

61. Castioriadis, "From Ecology to Autonomy," 20.

together. Taking its point of departure from the—natural—dependence of knowledge claims upon one another and upon and within sociality and place, it *situates* the negotiations that a renewing empiricism requires in matters of both knowledge and subjectivity. The point is to show how situation-sensitive knowledge making refuses the unimaginative, dislocated reductions and abstractions performed by the epistemologies of mastery, in order to negotiate the contributions of circumstance, subjectivity, and place to knowing conceived as process and as product. Since negotiating through differences figures prominently on its agenda, ecological naturalism turns to the contributions bioregional narratives can make to the internal regional and demographic mappings of the local "field" of inquiry it requires: mappings attentive to the surface and the less immediately visible aspects of the region, to the detail of its habitus and ethos; and intermappings from location to location from which analogies and disanalogies from place to place, subject matter to subject matter derive, that are equally integral to knowing well. Such negotiations involve attempting, imaginatively and critically, to understand the significance of resemblances and differences,[62] honoring them where engaged analysis shows them worthy of preservation, interrogating them where necessary, yet neither in stasis nor in isolation. The negotiations also, and sometimes urgently, reveal a need for careful, sensitive *advocacy*[63] by, for, and on behalf of those who have to seek acknowledgment from an often-intransigent orthodoxy for the subjugated or sedimented knowings that negotiation brings to light: knowings that promise—or threaten—to disrupt a comfortable stasis, thus requiring people to revisit their cherished beliefs, to reexamine habitual or stereotyped thinking. The erasures of female rationality performed by the "reasonable person" standard and the incredulity about women's cardiac symptoms occasioned by medical readings that rely only on statistical regularities determined by what is normal for male patients are but two striking examples of the reexaminations such an approach generates.

As I have shown, I conceive of this approach as a revisioned *naturalism*, because it locates epistemological inquiry within practices and institutions, of which law and medicine are two peculiarly apt examples, where people are engaged in producing and negotiating knowledge and from which they enact its effects. While making no before-the-fact assumptions about knowledge in general, it is committed to drawing (interim) conclusions to inform and enable more wide-ranging emancipatory projects, where the meaning of emancipation will

---

62. I pursue this line of thought more fully in chap. six.
63. I discuss advocacy at greater length in chap. five.

vary with regional and demographic diversity.[64] It is wary of the power-infused tendencies of racial-gender-class stereotypes and of essentialized conceptions of "science" and "nature" to take on the self-perpetuating, self-fulfilling qualities that foster illusions of sameness, and it takes steps to avoid complicity with them.

Such wariness is evident in the two examples I discuss in this chapter: of stereotype-sensitive legal and medical analysis. My reading of these examples is ecological, also, in its attention to the part played in each domain by an emblematic, exemplary figure—"the reasonable man" and the scientifically credentialed doctor—and that played by those whose epistemic lives are illumined, shadowed, or rendered invisible in consequence of her/his positioning, stature, and authority: the female patient, the nonwhite, nonaffluent patient discredited, the female/nonwhite/inarticulate rape victim disbelieved. It is ecological, too, in its dependence on and responses to the prevailing institutional habitus and ethos, as subtly shaping judgments of legitimacy and illegitimacy in conferring or withholding acknowledgment, and in its attention to how situation, variously construed, contributes to or thwarts knowledge gathering. Ecological naturalism reads and analyzes episodes of knowledge making in such institutions from a recognition of the contingent salience of purposes, webs of assumptions, and sedimented beliefs as they inform the underlying structures of each, to foster or block lines of inquiry. Hospitable as they are to the effects of power-infused reliance on stereotypes in western societies, these two institutions in their preecological mode can be as oppressive as they are conducive to the democratic cohabitability that is the goal of this project, and thus of ecological thinking at its best. They can be epistemologically oppressive at the traditionally most basic level, of factuality where, ecologically speaking, the seemingly simplest of "facts" has to be read bioregionally, all the way down, if knowledge is to be responsible of its kind.

Knowing or claiming to know is thus both a synchronic and a diachronic project that draws numerous intersecting strands together at one place, one nodal point, which for purposes of inquiry is separated from and connected to other places according to ongoing evaluations of pertinence and/or irrelevance. It observes how medicine and law, in these examples, can be so alike in the way factuality is inflected by gendered/racial/economic and other lines; in the way scientific and social scientific knowledge informs them; and in the manner of their authoritative positioning within a social imaginary as institutions of

64. I appeal here to Cheney's idea of bioregional narratives, elaborated in "Postmodern Environmental Ethics." See also my "How to Think Globally."

knowledge production. It is equally attentive to the differences that separate them according to the relative salience of each of these and other factors, within their structure. Comparable similarities and differences inflect Carson's and Messing's projects, both drawing them together and holding them separate. They learn from one another, as do law and medicine; yet the findings and practices of one do not translate without remainder into the presuppositions and methods of the other. The language of knowing is neither incommensurable nor univocal from place to place. Ecological naturalism draws issues together to discern their commonalities, holds them apart to remain cognizant of their distinctive aspects.

Indebted to natural and social scientific evidence in working to determine how survival and cohabitability are best enhanced, not just quantitatively but qualitatively, ecological naturalism works with a conception of embodied, materially situated subjectivity for which locatedness and interdependence are integral to the possibility of knowledge and action: an ecological human subject made by and making its relations in reciprocity with other subjects and with its (multiple, diverse) locations,[65] who requires a robust conception of epistemic responsibility to animate, and temper, its knowledge-making projects. This subject, who appears both as judge and judged, as doctor and patient, in this chapter will, in different guises, be the focus of analysis in the chapters that follow. In this renewed approach, epistemological evaluation will have to stretch to address the (empirically demonstrable) effects of putative knowledge, the materialities it produces, the meanings it makes and sustains, the practices it legitimates, the values it embodies and conveys. Responsibility and accountability requirements join verifiability high on the epistemic agenda as epistemic and moral-political issues coalesce and as statements of fact take on a less self-evidently factual demeanor.

65. For Conley, ecological subjectivity involves relating "consciousness of the self to that of being attached to and separated from the world" (*Ecopolitics*, 10).

If there is no action which takes place outside the framework of social practices, and if the object world is understood only in terms of its meaningful insertion within particular discursive practices, then why should we assume a unique and singular developmental path, a unique and singular subject?

—Valerie Walkerdine, The Mastery of Reason

4

ECOLOGICAL SUBJECTIVITY IN THE MAKING

"The Child as Fact and Artifact"

Epistemology and Developmentality

The epistemologies of mastery that occupy pride of place in Anglo-American professional philosophy and the dominant theories and practices of post-Piagetian developmental psychology echo and sustain one another across a range of methodological assumptions and substantive issues. Enactments of the central components of epistemological orthodoxy are in evidence throughout the practices of mainstream developmental psychology, which, in their turn, exemplify the effects of epistemology's normative claims and contribute to exposing their limitations. And mainstream developmental psychologists find their established practices vindicated in the equally well-established theories of knowledge that govern "normal" scientific and social scientific practice and "knowledge in general," while their practices confirm the viability and hegemonic status of those very theories. Even if developmental psychologists rarely read epistemology, even if epistemologists rarely read developmental psychology, these reciprocal effects are instructive. In this chapter I engage in an exploratory investigation of this relationship, informed by a critical feminist consciousness and intended to move toward an ecological reconfiguration of the conceptions of subjectivity integral to Anglo-American developmental psychology. Indicating how conceptions of knowledge and subjectivity central to both domains are implicated in sustaining androcentric, patriarchal, class-based, racist, and other asymmetrical distributions of power and privilege, my analysis opens space for ecologically informed, socially-politically transformative successor projects in epistemology and developmental theory,[1] attentive to matters of ethos in a sense continuous with Gilles Deleuze's conception of ethology, which, as I note in chapter one, refers to "the capacities for affecting and being affected that characterize each thing," which studies "the compositions of relations or capacities between different things . . . of sociabilities and communities."[2] Concerned to understand something about how children come to, are brought to, are enabled or rendered unable to enter, or to alter, sociability and community relationships, variously according to the specificities of their corporeal-cultural-intellectual-emotional being and to the material specificities of their situatedness, my investigation is critical of certain sedimented assumptions in mainstream white western developmental psychology about the capacities, powers, and possibilities of "the child."

As I have observed in the first three chapters of this book, orthodox Anglo-American epistemology seeks to determine universal, necessary and sufficient conditions for knowledge in general and to silence the skeptic who doubts that knowledge is possible. It is both a priori and normative: guided by a formal conception of knowledge, it works to determine standards for justifying claims to know and for distinguishing bona fide knowledge from belief or conjecture, to establish criteria ubiquitously valid across epistemic domains, thus neither deriving from nor dependent upon certain ways of knowing, the capacities of particular knowers, the particularities of epistemic location, or the purposes of specific epistemic projects. Such epistemologies have commonly modeled their inquiries on simple, everyday sensory perceptions of

---

1. An early, shorter version of this chapter was published as "Naming, Naturalizing, Normalizing."

2. Deleuze, *Spinoza*, 125–26.

"medium-sized" physical objects or on stylized, idealized conceptions of science and scientific method. Commonly, too, they presuppose an autonomous, rational, adult, individual knower who is everyone and no one, but whose identity is epistemologically irrelevant.

Analogous assumptions structure the developmental psychology informed and governed by the legacy of Jean Piaget, which is my main critical focus in this chapter. With the goal of demonstrating the emergence and evolution of universal cognitive and moral structures, presumed to be alike in all children, Piagetians and their successors depict developmental stages as steps on a ladder ascending toward rational maturity and marked by increasing evidence of achieved "logicality." Commonly they, too, model cognition on perceptually based abilities to distinguish, arrange, and manipulate medium-sized physical objects. They work with a conception of "the child" who is every child and no child in particular, details of whose identity or location should make no difference to the processes or products of inquiry. Despite some attempts to produce social accounts of development, of which L. S. Vygotsky's is the best-known classical example,[3] a belief that children can adequately be studied individually, in abstraction from their family, community, culture, and everyday activities—from their habitat and its prevailing ethos—governs large areas of developmental psychology. Even as some present-day developmentalists herald the collapse of Piagetian theory,[4] the territory mapped out in his project is a still-fertile theoretical ground. Still worthy of acknowledgment—recalling Annette Baier's reminder that a person is "marvellously corporeal"—is the point that, for Piaget, knowing is clearly an embodied activity. Thus, Christopher Preston notes that cognition, for naturalized epistemology, is "not only *in* and *of* the world, as Quine had wanted; it is also *in* and *of* a body that acts in the world as Piaget had insisted."[5] He is right to highlight this point, given how Piaget grounds knowledge in sensorimotor activity that is, by definition, embodied. My critical reading of Piaget in this chapter does not lose sight of his contribution to naturalistic inquiry, as evidenced most famously in his pathbreaking studies of his own children's language at home, in everyday conversation.[6] His failure to consider differences among children, however, and thus to take

3. See, e.g., Vygotsky, *Thought and Language*; and idem, *Mind in Society*.
4. See Gopnik and Meltzoff, *Words, Thoughts, and Theories*, 221. Yet the authors comment: "Nonetheless, . . . we and other theory theorists are staking out the same conceptual territory as Piaget. . . . Many of those working in this area come out of a broadly Piagetian tradition and see themselves as Piaget's inheritors" (221).
5. Preston, *Grounding Knowledge*, 33.
6. Piaget, *Language and Thought of the Child*.

into account how the specificity of *his children's* situation, sociality, class, race, and the material circumstances of an affluent, educated Swiss family must circumscribe the legitimacy of generalizing from their language to *the* language of *the* child, tempers the larger naturalistic promise.

The levels of abstraction that orthodox epistemologists work with often seem at best elusive, at worst absurd, to nonphilosophers, and I have taken issue with their reductive effects in earlier chapters of this book. Nonetheless, the goal of establishing reliable criteria for disinterested knowing, capable of resisting the persuasions of partiality and vested interests, is a worthy one, despite the scientistic and other excesses to which it is prone. Cognizant of the part played by standards of ideal objectivity and certainty in separating knowledge from power-driven struggles for epistemic ascendancy and authority—from conjecture, propaganda, whimsy—epistemologists rightly caution against the chaos that would ensue if "man" were indeed, idiosyncratically or even collectively, "the measure of all things," while feminists have deconstructed the very idea of this putatively "generic man" to expose its specific reference to a select group of white men. Thus, together with other postcolonial theorists engaged in transformative-emancipatory critique, feminists have shown how the neutral demeanor of these theories of knowledge masks their complicity in sustaining a hierarchical social order marked by radically uneven distributions of power and privilege. They have traced the genealogy of the ideals of knowledge, rationality, and agency that infuse these epistemologies and the practices they inform, to the lives, sociabilities, and communities—the habitus and ethos—of affluent educated adult white men. Their positioning as established authorities and experts may be a historical-sociological accident, but its effects are constitutive of the regulative epistemological and moral ideals of affluent white western societies. In the epistemic imaginary of such societies, these are the authorities who determine and defend the standards by which knowledge claims are (often tacitly) adjudicated, credibility conferred, and moral judgments enacted and evaluated.

Analogously, the levels of abstraction and assumptions of universality in the received practices of developmental psychology may seem at best artificial, at worst absurd, to readers cognizant of the diversity of children's lives. But the goal of determining whether a conceptual frame can be constructed, sensitive enough to catch what—if anything—is common to children *as children*, thus looking beneath surface inequalities to develop adequately informed responses to needs and deprivations, favoritism, or special interests, is likewise a worthy one. Yet feminists and other postpatriarchal developmental theorists, committed to eradicating the injustices its universalist pretensions sustain, have shown that the abstract impartiality of Piagetian developmentality and its

successors and cognates likewise masks their complicity in sustaining a patriarchal, Eurocentric, capitalist social order insufficiently attentive to structural differences and to the affective-situational-material-psychological-racial
specificities that shape the lives of children who fall outside "the norm." Thus
in her gender- and class-sensitive reading of Piaget, Valerie Walkerdine argues
that "what is taken to be universal is itself the imposition of a particular
truth,"[7] a truth neither apolitical nor otherwise neutral or innocent.

It may seem to be a large step from my initial polite sketches of orthodox
epistemology and developmental psychology to casting them, thus, as contributors to practices of privilege. Epistemology's self-presentation as the
proponent of a view from nowhere, a god's-eye view of the world, and developmental psychology's universality claims seem to hold them at such a
distance from concrete particularities as to exonerate both lines of inquiry
from the charge that they sustain practices and structures of inequality. Yet
I am proposing that the social-political effects of these epistemologies and
psychologies feed into and are fed by the *instituted social imaginary* of mastery
and domination I have been discussing in the preceding chapters. This is the
imaginary that values knowledge, too simplistically, too cursorily unified, for
its power to predict, manipulate, and control the objects of its study, be those
"objects" material or human. It represents knowers as infinitely replicable,
rational, self-reliant, dislocated, and detached individuals face to face with inert
and indifferent objects of knowledge to which their attitude, too, is and should
be one of indifference. It sustains and indeed celebrates the unquestioned
assumption that the child developmental psychologists study is the father of
autonomous *man*, the man of reason, who claims the principal speaking parts
in the discourses of orthodox epistemology and realizes his full potential to the
extent of his success in achieving the autonomy that a liberal democratic
society holds out to him as a goal and a character ideal. Distancing themselves
from the particularities of materiality, physicality, and all other circumstantial
contingencies shields autonomous practitioners of psychological research from
any need to address the differences difference makes.

Situated Knowing, Individualism, and Mastery

In this chapter, I am interested in how this social-epistemic imaginary constructs "the child" as an object of inquiry and as a (potential) knower whose

7. Walkerdine, *Mastery of Reason*, 193.

cognitive development follows a path of "natural" maturation into autonomous man, the fictive character who occupies center stage in this same imaginary. My inquiry thus participates in what, for Cornelius Castoriadis, would count as constructing a genealogy of the *creation* of the "individual" complete with his needs, within the dominant social imaginary. It is directed toward exposing the contingency of the process and the interests that this creation tacitly serves.[8] Indeed, in the privileged parts of the western world, a narrowly delineated achievement of autonomy counts as the *telos* of normal development for white affluent (male) children as its descriptively natural and prescriptively fostered goal. Discourses of development and maturation represent the child as a being who unfolds out of an infancy in which he is vitally dependent on nurturant others to a place of full individual autonomy where he becomes his own person, renouncing dependence to emerge as a self-sufficient individual.[9] Thus represented, development is a linear process: it achieves completion at "the age of majority," having passed through well-marked way-stages or levels en route to this fully separated moment.[10] Cognitive and moral maturity, then, marks an end to infant and childhood dependence. It manifests itself in the achievement of mastery: mastery over one's own body, which is so taken for granted as rarely to receive mention except as a precondition for all the rest, or when it fails so dramatically as to require special attention or intervention. Mastery over the emotions aligns closely with bodily mastery, as does mastery over the becoming-adult's physical, social, cultural, and natural surroundings—a complex of masteries indicative of a solitary coming of age in matters moral, epistemological, social, and personal. This masterful self, then, is the autonomous individual whose makings I discuss here.

Picking up a doubled thematic that runs throughout my work on knowledge and subjectivity,[11] in this chapter I examine the uneasy fit between epistemologically endorsed knowledge and the human subjects—the children—who are the objects of knowledge in developmental psychology. Concomitantly, I examine some assumptions central to these theories and practices: about what

8. Castoriadis, "From Ecology to Autonomy," 20.

9. The masculine pronoun signals the masculine character of autonomy in western post-Enlightenment discourse, a claim integral to my analysis in chap. five. For a fine discussion of the bounded masculine separateness fostered by autonomy ideals, see Schmitt, *Beyond Separateness.*

10. Classical U.S. child-raising manuals such as those of Spock and Gesell and the philosophical views of Rousseau, Durkheim, Kohlberg, and Piaget represent development thus. Chodorow, in *Reproduction of Mothering*, contrasts a putatively female connectedness with the autonomous disconnectedness fostered in male children.

11. See the introduction to my *Rhetorical Spaces* for a sketch of this thematic.

kind of being "the child" must be if she or he is to be knowable through the methods these assumptions sanction; what kinds of knowing he or she must manifest in order to achieve recognized "stages" on the way to maturity; what kind of knower an epistemologist-psychologist must be in order to produce developmental knowledge recognizable as "normal science." For although neither parents nor developmental psychologists may count themselves among the regular readers of epistemology texts, established theories of knowledge are widely enacted in everyday beliefs about which claims deserve the status "knowledge" and who merits acknowledgment as a knower and/or knowledgeable moral agent in the governing ideals of developmental theories and practices. Feminist critiques of the epistemologies and ethico-politics of mastery have exposed the silent agendas that underwrite these developmental disciplinary practices, inculcating children and inducting parents into this imaginary in which mastery in its multiple modalities stands as the mark of a successful human life. Here I examine naming, naturalizing, and normalizing as practices constitutive in their form, content, and social-political enactment of these modes of developmental inquiry. Reconfigured, these same practices might interrupt the self-certainties of received developmentality, contest its fundamental premises, and thus begin to disturb the neutral, disinterested self-conception that holds mastery in place as an often-oppressive regulative ideal. They might begin, also, to generate social-psychological knowledge capable of establishing ecologically reconstructed principles for responsible ethico-political cohabitation with one another and with/in the natural world.

As I will argue in more detail in the following chapters, post-Enlightenment, post-Kantian western philosophers often work with a curious, if standardized, conception of the (largely invisible) human subject who is their main protagonist. Although details of his identity rarely figure explicitly in colonial and pre-second-wave feminist theories, this subject is presumptively adult (but not old), white, affluent, and male. The governing assumption is that his natural epistemic maturation will follow the exact same path regardless of its cultural, familial, social, geographical, or material location. For positivist-empiricists, neither the developmental processes that shape the adult masculinity enacted in the life of this "rational self-conscious agent"—this man of reason—nor the situations, places, and circumstances in which his knowledge is produced claim epistemological significance. Those who argue otherwise risk committing the "genetic fallacy": the fallacy of resting justification or explanation upon such merely contingent, nonepistemic details as the provenance—the genesis—of reason and of knowledge claims, thus bypassing accredited justificatory strategies. In consequence, the relationship between developmental psychology

and epistemology as practiced by professional philosophers has been an uneasy
one. When children figure in canonical philosophy texts—with two notable
exceptions, in Jean Jacques Rousseau's *Émile* (which is "really" about education, thus allegedly not about epistemology) and in the later work of Ludwig
Wittgenstein—they tend to appear in retrospective extrapolations where autonomous man reconstructs his own adult knowledge from "primitive simples."
Thus, not atypically, D. W. Hamlyn accords Piaget's "genetic epistemology" no
philosophical significance whatsoever. Reiterating an entrenched conviction that
introspective reconstructions of childhood cognition provide everything an
epistemologist could need, he writes: "The priority of the concrete to the abstract
is something that all normal human beings *could discover by reflection* on what
they know about the nature of human development, of human learning: it needs
no further empirical investigation."[12] Thus, he believes, epistemologists are well
advised to resist any temptation to study empirical particulars as a prelude to
their normative, a priori inquiries: everyone, simply as a matter of course, is an
authority on childhood, for everyone has firsthand knowledge of it.

A notable exception to this disdain for developmental and situational
questions is the later Wittgenstein. Consider the following:

> We are brought up, trained, to ask: "What is that called?"—upon
> which the name is given. . . . Now one can ostensively define a proper
> name, the name of a colour, the name of a material, a numeral, the
> name of a point on the compass and so on. The definition of the
> number two, "That is called 'two'"—pointing to two nuts—is
> perfectly exact.—But how can two be defined like that? The person
> one gives the definition to doesn't know what one wants to call "two";
> he will suppose that "two" is the name given to *this* group of
> nuts! . . . That is to say: an ostensive definition can be variously
> interpreted in *every* case.[13]

Wittgenstein is no developmental psychologist; and his remarks rely on everyday observation, thus not on experiment—but also not on mere reflection.
Yet the passage stands as an implicit critique of Hamlyn's dismissal of such
insights as epistemologists might gain from developmental studies, and thus
also of developmental psychology's focus on the generic individual child, separated from the affective, locational, and material particularities that promote
or thwart her/his cognitive development. Even so apparently basic a cognitive

12. Hamlyn, "Logical and Psychological Aspects," 42 (emphasis added).
13. Wittgenstein, *Philosophical Investigations*, §§27–28.

practice as teaching a child, ostensively, the name of a color contests any claim that people "can discover by reflection" anything they need to know about child development. It emphasizes the complexity of even so simple an act as showing the child it is the *redness* of the book, the sweater, the crayon, that I am teaching her to name. How can she discern that my gestures mean the color, not the object itself, or its location, or its shape? Because acts of naming are socially-culturally embedded all the way down to the traditionally most basic level, it is impossible to represent the process as simply as philosophers wedded to the myth of the given,[14] the certainty of a retrospective glance and the idea that we all have equivalent "privileged access" to the nature of our childhood knowings, evidently think possible. In the epigraph to this chapter, Walkerdine, provocatively, asks: "If there is no action which takes place outside the framework of social practices, and if the object world is understood only in terms of its meaningful insertion within particular discursive practices, then why should we assume a unique and singular developmental path, a unique and singular subject?"[15] Here I am endorsing her contention that all actions, all meanings, occur and indeed are *made* within social practices: a claim that marks a radical departure from the individualism of orthodox western epistemology and psychology. Although Vygotsky's work, also, affords evidence that developmental psychology has not been unrelievedly individualistic, especially given his emphasis on social, communicative as contrasted with egocentric language development, it is worth noting how investigations framed in the language of social-cultural influences *on* the child or interactions *with* the child still, subtly, hold to the conception of a self-contained *individual* who is subject to, but can be extricated from and purged of, those influences.

Nor does the color-naming episode unequivocally mark a standard, universal stage in conceptual achievement, a ubiquitous readiness for the next stage of learning: it, too, can—and must—be variously interpreted. In an epistemology of mastery, as in developmental psychology informed by it, such learning to *name*, the achievements of such "referential-nominal children,"[16] attests to a degree of success in mastering the environment, a level of control over objects. Nor is such a reading implausible or troublesome. But it is as much an artifact of the social imaginary that normalizes individual mastery as it is a neutral reading of naming activities. A less individualistic, more socially embedded analysis might, for example, read learning to name or to use language in

14. See again Sellars, "Does Empirical Knowledge?"
15. Walkerdine, *Mastery of Reason*, 30.
16. The phrase is from Burman, *Deconstructing Developmental Psychology*, 130.

other ways as a mark of, and integral to, a child's entry into a family, a group, a community where she establishes her place linguistically as she learns to name—both how to name and what is worth naming—within the form of life where she thus begins to claim membership. Here, again, is Wittgenstein: "When a child learns language *it learns at the same time what is to be investigated and what is not.* When it learns that there is a cupboard in the room, it isn't taught to doubt whether what it sees later on is still a cupboard or only a kind of stage set."[17] Wittgenstein's insistence that to learn a language is to learn a "form of life" amounts to a denial that naming and more elaborated learning-knowing processes speak for themselves: rather, they acquire meaning—and hence theoretical and practical significance—out of the social-cultural-ecological locations where they occur. He thus relocates childhood cognition within situations, communities, social-political practices—within a habitus and ethos—where naming is neither a solitary nor a simple act.

Indeed, despite the centrality to developmental psychology of the line that runs from Rousseau through Kant to Piaget and, subsequently, Kohlberg, there are other ways of thinking philosophically about childhood—of which Wittgenstein's counts as one—and other naturalistic approaches to child development that are sufficiently attentive to the sociability and community that Piaget so strikingly neglects as to unsettle Piagetian hegemony, or at least to highlight its strangeness. It is not my intention to draw up a list, but it is worth considering different paths that might have been taken, as further evidence for the contingency of the one most traveled. Thus, for example, where Piaget and his successors follow a Kantian line from the Enlightenment forward, Axel Honneth, reading George Herbert Mead, follows a Hegelian line. In *The Struggle for Recognition*, Honneth discusses "Mead's naturalistic transformation of Hegel's idea," in an analysis focused on Mead's having "inverted the relationship between the ego and the social world . . . [to assert] the primacy of the perception of the other to the development of self-consciousness."[18] For Honneth, children learn to see themselves as "independent subjects" through emotional (hence not exclusively cognitive) relationships to/with other people: thus he, too, is critical of research that studies infants "in isolation from all significant others."[19] While the centrality he accords to struggle and conflict in developmental processes, and his references to "the generalized [rather than the 'concrete'] other," may tell

17. Wittgenstein, *On Certainty*, §472 (emphasis added).
18. Honneth, *Struggle for Recognition*, 75. "Mead's Naturalistic Transformation" is the title of chap. 4.
19. Ibid., 97–98.

against feminist willingness to draw extensively either on Honneth's own theoretical position or on his reading of Mead, his careful attention to the primacy
of attachment and to "second person" modalities could sit very well with some
feminist and other anti-individualistic projects. Moreover, Honneth is one of
only a few theorists to appeal to ethological investigations to support his claims
for the developmental primacy of sociality.[20] With its focus on the socially
mediated character of development, Honneth's reading of Mead situates his
work close both to Vygotsky's and to Jerome Bruner's studies of how sociality
contributes to making individuality possible, which I discuss in chapter two.
Thus he presents a naturalism less scientistic and less individualistic in its
founding presuppositions than Quinean naturalism. So, too, does George
Butterworth in an explicitly ecological reading of the origins of self "as both
a process and a product of embodied perception," where he emphasizes the
constitutive relationship between "the embodied self and physical reality" and
"the infant's relationship with other people, which situate her in social reality."[21]
I cite these examples merely to indicate that Piaget's is not the only available
conceptual apparatus for addressing cognitive development naturalistically and
to suggest that, phenomenologically, the isolated Piagetian subject, "positioned
outside history and society," is less plausible than the subject of some more
explicitly socially-ecologically grounded conceptions that, for reasons difficult
to fathom, have failed to claim ascendancy. Still now, according to Erica Burman, "Piaget remains the dominant *psychological* resource for professionals who
want to know how children think."[22]

Walkerdine is one of Piaget's most cogent critics on issues of gender, class,
and race. She develops an explicitly situational-political-material critique of
the assumptions underwriting his project: a sustained, provocative genealogy
of how Piagetian psychology reinscribes and reinforces the rhetoric of mastery as a universal *Leitmotiv* of developmentality. In an analysis with clear affinities to Susan Buck-Morss's now-classic exposure of socio-economic bias in
Piagetian theory and to Cathy Urwin's and her own earlier social-material
analyses, Walkerdine maps the narrowly local specificity of Piagetian theory:
its situatedness within, as a product of, and as a disciplinary matrix regulative for the lives of affluent white middle-class children and parents.[23] She

---

20. Ibid., 96–97. See also Butterworth, "Ecological Perspective," 94.
21. Butterworth, "Ecological Perspective," 87, 102.
22. Burman, *Deconstructing Developmental Psychology*, 154, 151 (emphasis original).
23. See Buck-Morss, "Socio-Economic Bias in Piaget's Theory." See also Urwin, "Power
Relations"; Walkerdine, "Developmental Psychology"; and Burman, *Deconstructing Developmental Psychology*, chap. 10.

takes issue with Piagetian theory's universalist pretensions even within western societies, offering a critical reevaluation of the scope, limits, and political consequences of its oft-declared neutral, politically innocent theoretical apparatus. Its tacit political intent, she convincingly argues, is to promote "the triumph of reason over emotion through stressing the naturally adaptive processes of organisms . . . [so that] animal passions would be left behind to found a better world in reason."[24]

Such a project might seem at first glance to advocate an incontestably commendable goal, nor does Walkerdine deny its promise. Her quarrel is with its implicitly naturalizing-normalizing agenda and with the suppressions and silencings of Otherness effected by its promotion of a formal reason, assumed without contest to be alike in all *men*.[25] Among the consequences of such celebrations of the power of reason over emotion is a failure to take adequately into account the sociality—the radically diverse "practices of everyday life"—that makes rational development *variously* possible, fostering or thwarting its multiple modalities. Co-opted into "bourgeois and patriarchal rule by science," Walkerdine contends, "the 'reasonable person,' in Piaget's terms, is 'in love with ideas' and not bodies."[26] This suppression of affect, thence of sociality, and of affective connections with other people and with the differences that the diversity of human embodiment entails is a significant cost exacted by ideal mastery over the self and the physical/social world. It at once informs the naturalizing-normalizing I will go on to discuss and renders epistemologies and psychologies of mastery inimical to feminist and other postcolonial emancipatory projects (although I must emphasize that this criticism is not meant as a plea for aligning an *essential* femaleness-femininity with affect).

Naming, Naturalizing, Normalizing

My intention here is not to enlist Wittgenstein as a protofeminist or protodevelopmentalist, but to read passages in his later work (which can also be "variously interpreted") as marks of a departure—partially congruent with Walkerdine's critique—from certain constraints generated by received epistemological orthodoxy. For Wittgenstein, entering a language game, a form of

24. Walkerdine, *Mastery of Reason*, 5.
25. See Lloyd, *Man of Reason*.
26. Walkerdine, *Mastery of Reason*, 186.

life, could well be characterized, following Deleuze, as "a matter of sociabilities and communities": he examines social practices as locations where truths about childhood cognition are produced and which (to borrow Walkerdine's words) create "a normalizing vision of the 'natural child.'"[27] Thus I am reading Walkerdine and Wittgenstein through one another, as contributors to a *natural history* of knowledge-and-subjectivity in child-adult-world cognitive relations. The analysis contributes one more piece to this articulation of an *ethologically* and *ecologically* sensitive naturalized epistemology: its aims are to discern what epistemologists—especially naturalistic epistemologists—can learn from developmentalists about the production of knowledge and subjectivity and to show why a critical stance toward Piagetian orthodoxy and its successors and analogues matters to feminists and participants in other successor epistemology projects, who are likewise working to undo the damage consequent upon an excessive veneration of mastery.

As I have observed in earlier chapters, naturalists relinquish mainstream epistemology's search for a priori, necessary and sufficient conditions for knowledge in general, to examine how people go about knowing, variously, within the scope and limits of their (experimentally revealed) cognitive capacities. As I have also noted, Quinean naturalism's title and its guiding principle originate in W. V. O. Quine's landmark claim: "Epistemology, or something like it, simply falls into place as a chapter of psychology and hence of natural science. It studies a natural phenomenon, viz., a physical human subject."[28] Its agenda-setting questions, according to Hilary Kornblith (in a more secular, everyday articulation than the one I cite in chapter two), are "What is the world that we may know it? And what are we that we may know the world?"—for which answers will be found where the best theories of physical reality and the best psychological theories dovetail: in studies of "how we are adapted to the structure of the world around us" so that we can rely on perceptual information and the conclusions of inductive inferences.[29] Yet as I have also argued, its *scientism*—that is, its adherence to a strictly power-, affect-, and value-neutral conception of scientific inquiry as the only inquiry capable of yielding knowledge worthy of the name—limits Quinean naturalism's promise for feminist and other postcolonial projects. It bypasses that promise still further in its failure to engage in material analyses of the institutions of knowledge production or to examine the unequal part played

27. Ibid., 5.
28. Quine, "Epistemology Naturalized," 25.
29. Kornblith, "Naturalistic Project in Epistemology." 3, 15.

by diverse social groups in determining standards of judgment. As I suggest in chapter two, a principal effect of Quinean analyses of self-contained observer-observed experiments is to "denature" both knower and known. The knower, who can be everyone or anyone, is a neutral placeholder, isolated from all "natural" knowledge-enhancing or knowledge-thwarting factors; and the "known" manifests the purity of a statistical formalism that glosses over differences and specificities within "natural kinds." Thus Quinean naturalists presuppose the objective validity and exemplary status of the scientific knowledge they study. Restricting their observations to experimentally demonstrated knowing in the scientific laboratory where the situation is contrived and controlled to erase any concern about "the unequal part played by different social groups in determining standards of judgement" (recalling Sabina Lovibond),[30] they proceed as though values, ideology, power, and privilege have also been left behind at the door. In consequence, they are unable to realize naturalism's naturalistic potential.

The effects of these limitations are starkly apparent in Alison Gopnik and Andrew Meltzoff's commitment to scientistic literalness, in their "theory theory," where they cast developing children as miniature rationalistic scientists, their cognitive activity as theory-constructive from earliest infancy, and old-style mastery as their ultimate developmental achievement.[31] Of particular significance for feminists is the unaddressed implication that this "budding scientist" who, even when he is studied outside the confines of the laboratory is still engaged systematically in "encountering problems in the material world, developing hypotheses and learning by discovery and activity," is represented as quintessentially male (and presumptively both affluent and white), and his quest for knowledge is incorporated into the discourse of science, itself a "gendered practice."[32]

Here I am reading Wittgenstein as a more secular naturalist, whose contributions to a natural history of everyday epistemic life generate neither a full-blown theory nor a scientistic reductionism. Yet both Wittgenstein's work and Walkerdine's—albeit quite differently—succeed in "making strange" certain sedimented epistemological assumptions, revealing their incongruity with everyday (diverse) epistemic lives; while Walkerdine exposes the ideo-

30. Lovibond, "Feminism and Postmodernism," 12–13.
31. See Gopnik and Meltzoff, *Words, Thoughts, and Theories.* In an earlier piece, Gopnik's analysis is more hospitable to folk psychology's capacity to contribute a basis for cognitive scientific inquiry; see her "Developing the Idea of Intentionality."
32. The phrases cited are from Burman, *Deconstructing Developmental Psychology,* 157.

logical complicity of the value system implicit in the work of Piaget and his successors, observing that "experimental studies, while they are an important source of data... reveal relatively little about how non-experimental contexts operate."[33] (Her hesitations are continuous with those Messing voices about translating information derived from studying Chinese hamster ovary cells into conclusions about human workplace health.) Feminist commitments to eradicating real-world injustices preclude such reliance on an overblown estimation of the reach of experimentally derived conclusions: the gap between theory and practice, between laboratory and habitat, is too wide. Thus, again, I am casting these forms of scientism as inimical to feminist naturalistic projects because of their evident conviction that natural science is in order as it stands; hence there is no need to interrogate the universal applicability assumptions of scientific orthodoxy, whose claims to account for everything worthy of the honorific status "knowledge" mask its power-privilege sustaining agendas. Nor is there any need to question the abstract individualism it takes for granted, in which "the knowing subject" figures only incidentally, and inconveniently, as the producer of the knowledge that matters: he need not be identified because knowers are perfectly interchangeable. Nor, for Piagetians, is there any need to contest the status of formal logic "as the normative end point of cognitive development" with its aim of "providing complete closure, capturing unshakable truths," a goal Rachel Falmagne persuasively casts as hegemonic in its intolerance of "concrete content, nuance, pragmatic context, rhetorical force."[34] Within such frames there is no place to ask "whose knowledge are we talking about?"—a question pivotal to feminist and other postcolonial epistemologies and to the disciplinary projects they inform.

Wittgenstein takes neither equality nor ideology into account, but his observations of how children know within "forms of life," as I read them, count as contributions to a "natural history of human beings" with a capacity to radicalize the potential of a science-derived naturalism prepared to look only occasionally to developmental psychology—and, when it does so, to a

33. Walkerdine, *Mastery of Reason*, 11. See also Nelson et al., who comment: "It is not surprising... that children at home in everyday situations may display greater knowledge and interpersonal competence than they do on laboratory tasks.... The... laboratory may pose formidable problems of interpretation for the very young child" ("Entering a Community of Minds," 70).

34. Falmagne, "Positionality and Thought," 202–3. For Falmagne, and I concur, "formalism [is] oppressive by virtue of its epistemic status rather than being oppressive quintessentially."

mode of developmental practice (of which Gopnik and Meltzoff's 1997 text is a representative example)—that characterizes itself as a "specific version of the naturalistic-epistemology story."[35] Their project is almost as reductively scientistic as the other sources to which Quine-line naturalists appeal, for they enter these debates fully equipped with before-the-fact assumptions about the child as a little scientist and about the naturalness both of laboratory life and of solitary, self-reliant information-processors as paradigmatic knowers. This is the scientism that Jeanne Marecek discerns in mainstream psychology, historically "committed to the discovery of presumed universals in human experience—'laws of human behavior' that transcend history, culture, class, caste, and material circumstances. Thus, the valued means of producing knowledge has been the experiment, in which behavior is extracted from its usual social context."[36] Yet investigation need not be confined to the laboratory; Walkerdine, for example, relocates it in the schoolroom (rather as Carson looks to the world around her, and Messing to the workplace). Even there, she cautions, universalistic assumptions could function reductively, as a prefabricated grid, if an inquiry were treated simply as a means for producing quantifiable analysis and the classroom as a site for straightforwardly *scientific* naturalistic observation. In such circumstances, Walkerdine suggests, the process of inquiry "evades and elides" issues of how the truth of specifically located practices is produced and fails to address how that truth is registered in the institutionalized aptness of certain kinds of response.[37] Yet she also shows how such assumptions can be problematized in observations whose departure from empiricist orthodoxy allows them to participate in a critical, *negotiated* empiricism, where perceptual "data" and "statements of fact" have always to be debated, interrogated, interpreted, analyzed— thus neither merely "read off" the surface of events and practices nor discounted for the information they afford about the world, both animate and inanimate.

With these thoughts in mind, in the following subsections I give content to the concepts in the title of this section: naming, normalizing, and naturalizing. My intention is to show how these practices figure emblematically and often coercively within the instituted developmental imaginary of the affluent white western world and to suggest how they might be reimagined, reconfigured in ecologically conceived developmental projects.

35. Gopnik and Meltzoff, *Words, Thoughts, and Theories*, 18.
36. Marecek, "Psychology and Feminism," 110.
37. Walkerdine, *Mastery of Reason*, 51.

Naming

Naming in the title of this section and in Wittgenstein's reminders about the ambiguity of ostensive definition is a trope for the "primitive simples" that classical and some later empiricists represent as the basics, the givens, of human knowledge. Likewise in the assumed (imagined) immediacy, simplicity, and atomicity of childhood knowing in the western world, simple, prepropositional naming of discrete physical objects has tended to count as an originary cognitive moment. Rhetorically, it functions as the moment where it all began, a moment recuperable in analyses rigorous enough to reconstruct the discrete building blocks from which knowledge can be rebuilt "from the bottom up" to reveal the temporal and logical conditions of its possibility. Classical empiricists, as I have noted, arrive at these simples by introspecting retrospectively to what a child "must have known for certain." Thus the early-twentieth-century thought experiments of such sense-data theorists as Bertrand Russell and H. H. Price strip observations of medium-sized material objects down to their barest presentational moments; while logical positivists contrive sanitized observations where simple propositional knowledge claims map perceptual givens to yield protocol statements straightforwardly verifiable by checking for correspondence against those percepts.[38] Analogously, laboratory psychology favors experiments designed to elicit simple verbal responses, where the point is to name sensory input so clearly as to allow for minimal interpretive variation. The belief is that in honoring such requirements, cognitive/social science displays its true scientificity. Rarely, in these traditions, is epistemological significance accorded to the possibility that naming practices might vary, even dramatically, perhaps incommensurably, according to race, gender, class, material-geographical location, culture, ethnicity, or any of the other ecological specificities that radically shape and inflect cognitive processes in the everyday world. Appeals to the logical possibility of universal replicability are invoked to override such situational contingency.

The pivotal place epistemologists and developmental psychologists accord to naming as a paradigmatic act of knowing, indicative of an achieved moment of mastery, both naturalizes and normalizes the picture of the abstract, interchangeable knower—of the *individualism*—which, in a complex feedback loop, gives content to and acquires content from a conceptual apparatus whose central pillar is a form of objectivity possible only through the autonomous

38. See Russell, *Problems of Philosophy;* Price, *Perception;* and Ayer, *Language, Truth, and Logic.*

exercise of reason. Developmentalists' chartings of rational progress attest amply to this point. Thus, representing quantifiable input-output experiments designed to chart the ability to name as exemplary of "ordinary" human knowing attests to the residual power of a positivistic unity-of-science credo, even after "the naturalistic turn." With its emphasis on language as a naming, referential activity—on language "as object rather than relationship"[39]—it fosters the formalist emphasis that Falmagne interrogates[40] and has the further effect of sustaining an image of language as only *representing* rather than also *producing* truths and of erasing affect from processes of learning to talk, to communicate, and to express thoughts and feelings. When developmentalists rely on uninterpreted, uninterrogated namings as demonstrations, for example, of a child's having achieved a cognitive level marked by a readiness to pick out objects in her or his surroundings or to make comparative "bigger/ smaller," "more/less" judgments, they perpetuate these same assumptions, oblivious to observations such as Wittgenstein's about the radical interpretability of the simplest naming practices.

Walkerdine, in an instructive contrast, details experiments with children's responses to the story of the three bears, in studies designed to confirm their readiness to proceed to complex object comparisons once they have demonstrated an ability to distinguish "small/bigger/biggest." The unquestioned—and seemingly neutral—background assumption is that *all* children will recognize baby bear as smaller than mommy and daddy bear, mommy bear as smaller than daddy bear, and daddy bear as the biggest of the three. Walkerdine notes how seriously observers had to challenge their own fundamental, governing imaginary just to be able to *hear* answers that spoke against these sedimented assumptions, to understand how, conceptually-psychologically, affectively, and physically, children who kept insisting that mommy bear was bigger than daddy bear often made sense, even if objective measures showed mommy bear to be (physically) smaller. These children's answers expose a range of variations—emotional, situational, empirical—on presumptively normal patriarchal family structure: variations in which daddy is not present at all; in which daddy's is an insignificant, minimal presence; in which mommy is physically or affectively/psychically bigger; and so on. Here not even measurable size is simply a given physical attribute or a natural, nameable trait innocent of class and patriarchal assumptions, nor is knowing so straightforward as sanitized, standardized, polite

---

39. The phrase is Burman's, *Deconstructing Developmental Psychology*, 117. In my thoughts here I am indebted to her chap. 8, "Language talk."
40. See Falmagne, "Positionality and Thought," 202–3.

accounts assume. Burman, for example, notes that even when studies of naming make space for evaluating the significance of emotions in cognition, only the "nice" emotions are considered; and in their depictions of caring-teaching mothers, they "present an overharmonious view of parent-child interaction."[41]

Of the children who participated in the three bears study, Walkerdine remarks: "These children can clearly make size comparisons, but these comparisons are relations within particular and specific practices."[42] The experiment confirms the minimally informative potential of the disembedded, label-eliciting question; it shows how a complex interplay among observer, observed, and the politics and ecological patterns of larger social-cultural situations inserts itself into the negotiative interpretation of empirical observations. Yet—and this point, too, must be taken very seriously—it cannot adequately be explicated in the language of context and contextualization, where text and context are represented as separable, with text explaining itself better, more easily when it is inserted into or placed back in context, while each remains distinct in itself. As Cathy Urwin convincingly observes: "The appeal to context not only fails to explain; it also conceals. . . . [It] puts the context outside the child, who is viewed as a point of origin which interacts with or is affected by external factors. . . . The relation between the situation and the process of production is left out of the account. So, too, is the child's motivation or power to speak."[43] It is for reasons consonant with these that the conceptual apparatus I am developing throughout this book derives, both literally and metaphorically, from ecological thinking: as I have explained, the position I am developing is more, and other, than one of simply contextualizing knowledge and subjectivity.

In the practices Walkerdine details, "kinds," namings, practices, situations are mutually constitutive in ongoing interpretive negotiations. Thus consider also bell hooks:

> We are so confused by this thing called Race.
>   We learn about color with crayons. We learn to tell the difference between white and pink and a color they call Flesh. The flesh-colored crayon amuses us. . . . Flesh we know has no relationship to our skin, for we are brown and brown and brown like all good things.[44]

41. Burman, *Deconstructing Developmental Psychology*, 117.
42. Walkerdine, *Mastery of Reason*, 72.
43. Urwin, "Power Relations," 273.
44. hooks, *Bone Black*, 7–8.

What better example of the cultural-locational saturation of simple names, of the co-opting of everyday naming practices into the language of the dominant, of the power-infused nature of the putatively simplest of knowings and not-knowings?[45] In like vein, Burman urges language researchers to take into account the legacy of colonialism and imperialism, both territorial and cultural, embedded in the tendency of psychological research to presuppose a monolingual language learner.[46] The issue in these examples is not just about naive naming (analogous to naive realism), but about how culturally specific, raced and gendered beliefs are entrenched even in traditionally basic perceptual-naming practices. Nor could simple translation bridge the divide in every case, for it leaves systemic power-knowledge relations that structure these differences completely *hors de question*, preserving the dominant wisdom of materially replete white societies about disinterested observations and manipulations of objects generating uniform, straightforwardly translatable naming practices so common as to stand exempt from any need to examine their assumptions of mastery or their built-in exclusions, even as invoking them presupposes an ecologically neutral interchangeability of experiences and perceptions.

Naming, then, is emblematic of the dislocated one-liner responses in input-output experiments and simple everyday paradigm-generating knowings. Disengaged from the social-cultural-material practices and from the habitat-specific circumstances that generate them and make them meaningful, such practices appear in the epistemologies of mastery as neutral, apolitical, and thence universal markers of a uniform developmental progress. Yet these practices are embedded in and constituted—though not determined—by their epistemic and linguistic community of origin: nor could they be otherwise, the cleansing and disentangling steps taken to present them as ostensibly free of cultural or any other taint notwithstanding.

Whereas Gopnik and Meltzoff comment "even extremely young children appear to organize their categorization in terms of 'natural kinds,' underlying essences with causal efficacy,"[47] Walkerdine contests the very idea of a dislocated "natural kind," observing the "multiple signification of many signs within particular practices [that] demonstrates ... the way in which the

---

45. Striking, too, is Morrison's account of a dispute between a white man and a slave over whether the slave's killing and eating a hog counted as theft or, as the slave claimed, as "improving the Master's property." "Clever," Morrison writes, "but schoolteacher beat him anyway to show him that definitions belong to the definers—not the defined" (*Beloved*, 190).

46. Burman, *Deconstructing Developmental Psychology*, 121.

47. Gopnik and Meltzoff, *Words, Thoughts, and Theories*, 31.

participants are positioned and regulated, and how emotionality and desire are carried within these relations themselves."[48] I am suggesting that Walkerdine's critical stance—her down-on-the-ground experiments in naturalizing to working-class lives rather than to putatively normal bourgeois lives or lives imagined as classless—at once refuses to hegemonic practices an exclusive power to supply the contents of "the natural" and keeps her investigations truer to the subjects they study than unnegotiated empirical studies claiming to read results neat, from a smooth, seamless surface, can be. Her practices of inquiry, as I read them, display ecological thinking at work, exposing human subjectivities with their multiple, diverse "capacities for affecting and being affected," as artifacts of sociability and community, as shaped by the geographical-material-cultural locations of their making. Their multiplicity adds confirmation to Kristin Shrader-Frechette's proposal that "ecological applications arise when (and because) scientists have a great deal of knowledge about the natural history of the specific organisms investigated in a particular case study," which I cite in chapter one.[49]

Naturalizing

Naturalizing, as I argue in chapter two, is a term I invoke in two senses in this inquiry. First, in its critical dimension, it interrogates the implicit, subterranean naturalizings both of human knowers and of exemplary modes or moments of knowing within the very scientific psychology from which Quinean naturalists and their successors draw their evidence about who/what "we" are. Second, in a different and more positive register, this analysis catches the promise for feminists and other postcolonial theorists in naturalism's turning away from speculation to relocate theoretical inquiry within the habitats and epistemic practices of real, specifically situated natural knowers.

With reference to critiques of implicit naturalizing, I have recalled Naomi Weisstein's now-classical feminist text "Psychology Constructs the Female," where she argues that natural (female) human "kinds" are as artifactual as they are factual: constructs of the very experiments and studies, and projections of an imagined sameness with the very inquirers who claim to know them.[50] In like vein, Walkerdine observes: "The liberal order of choice and free will had to be created by *inventing* a natural childhood which could be produced and

48. Walkerdine, *Mastery of Reason*, 93.
49. Shrader-Frechette, "Ecology," 313.
50. See Weisstein, "Psychology Constructs the Female."

regulated in the most invisible of ways...it is mothers who are held responsible for the emergence of the 'natural.' "[51] For these theorists, it would strain credulity to suggest that "natural" femaleness-femininity can simply be read off the surface of child or adult bodies, of events, and of practices: assumptions constructed on a presumed-natural foundation have in fact to be interpreted, negotiated, interrupted in every case. Indeed, readings of "the natural"—of natural human, and other, kinds—and the ensuing politics of knowledge vary radically across differences of class, race, gender, ethnicity, across the myriad differences masked by tacitly-presupposed direct observational access to reality and by a demeanor of dislocated ubiquity.

By contrast, although Wittgenstein is no psychologist, the naturalistic face of his thought reveals itself in specific appeals to what children *do*. He writes, for example: "Children do not learn that books exist, that armchairs exist, etc. etc.—they learn to fetch books, sit on armchairs, etc. etc." He observes: "The child, I should like to say, learns to react in such-and-such a way; and in so reacting it doesn't so far know anything. Knowing only begins at a later level."[52] Wittgenstein's repeated reminders that the norms of epistemic practice are fundamentally social have the effect again of making strange some abstract philosophical puzzles about knowledge and language use. The connections he draws between learning a language and learning a form of life contest the usefulness of dislocated practices of separating out the natural from the artifactual. Wittgenstein looks—perhaps at how his pupils go about knowing[53]—and he tests his thinking against observations of everyday practice. Thus, in naturalizing his inquiry, he interrogates by example the canonical individualistic assumptions of mainstream epistemology, showing how, in Peg O'Connor's words, the acquisition of self-identity "is a function of our social interaction and participation with other persons, broader communities, social institutions, and the world," how through learning a language people become aware that they are "particular people who stand in a multitude of relationships" and belong to "a variety of communities."[54] Thus, too, Wittgenstein becomes a distant ally for feminist naturalizing projects, while showing why epistemology cannot just fall into place as a chapter in

51. Walkerdine, *Mastery of Reason*, 212–13 (emphasis added). As I note in chap. two, naturalistic assumptions also pervade Philippe Rushton's studies of putatively natural links between brain size and genital size and the *Bell Curve* controversy.

52. Wittgenstein, *On Certainty*, §476, §538.

53. For an account of Wittgenstein's teaching experience see Monk, *Ludwig Wittgenstein*, 193–209.

54. O'Connor, "Moving to New Boroughs," 436.

psychology: neither epistemology nor psychology can be assumed to be in order as it stands.

In its more positive register, then, the version of naturalism I advocate reclaims a place for *everyday*—as opposed to standardized, sanitized— empirical evidence, within the confines of hitherto a priori epistemological projects. And in so doing, it alerts "us" to the necessity, always, of being mindful of *whose* "everyday" is being taken for granted. Equally significantly, this naturalism contests the orthodox theory-practice relation, where conflicts between practice and theory tend generally to come out in favor of holding established theory intact, thus bypassing practical occurrences that appear to challenge it or labeling them mere exceptions, aberrations.

In part because of its refusal to perpetuate a theory-over-practice ascendancy, Carol Gilligan's work claimed landmark status for feminist psychologists and philosophers (especially in North America) in the late 1970s and early 1980s. Gilligan's landmark achievement was to expose the experimentally demonstrated "fact" of women's natural moral immaturity as an artifact of the insensitivities of Lawrence Kohlberg's stage theory of moral development.[55] On tests designed to measure moral maturity, administered within the purview of this theory, female children and adolescents routinely achieved lower scores than male children and adolescents, while those (few) who attained the highest level of mature, autonomous, principled moral reasoning were uniformly male. Gilligan's innovative move was to examine the structure of the theory itself, especially the presuppositions that positioned certain kinds of response as evidence of moral maturity, while discounting others. Coincidentally or otherwise, styles of moral reasoning that earned low scores matched responses to moral dilemmas typically fostered in female children—responses that, in the discourse that evolved out of her work, came to be labeled "care" responses. These contrasted with the more highly esteemed "justice" responses male children typically offered. Rather than reading female subjects' "failure" to measure up to the demands of the Kohlbergian scale as proof of women's "natural" incapacity for moral autonomy, Gilligan's work critiques the model itself, with its in-built devaluation of women. Equally deserving of critique is Kohlbergian theory's incapacity to take the social-political-material production of male/female gendered children into account as constitutive of gender-related developmental differences, rather than reading those differences as signs of "natural" (in)ability. The stark individualism at its core prevents the theory's practitioners from according sociality and situation their due; for in

55. See Gilligan, *In a Different Voice.*

its veneration of autonomy as the goal of development, the theory works with an asocial view of the individual, while promoting "a form of conceptual imperialism" in applications to cultures where autonomy does not count as the highest developmental achievement. Burman observes, for example, that many cultures "value obedience and respect for elders and tradition over personal [autonomous] conviction,"[56] characteristics that do not claim comparable approval in Kohlberg's ranking.

Gilligan's work of the early 1980s does not escape the naturalizing assumptions constitutive of white bourgeois patriarchy. From its origins in the philosophy of Rousseau and Kant, the developmental narrative that runs through twentieth-century psychology after Piaget, to reemerge in Kohlberg's stage theory and thence to inform numerous popular child development manuals, is complicit in legitimating the ongoing hegemony of the status quo of the white middle-class western world. The values of the middle-class, white, homophobic, patriarchal nuclear family in Cold War (Norman Rockwell) America are inscribed in Kohlberg's developmental stages, as are the disciplinary practices of the (masterful) father and the complementary acquiescence, albeit often silently coerced, of the stay-at-home care-giving mother.

Gilligan (following Nancy Chodorow) reclaims a place for maternal agency in "the" relatively uncontested—presumptively natural—family arrangement, even as she pays unprecedented heed to the voices of female children. Yet her analysis, radical though it was in its early articulations, concentrates more closely on the internal dynamics of a naturalized and idealized heterosexual nuclear family structure than on the social-material locations and the power-infused relations that permeate and sustain it. It is not easy, within these naturalizing processes, to see how same-sex relationships could claim recognition except as unnatural practices or how same-sex parents, and their children, could fail to be judged aberrant. Nor is it easy to see how single-parent families could find a place in the script. Gilligan exposes gendered texts and subtexts in the entrenched developmental practices that enable (some) girls to bring to their moral and cognitive lives a caring stereotyped as "natural" within the dominant social imaginary: texts and subtexts absent from and/or devalued in the rights-and-justice-based, autonomy-promoting lives constitutive of the template for male development in those same segments of society. Thus she prepares the ground for renewed interrogations of nature and nurture, gender essentialism, difference, and power—debates as crucial for feminist developmental psychologists as for feminist epistemologists. But the

---

56. Burman, *Deconstructing Developmental Psychology*, 183.

social imaginary she constructs is so generally polite, so benign, that the wide diversity of infant-caregiver relationships fails to find an analytic place within it. Nor, in a different and more sinister register, is there analytic space to address the darker emotional and power-infused side of adult-child relations, especially as it manifests itself in patterns of child abuse. Where analysis focuses on the adult-child dyad in which children are taught to obey their elders and recognize their authority, it is difficult for an abused child to withstand her or his abuser's power to determine "whether the child is good or bad, what kind of 'love' or 'punishment' is deserved, what count as 'natural" and 'special' ways to love."[57] Nor can wider social patterns of child neglect, or of spousal abuse, easily be addressed except as individual failures to realize the potential that a well-meaning liberal democratic society allegedly makes available for everyone.

Gilligan's early texts are as markedly *white* as they are middle-class and heterosexual, two-parent family centered. Their racial specificity contrasts sharply with developmental stories from other racial and cultural locations, of which a salient example again comes from hooks's *Bone Black*: "In traditional southern-based black life, it was and is expected of girls to be articulate, to hold ourselves with dignity.... These are the variables that white researchers often do not consider when they measure the self-esteem of black females with a yardstick that was designed based on values emerging from white experience."[58] Naturalizing female development as it is fostered in affluent segments of white societies can only render such expectations "unfeminine," and hence again "unnatural." When it builds on such values, developmental theory cannot easily avoid legitimating deep social divisions, leaving the white western well-behaved individualistic "I" intact throughout the story it tells: the individual following a scripted trajectory of gender-, class-, sexuality-, and race-specific development toward a goal of autonomous self-sufficiency. This subject is imagined, also, to be so transparent to her/himself as readily to see the conditions of her/his oppression, to be able to transcend or disarm them through acts of individual will, and to deserve blame when her avoidance strategies fail. Structural, systemic oppression recedes from view in such tellings.

Whereas orthodox Quinean naturalists assume homogeneity within the "natural" kind *human*, then, feminist naturalistic studies of cognitive and moral practices have to be simultaneously gender-sensitive and multiply aware of the diverse axes along which, and the ecologically specific habitus and ethos

57. O'Connor, "Moving to New Boroughs," 438.
58. hooks, *Bone Black*, xiii.

within which, gender is enacted. Feminists cannot operate effectively with a model of vision as a passive, unnegotiated mirroring of empirical reality, achieved by a dislocated, anonymous spectator; they cannot assume that people, simply by looking, will see things as they are. Yet orthodox psychology assumes they can do just this. Feminists, by contrast, in Donna Haraway's words, are caught up in "the problem of responsibility for the *generativity* of all visual practices...answerable for what [they] learn how to see."[59] Thus feminist-informed naturalistic research requires a sensitively focused methodological vigilance. It has to be sufficiently perceptive to notice and contest theory-constitutive assumptions permeating everyday lives and professional psychological discourses alike, about the naturalness of feelings, traits, behaviors, dispositions. It has also to be prepared to submit research hypotheses, projects, and methods to scrutiny for tendencies toward androcentrism, parochialism, and imperialism, just as meticulously as it has to urge respectfully engaged observational and communicative practices for studying the subjects research takes as its objects.[60]

Cynthia Willett's subtle analysis of mother-infant relations offers one pertinent example of what a difference it would make to studies of cognitive development were they prepared to see the infant, from the beginning, as a social, erotic, desiring, and creative being, learning to live in an affect- and meaning-saturated world, embedded within habitus and ethos. The contrast with the mastery-oriented (Kantian-)Piagetian-Kohlbergian story is stark; as is the contrast with appeals to the retrospective reflection of disengaged, disinterested adults and with the restriction of (Quinean) attention to visual observations of "a *physical* human subject." These more orthodox framings, albeit variously, reduce the child to mere appetite needing to be disciplined, mastered, even as the developmental significance of the social eroticism that, from the beginning, binds together mother and children, care-giving fathers, same-sex spouses, nannies, daycare workers, teachers and children, falls below the threshold of theoretical notice. Crucially, too, the extent to which the child's agency itself shapes developmental processes, from earliest infancy, drops out of sight. Furthermore, in theories for which cognitive developmental significance is accorded neither to touch or gesture nor to modes of communication and listening that—phenomenologically—are at once enfolding and visually engaged, nurturing a child reduces to abstract, distanced, mechanical activity. In these early expressive relationships, infants and children

---

59. Haraway, "Situated Knowledges," 190 (emphasis added).
60. See in this regard my "How Do We Know."

develop, or are thwarted in their efforts to develop, faith in their surroundings and trust in other people and in themselves. As Willett observes, "By 'naturalizing' the work of the nurturer, patriarchal institutions of motherhood subject the nurturer to the same subjectless asociality as her infant. Together parent and infant are rendered mute before the forces of a masculinized reason and an oppressive social system."[61] It requires a full acknowledgment of these affective-erotic processes to foster in children the mature capacity for affectivity, integral to genuinely *communal* lives and practices. Cathy Urwin makes a related point: "The separation between affect and cognition in Piaget's theory by-passes the question of what actually motivates children's communications; and the universalist paradigm . . . renders the study of systematic differences in development inaccessible within the account."[62] The alienated and estranged autonomous individual who is the exemplary mature adult for Piaget and Kohlberg—the end product of the "natural" maturation process—emerges as a solitary creature on an indifferent landscape peopled by rational Others with whom his contact is primarily competitive and otherwise largely devoid of meaning. Experientially, in the gendered imaginary of predominately white patriarchal societies, such forms of estrangement will seem unnatural to many women and other Others: morally-politically it is not easy to see how they can conduce to the viable, productive, and respectful cohabitation with one another and with(in) the world where "we" live, which is the goal of many feminist, ecological, and other postcolonial projects.

Normalizing

Normalizing consequences and naturalizing practices are inextricably intertwined, as naturalistic inquiry normalizes certain experiences, certain ways of being, and in so doing puts in place standards according to which behaviors, among them putative knowings, can be cast as acceptable, "normal," or aberrant. Developmental analyses normalize the trajectory toward maturity fostered in a "normal" affluent white heterosexual two-parent patriarchal family, reading past the power relations patriarchy enacts and the abuses of women and children it condones within the confines of a protected, private domain. Yet the often-invisible ubiquity of patriarchal power relations makes of the idea of a "normal," situationally neutral developmental line more a fiction (a fabrication) than a natural fact. (The variations exposed in Walkerdine's three bears

61. Willett, *Maternal Ethics*, 32.
62. Urwin, "Power Relations," 269.

study illustrate this point.) Feminist developmentalists have to look at power in a new way within child raising situations, to show (again in Urwin's words) how "desert-islanded" images of mother-child relations preempt "any examination of material conditions, ideology and questions of power."[63]

In short, "normal" rarely functions as a simple descriptive in philosophy, psychology, or everyday discourse: deviations from or failures to achieve the putatively normal—whether it is a cognitive-developmental stage, an IQ score, an acceptable sexuality, an achieved femininity—invite disapproval and evoke strategies for improvement or correction. The very idea of "the normal child" performs a powerful regulative function, generating acute anxieties, constant monitoring, and a range of compensatory measures when a child appears not to fit within it.[64] A normal girl and a normal boy are likewise imagined and fostered in developmental practices, with ensuing coercive pressures to conform to gender-specific patterns. Thus although some critics take naturalistic epistemology to task for being merely descriptive, claiming that it falls short of the normative, criteria-establishing demands a real theory of knowledge should address,[65] my interest, by contrast, is in the normative force of the descriptions by which it tacitly normalizes a certain set of mothers, fathers, and infants/children, together with familial-social, teacher-pupil, and other comparable relationships. My intention in this chapter thus has been to ask what kind of engagement with childhood—childhoods—an appropriately power-sensitive developmental epistemology must promote if it is to avoid gross reductionism at one end of a spectrum and anecdotal randomness at the other, so that it can foster better, more responsible cohabitation than individualistic thinking can allow.

Given the complicity of mainstream epistemology and psychology in sustaining a patriarchal social order; given the extent to which that very social order underwrites "pure white," humanly and ecologically exploitative practices, *feminist* epistemology, even naturalized, cannot simply "fall . . . into place as a chapter of psychology and hence of natural science,"[66] as Quine would have it, for the gender politics of psychology and natural science are plainly not in order as they stand. In this chapter I have looked at the theoretical assumptions and practices of Piagetian developmental psychology and its successors, from which "the natural child" emerges more as a construct according

---

63. Ibid., 270.
64. See, e.g., Wong, "Adventures in Socio-Historical Meta-Epistemology."
65. See, e.g., Kim, "What Is 'Naturalized Epistemology'"?
66. Quine, "Epistemology Naturalized," 25.

to a preexisting model than as a discovery, although my purpose is not to essentialize developmental psychology by representing it as a unified project or its practices as uniform or univocal. I have offered a sampling of projects—Wittgenstein's observations of childhood participation in forms of life and the feminist work of Burman, Walkerdine, hooks, Willett, and others—which I read ecologically, if variously, for how they situate childhood within larger structures of habitus and ethos, where place, language, sociality, affectivity, culture, race, and other ecological specificities inflect and inform development both as theory and practice. In exposing the partiality of its universalist pretensions, these theorists' innovative readings of developmentality are unsettling to Piagetian orthodoxy. I have, moreover, criticized epistemologists' dismissals of appeals to psychology as "psychologism" and taken issue with psychological practices whose effects are to normalize and naturalize the abstract individuals who are the subjects-objects of their inquiry and hence to preserve conceptions of human development that erase the differences and the ecological particularities integral—on my view—to human corporeal, cognitive, moral, and affective experiences.

"The Child as Fact and Artifact"

Who, then, or what is this child whom I represent as both fact and artifact, both found and made? Just as, for Quinean naturalists, the human knower is a *factual* physical entity, a natural kind whose cognitive processes are available to objective inspection, so, too, for Piagetians and their successors the child is the natural, *factual* given in genetic inquiry. Neither Piagetians nor Quineans consider the possibility that this very "natural" kind—this human knower, this child—might be *as much* an *artifact* of experimental settings and observations as a natural given. Hence the background assumptions that govern Gopnik and Meltzoff's studies of the child who emerges as a little theorist—in their "theory-theory"—work from a template that naturalizes this picture of the child, both before and after the fact, much as Quinean naturalism naturalizes its subject and its object. The template stylizes "the child," and aggregates real children, around attributes and relationships to their human and other surroundings that are commonly found and nurtured in "normal" white, middle-class, male infants and children.

Nor do intimations of social constructivism sit well with cognitive-science-based developmental theorists, who tend to caricature it as antithetical to realism, hence symptomatic of a postmodern slide into chaos. Again, Gopnik and Meltzoff are typical in this regard. They deflate constructivism into socialization and chide would-be constructivists as follows: "Assimilating *all* cognitive development to the model of socialization is, however, a dreadful mistake, allied to the dreadful mistake of postmodernism in general. . . . Purely social-constructivist views discount this fundamental link between mind and the world."[67] Were this view not so common a misreading of social constructivism in its multiple modalities, it would merit no further comment. Nothing in the contra-Piagetian positions I have discussed attributes *all* cognitive development to socialization or disregards the child as an embodied, feeling, needy being who is really, corporeally, materially, *there*, part of the social and physical world in which it learns to *be*, where its knowing, doing, feeling, and judging come to be possible. Nowhere do Gopnik and Meltzoff offer an account of the "postmodernism in general" that they cast as a dreadful mistake; hence it is impossible to agree or disagree with them. But the successes of some postmodern theories in opening out and exposing the oppressions, exclusions, and colonizing practices, and the narcissism consequent upon humanistic assumptions of universal human sameness, caution against so peremptory a dismissal. The range of positions characterized, and characterizing themselves, as postmodern—of which feminism itself, on many readings, including my own, counts as one—leave references to postmodernism in general as empty as they are unilluminating. Thus it is impossible to take this condemnation seriously.

For the positions I have drawn on for positive insights in this discussion, the child is at once thrown into and shaped by the world of which it is a part: made but not determined; yet not merely influenced superficially, as the language of socialization implies, with the sense that its effects are mere accretions to a core being who remains somehow discoverable beneath them: accretions that could be stripped away and the "real" child, or adult, would emerge. Children—real, embodied, feeling, and feeding children—are born into complexes of familial-social-material-cultural-affective meanings and expectations and studied within disciplinary expectations sufficiently powerful to shape, *even if they do not determine*, who the child can be, what she can know, how she can respond and negotiate with and within the affective, social, geographical, and ecological situations where she participates in constructing her becoming-adult subjectivity. The seemingly simple contrast between the interlocking grid of semantic, responsive, and material expectations in which white American girl children enact their subjectivity in Gilligan's account and those within which black American girl children enact their subjectivity in

---

67. Gopnik and Meltzoff, *Words, Thoughts, and Theories*, 72 (emphasis original).

hooks's example poses a telling challenge to any idea that "the child" could be extracted from the conditions that make her particularly realized maturation possible and could be transplanted to mature, interchangeably, in a frame so different that she could not *be* the same person within it. The normalizing assumption that she should, nonetheless, *want to* conform to the standard group—to be "just like *us*"—attests further to the colonializing effects of dominant norms. Why ever would she? An example Burman cites complements Walkerdine's three bears example and confirms the oddity of thinking she might: When the African Kpelle were asked "how a wise man" would organize piles of food and household items together, in a project designed to demonstrate that they had mastered Piaget-style classification by similarity, they consistently failed to sort as the researcher expected. Only when, in despair, the researcher asked how "a fool would do it" did they present a typical western classification by type, rather than sorting by function, according to how the items would be used.[68] Convincingly, Burman reads the example as further evidence of the incapacity of a unitary developmental model to deal with differences from a preexisting picture, from an instituted imaginary, except as aberrations, deviations, from a normal, linear path.

Disenchanted with post-Kantian "philosophical psychology's" speculative, introspective approach—its belief in "a power peculiar to philosophical thought, which, in determining the preliminary methods necessary for science, places itself above it"—Jean Piaget argues for the superiority of "scientific psychology."[69] Yet for all the differences in their conceptions of scientific psychology, Piagetians and post-Quinean naturalists work from assumptions of human sameness that block adequate engagement with the constitutive differences on which feminist and other postcolonial inquiry focuses. Claiming a formalistic advantage, Piagetians and Quineans stand outside the fray of knowledge making, as spectators "from nowhere." Thus dislocated, their specificities as inquirers need count for naught; and the specificities of objects of inquiry count likewise for naught, be they physical objects or human subjects. Scientific inquiry thus invoked is about uniformity, lawlike behaviors, deductively achieved conclusions, none of which need address the kinds of idiosyncratic, local variations that ecological thinking, both literally and metaphorically conceived, requires.

68. Burman, *Deconstructing Developmental Psychology*, 183, citing *Cultural Context of Learning and Thinking* by Cole et al.
69. Piaget, *Insights and Illusions of Philosophy*, 57.

There are indeed modes of inquiry in which abstract formalism, uniformity, and lawlike deduction are quite fitting: logic and mathematics are the most frequently cited, together with the processes integral to achieving good, reliable prediction. Yet once inquiry locates itself down on the ground, ecologically, in the midst of and answerable to the specific integrity of real people's cognitive practices and places, it faces imperatives extending as far beyond the walls of the laboratory as beyond those of the philosopher's study. These are about responsible inquiry, about being "true to" the experiential-material situatedness of everyday knowings. No longer can inquiry assume before-the-fact (= a priori) sameness of human subjects either as inquirers or inquired into/ about; nor can it assume before-the-fact (= a priori) objective rational sameness on the part of inquirers themselves, whose inevitable "situatedness" cannot, epistemologically, remain *hors de question*. Neither can it mask its artifactual side, casting its object of inquiry—"the child"—in a predetermined (a priori after all) image of a situationally indifferent, naturally developing biological organism.

Most strange is the support these assumptions have provided for the belief that *people*—subjects who are the objects of inquiry—can adequately be known in this disconnected way, a belief which I address more fully in chapter six, whose social scientific adherents must restrict their observations to separate, discrete behaviors and overt utterances of people extracted from the circumstances that generate those behaviors and make them possible, appropriate, and meaningful. Inquirers who endorse such an approach must extract their subjects-objects of study from their affective, cultural, racial, economic circumstances; from their corporeal specificities as variously gendered, raced, aged, abled beings; and from the narratives that carry their psychosocial histories, constructing and constantly reconstructing the meanings shaping their lives and making them who they are.

Most curious about these assumptions from a developmental point of view is that, in the affluent societies where most studies of "normal" children are—presumptuously—conducted and for whom most studies are written, recognizing nurturant others, learning what she or he can expect of them, comprises the very earliest infant learning.[70] An infant learns to respond affectively-cognitively, and insistently, to carers who touch, hold, and feed her long before she can name the simplest physical object: her access to the objects she comes to know is embedded in and mediated by affective-linguistic-cognitive relations with carers, and not just intersubjectively, but

70. I argue this point more fully in my *What Can She Know?* chap. 2.

within and in relation to culturally, situationally, and historically specific social practices. Studies of the effects of sensory-emotional "deprivation" in the development of subjectivity, sociality, and agency (of which the example of the Wild Child of Aveyron is best known to western theorists) show how closely a child's growing capacity to make trusting sense of and within the world, both physical and personal, is bound up with her caregivers' capacity to offer nurturance[71]—a capacity shaped, enabled, and/or thwarted, in its turn, by the material-social-educational value-saturated situations where their (attempted) caregiving occurs. Western-designed studies of childhood in so-called developing countries complicate the issue radically in their efforts to translate this culturally specific model of childhood innocence and unimpeded progress into social situations where children may have to be differently savvy, and often reliant on their own devices, just in order to survive.[72] There is no neutral originary place, no untouched "individual," no pure moment amenable to being separated out for study.

Yet there are practices, myriad practices, communal, collective, and loving practices, isolated, fearful, and desperate practices: these are the places where ecological subjectivity begins and is encouraged, ignored, or impeded; where knowledge is produced and where, I am urging, it has to be studied, developmentally. Nor can the idea that knowledge, necessarily, grows out of or is blocked in such a range of practices and places be read as a simple amendment to or expansion of established epistemological wisdom. As all ecological thinking must, it poses a radical challenge to the individualistic tradition of unnegotiated empiricism, resituates and reconfigures it, rewrites its agenda. Taking seriously Wittgenstein's demonstration that the norms of cognitive practice are fundamentally social, Walkerdine's and Burman's that they have to be studied in their material-cultural situatedness, and Willett's that they are as affective as they are rational, I have offered some suggestions as to how feminist developmental psychology and feminist epistemology can work toward an ecologically naturalized approach to questions of developing subjectivity and agency. One of the principal pieces of that project will be to interrogate the unquestioned veneration of autonomy as a goal of individual development and as an often-imposed if not coerced goal of policies designed to promote development for the people and places a well-meaning liberal democracy represents as "less fortunate"—than *we* are.

71. A classic study is Goldfarb, "Effects of Psychological Deprivation."
72. See in this regard Burman's astute analysis of the cultural imperialism of Anglo-U.S. developmental psychology, *Deconstructing Developmental Psychology*, 183–89.

*What have I to say about freedom and the self? I wondered whether I should not
point out that all the components of the philosophy of the self in the West
have . . . had a liberating effect . . . but point out, too, that this philosophy was
undermined by aspects unforeseen and at the time unforeseeable, repressive
aspects having to do with phallocentric and colonial patterns of speech. . . . Might it
not be necessary to do two things at once: to emphasize both the permanent value
of the philosophy of rights, and, simultaneously, the inadequacy, the limits of the
breakthrough it represented?*

—Hélène Cixous, "We Who Are Free, Are We Free?"

5

PATTERNS OF AUTONOMY,
ACKNOWLEDGMENT, AND ADVOCACY

The Perversion of Autonomy

Autonomy, at once a goal of individual development and, latterly, of policies
designed to promote "development" for people and places that a well-meaning
liberal democracy sees as "less fortunate" than *we* are, stands as a cornerstone of
Enlightenment thought, whose developmental imaginary I discuss in chapter
four. It has figured, also, as an emancipatory ideal in feminist, antiracist, and
postcolonial analyses of oppression, subjection, subjectivity, and agency—the
inheritors of the philosophy of rights—and in activism informed by these analyses. Yet even while acknowledging autonomy's incontestable liberatory appeal
in the post-Enlightenment, postcolonial social imaginary, in this chapter I
engage critically with it, prompted by an unease with the autonomy-saturated
theories and rhetoric that infuse affluent western social-political spaces at the
beginning of the twenty-first century. This rhetoric, I will argue, holds in place a
regulative autonomy ideal whose effects, paradoxically, are as coercive as they

are liberating, as effective in sustaining oppression and subjection as in inspiring release from heteronomy. Yet, consciously generating a tension as it does so, my inquiry confirms the very point it challenges: autonomy's emancipatory promise for women and other Others who, in their marginality, have had scant access to the autonomy that members of advantaged social groups take unquestioningly for granted.[1]

While it carries a fairly traditional core sense of self-reliance, of self-determination, of shaking off the fetters of heteronomy so as to be able to reason, judge, act for oneself, autonomy figures in my analysis here in variations on, shadings and derivatives of, that central concept. One cluster of meanings is primarily epistemological, another is social and economic, yet these are not distinct and separate one from the other: they are mutually, reciprocally constitutive, often working together in autonomy-promoting actions even though they can be separated for purposes of analysis. The meanings that bear on epistemic autonomy have to do with thinking for oneself and being able where necessary to distinguish knowledge issues, judiciously, from values and vested interests, with not being unduly reliant on others' testimony or tutelage or unduly in thrall to emotions or passions. Thus they are about people's capacity to regulate their actions and practices by principles they are ready to own, to avoid being swayed by impulse alone. In all of these modes, autonomy requires an ability to distinguish a just measure of influence from a reversion to heteronomous dependency. The term's social-economic connotations are about freedom from oppression, where autonomy refers to a self-sufficiency, manifested in access to the social freedom, material resources, and other supports required to make and act upon decisions about how to live. Both epistemic and social, in a sense especially pertinent to my argument in this book, is a mode of autonomy realized in being appropriately knowledgeable and well situated to invite and expect the *acknowledgment* for knowledge claims, testimony, both public and private, for which social-political credibility and authority seems to be a sine qua non in the imaginary of hierarchically ordered societies. Moreover, in thinking ecologically about autonomy, I understand it as not an exclusively individual achievement or attribute, but as a characterization also appropriate for social groups and even societies—recalling and elaborating Castoriadis's reference, which I cite in chapter one, to the critical-creative activity of a society that exhibits its autonomy in its capacity to put itself in question.[2]

1. Parts of this chapter are drawn from my "Perversion of Autonomy."
2. See Castoriadis, "Radical Imagination."

My analysis, then, thinks through some enactments of autonomy from the standpoint of an ecologically conceived sociability and community to show how, as an ideal, autonomy can in fact be as complicit with larger oppressive structures as it can be subversive of them. Yet my intention is not to resolve this tension, but to think productively within it. Focusing on *advocacy* relations, I will engage critically with certain "perversions" that currently season autonomy's capitalist patriarchal enactments, in an attempt to disentangle its aspirational-inspirational appeal from its repressive dimensions.

Advocacy, likewise, carries multiple connotations, derived initially from its legal usage where an advocate pleads—argues—the cause/case of another before a court or a tribunal. In the extended meanings that inform my argument in this chapter, it moves from the courtroom to everyday lives, where it has to do with defending or espousing a cause by arguing in its favor; speaking on behalf of, supporting, vindicating, recommending someone, some project, some policy, in respect to a particular issue or point of view; representing someone/some group in order to counter patterns of silencing, discounting, incredulity, and other egregious harms. It can take place in individual and communal practices: someone may advocate on her own behalf or on behalf of (an)other person(s), may advocate in favor of the significance, cogency, validity, credibility of another person's testimony, of the testimony of several people, a group, institution, or society. It is particularly in this last range of practices that advocacy carries epistemological force within the power and privilege structures of hierarchical societies: as a cluster of liberatory practices whose goal is to (re)enfranchise epistemically disadvantaged, marginalized, disenfranchised Others.

Working with these conceptual resources, my principal contention in this chapter is in fact a contentious one: I will propose that *practices of advocacy often make knowledge possible* within hierarchical distributions of autonomy and authority and in institutional divisions of intellectual labor in western societies, where those lacking the autonomy that social and economic self-sufficiency provides tend in consequence to be excluded from the epistemic autonomy that would ensure and secure their recognition as knowers whose claims to know are to be taken seriously. Advocacy, in such situations, performs a liberatory function. It counts as a main ingredient in the medical and legal epistemic negotiations I discuss in chapter three; advocacy practices are integral to the work of Rachel Carson and Karen Messing, and thence to the promotion of ecologically conceived epistemic community, where the interdependence and trust integral to ideal cohabitation are valued and practiced. Moreover, advocacy at its best can, I believe, preserve autonomy from certain perversions to which it is prone in early-twenty-first-century societies.

The tension I have generated signals a rupture between sedimented conceptions of a unified subjectivity of Kantian origin and late-twentieth-century decenterings of the human subject that unsettle some of the founding assumptions of Enlightenment-liberal autonomy, whose effects I discuss in a different register, in chapter six.[3] Variations—often hyperbolized—on notions of self-transparency and self-reliance frame the picture of human selves regulatively operative in the instituted social-political imaginary of liberal democratic societies, a picture remarkably resistant to acknowledging the "repressive aspects," the "inadequacy" that Hélène Cixous mentions. Yet as I will argue both here and in chapter six, it is hard, now, to believe that this western self with its constitutive rights and responsibilities can go on claiming to be the self, or indeed that (anthropologically-geographically) it ever was the self for whom autonomy ideals were, and still often are, imagined. Consequent upon the influences of Freudian theory, Nietzschean genealogy, and postcolonial, post–World War II, and post-1968 political upheavals, late-twentieth-century social theory has radically unsettled the ideal unified, self-determining subjectivity whose achievement is the *telos* of Piagetian developmental processes. It evinces skepticism about the "controllability of our own doing" that makes self-determination a plausible goal and interrogates the very idea of a subject so transparent to her/himself as classical autonomy ideals assume. Conjoined with a post-Wittgensteinian, post-Saussurean linguistic turn that contests the subject's presumed capacities to "constitute or exhaust meaning" and thus to claim authorship of its own being,[4] such challenges destabilize liberal assumptions of self-ownership and self-mastery. Together with historical-material interrogations of classical autonomy's imagined basis in circumstantial-locational homogeneity, these lines of thought tell *against* the plausibility of the self-conception orthodox autonomy theories presuppose.

The tension I engage with, then, sets up an opposition between an entrenched, indeed escalating, promotion of autonomy ideals in the social rhetoric of white affluent liberal societies and practical-empirical demonstrations that the ideals cannot hold. A hyperbolized vision of autonomy tenaciously dominates the social imaginary—the common sense—of affluent white western

3. See Honneth, *Fragmented World*, chap. 16, "Decentered Autonomy." Hiley examines tensions between autonomy and community in *Philosophy in Question*, chap. 2: "We have retained eighteenth-century conceptions of freedom which have as their central feature the idea of individual self-determination, yet we seem no longer able . . . to support both our autonomy and genuine community" (63).

4. The phrases cited are Honneth's, *Fragmented World*, 261, to whom I am indebted in framing these issues. See also chap. 14, "The Limits of Liberalism."

societies, descriptively configuring and prescriptively animating discourses of self-sufficient individualism where "autonomous man" stands as an iconic figure, emblematic of self-reliant self-making.[5] Talk about having a "life plan," "being one's own person," infuses social-political discourse, urging self-determination as though it were, without question, desirable *and* possible.[6] This gap between empirical exposures of structural impediments to achieving it and a social rhetoric persistently heralding it as a universal entitlement holds ideal autonomy at such a distance from everyday lives and practices that, for many feminists and other Others, it reduces to a hollow promise from a bygone era.

In that era—in its Kantian origins—autonomy is imagined as man's *"emergence from . . . self-incurred immaturity,"* an immaturity endemic to heteronomy manifested in an "inability to use one's own understanding without the guidance of another." As the Kantian motto *"Sapere aude!*—have the courage to use your *own* understanding!"—announces, emancipation is a task "for each separate individual." It is the "duty of all men to think for themselves," to cultivate "their own minds,"[7] so as to escape the shackles of heteronomy. Yet noting the limited reach of the "all" in his 1984 reading of Kant's essay, Michel Foucault asks, "Are we to understand that the entire human race is caught up in the process of Enlightenment?"[8] Kant's remark that, for the majority of people, "*including the entire fair sex,*" the move to maturity will be too difficult and dangerous[9] anticipates the negative answer Foucault expects. Neither is the "freedom to make *public use* of one's reason in all matters"[10] universally available in societies whose hierarchical social arrangements determine *whose* rational utterances are worthy of a public hearing, whose voices merit acknowledgment, thus preserving areas of heteronomy even where autonomy is touted as a universal option. Such exclusions work differently in diverse cultural-historical-ecological situations, running as much along class,

5. Note that individual*istic* subjectivity and agency (and thus also individual*ism*) contrast with North American vernacular talk of "individuals" to mean "people." They contrast also with individual*ity*, which is not under threat in these contestations of its boundary claims.

6. Schmitt discusses how the "autonomy of the philosophers" culminates in the need for a "rational life plan" in *Beyond Separateness*, 4–6. See also Walker, *Moral Contexts*, chap. 6, "Career Selves," where she develops a trenchant analysis of how "career selves," with the autonomy they require, are out of reach for many people—especially in this chapter, older women.

7. Kant, "What Is Enlightenment?" 54–55 (emphasis original).

8. Foucault, "What Is Enlightenment?" 35.

9. Kant, "What Is Enlightenment?" 54 (emphasis added).

10. Ibid., 55 (emphasis original). "Freedom to make *public use* of one's reason" is Foucault's gloss on Kant's *sapere aude!* injunction.

race, and other lines of power and privilege as along lines drawn by membership in "the fair sex." They count among the reasons why advocacy claims a central place in my argument here. Yet for autonomy's defenders, these exclusions are inconsequential to a universal release from thralldom, to a stark individualism fueled by the assumption that autonomous man in his radical self-making is free to sidestep the constraints of materiality and the hegemony of instituted social-political structures and *should* act accordingly.

In *The Unnatural Lottery*, Claudia Card discusses feminist disenchantment with this Kantian—and latterly, Rawlsian—assumption that "we can all act as duty requires, come what may," that "our goodness (or badness) is entirely up to us," a conviction whose effects are to banish people whose circumstances are so oppressive and damaging, so immobilizing as to block all routes to autonomous agency, behind a (different, non-Rawlsian) veil of ignorance where they need not be known and cannot claim acknowledgment as knowers. She is "skeptical of Kant's apparent assumption that the same basic character development is accessible to everyone."[11] Guiding her project, Card explains, is a belief that

> it is not enough to confront the inequities of the "natural lottery"
> from which we inherit various physical and psychological assets and
> liabilities. It is important also to reflect on the *unnatural* lottery
> created by networks of unjust institutions and histories that bequeath
> to us further inequities in our starting positions and that violate
> principles that would have addressed, if not redressed, inequities of
> nature.[12]

In the "perversion of autonomy" I name in the title of this section, these circumstances figure not merely as descriptive but as prescriptively coercive, in societies permeated by the imperatives of an overblown, ecologically insensitive autonomy ideal, conjoined with a stark individualism. It demands a level of physical, psychological, situational, material overcoming of real obstacles that are insurmountable except for a privileged few. In so doing, it distorts, undermines the liberatory promise of the Enlightenment ideal by condemning to failure those who, in good faith, endeavor to realize its promise. Hence its

11. Card, *Unnatural Lottery*, 3–4. The title plays on Rawls's claim that the distribution of natural human assets is decided by a "natural lottery" that is "arbitrary from a moral perspective" (*Theory of Justice*, 74). The members of a society "satisfying the principles of justice as fairness... are *autonomous* and the obligations they recognize self-imposed" (13, emphasis added).

12. Card, *Unnatural Lottery*, 20 (emphasis original).

"unforeseeable, repressive aspects," of which Cixous speaks. In what follows, I try to think through the autonomy-*thwarting* effects of some of these unjust coercions. Autonomy in its hegemonic modes, I suggest, is a locally specific ideal, prone to exceed its reach. Margaret Walker aptly notes: "A certain kind of society holds out to us, and gives some of us, to varying degrees and at different costs, the gift of (roughly) autonomous lives."[13] Because the scope of its easy realization encompasses most of the social spaces inhabited by the upholders of individualistic autonomy—whom Sabina Lovibond aptly dubs "worshippers of the individual"[14]—its local specificity tends to recede from view.

In this chapter, then, I highlight a curious rhetorical genealogy in which a hyperbolized version of autonomy has become a controlling, even a dystopian ideal, particularly in the United States and, derivatively, in Canada. This powerful (regional) confluence of autonomy and individualism issues in a cluster of regulative principles whose effects are as negative as they are positive for hitherto marginalized people. Epistemologically and morally-politically, it casts advocacy, epistemic negotiation, and other forms of interdependence as marks of weakness, of immaturity, as falling beneath the threshold of rational respectability. It nourishes a social-political-epistemic imaginary visibly peopled by the self-reliant rational maximizer, the autonomous moral agent, the disinterested self-sufficient knower, and the rational economic man of late capitalism, to name only the most familiar tropes, *invisibly* peopled by less consequential, because less perfectly autonomous, Others. My autonomy-skepticism echoes the title of Willard Gaylin and Bruce Jennings's book, *The Perversion of Autonomy*, whose authors contend, and I concur: "Autonomy's success in the struggle for the American moral imagination has made it overbearing and overweening"; and "the imperialism and arrogance of autonomy must be bridled."[15] Although my reading of its implications differ from theirs, this imperialism fuels the tension I have signaled, as women's (and other Others') legitimate struggles to claim an autonomy that has never been theirs confront *perversions* of autonomy in affluent parts of the western world.

Ecologically speaking, the terms of this tension are writ large in an opposition between stark autonomy and what I am calling "advocacy practices," which include representing, arguing for, recommending, acting or engaging in projects of inquiry and intervention in support or on behalf of someone or some group of people. These practices, I propose, are integral to the very

13. Walker, *Moral Understandings*, 151.
14. Lovibond, *Realism and Imagination*, 169.
15. Gaylin and Jennings, *Perversion of Autonomy*, 5, 24.

possibility of developing an *instituting* social imaginary that is capable of promoting social conditions of cohabitability in the best sense, upheld by networks of responsible epistemic practices. My principal interest in this chapter is in how advocacy plays into a politics of knowledge where "advocacy research" tends to function as a derogatory label, to be invoked to dismiss research apparently undertaken to serve "special" as contrasted with universal (read: "dominant") interests, and where credibility is conferred or withheld in unevenly distributed patterns of acknowledgment: recognizing or discounting the experiences of certain would-be knowers as knowledgeable, granting or refusing their testimony fair hearing, facilitating or blocking their participation in authoritative, emancipatory epistemic practices. Nonstandard (= nonmale, nonaffluent, nonwhite) members of epistemic communities often occupy starting positions from which it is literally impossible (practically, if not logically) for them to achieve positive outcomes "without the guidance of another," while offering "guidance" can itself mutate into an exploitative move.

Advocacy and autonomy function oppositionally in the individualistic discourses that permeated the social-welfare debates of the 1990s, where the mythologized "individual" achievements of autonomous man produced as their foil and negative counterexample a reinstituted *subjection* of women, in a process that, structurally, recapitulates the subjection to paternalistic tutelage John Stuart Mill sought to counter in the mid-nineteenth century.[16] Women tend, variously, to be discounted as unreliable narrators-knowers of their experiences and circumstances, women on welfare as failing to meet certain standards of civic self-sufficiency, women seeking child care as inadequately autonomous in assuming responsibility for their own choices, all represented as "entirely up to them." All of these modalities are exaggerated for nonwhite, nonheterosexual, non-middle-class and untold numbers of otherwise "othered" women (and men), socially positioned so that they cannot readily use their own understandings without the guidance of another and claim a serious, respectful hearing, and so that they are especially vulnerable to unscrupulous offers of guidance.

With its focus on sociability, community, and ideals of responsible cohabitation, the ecologically modeled conceptual apparatus I am constructing in this book works against the autonomy/advocacy opposition thus produced, to counter autonomy's hyperbolic excesses, while demonstrating the power of judiciously realized interdependence to foster livable sociality and community. It is both diagnostic and prescriptive: locating itself down on the ground, it is

16. Mill, *Subjection of Women.*

informed as much by the rhetorical effects of autonomy imperatives for peoples' lives and situations—their habitat in Raymond Williams's sense, which I discuss in chapter one[17]—as by philosophical-conceptual analyses of autonomy "as such."

Epistemic Autonomy, Testimony, and Advocacy

The hyperbolized autonomy ideal I have been discussing permeates the epistemologies of mastery that trade upon an image of autonomous man: the ubiquitous, invisible expert/authority, who stands above the fray to view "from nowhere" the truths the world reveals to a mind prepared. Epistemic autonomy is a complex ideal that I paint here with broad strokes. The autonomous knower escapes the governance of the body, thus transcending reliance on the senses, to cultivate reason freed from distracting influences. Neither for a Cartesian disembodied reasoner nor for a merely incidentally embodied empiricist knower can knowledge-productive effects derive from the specificities—the physicality and physical locatedness—of embodied existence. Epistemic autonomy celebrates an escape from the influences of Bacon's "Idols,"[18] from the particularities of location, experience, and identity. Hyperbolized, it shapes the stark objectivism of twentieth-century scientistic positivism, where it is abstract individuals who know, each a potential surrogate for every other because they are never individuated. Continuous with Kant's injunctions, autonomy is also about thinking for oneself, having the courage to use one's own understanding. Epistemic self-reliance is its watchword: freedom from dogma, opinion, or hearsay and from subjection to the heteronomy of higher authority, whether sacred or secular. In its everyday moments, it translates into a reluctance to consult, and especially to rely on, other people in knowing, thinking, and doing.

The appeal of epistemic autonomy is clear. Transcending the confusion of sensory, social, emotional, locational particularity promises the certain knowledge that only objective detachment can deliver. And within controlled circumstances, success has seemed to be achievable: physical and technological science extend "man's" mastery and control to fuel this autonomous dream,

17. I use the term to capture the social-material-historical-ecological dimensions of situatedness. See chap. one, n. 3.

18. According to Tiles and Tiles, Bacon's four "Idols"—the idol of the tribe, the theater, the marketplace, and the cave—classify "the various false ideas which obscure and interfere with our grasping the true objects of knowledge" (*Introduction to Historical Epistemology*, 37).

perpetuating the social imaginary that sustains it and disqualifying more frankly *situated* contenders from recognition as knowers.[19] Thus epistemic autonomy generates structures of authority and expertise where the power to predict, manipulate, and control objects of knowledge—both human and nonhuman—informs and guides inquiry. As the histories of paternalism and colonialism in white western societies amply demonstrates, it is but a short step to the place where autonomous man in his epistemic robes claims a responsibility to think and know for Others too immature to escape the constraints of heteronomy, thus to know their own interests or understand their experiences. Epistemic heteronomy has long been women's lot under patriarchy, manifested at its most outrageous in a conviction that women cannot know the truth even of their own experiences. Autonomy's persistence as a feminist goal is thus easy to understand, despite the antifeminist consequences of its hyperbolic invocations. Systemically, it has remained out of reach for many women and other Others. Small wonder, then, that successor epistemology projects committed to destabilizing power-infused patterns of epistemic authority often incorporate strategies for achieving epistemic autonomy by or for those who still dwell in (enforced) tutelage: for autonomy as the "freedom to make public use of one's reason," the "courage to use [one's] own understanding."

Testimony's uneven reception merits special attention in this regard. As I have argued elsewhere and maintained in earlier chapters of this book, of the classical sources of empirical knowledge, testimony has long ranked a distant third on a scale of epistemic respectability, yielding pride of place to the putatively more direct, more self-reliant, and putatively reliable, processes of perception and memory.[20] Its source in experiential specificity puts testimony's detached replicability in question; and its *situatedness*, its positioning as *someone's* speech act, places it closer to opinion, hearsay, than to sanitized—thus again putatively more trustworthy—sources of knowledge. Hence denigrations of testimony in epistemology and the politics of knowledge insist on and reinforce an imagined cognitive autonomy. Testimony challenges this imaginary, for it functions as a constant reminder of how minuscule a proportion of anyone's knowledge, with the possible exception of occurrent sensory input, is *or could be* acquired independently, without reliance on

19. Recall Haraway's "situated knowledges," which I discuss in chap. three, where she rejects any suggestion that knowers can perform "the god-trick" of extracting themselves from the world to know "from nowhere," and her elaboration, in *Modest_Witness*, of the conception of situated knowledges that eschew illusions of epistemic autonomy.

20. See my *Rhetorical Spaces*, chap. 3, "Incredulity, Experientialism, and the Politics of Knowledge."

others. In an elaborated sense of learning from other people, from cultural wisdom embedded in everyday language, from books, media, conversations, journals, standard academic and secular sources of information, testimony makes knowledgeable living possible. Thus it is curious for epistemologists to discredit testimony for offering evidence *not* achieved independently, at first-hand, given its function as the starting point for so many epistemic negotiations and justificatory projects. Such negotiations are commonly as dependent upon testimony's variable credibility as on perception and/or memory singly conceived. Yet despite overwhelming everyday evidence of "our" fundamental reliance on testimony, and indeed on advocacy, the image of the self-reliant knower directly confronting the world continues to play a regulative part in mainstream epistemology such that, if the image could not be held intact, the basic tenets of the system would no longer hold. With other feminist epistemologists, I am contending that indeed they cannot continue to hold.

In its "flattened" moments, when it replicates simple ("*S*-knows-that-*p*") knowledge claims and can be assimilated to aural perceptual-observational knowledge, testimony is most amenable to formal epistemological analysis: "Jane said she knew that Sally had fed Spot."[21] Here it finds its greatest credibility, at scant remove from perception and memory. But when it moves closer to frankly and more elaborated personal reporting, testimony no longer claims the replicability required of orthodox empirical knowledge claims, and its credibility diminishes. Testimony is seldom concerned with generalities, universals. More commonly, it is about particularity, about concrete things that "merely happen," a feature that contributes to its uneasy relations with objectivist theories. Curiously, as Thomas Nagel notes: "Something in the ordinary idea of knowledge must explain why it seems to be undermined by any influences on belief not within the control of the subject—so that knowledge seems impossible without an impossible foundation in autonomous reason."[22] Hence a sensitive epistemology of particularity, responsibly attentive to testimony, appears to face two choices: it must either relinquish its claims to count as an epistemology or push against the boundaries of the orthodoxy to demonstrate its own peculiar effectiveness in addressing issues on which epistemic and moral agents require guidance. Here I opt for the second alternative: for an epistemology-morality that (borrowing Margaret Walker's words) "bears a far greater *descriptive* and *empirical* burden,

---

21. For such analyses, see Fricker, "Epistemology of Testimony"; and Coady, "Testimony and Observation." For a fuller account of his position, see Coady, *Testimony*.

22. Nagel, *Mortal Questions*, 36.

in pursuing details of actual moral [and epistemic] arrangements, than it is commonly thought to entail."[23] And yet beginning in particularity need not entail remaining there, enmeshed in the minutiae of the concrete, unable to escape the merely experiential, a point I will develop further in chapter six. Anne Seller's claim that "as an isolated individual, I often do not know what my experiences are" and Ludwig Wittgenstein's that "knowledge is in the end based on acknowledgment," which I have cited elsewhere, capture the limitations of the autonomy-of-knowledge credo.[24] In a hegemonic social imaginary where testimony risks being discounted because of the testifier's disenfranchised position in the social-epistemic order or because of her/his failure of self-reliance, gaining acknowledgment requires more than the courage "to use one's own understanding," more than an individual resolve to make free "public use of [one's] reason." Membership in "the fair sex" has counted as but one such disenfranchised position: a sex whose very "fairness" annuls expectations of fair acknowledgment.

Advocacy, like testimony only more so, seems to defy the Kantian injunction that requires using "*one's own* understanding without the guidance of another." Nor is it surprising that it should, in media-saturated societies familiar with tales of lawyers' advocating *for* their clients, with the overriding goal of winning, even within the dictates of legal limits on misrepresentation. Beliefs that advocacy, by definition, abdicates respect for truth gain in plausibility from such practices. Analogously, as my chapter three discussion suggests, in received medical discourse, a sharp distinction between measurable, diagnosable symptoms and experientially based personal narratives equates narrative with advocacy, thereby disqualifying both together as potential sources of medical evidence.[25] In moral-political discourse, advocacy is the putative villain behind conflicts of interest and ideologically driven lobbying, evoking the "interest group" label that invites condemnation in the social rhetoric of equal (impartial) treatment for all, where impartiality is objectivity's analogue. And in philosophical discussions more generally, advocacy and rhetoric tend to be linked together as modalities of sophistry and emotive persuasion, contrasted with philosophy proper's logical, rational

23. Walker, *Moral Understandings*, 13 (emphasis original).
24. Seller, "Realism versus Relativism," 180; Wittgenstein, *On Certainty*, §378.
25. It will be evident that narrative in this setting often amounts to elaborated, extended testimony. The idea that stories evade the strictures of objective evidence, and that patients cannot be objective about their own symptoms, prompts implausible charges that narratives reduce to the kind of truth-manipulating strategy commonly deemed characteristic of legal advocacy.

demeanor in which truth is sought for its own sake and set out dispassionately to await reasoned assent. Lynette Hunter's provocative observation, which I cite in chapter one, is equally salient here. Modern science and orthodox epistemologies established themselves, she claims, in a founding gesture in which

> neutral logic and pure language replaced "rhetoric." ... [And science assumed] a rhetorical stance that denied that the rhetoric of social persuasion in historical context was needed, even denied that it existed. ... Built upon the concept of the "universal autonomous man," able to communicate infinitely replicable experience [and] isolated from the social world, which might contaminate the purity or challenge the totality of explanation. ... *Its rhetoric claims that there is no need for rhetoric.*[26]

With testimony at its epistemic core, advocacy defies these assumptions: transgressing the boundaries imagined as separating objective knowledge claims from rhetoric, it moves to the margins of epistemic legitimacy. Endorsing that "founding gesture," orthodox epistemologists for whom facts are self-presenting—requiring neither advocacy nor negotiation—confirm advocacy's propensity to obstruct objectivity. There is no need to resort to social persuasion, they argue, nor to see facts through anyone else's eyes, to appeal to diverse interpretations, to test them or debate them in the social world: an autonomous knower will refuse such (heteronomous) dependency. These assumptions fuel charges that represent advocacy research as committed to serving "special interests" and, when expedient, to sacrificing objectivity to those interests. Peter Novick, referring to historical knowledge, summarizes the position well: "The objective historian's role is that of a neutral, or disinterested, judge: it must never *degenerate* into that of an advocate or, even worse, propagandist."[27] The juxtapositions he invokes display advocacy's proximity, in the dominant epistemic imaginary, to the worst rhetorical excesses.

It would be naive to dismiss such worries as unfounded. Advocacy operates variously: sometimes, undoubtedly, it shapes the truth to serve specific ends; truth becomes subservient to those ends (which may be reprehensible); propaganda is the appropriate label, exposure and censure the only reasonable responses. Yet it is curious that advocacy's least responsible moments should be taken for its essential, inevitable characteristics: shaping the truth in these ways is neither its only nor even its principal function. In the examples I will address,

---

26. Hunter, *Critiques of Knowing*, 30–31 (emphasis added).
27. Novick, *That Noble Dream*, 2 (emphasis added).

advocacy practices work to *get at* truths operating imperceptibly, implicitly, below the surface of the assumed self-transparency of evidence. They can be strategically effective in claiming discursive space for "subjugated knowledges," putting such knowledge into circulation where it can claim acknowledgment, working to ensure informed, emancipatory moral-political effects.[28] Advocacy is at once dependent on the quality—the careful sensitivity—of the knowledge informing it and on the level of epistemic responsibility and the climate of trust where it circulates: since its epistemic and moral-political aspects are so closely intertwined, responsibility issues are central to its sensitive functioning. Advocacy practices rely for their "goodness" on the epistemic credentials of the advocate(s) and their responsiveness to testifiers who indeed, in diverse modalities of isolation and/or silencing, often require the guidance of others to understand and know how to articulate their own experiences. To work effectively, advocacy needs to operate as much in the second person as in the third person: speaking, engaging in ongoing dialogue *with* the other as a particular "you" whose circumstances matter in their (relevant) detail, and for the other(s) as a "she," a "he," a "they" in places where they themselves may not be authorized, credentialed, confident enough to speak (as is so for many of the workers Messing represents) or may otherwise require expert advocates. Relevance, in such processes, is a subtle matter and cannot be foreclosed before the fact: this, again, is an effect of the sometimes remote and often obscure causal or contributing factors expert advocacy can trace. Advocacy makes candidates for truth available for negotiation with, by, and for people diversely positioned on epistemic terrains whose gatekeepers mistakenly imagine a uniform homogeneous population and universal, autonomous access to the evidence and acknowledgment on which knowledge depends. At its best, advocacy can counterbalance the social-political patterns of incredulity into which the testimony of marginalized knowers tends to fall and can thereby contribute to an enhanced sociability and community. Yet the level of trust, and of exposure, advocacy requires makes of it a fragile, delicate process which participants have to enter in cognizance of the vulnerability it commonly produces.

At the confluence of ideal autonomy and *individualism*, the epistemic dichotomy between autonomy and advocacy runs parallel to two further

28. "Subjugated knowledges" is Foucault's term in *Power/Knowledge*. It refers to "a whole set of knowledges that have been disqualified as inadequate to their task or insufficiently elaborated: naive knowledges located low down on the hierarchy, beneath the required level of cognition or scientificity." Foucault claims, "it is through these . . . disqualified knowledges, that criticism performs its work" (82).

regulative dichotomies: fact versus value, and justification versus discovery. Within the confines these dichotomies produce, bona fide knowers stand impartially apart from processes of discovery, represented as temporally prior to and substantively distinct from knowledge proper. They distance themselves from the guesses, trials and errors, persuasions and negotiations, diverse contributions, hypotheses, and proposals integral to discovery, which is imagined as a messy process whose planned obsolescence assures its invisibility in "contexts of justification," in the confirmation and/or falsification that are epistemology's proper business, where values and human interests are rigorously expunged to allow facts to stand forth in their crystalline purity. Even if values should permeate the discovery process, an assumption prevails that knowledge as product can be cleansed of their distorting, discrediting influence.

Yet feminist epistemologists, with naturalistic and other successor epistemologists, have argued that neither institutional nor everyday practices of discovery can be granted immunity from epistemic scrutiny, thereby moving them into critical focus as places where situational specificities have ample room to shape knowledge-producing projects. Showing how politically infused assumptions infiltrate and shape an impressive array of research projects from the bottom up, if sometimes tacitly and by no means always reprehensibly, feminists have exposed the illegitimacy of assuming value neutrality before the fact and have shown mainstream epistemology to be as value-laden as the so-called special-interest projects whose explicit commitments to values and interests it denigrates. Donna Haraway, with characteristic irony, notes: "The messy political does not go away because we think we are cleanly in the zone of the technical."[29] Values, background assumptions, and specificities of situation and place commonly inspire and inform inquiry: they are as open to critical evaluation as its products. Hence, for example, as Sandra Harding characterizes it, the "strong objectivity" of standpoint epistemology refuses to allow inquirers "to be unconcerned with the origins or consequences of their problematics and practices or with the social values and interests that these problematics and practices support."[30] To make good its claims for the capacity of avowedly engaged, politically committed investigations to yield well-warranted conclusions, strong objectivity demands a breadth of scrutiny encompassing, at minimum, the standpoint of the knower and the "nature" of the known. Further reconfigured as a potential contributor to ecological thinking, it demands reimagining standpoints and subjectivities in order to

29. Haraway, *Modest_Witness*, 68.
30. Harding, "Rethinking Standpoint Epistemology," 71.

investigate the specificities of place, habitat, habitus, and ethos in the construction of putative knowledge, mindful of their pertinence for adjudicating
epistemic projects, negotiations, and claims to know. Such reconfigurations
again claim a debt to naturalized epistemology, while loosening the connections between naturalism and laboratory science, turning to secular knowledge
making in search of "more natural" sites for studying knowledge production
in its situated specificity and its wider effects. In this chapter, advocacy relations tie those sites loosely together: they are exemplary of places and processes
where knowledge is collaboratively negotiated.

As a lattice of practices, advocacy in its always-particularity (albeit differently from place to place) has to be so carefully, specifically situated as—
often—to require mappings across a range of issues, many of which, initially,
may seem not to be spatially or temporally close enough to the object of study
to count even as tangential, and few of which will be precisely replicable from
situation to situation. Recall Carson's tracking of the Japanese beetle's natural
predators, Messing's of intra-actions (borrowing Barad's term) between mys-
terious ailments and the structures of equipment or workplaces, Walkerdine's
urging researchers to map "outward" across complex habitat conditions to see
why daddy bear might not be bigger, for some children. Striking in each of these
examples, albeit variously, is the need to push against intransigent imaginaries,
systemic incredulity, rhetorical barriers blocking acknowledgment, whose effects are to render such knowings aberrant, to dismiss the evidence as flimsy,
thereby refusing to allow putative knowings to go through into places where
they could generate reimaginings, action, policy changes—how they confound
negotiations of which advocacy is both a catalyst and a consequence.

In "The Possibility of Feminist Theory," an essay I read as signaling
advocacy's crucial significance for feminist and other postcolonial inquiry
(though "advocacy" is not her term), Marilyn Frye observes:

> In the light of what is generally considered common knowledge...a
> great deal of most women's experience appears anomalous, discrep-
> ant, idiosyncratic, chaotic, "crazy." In that dim light our lives are to
> a great extent either unintelligible or intelligible only as pathological
> or degenerate. As long as each woman thinks that her experience
> alone is thus discrepant, she tends to trust the received wisdom and
> distrust her own senses and judgement...[to] believe that her
> "inexplicable" pain is imaginary, a phantasm.[31]

31. Frye, "Possibility of Feminist Theory," 34.

Cognizant of the cogency of this point, advocacy practices and the negotiations they entail defy that "founding gesture" of which Hunter writes, insisting that it is indeed no mark of rational immaturity to be unable to use one's own understanding without the guidance of another. They demonstrate in practice that learning how to negotiate across and through an epistemic terrain, seeking and giving appropriate guidance where and as one can, developing political and other cooperative/collective strategies to circumvent obstacles, is integral to mature sociality and viable community. Hierarchies of epistemic power and privilege are sustained, far more complexly than standard monologic models assume, by patterns/structures of unknowing, in which those least well situated in relation to multiply intersecting lines of "facts" and potential negotiations are immobilized at a level where even the simplest negotiations exceed their reach. Good, responsibly knowledgeable advocacy endeavors to remedy such immobilization.

The point, then, is not to overestimate the link between autonomy and self-reliance, but to show how self-other(s) mappings of reliability, responsiveness, responsibility, narrative, dialogue, interpretation, deliberation, and conferrings and/or withholdings of trust make knowledgeable, ecologically manageable living possible. It all depends on judicious readings of multiple and often multiply *ambiguous* mappings of the intricacies of place, people, and circumstance, of their constitutive part in making knowledge possible, and of the *need*, which need not be repudiated in hollow gestures of pseudo-self-reliance, for consultation, recognition, debate to and fro. These are some of the principal ingredients of the negotiations I recommend. Some of Messing's subjects, Carson's secular witnesses, Candib's and Malterud's patients could not (in a strong sense) claim a hearing, hence could not know *that they know* without the negotiations to which their own experiential expertise and testimony contribute in deliberations around the reports they bring to an encounter, in concert with the kind of advocacy that Carson's, Messing's, Candib's, and Malterud's scientific and political expertise can inform and guide. Often, their knowledge could not claim acknowledgment and thus count as knowledge, beyond their own (often tentative) experiential confines, without advocacy. Advocating advocacy as it emerges from such imagined negotiations is again a delicate matter, for among the obstacles it faces, two are especially salient here: it requires reading past entrenched views, first, that advocacy cannot be truth-conducive for it aims, usually, to win rather than to know, on the model of Plato's warnings against being swayed by the sophists; and, second, that advocacy is tantamount to paternalism. Both, indeed, are dangers, and I have had something to say about the first. With respect to paternalism, to which I also allude earlier, it, too, hovers as a possibility, but not an inevitability. The force of my claim for epistemic responsibility as integral to the kind of thinking and knowing enacted in such practices is that they depend, qualitatively, on a vigilant and sensitive ethical stance vis-à-vis the encounters, debates, consultations, or lobbying they may generate, to guard against abusive/coercive paternalism by preserving and respecting self-reliance where it is reasonable to expect it and working to foster it when it is not. When advocacy is effective, those advocated for may come to be well placed to claim the autonomy of acknowledged knowledgeability, which will be no less theirs, no less autonomous in the *sapere aude!* sense, for the advocacy that has helped it reach this point.

Autonomy and Social Advocacy

Gaylin and Jennings's *Perversion of Autonomy* locates itself within the autonomy-versus-coercion debates spawned by 1960s protests against paternalism in medicine and elsewhere. Yet it does not engage with advocacy. Autonomy run wild, the authors suggest,[32] denies *coercion* its necessary function as a promoter of human well-being. Coercion, in the guise of a "community-oriented" paternalism, tailored—and "softened"—into a technique for showing people what is best for them is, the authors argue, justifiable coercion.[33] Their argument, like Rawls's "natural lottery," tacitly assumes a starting place where positions of expertise and its opposites are naturally fixed and from which people (read: "some people") can thus, justifiably, be coerced, while others, as a matter of course, know what is best for them. Taking human homogeneity tacitly for granted, the authors neither analyze nor critique social-locational asymmetries of power and privilege. Because they fail to take account of patterns of incredulity prevalent at a much deeper level than the place where their deliberations begin, they leave open no space between "the perversion of autonomy"—about whose features they are often right—and "the proper uses of coercion"—where they evidently focus on social-political situations that could be anywhere, or nowhere, and whose just ordering their argument fails either to interrogate or demonstrate. It is not surprising that advocacy does not figure in their discussions, for individualism and epistemic power structures remain largely uncontested, despite the authors' critical view of autonomy.

32. Gaylin and Jennings call it "autonomy gone bonkers" (*Perversion of Autonomy,* chap. 10).

33. Ibid. (chap. 9: "In Defense of Social Control: The Ethics of Coercion").

As I read it, a false dichotomy between autonomy hyperbolized and re-claimed practices of social control designed to promote "the good of the individual" structures Gaylin and Jennings's analysis.[34] The authors do not even consider the possibility that autonomy could be as much a collective as an individual goal and achievement. They are less concerned with the spaces and social structures where critical interpretive-testimonial projects, both coopera-tive and solitary, can be developed for, by, and with people resistant to or con-strained by the impossible demands an autonomy obsession exerts, than they are with justifying paternalistic coercion. Yet those are the spaces where the open, creatively critical democratic deliberation can take place, on which viable community depends. Gaylin and Jennings's quest for proper uses of coercion enlists a stark, if tacit, condemnation of advocacy that reinstates autonomous man as a regulative exemplar: the central figure in a discourse where stereotypes, posing as knowledge achieved, short-circuit any need to know people and their circumstances well, thus nullifying the very negotiations capable of making more responsible knowing possible and of tempering autonomy's "imperialism and arrogance."

Examples abound in the politics and rhetoric of social welfare, where an assumed equality-of-access to social goods for which no advocacy is required underwrites an entrenched—and itself coercive—belief that individual failure to achieve autonomy is a social sin. Thus, public measures are enacted to en-force self-sufficient autonomy after all, while reliance on social services pre-sumptively "available to all" slides rhetorically into a weakness, a dependence on social advocacy and support that, paradoxically, invites—and receives—judgments of moral turpitude. Strikingly, in her poignantly titled essay "The Unbearable Autonomy of Being," Patricia Williams shows how the entrenched stereotype of "the black single mother" in the United States is invoked to disguise "the class problems of our supposedly classless society . . . by filtering them through certain kinds of discussion about race and the shiftless, unde-serving, unemployable black 'underclass.' "[35] In consequence, single mothers (who are *not*, she observes, predominantly black or "teenaged") are left res-olutely to their own devices, as the informed advocacy that might elicit more responsible responses from an affluent society is condemned as special pleading for members of "interest groups" who have not made the right choices, have failed to exercise self-restraint and self-reliance, or to contribute appropriately to a society bent on demonizing them. Arguments, supported by

34. Ibid., 182.
35. Williams, *Rooster's Egg*, 177.

good evidence, of the extent to which single mothers "now bear a greater responsibility than at any time in our history for raising the children of this society," hence everyone has a stake in these children's well-being—arguments that ought therefore to awaken the self-interest of the affluent even if they remain otherwise unmoved—are reconstructed in the instituted social imaginary as truth-ignoring advocacy for the "shiftless welfare queen who always gets more than she deserves."[36] The imagined moral and epistemic autonomy of the affluent sex, class, and race allows them to "know" her thus. It produces and condemns a new heteronomy of others who fail by its own unexamined, imperialist standards.

Cornel West offers an analogous example, where an ever-vigilant individualistic and coercive imperative takes on a censorious demeanor, also suppressing any thought that such responsibilities might be more collective than individual. He observes:

> The new black conservatives claim that transfer payments to the black needy engender a mentality of dependence which undercuts the value of self-reliance and of the solidity of the black poor family. . . . [Yet] in the face of high black unemployment, these cutbacks will not promote self-reliance or strong black families but will only produce even more black cultural disorientation and more devastated black households.[37]

A set of intransigent assumptions about the universal, matter-of-course possibility of self-reliance, both epistemic and practical, thus keeps in circulation the prescriptive effects of a hyperbolized ideal of autonomy as equally and equivalently accessible to everyone, if they just try hard enough. Such assumptions bypass empirical evidence of how the material consequences of "the unnatural lottery" count among conditions that make knowledge and authoritatively informed practices possible, or block their passage altogether. These rhetorical shifts reinforce the coercive power of an old-style autonomy whose effects are to discredit the very advocacy practices integral to the idea(l) of community as a locus of respectful cohabitation, mutual support, and concern.

Social welfare, in Canada and the United States as elsewhere in the western world, came into being because of *advocacy* (often by women) to members of

---

36. Ibid., 174–75. Ross observes: "The rhetoric of poverty of the 1980s was exemplified by the various forms of the narrative of a black woman receiving fraudulently obtained public assistance and driving away in her Cadillac" (*Just Stories*, 63).

37. West, *Race Matters*, 86.

the privileged classes, who were themselves able, without question, to expect social benefits that for those in less affluent positions earned the label *welfare.*[38] The rhetoric of self-reliance, sanctimoniously manipulated, enforces a stoic version of autonomy, separately and collectively, upon people who are thwarted in their efforts to achieve it by the very free-market society whose "just" distributions of power and privilege produce their deplored "inability." As Susan Wendell notes: "When governments want to make cutbacks in social services, they may 'release' people from institutions without adequate support to enable them to live on their own..., describing the changes they make as creating more 'independence.' "[39] And noting another facet of autonomy's imagined necessity for maintaining "a liberal, 'free' society," Erica Burman reports U.S. President Nixon's having vetoed proposals for daycare provisions (in the 1971 Child Development Act) "on the grounds that [it]...threatened the traditional (North) American family and (North) America's tradition of individualism."[40] Ironically, such perversions of autonomy reproduce or re-inforce patterns of subjection, after all.

Just as ironically, the 1990s rhetoric invoked in favor of dismantling the welfare state reiterates the 1920s rhetoric of opposition to its creation. Martha Minow writes: "To many observers, state-supported social welfare jeopardizes individual autonomy, independence and freedom."[41] Opponents inveighing against the (1927) infant and maternal health legislation in the United States chose "socialist" and "communist" as their favored terms of invective, in support of their position that the legislation allegedly "inter-fered...with the free-market economy." They feared that "*the act's encour-agement of women to seek information about their own bodies and health*" would prompt them to reject their traditional roles.[42] *Sapere aude!* indeed. The co-ercive voice of autonomy is as audible here as in California's 1994 cessation of welfare provisions for single mothers, where the argument that welfare thwarts their autonomous self-reliance sounds a similar note to the Ontario Conservatives' 1995–96 assault on social welfare for "interfering" with per-sonal autonomy. Welfare as a vehicle for a "free ride" is the guiding nega-tive metaphor: an image capable also of masking the extent to which welfare humiliates and coerces, even as it helps. As Minow says: "Public assistance

38. Gordon notes that "the meaning of 'welfare' has reversed itself. What once meant well-being now means ill-being" (*Pitied But Not Entitled*, 1).
39. Wendell, *Rejected Body*, 148.
40. Burman, *Deconstructing Developmental Psychology*, 167.
41. Minow, *Making All the Difference*, 268.
42. Ibid., 248–49 (emphasis added).

and social work interventions too often...controlled and restricted... people ['in need'] and subjected them to governmental regulation without protection against power imbalances";[43] and Linda Gordon observes: welfare "humiliates its recipients by subjecting them to demeaning supervision and invasions of privacy."[44] What autonomy discourse initiates as an entitlement mutates into a disempowering gift, imposing obligations its recipient cannot honor for the very reasons that brought her to seek assistance in the first place.

Welfare issues, then, are about relations to and within intransigent systems and social orders informed by stereotypes of subjectivity and agency that continue to hold autonomous man in place as a regulative fiction, while subjecting women, and others who cannot measure up, to the dictates of an impossibly coercive imperative. This putative knowledge of what people are and what they can and must do is invoked to legitimate policies, actions, treatments modeled on *his* experiences and options, glossing over the extent to which autonomous man is himself dependent upon patterns of structurally invisible advocacy for his own putatively autonomous achievements.[45] These examples convey a sense of how, in discourses of social welfare and in anti-poverty discourses, a presumption of individualistic self-reliance generates coercive, regulative autonomy imperatives. Yet especially where hierarchical divisions of epistemic power and privilege structure the constitutive relations, it is impossible in practice—and logical possibility is truly irrelevant—for people relegated to disadvantaged positions, or even occupying them by choice (recall Patricia Williams), to claim the benefits to which they are seemingly entitled, without advocacy. Nor am I imagining advocacy as a once-and-for-all, automatic solution that, once it is in place, will solve all the problems. The issues are far more complex, fraught with competing arguments, prejudices, stereotypes, and entrenched convictions (in putatively democratic, liberal societies) about the moral opprobrium due to interest-group politics—a rhetorical space into which advocacy is readily, if carelessly, slotted. Thus, any defense of the power and epistemic significance of advocacy has also to be cognizant of the power of stereotypes to block the best efforts even of socially well-positioned advocates.

43. Ibid., 267. See also Ferguson, *Feminist Case against Bureaucracy.*
44. Gordon, *Pitied But Not Entitled*, 2. Ross, too, notes that a dichotomy drawn between social insurance and public assistance "served to underscore the undeserved quality of the benefits extended to recipients of the latter" (*Just Stories*, 62).
45. I am thinking here of Hunter's reference to the masculine "club culture" of laboratory science in *Critiques of Knowing*, 30.

Knowledge and Credibility in Medicine

Medicine, the domain from which Gaylin and Jennings develop their argument, is a crucial site for engaging in advocacy practices, contesting a social imaginary for which "the facts" of pain and physical suffering—medical facts—seem without further ado to stand forth in their clear, incontrovertible factuality, requiring neither negotiation nor advocacy. Knowing that one is in pain is commonly assumed to be the clearest, most doubt-immune knowledge anyone could have. But here, too, things are not so simple: the worry I have mentioned, to the effect that infant and maternal health legislation would encourage women to seek information about their own health, thus prompting them to reject their (appropriate) traditional dependence on those positioned as more knowledgeable, exposes still more complex power-knowledge interconnections between expert knowledge and experiential acknowledgment in hierarchical social structures. Even pain does not claim such ready acknowledgment as one would expect: recall Susan Wendell's remark cited in chapter three: "My subjective descriptions of my bodily experience need the confirmation of medical descriptions to be accepted as accurate and truthful."[46] In the hierarchies of institutional medicine, one solitary, even one putatively *autonomous* voice, often fails to gain the hearing it requires: these are the locational structures whose navigational issues an ecological naturalism has, for better or worse, to take into account. The autonomy-of-knowledge credo cannot explain how such subjective, experiential knowledge could fail to achieve acknowledgment without advocacy, in this instance in the form of a physician's preparedness to listen, to find the patient's testimony credible, to acknowledge her symptoms and think carefully with her about how to act upon them.

Lucy Candib, for example, in an analysis with many features I regard as ecological, argues against reading medical symptoms by glossing over narrative accounts drawn from the patient's habitat, both physical and social, that could be crucial to responsible diagnosis. Connecting believability to advocacy, she writes: "Patients subject to abuses of power bring their stories of vulnerability to clinicians every day.... Advocacy means arguing for the believability of those stories."[47] Women, she notes, can experience chest pain, and many other symptoms, as a result of abusive practices that permeate their lives. Mapping the effects of these oppressions for this patient, abdicating the "disinterested posture" expected of family physicians—a posture that "corrupt[s] the idea

46. Wendell, *Rejected Body*, 122.
47. Candib, *Medicine and the Family*, 159.

of advocacy"[48]—allows a physician and patient (sometimes in concert with members of the patient's family, friends, or community) to collaborate in making sense of her symptoms; refuses to hold her autonomously responsible for their occurrence or to treat problems merely as mechanical failures; and allows doctors and patients to think differently about causes and cures, yet in the end makes it possible for a patient to work cooperatively with the physician, toward being able to claim a more manageable, advocacy-fostered autonomy.

The truth is, even in pain and suffering—experiences philosophically imagined as quintessentially "my own," cornerstone examples of epistemic "privileged access"—I cannot, as an autonomous knower, always know what my experiences are, and contributing causes can be so remote and seem so implausible that, without advocacy, I could not even imagine their pertinence. For people traditionally silenced, marginalized, discredited—women, blacks, the poor, the disabled, the inarticulate, the elderly—these problems are doubly acute. Elaine Scarry confirms the isolation of experiential certainty: "For the person in pain, so incontestably and unnegotiably present is it that 'having pain' may come to be thought of as the most vibrant example of what it is to 'have certainty,' while for the other person it is so elusive that 'hearing about pain' may exist as the primary model of what it is 'to have doubt.' "[49] Monologic, solitarily achieved acknowledgment is far more elusive than arguments from first-person privileged access imagine, as epistemic autonomy recedes to a vanishing point. Here again is Scarry:

> The success of the physician's work will often depend on the acuity with which he or she can *hear* the fragmentary language of pain, coax it into clarity, and interpret it.... Many people's experience... would bear out the... conclusion that physicians do not trust (hence, hear) the human voice, that they in effect perceive the voice of the patient as an "unreliable narrator" of bodily events, a voice which must be bypassed... so that they can get around and behind it to the physical events themselves.[50]

48. Ibid., 76.

49. Scarry, *Body in Pain*, 4. Scarry's comments bear on the idea that patients cannot be objective about their own symptoms, which prompts the charge I have cited, that narratives belong to the truth-manipulating strategies commonly deemed characteristic of legal advocacy.

50. Ibid., 6 (emphasis added).

When that voice speaks from within sedimented patterns of incredulity accustomed, in the dominant social imaginary, to tell against the veracity of its tellings because of the (inferior) social status of the teller, it is no wonder that autonomously knowing even one's own experiences can neither be taken for granted nor achieved, as a matter of course, without advocacy (recall Anne Seller: "As an isolated individual, I often do not know what my experiences are").[51] Some people—especially the educated, articulate, privileged—may be able to inform themselves well enough to perform as their own knowledgeable advocate: many work to become medically and scientifically literate for this very purpose, and their efforts are epistemically commendable. But for just as many others this process is not an option, either because of the aura of mystification medical expertise tends to convey, whose disempowering effects for women and other Others cannot be gainsaid, and/or because they live in situations of oppression, marginality, illiteracy, poverty, or a range of other circumstantial social-material-economic contributors to epistemic timidity. Such people are fortunate if they can find a physician prepared to look beyond the one-size-fits-all diagnosis to take wider, more subterranean, more situationally remote ecological contributors into account.

In the literature of theoretical medicine, advocacy commonly appears as an ethical issue with the most frequently named advocates being nurses, patient or lay advocacy groups, lawyers, pharmacists.[52] Sometimes they, especially nurses, act as intermediaries from patient to doctor or to other members of the medical establishment, representing patients' interests that, for structural reasons, they may be unable to represent autonomously (= for themselves). Often (if less so in patient advocacy groups), the relationship is structured around patients' assumed passivity, with autonomy again standing as the preferred contrast, and advocacy the route by which it will be achieved. Although the language of "representing interests" may appear to locate the issues within a moral-political frame, a closer reading shows them to be at least as significantly about knowledge—experiential knowledge—about facilitating its passage through structures of public visibility, scientificity, and incredulity en route to claiming the acknowledgment essential for informed moral-political deliberation and care.

51. See Seller, "Realism versus Relativism," 180.

52. See, e.g., Herb, "Hospital-Based Attorney"; American Medical Association Council, "Ethical Issues in Managed Care"; Rosenberg, "Delaying Approval"; May, "On Ethics and Advocacy"; Abrams, "Patient Advocate or Secret Agent?"; and Jecker, "Integrating Medical Ethics."

Some feminists have traced a path running from inarticulate patient to appropriately experienced nurse to scientifically knowledgeable doctor, following an ascending line of legitimation to culminate in and confirm the commonsense belief that "doctor knows best," while tacitly installing a hierarchical contrast between experience, as a lesser mode, and knowledge, as a greater, more powerful achievement. Hence the (presumptively) female, experienced nurse is positioned as an intermediary, advocating from patient to (presumptively) male, knowledgeable doctor. Assuming that a nurse's "special understanding" enables her to promote the patient's "autonomy, dignity, and best interests," this picture confirms her subsidiary position within a caregiving sphere, contains her within gender-specific deference to the doctor's acknowledged expertise.[53] Peta Bowden's nuanced analysis shows how, nonetheless, sensitive nursing practice at its best can perform respectful yet knowledgeable *advocacy*, well enough attuned to experiential and ecological particularities to enable patients to "interpret their dependency as harmonious with an established context, yet free of conflict with celebrations of autonomy and independence in the wider culture."[54] From a feminist point of view, the politics of these issues—of which Bowden is well aware—are contestable in their confirmation of the power structures of traditionally gendered divisions of labor and epistemic authority. The issue of how testimony-based knowledge can cross the threshold of acknowledgment is the salient one: clearly the autonomous knower—even of his or her "own" experiences—is a rare bird. The goal is to develop collaborative advocacy practices where divisions of intellectual labor and expertise disenfranchise neither the advocate(s) nor the one(s) for whom they advocate.

Syndrome X and fibromyalgia, which I discuss in chapter three, attest further to advocacy's constitutive role in making knowledge possible. Both, as I have noted, have been more common for women than men;[55] and since neither condition is readily detectable in standard diagnostic procedures, patients who present their symptoms to a physician—because (experientially, phenomenologically) "they *know* there is something wrong with them"—are frequently dismissed as complaining of a pain that is "all in their minds" and

53. The quoted phrases come from Theis, "Ethical Issues." See also Bernal, "Nurse as Patient Advocate."

54. Bowden, *Caring*, 124.

55. I discuss the politics of syndrome X in "How Do We Know?"

therefore not *real*.[56] Ironically, they cannot know *that they know* without the deliberations and negotiations that take place in the physician's consulting room, around the testimony they bring with them, which, from a receptive encounter, can prompt the kind of advocacy physicians are best placed to initiate.

Stereotypes of women's lives as, in Frye's words, "unintelligible or intelligible only as pathological or degenerate" block epistemic autonomy as effectively as any of the other social-structural factors I have named. Advocacy is again the politics-of-knowledge issue, but its starting point is not in a conviction that practitioners of "normal science" (normal medicine), where male symptoms and bodily experiences silently establish the norm, *should* have expected women's symptoms and bodily experiences to manifest differently from men's, thus that women *should not* merely have received instructions to live with their symptoms. In a social environment informed by an epistemic imaginary where the authority of (medical) textbook interpretation confirms and is confirmed by the best scientific standards, making it reasonable to read symptoms that do not fit as aberrant, anomalous, or to discount them all together, these are hollow "shoulds." The force of the paradigms governing practices and institutions of medical knowledge production is such that *individual* different or dissenting voices, both of patients and of physicians, have scant hope of claiming a hearing.[57] Only a substantial, authoritative critical mass of interrogating, urging, advocating voices can hope to initiate research and other policies capable of dislodging an established procedure or checking the inertia of instituted practices. Thus again, it is not enough even for people in pain *autonomously* (= separately) to maintain the veracity of their own experiences; nor is women's failure singly and separately to gain autonomous acknowledgment a sign of their immaturity as members of the fair sex, dwelling still in tutelage. Hence again the pertinence of Frye's observation about women's experience as "anomalous, discrepant, idiosyncratic, chaotic, 'crazy'" by received standards of knowledge. Her reference is to a generalized

---

56. Of syndrome X, Kathleen King wrote in 1993: "Men often experience... 'textbook' cases of angina and other heart-disease symptoms because the textbooks are written to describe men's symptoms.... You're not going to think of heart disease unless the symptoms fit the classic picture. And... we don't know what the classic picture for women is" (quoted in Henig, "Kind Hearts and Coronaries"). Such studies—which count as an essential step in a larger advocacy process—have drawn sufficient attention that, more than a decade later, the face of cardiac medicine is changing.

57. The reference is to Kuhn's claims about the intransigence of paradigms in *Structure of Scientific Revolutions*.

pain, produced by oppressions in which most women, diversely and often imperceptibly, live their lives. But the argument translates into the language of pain as medically conceived and read, and into feminist connections that Lucy Candib and Kirsti Malterud (whom I discuss in chapter three) draw between larger settings of pain and the more traditional medical symptoms that women present in a physician's consulting room.[58] Analogously, Scarry's remark about the "fragmented language of pain" takes on a special urgency when the "voice" she refers to speaks from the confines of social stereotypes—of women, blacks, the poor, the old, the disabled, the illiterate and uneducated, and/or the otherwise marginalized—voices that tell against the *acknowledgment* the speaker requires in order to trust "her own senses and judgment."

Advocacy and Trust

Trust, and the politics of trust as it surfaces in Frye's and Scarry's observations, is integral to advocacy practices. These practices address contrasting, yet interrelated, senses of trust: trust in authorized expertise, in the reliability of institutional scientific knowledge, in its presumed capacity to trump personal knowledge, contrasted with lack of trust in oneself and in narrative, experiential knowledge. (Trust is again a central issue in the example I will discuss in chapter seven.)

Frye attributes the possibility of feminist theory to consciousness-raising with its capacity to confer upon women's "sense-data . . . body-data" a cogency that "makes it possible to trust it," where trust had hitherto eluded them. Neither unifying nor aggregating women's experiences in an analysis that counters the "homogeneity of isolation" in which "one *cannot* see patterns and . . . remains unintelligible to oneself,"[59] Frye works generality and specificity together without losing the force, or the fine-tuning, of either. Thus her analysis can be brought to bear on the need for medical practitioners to resist a false dichotomy that (recalling Scarry) would require them to bypass patients' individual voices in favor of attending exclusively to observable physical events. That dichotomy offers only two, equally immobilizing options: either reduce concrete specificities to cases that fit an *objective* rubric and cannot be treated unless they do, or settle for a "retreat into autobiography" where experiential voices remain idiosyncratically *subjective*, untrustworthy contributors to theory

58. For a further discussion of these issues see Malterud, Candib, and Code, "Responsible and Responsive Knowing."

59. Frye, "Possibility of Feminist Theory," 37, 39, 38.

or practice. Politically, each option serves only to uphold an instituted social-epistemic imaginary of entrenched expertise encountering and discounting the believability of aberrant "differences." And while expertise is indeed what patients rightly seek in and require from physicians, I am proposing that expertise functions most effectively when it is mixed with thoughtful, compassionate acknowledgment.

The very possibility for women or other marginalized and oppressed Others to *trust* their "own senses and judgment" depends upon delicate negotiations between/among patients and doctors and within wider social-ecological situations. Negotiations designed to issue in effective advocacy require a minimal presumption of trust—something like a principle of charity—from the outset, for they commonly start from and generate vulnerability not only for the patient, but often also for nurses or doctors who may have to put their own professional credibility on the line in order to participate effectively in advocacy projects. Even if, according to the common wisdom, it is physicians who occupy the positions of epistemic power in a society or institution, they, too, can be immobilized within standard diagnostic procedures by requirements that they demonstrate their credibility *as* diagnosticians and practitioners, answerable to the state-of-the-art normative, often legally enforced, requirements of the profession.

The multiple practices of empowerment set in motion by feminist and other politically progressive medical practitioners engage with the diverse workings of power in institutional knowledge, where doctors, too, can be caught within formal constraints and sedimented patterns of disbelief when they challenge established knowledge, offer treatment contesting its hegemony, or advocate for anomalous diagnoses, procedures, or practices. The issue is a delicate one: the assumption prompting my discussion here is emphatically *not* that trust is missing, as a rule, from standard medical consultations or that physicians generally give it no thought. Patients would gain nothing from physicians if they could not, ordinarily, enter the consulting room with a modicum of trust, even if it is sometimes mixed with cautious, strategic skepticism. Trust, in this regard, is not just, or even primarily, about the physician's professional ethics. It has more to do with her or his presumed knowledge, expertise, whose legitimacy most patients, almost by definition, can take only on trust given the usual habitat conditions: most notably, given most patients' distance from the sources of knowledge, the difficulty of comprehension for those not trained, the profession's well-known investment in sustaining a certain opacity around putatively esoteric knowledge.

Trust also contributes to the physician's positioning in the consulting room: trust in her or his own knowledge, however tentative, underdetermined it sometimes may be; trust or (following Scarry) lack thereof in the reliability of the patient as narrator; trust in the capacity of the consultative encounter to elicit readable signs, even though they may be invisible at first glance. Nor need trust in these multiple modalities always be individually realized or possessed. Presumptions in favor of trust are carried in the dominant epistemological imaginary that confers on scientific and thence on medical knowledge the status of arbiter of truth; presumptions in favor of trusting physicians are integral to accreditation practices that grant and sustain their professional status. These presumptions may be shaky, provisional, contestable for members of oppressed and marginalized groups and, conversely, for an educated laity, critically aware of the limitations of scientific knowledge and its availability for misuse, despite its overwhelming successes and powers. It is within this tangled web of trusting relations that acknowledgment and advocacy have to be negotiated for the medically unexplained disorders whose signs Kirsti Malterud seeks to read, as for the experiences that Wendell refers to and the pain of which Scarry writes. Trust as I am thinking of it, and the acknowledgment that it produces and is produced by it, works in multiple directions in doctor-patient relationships; nor can these relationships be isolated from the *situations*—the myriad complex social-political-cultural-ecological situations—where knowledge is claimed, established, and enacted and where power asymmetries prevail.

In my discussion of *The Perversion of Autonomy*, I noted that in medical ethics many of these issues used to play themselves out in sharply bifurcated debates about patient autonomy versus practitioner paternalism, dichotomously construed.[60] Here, inspired also by Frye's reference to the "novel acts of attention" necessary for "discovering patterns" of oppression,[61] I am proposing trust, acknowledgment, and effective advocacy as ingredients well designed to fill some of the spaces left vacant in the in-between ground of this stark opposition, advocating trust, and the responsive listening, sensitive interpretation, and responsible knowing that count among the conditions of its possibility.

My discussion in this chapter and throughout this book proposes that the stripped-down fiction of uniformly perceptive, autonomous knowers confronting self-announcing facts should yield to an imaginary of knowledge construction as a social-communal-political process, where items of would-be

60. See, e.g., Callahan, "Autonomy"; O'Neill, "Paternalism and Partial Autonomy"; and Sherwin, *No Longer Patient*, esp. chap. 7.
61. Frye, "Possibility of Feminist Theory," 40.

knowledge are embedded in discourses, informed by interests that are them-selves open to critical scrutiny and by hierarchies of power and privilege, uneven credulity, and the pragmatics of conferring or withholding trust. Such an epistemic terrain, for all the complexities of negotiating it, becomes a fertile ground where advocacy can demonstrate its effectiveness in opening out rhetorical spaces to accommodate *"the insurrection of subjugated knowl-edges."*[62] The consequences can be gratifying. For example, in a 1993 article discussing syndrome X, science journalist Robin Henig notes that in response to persistent and growing patient and practitioner advocacy, "a handful of cardiologists" had begun to hear the hitherto muted voices of these "frustrated heart patients," with the consequence that by the time she was writing, a massive clinical trial was under way in the United States, all of whose 140,000 subjects were women.[63] Analogously, when *Harvard Women's Health Watch* corroborated these women's experiential reports, the credibility index of the syndrome X story began to rise.[64] The conclusion is hard to resist: advo-cacy research, empirically grounded, scientifically conducted, and politically enacted—but *advocacy* nonetheless—is necessary if such breakthroughs are to disrupt the sedimented knowledge-sustaining institutional power structures.

Yet for feminism's detractors, any hint that research is advocacy driven condemns it as deficient in objectivity, thence in credibility, and therefore as prone to ideological excess. For instance, Christina Hoff Sommers criticizes a study of rape in contemporary U.S. society, as follows: "High rape numbers serve gender feminists by promoting the belief that American Culture is sexist and misogynist," contending: "We need the truth for policy to be fair and effective. If the feminist advocates would stop muddying the waters we could probably get at it."[65] The tacit contrast is instructive: Sommers assumes that research that is *not* explicitly feminist operates from no preconceived agenda; hence, apparently, such objective inquiry amounts to random fact finding, designed to serve no specific ends. Yet this same assumption sits oddly with her faith in projects designed to show that rape statistics are unrealistically high: by contrast, she believes, *they* will be innocent of political commit-ments.[66] The contrast is a curious one, yet it is commonly drawn to distin-guish research implicitly working to confirm the status quo (and thus claiming

62. Foucault, *Power/Knowledge*, 81 (emphasis original).
63. Henig, "Kind Hearts and Coronaries."
64. *Harvard Women's Health Watch* 1.6 (February 1994).
65. Sommers, *Who Stole Feminism?* 103.
66. I am indebted in thinking about this example to Davion in "Listening to Women's Voices." The report discussed is Koss, "Hidden Rape."

apolitical innocence) from research contesting received truths from an explicitly declared standpoint or situation. The rhetoric of "interest-group advocacy" preserves an implausible presumption of disinterestedness on the part of unmarked, dominant inquirers, while casting inquiries that wear their politics on their sleeve as always, for this very reason, bound to yield skewed results.

The issue is complex. Politically informed theorists are well aware of the advocacy research that (often covertly) promotes the interests of pharmaceutical companies,[67] the arms industry, genetic engineering, governments, and multinational corporations, with research designed and often slanted to demonstrate the harmlessness of toxicity-producing practices too numerous to mention. On the basis of such examples alone, it is no wonder that advocacy research counts in the public eye as a practice of ill repute. But advocacy research is multifaceted in its aims and agendas. It is as frequently benign as it is malign in its purposes and findings. Think, by contrast, of the advocacy research devoted to developing safer and more reliable contraception, seeking effective cures for HIV/AIDS, studying environmental and workplace harms, fighting to eradicate pollutants and toxic substances, promoting the licensing of midwifery, arguing for ecologically sensitive "development" and fair trade coffee. The issue is not about condemning advocacy *simpliciter* but about establishing deliberative communities where inquiry becomes subject to public scrutiny devoted to evaluating agendas according to larger criteria of social-politically responsible epistemic practice.[68] Without advocacy, phenomena such as syndrome X could not have achieved recognition as pathologies deserving of major reconfigurations in "normal medical science."

Advocacy is thus both an epistemic and an ethico-political issue. Without advocacy, few of "us" could claim sufficient credibility to challenge the combined force of the scientific paradigms and hegemonic social imaginaries sustaining the received politics of knowledge.[69] Nor is the problem with expertise

67. See, e.g., Healy, "Conflicting Interests"; and Lemmens, "Confronting the Conflict of Interest Crisis."

68. Haraway's account of how Danish panels of citizen deliberation contribute to shaping democratic science and technology policies offers an impressive example of how such a process could work. It encourages a remarkable "degree of scientific and technical literacy ... in ordinary people" (*Modest_Witness*, 95–96).

69. Think of Messing's comment about activist projects tending, in the public eye, to corroborate a suspicion that "they will fake symptoms to gain their point ... even when the patterns of physiological change are so specific to the toxic effect that the worker would have to be a specialist ... to produce them" (*One-Eyed Science*, 69).

and authori*tative* practice *tout court*, but about occasions where authori*tarian* expertise operates behind a screen of proclaimed autonomous objectivity to paper over the gaps, the breaks in the putatively seamless imaginaries that legitimate it. Ignorance unacknowledged becomes the thematic issue: it takes expert advocacy to expose gaps in the knowledge of accredited and acknowledged experts. What has long been imagined as women's and other underclass knowers' lack of courage to use their own understanding ("*sapere aude!*") emerges as a demand that is unrealizable, universally, and for many people literally *impossible*; whereas (some, usually white) men's apparent successes in doing just that hark back to Claudia Card's remarks about the effects of the unnatural lottery. The ease with which so many such people fit standard textbook descriptions, the ease with which their experiential utterances are taken on faith and their testimony receives acknowledgment, the presumption of veracity that greets their every utterance, has as much to do with the starting positions they occupy in the "unjust institutions" they are positioned to call "their own" as it does with their autonomous rational achievements.

In the relational complexes I have highlighted, advocacy may seem to be directed toward securing the very autonomy that has eluded the grasp of those advocated for; and indeed, advocacy practices enjoined and engaged often explicitly aim to promote autonomy. But this is autonomy remodeled from the bottom up: dis-individuated, decentered, reconfigured across patterns of mutual and crisscrossing recognitions and responsibilities, no longer constrained to define itself in opposition to the caricatured paternalism that Gaylin and Jennings invoke. It is multiply, relationally structured all the way down, eschewing the individualism around which hyperbolized autonomy defines itself, together with the overriding goal of mastery and control it promises. Thus reconfigured, it is consonant with the autonomy Castoriadis applauds in his reference to the critical-creative activity of a society exhibiting its *autonomy* in its capacity to put itself in question, prompted by a (collective for some collectivity) recognition that the society is incongruous with itself, with scant reason for self-satisfaction.[70] As Jane Flax rightly observes: "The success of feminist projects does not depend on the acquisition of an autonomous agency some white men can pretend to exercise." She notes how "the *appearance* of stability, autonomy, and identity is generated and sustained by relations of domination, denial of aspects of subjectivity, and projection of contradictory material onto marked others."[71] These issues prompt me to read

70. In Castoriadis, "Radical Imagination."
71. Flax, "Displacing Woman," 152 (emphasis original).

the perversion of autonomy across a much broader terrain than the book's authors have mapped.

Feminists are well aware that within the insider/outsider structures that frame the politics of public knowledge and the prestige of scientific knowledge, "ordinary" women's voices—like those of other disenfranchised knowers—often go unheard and fail to achieve autonomous acknowledgment. Their reports of violence, sexual assault, domestic abuse, racism and sexism in the work place and in the world, are as often discredited as acted upon. Such patterns of incredulity prompt the *uneasy* suggestion I have elaborated, that first-person experiential reports often require expert or accredited *advocacy* in order to claim a serious hearing. It is uneasy because of the delicacy of speaking for others. Questions about who can/should speak for whom run through a long history of propertied white men speaking for, thinking for, voting for, making decisions for "their" women and their alleged inferiors, while appropriating women's experiences, even as they claim to know women and other Others better than they can know themselves. (Note, too, that there are as good reasons for wariness about women speaking for one another as of men's presumptions to speak on their behalf.) Thus advocacy seems to erase (some) women's hard-won capacity to speak in their own voices, to produce a renewed silencing that would replicate oppressive patterns of hierarchical expertise. Small wonder that the politics of advocacy are among the most contested issues in present-day activism and research. The challenge is to devise strategies for distinguishing responsible advocacy from inappropriate intervention and appropriation: to acknowledge that "we" cannot always speak for ourselves, yet people who speak for us, on our behalf or about us, are as often underinformed, self-interested, and imperialistic as they are supportive and empowering. Although it would be impossible to spell out rules for responsible advocacy or for protection against its abuses and misuses, clear violations of the trust, sensitivity, and integrity on which it relies are constantly exposed in feminist-informed deliberation. Once acknowledged, they can begin to indicate, by contrast, how responsibilities might be entered differently. Knowing what is wrong does not always show, automatically, what would be right; but it opens the way to clearer deliberation toward that end, after the fashion of the detective story I mention in chapter three. Thus, the failures of "one policy, one diagnosis fits all," vividly apparent in my welfare and medical examples, become catalysts for transformative advocacy. In guiding that effort, ecological thinking offers a more responsible approach than those mandated by the discourses of disinterested autonomy.

Ecological Implications

The decentering of the subject, gained by the labors of structuralism and

poststructuralism, leveled hierarchies and shifted a vertical vision of the world toward

a more horizontal one, so important for feminism, that places on the same surface

both multiculturalism and ecology.

—Verena Conley, Ecopolitics *(emphasis original)*

When I do not see plurality stressed in the very structure of a theory, I know that

I will have to do lots of acrobatics—like a contortionist or tight-rope walker—

to have this theory speak to me without allowing the theory to distort me

in my complexity.

—María C. Lugones, "On the Logic of Pluralist Feminism" *(emphasis original)*

Revisionary projects of thinking through the subjections consequent upon perversions of autonomy can be only minimally transformative so long as they remain framed within the confines of an individualistic imaginary where, as Val Plumwood persuasively observes, the subject "loses a sense of itself not only as an organic but as a social being, as an agent in and chooser of political, economic and technological frameworks."[72] Softening the coercive force of individualism's social imperatives, elaborating individual selfhood into social, intersubjective multiples of the Same, may perhaps unsettle the hegemony of the framework. But the discourses of mastery spawned and nurtured at the confluence of individualism and hyperbolic autonomy permeate the instituted social imaginary so thoroughly that internal tinkering with their detail cannot achieve the transformative effects that revisionary politics so urgently require. Ethical self-mastery, political mastery over unruly and aberrant Others, epistemic mastery over the "external" world, pose as the still-attainable goals of the philosophy of rights. They maintain the tensions between autonomy and advocacy I have discussed and sustain hierarchical, often exploitative relations between members of privileged cultures and members of nonaffluent, non-western/non-northern societies and cultures both at home and abroad.

72. Plumwood, *Feminism and the Mastery of Nature*, 119.

These relations are configured into top-down (= vertical) patterns of authority and expertise that work to legitimate domination in the name of an achieved *mastery of* the human and natural world and *mastery over* the personal idiosyncrasies of the masters.[73] They endorse exaggerated proclamations of the "permanent value" (in Cixous's words) of the abstract autonomous agency integral to the philosophy of rights, which reduces plurality to variations on the Same, substitutes instrumental policy decisions for open, deliberative democratic practices, and distorts the complexities of specific positionings and allegiances in the name of universal, impartial rights, obligations, and duties. These discourses underwrite an equivalently reductive picture I will sketch in chapter six, of epistemic agents as isolated units on an indifferent landscape, to which their relation is one of disengaged indifference.

In contradistinction to discourses of mastery and domination, in the preceding and the following chapters I enlist the ethico-political potential of ecological thinking to reconfigure knowledge, sociality, and subjectivity.[74] This proposal, I have noted, is not merely about injecting an "alternative" social imaginary into the old-but-not-tired hegemonic imaginary, by way of offering a choice, for it reconceives human locations and relations all the way down. It infiltrates the interstices of the social order, where it expands to undermine its intransigent structures, as the ice of the Canadian winter expands to produce upheavals in the pavements and roads, working within/against these seemingly solid structures to disrupt their smooth surfaces.

The decentering that ecological thinking sets in motion is enacted in its refusal to continue silently participating in a philosophy tacitly derived solely, if imperceptibly, from the white, affluent, western, male experiences that generate hyperbolic autonomy ideals. It displaces "man" from his central position in the world and in himself and disturbs the (often narcissistic) inwardness of autonomy in its self-transparency aspect. Hence my claim, in the introduction, that ecological thinking's revolutionary potential recalls Kant's Copernican revolution, which moved "man" *to* the center of the philosophical-conceptual universe. It redirects the focus of epistemic analyses toward situated knowledges, situated ethico-politics, where situation is constitutive of, not just the context for, the backdrop against which, enactments of subjectivity

---

73. Plumwood writes of "variations on the reason/nature story which develop in tandem with the emerging [capitalist] systems of individual appropriation and distribution [and] turn on a concept of...individual rationality, which denies both human and social others and earth others in its concept of the rational egoist subject of social and economic life" (ibid., 141).

74. As I indicate in the introduction, I take the term *ethico-political* from Bar On and Ferguson, *Daring to Be Good.*

occur. (Donna Haraway comments: "I have a body and mind as much constructed by the post–Second World War arms race and cold war as by the women's movements.")[75]

In this chapter, I have represented advocacy relations as micropractices that challenge the hegemonic social imaginary of autonomous individualism. They initiate disruptions through critique enacted in oppositional praxes, not merely for the sake of refusal but to demonstrate ways of working toward more habitable habitats in which to acknowledge and make space (rhetorical, physical, *agenda* space) for subjugated knowledges such as women's inexplicable medical disorders; habitats where the modes of being on which perversions of autonomy rely will no longer find so comfortable a place. In its sustained critique, this work aims not just to enable the epistemically disenfranchised to gain a hearing, although that counts among its most noble practical goals. But, conceptually, it engages with the social imaginary of autonomy and mastery—and the philosophy of the self it engenders—with the deeper, more wide-ranging intention of bringing to critical social awareness what Cixous calls "the limits of the breakthrough it represented." It contributes to enabling a creatively interrogating, *instituting* social imaginary to undermine and begin to displace an *instituted* imaginary whose claims to represent the natural way of being and knowing cannot be condoned in societies committed in their thinking and acting to honoring principles of ideal cohabitation.[76]

In its respect for particularity, ecological thinking is committed to a methodological pluralism. Thus advocacy becomes neither a new paradigm nor a universally valid method simply to be applied across the places where ecological thinking makes a difference. Nor are all advocacy relations alike, all advocacy practices homogeneous. They may have to produce multiple studies of (often linked, sometimes markedly differing) oppressions, multiple studies of "the same" oppression from various locations and implications, with attention to different evidential repertoires; they generate multiple coalitions and forms of activism, where the trick is to understand the connections that grant the myriad oppressions of white patriarchal capitalist societies their mutually reinforcing power and to develop disruptive, liberatory strategies.[77]

75. Haraway, "A Cyborg Manifesto." In *Simians, Cyborgs, and Women*, 173.
76. Castoriadis, as I have noted, discusses the creative power of the instituting imaginary in "Radical Imagination."
77. See also Cuomo, *Feminism and Ecological Communities*, esp. chap. 7: "Activism That Is Not One."

Where a relational autonomy drawn from the polite relations of ordinary liberal societies starts well above the bottom line of struggles for autonomous control even over one's body that sickness, poverty, malnutrition, and oppression can erase or render impossible, in ecological thinking places of excess in the negative effects of the unnatural lottery become starting places for investigation and critique, yet not for blame, or for subjection within an illusory autonomous sameness. With its conception of materially situated subjectivity for which embodied location and deliberative interdependence are constitutive of the very possibility of knowledge and action, ecological thinking opens the way to a renewed conception of responsible citizenship, as responsible in its knowing as in its doing.

*Il est plus aisé de connoître l'homme en général que de connoître un homme
en particulier.*

—*La Rochefoucauld,* Maximes (1665), *no.* 436

6

RATIONAL IMAGINING, RESPONSIBLE KNOWING

How Far Can You See from Here?

In the introduction to *Freedom and Interpretation: The Oxford Amnesty Lectures
1992,* Barbara Johnson writes that contributors to the lecture series were asked to
"consider the consequences of the deconstruction of the self for the liberal tradition," to think about whether the self "as construed by the liberal tradition still
exist[s]" and, if it does not, "whose human rights are we [= we Amnesty activists]
defending?"[1] They were to address an apparent conflict, then, between the defense
of human rights at the core of Amnesty International's mandate and postmodern
deconstructions of the humanistic subject, which contest the very idea of the
unified, autonomous, self-reliant rights-bearing self whom "rights talk" commonly
presupposes and thus of a moral-political agent responsible for respecting or entitled
to claim those rights. Because the self of the liberal-Enlightenment tradition is the

1. B. Johnson, *Freedom and Interpretation,* 2.

selfsame self who is the taken-for-granted knowing subject in orthodox Anglo-American theories of knowledge and because fulfilling its own mandate requires Amnesty to know, responsibly and well, the persons for whom and the situations in which it intervenes, these issues are as epistemologically significant as they are morally and politically urgent. They pose a range of equally complex questions about the intricacies of situated *epistemic* subjectivity: of subjects knowing and subjects known. This chapter engages, ecologically, with these questions.

Pertinent to this engagement is a conceptual contrast Johnson draws:

> While the Anglo-American ("liberal") tradition tends to speak about
> the "self," the French tradition tends to speak about the "subject."
> The concept of "self" is closely tied to the notion of property. I speak
> of "my" self. In the English tradition, the notions of "self" and
> "property" are inseparable from the notion of "rights." . . . The
> French tradition, derived most importantly from Descartes's "I think,
> therefore I am," centers on the importance of reason or thought as the
> foundation of (human) being. Where the "self," as property,
> resembles a thing, the "subject," as reason, resembles a grammatical
> function. . . . In the sentence "I think, *therefore* I am," what is posited
> is that it is *thinking* that gives the subject being.[2]

This self-or-subjectivity dyad forms the backdrop for my examination of some moral-political-epistemological implications of Amnesty's question to its contributors as it bears on issues connected with the epistemic subject, individuality, acknowledgment, and the place of imagination in the construction of knowledge. Yet even in discussions of the self as property—as a thing—in the English tradition, "the body" tends (implausibly) to figure as a standardized, generic body; and the Cartesian "thinking thing" maintains a principled distance from physicality. Thus my analysis is as skeptical about the political implications of conceiving the self as property as it is reluctant to represent thinking as the sole practice that gives the subject being. For, as I have indicated, the ecological subject who inhabits the pages of this book is both more and other than a rights-bearing thinker, even though it is both of these as well. It is, as Annette Baier, following Montaigne, puts it, "marvellously corporeal,"[3] ineluctably embodied: its spatially and temporally situated corporeality are as constitutive of the modalities of its being as its thoughts, feelings, and other "inner" processes.

---

2. Ibid., 3.
3. Baier, *Moral Prejudices*, 316.

It should be noted, moreover, that asking whether the self of the liberal tradition (the morally and epistemically autonomous bearer of rights, the rational self-conscious agent, and thence the orthodox empiricist knower) *still* exists is question-begging in its assumption that he has in fact ever been more than a fictive creature. My underlying thesis is that he has existed only in narrowly conceived theoretical places, abstracted and isolated from the exigencies and vagaries of human lives; and whenever he has figured in philosophical-political theory, he has been presumptively male, usually white, privileged, able-bodied, articulate, and educated. Of particular significance for my purposes is his principled isolation from the implications of corporeality, from the minutiae of individuality and situatedness, and from affectively informed or motivated participation in concerns that surface insistently in everyday interactions marked by vulnerability and trust and/or in experiences of trauma and crisis, where the requirements of responsible knowing are particularly urgent. The deconstruction of the self in postmodern thought, I am suggesting, is matched if not exceeded by ordinary and extraordinary contestations of the very possibility of integrated subjectivity and self-ownership, occurring routinely below the polite surface of the liberal tradition, for which "autonomous man" is emblematic of everything humanly admirable[4] and whose personal-social-material-ecological circumstances are presumed to be uniform, and so benign as to require no mention in analyses of rights-enabling or rights-thwarting projects. Thus Amnesty's question to its contributors confines the knowings it problematizes to deconstructions and fragmentations of selves at a level more abstractly theoretical, less experientially basic than the climate of oppression, torture, abuse, and rape its mandate requires it to address, where victims/survivors and others who attempt to know them and their circumstances well must deal with systemic assaults on "the self" far more radical than theoretical deconstruction and where people are more vulnerable than autonomous man ever seems to be. Everyday vulnerability and experiences of trauma make owning one's capacities, emotions, and actions far less matter-of-course than liberal assumptions about the self-sufficient self-as-property assume; yet, phenomenologically, such experiences are as central as autonomy to human being. Hence again the need to engage with the intricacies of epistemic and moral subjectivity.

---

4. In the liberal tradition, knowers were—and often still are—presumptively male: hence the masculine pronoun. This chapter is revised from my "Rational Imaginings, Responsible Knowings."

Nonetheless, some minimal version of rights talk as a court of legal and political appeal, together with the cognate language of rationality-as-objectivity, remains integral to this inquiry, for many of the fundamental rights, and much of the commonsense knowledge that privileged inhabitants of the "first world" take unthinkingly for granted, function as an unseen frame within which postmodern deconstructions of subjectivity and agency occur.[5] And human rights are integral to the articulation of Amnesty International's mandate. Indeed, not only do rights comprise one of the elements that make deconstructive projects possible but more fundamentally, in social-political structures where rights and power are intricately interwoven, neither the oppressed nor their advocates can underestimate the significance of rights for the pursuit of justice. Analogously, challenges to the very possibility of objectivity commonly occur within a framework of tacit assumptions, more plausible in materially replete societies than elsewhere, that, at the simplest material level, everyday "facts" are so readily and ubiquitously accessible that conversations across geographic, political, cultural, and other differences do not risk dissolving into radical incommensurability, even if complete congruity remains an elusive possibility. My intention is to extract both modes of discourse—rights and objectivity—from their intrication with the implausible individualism at the core of liberal discourses of self-ownership and epistemic autonomy:[6] I read the liberal conception of the self against these ideas, to expose its limitations. But "self-or-subject" is not a tidy distinction, nor does it function dichotomously either in this chapter or in the social-political world. Both rights talk (= talk of liberal selves) and discourses of enacted, located, and fragmented subjectivity variously inform feminist and other antioppression, postcolonial analyses: there need be no forced choice between them, for selves are multifaceted in their responses to situations and other selves. Thus, the Amnesty question is partly about how these locutions—self-or-subject—function, against and within one another.

5. Honneth, in his discussion of George Herbert Mead, makes the point well: "Rights are, as it were, the individualized claims about which I can be sure that the generalized other would meet them. . . . For in realizing that they are obliged to respect one's rights . . . [members of one's community] ascribe to one the quality of morally responsible agency" (*Struggle for Recognition*, 79–80).

6. In his lecture "Self as *Ipse*," Ricoeur maintains, persuasively, that "human rights do not necessarily rely on the presupposition of a 'liberal' self . . . [on the] self that *atomistic* political philosophies take for granted . . . a rational self . . . equipped with rights prior to engaging in any form of societal life" (119).

As Amnesty activists also must, I examine how so-called limit experiences—those that traverse, exceed, and interrogate the viable extension of the norms embedded in the normalizing discourses of white western societies—contest a sedimented liberal ontology, epistemology, and morality of the self with its ingrained assumptions about the manageability and predictability of the world, both physical and human. Nor does the radical reconfiguring of subjectivity these experiences demand remain sealed within philosophy. It is operative in the *Lebenswelt* where it engages with lives in which the very possibility of achieving or maintaining a (liberal) "sense of self" would come under pressure from story lines too difficult to bear, sustain, or imagine from a position of taken-for-granted self-ownership—from an unmarked "here"—and where yearnings for a return to or a reconstruction of subjective stability often betray a nostalgic misremembering of events and histories, both private and public.

Yet it is also difficult to discern how a guiding conception of fragmented, dispersed, evanescent subjectivity could foster the political acuity Amnesty's mandate requires. Indeed, the question posed to the Amnesty lecturers may have the effect of urging a recuperation of a demonstrably hollow conception of subjectivity; may rest on a tacitly maintained quest for a self that never was; may be tailor-made to perpetuate an imaginary fundamentally limited in its emancipatory-liberatory potential because of the false hopes it engenders. Amnesty essayists and activists are enjoined to practice a peculiarly imaginative, responsive knowing, to be wary of replicating the very silencings and other oppressions that Amnesty aims to counteract. In consequence, questions about epistemic violence and imperialism, political oppression, and torture open out into vexed questions, continuous with some of the questions I raise in chapter five, about how practitioners and other putative activist-knowers situated in comfort and stability can know radically "other" selves and situations well enough to judge/advocate/intervene without appropriating or colonizing them. Sometimes they appear to do so, even in radical experiential incongruity: but such impressions have to be carefully monitored to discern whether they claim successful intervention only because they have somehow imposed their own values, their standards of freedom and interpretation, onto those for, or on behalf of, whom they have acted. How could they know well enough to avoid appropriation, from and within limits of locational specificity that constrain both the knower and the known?[7] Such questions, again, invoke an ecological imperative for which responsible knowing cannot restrict its focus to "the

---

7. I discuss this matter more fully in "How to Think Globally."

individual," but must take into account her/his circumstances and situation, habitus and ethos, in their ecological specificity.

As I have posed them, these questions generate two further, particularly vexed questions that need to be addressed at this juncture: What place can reasonably be claimed for imagination in the construction of knowledge; and what could it mean for knowing to count as peculiarly imaginative and responsive, in an emancipatory-liberatory sense? Given an entrenched normative epistemological distinction between knowledge and imagination, according to which imagination need not serve truth-seeking purposes and indeed very likely cannot, the case I am making for the epistemic value, often in fact the necessity of imagination requires special care. In light of my argument so far, making that case presents a peculiar challenge, for I have advanced this book's central thesis as designed to contest a governing, instituted imaginary so as to make way for a renewed, instituting imaginary and have spoken as though all thinking, knowing, doing occurred *within* an imaginary—as indeed I believe it does. In turning to discuss imagination as it figures in this chapter, I am introducing a further twist to that larger argument, maintaining that imagining, too, occurs within an imaginary even when, as I will argue, its purpose is to interrupt, destabilize, that very imaginary in demonstrating the necessity, and the difficulty, of thinking beyond its confines.

Especially for purposes of this chapter, imagination as it contributes to the construction of knowledge is to be read phenomenologically, as a practice that requires "bracketing" presumptions of sameness within or beneath surface differences, even though, perhaps paradoxically, it must also presuppose a certain human commonality if it is to perform its imaginative function well. So it is a delicate process, requiring the careful sensitivity integral, more generally, to the responsive-responsible knowing I have advocated in other situations, throughout this book. The power of imagination for the subject matter of this chapter is in its commitment to taking seriously the possibility—indeed, the high *probability*—of radical difference: the possibility that points of commonality across lives, circumstances, and responses to them, ways of living in and with them, experiencing them, might very well be far fewer than liberal theory and social-political policies designed according to its ready-made template often take, unimaginatively, for granted. But this is not the whole story. The phenomenological aspect is realized in imaginative efforts to understand something of how it *is* to be so differently positioned from the imaginer that nothing can be assumed before the fact: this is the point of the bracketing. Responsible imagining is unlikely to be a one-off achievement: it requires work, careful work, research, consultation, negotiation, interpretation. It is rarely a solitary endeavor and is less likely to be successful when it tries or purports to be, for it needs the voices of an interpretive community. Where possible (i.e., where the Other(s) is/are available and able to provide it) it requires constant checking for confirmation or misreading: it demands a certain epistemic humility prompted by wariness of premature closure and further complicated by a recognition that "we" cannot always know the truths of our own lives. Imagination here, then, is about making such attempts as are feasible to think one's way into the situations of differently situated Others, including principally (for this argument) but not exclusively, the marginalized, the otherwise damaged; and not just for the sake of it, but to attempt to undo some of the damage enacted by often-coercive presumptions of sameness. It need not be a top-down process, from the privileged to the not- or less-privileged; although in this chapter's analysis it mostly is. Either way, it is a liberatory project in its quest to avoid easy categorization, Procrustean processes of slotting people into conceptual boxes and kinds that are both crude and harmful as putative epistemic devices. It is liberatory, too, in its ecological commitments to understanding the implications for (a) human subject(s) of occupying social-political-economic positions radically different from the knower's and of assuming from the start that these are neither homogeneous nor interchangeable. Honoring this commitment requires circumspection in imagining how it is to be in that place and circumstance, with those conditions, however strange and improbable they may seem. My thesis is that starting from expectations of differences not immediately knowable in the way that classical empiricists claim to know unmediated facts can move toward an epistemic orientation that makes it possible to see far more than the "pair of glasses on my nose" whose effects are to make everyone, everything, everyplace, look simply like variations on the same.[8] Such a starting point could prompt the kind of sensitive imagining of other people's lives and what it is like to live them that is so palpably absent from knowing that attends merely to the barest outline of the situation or endeavors simply to remember that "they" might not proceed from the same assumptions "we" do (but really, they *should,* and would if they could!).

As I have observed, in orthodox Anglo-American theories of knowledge the liberal self appears as a standardized but barely acknowledged epistemic subject: a subject, as I observe in chapter four, who is everyone and no one. He is presumptively adult (but not old), able-bodied, white, and male, although even such minimal details of his physical being rarely figure explicitly in epistemology's theoretical apparatus. He is a dislocated, shadowy figure not merely by

---

8. The allusion is to Wittgenstein's reference to "a pair of glasses on our nose through which we see whatever we look at. It never occurs to us to take them off" (*Philosophical Investigations,* §103).

accident but by design, for the regulative assumption is that it would detract from epistemology's defining tasks to claim greater epistemic significance either for the specificities of his location or for the material, social-political, ecological, affective particularities that prompt, engage, or thwart his knowledge-making activities than one would claim for the color of his eyes. For epistemological purposes, he is and *should be* solitary, self-reliant, and rational, disconnected from accidents of embodiment, history, and place—both physical-geographical and social—and from the distractions of human relationships, affect, and personal, social, or cultural history. Evidence of his having yielded to the influence of such distractions risks discrediting his claims to know, compromising his credibility. Particularly salient for the issues I address in this chapter, as I have begun to show, is how a stark objectivity requirement—a condition sine qua non for knowledge in "the epistemological project"—underwrites the expectation that this putative knower both can and will expunge *imagination*, along with negotiation and interpretation, from his cognitive endeavors so as to escape their ineluctably subjective threat and that anyone in comparable circumstances could replicate his knowledge without variation or interference.

Although the "comparable circumstances" condition may seem to introduce the very situational detail I have been advocating throughout this book, for orthodox epistemologists the requirement is purely formal. It refers to observational circumstances arranged and controlled before the fact, a mere backdrop of no particular consequence, thus neither an integral nor a constitutive feature of the epistemic setting. Their formal character assumes that knowledge-producing projects conducted in such circumstances require no special imaginative effort or interpretive skill. As I have explained in chapter two, when observations move to the laboratory, a further presumption accompanies them, according to which information-processing from controlled input to statistically variant output offers the best available, standard-setting form of knowledge—thence the status of the laboratory as the privileged site of natural knowledge making. Ironically, then, the epistemic subject is imagined as an unimaginative, disembodied, faceless, placeless, affect- and interest-free "individual" who could be anyone or everyone, but is nonetheless presumptively male, albeit generically so.

From the logic of the model it follows that this knower would be unable to know things well enough to do anything with or about them, to engage with them, or to care about them either positively or negatively. Emphasis is placed (recalling Bruno Latour) on matters of fact, to the exclusion of matters of concern. The exemplary status accorded such knowledge claims fails to reveal what part empirical "knowns" could play in anyone's life outside a framework of circumscribed observational moments or beyond the confines of the laboratory.

In consequence, and not surprisingly, other people rarely figure in what this knower knows, except in perceptual recognitions—this is a man but that is a robot—or in laboratory experiments investigating standardized, quantifiable behavioral responses from which (subjective) specificities are erased. Rooted in his observation post, which is strictly separated from anything he claims to know, this epistemic subject is restricted in his knowings to what he can see from there.

Neither in the everydayness of "ordinary lives" nor in professional-institutional settings, therefore, can the hegemonic epistemologies of empiricist-liberal societies offer more than scant resources to situated epistemic subjects when, as in responding to Amnesty's question, they need to know other people responsibly, not only because their rights are under threat, but because their very being is under pressure. A set of—usually unstated—assumptions informs much prefeminist moral philosophy, to the effect that *moral* deliberation, as a matter of course, is adequately informed in its knowing of situations, actions, and states of affairs that require moral judgment.[9] A taken-for-granted, rarely articulated or interrogated empiricist-realist stance—almost a *naive* realism—implicitly allows most standard moral theories to work with a picture of knowledge for which right perception is alike in all moral agents, who therefore can readily "put themselves in anyone else's shoes." They will all see/know the same things, formulate problems in the same way, and thus start from the same place in moral deliberation. Yet the very possibility of approaching deliberation from so secure a sense that debate-generating situations are readily and uniformly *known* is, in large part, a function of the simplified, artificially self-contained problems and dilemmas that theorists commonly cite to exemplify moral conflict—between keeping an appointment and saving a drowning child; between an absolute duty not to tell a lie and a particular duty to a fugitive whose whereabouts one knows. Their exemplary role in the theory is intended to affirm their representative status: all knowledge properly so called will be like this, verifiable by any observer and foundational in that more elaborated bodies of knowledge can be based upon such propositional certainties. This tacit experiential-empirical standardization allows the often-unarticulated commonsensical knowings that inform moral deliberation to claim a degree of plausibility in consequence of which, it seems, no *negotiation* is required to establish the knowledge base from which it works (recall my note about the doctrine of judicial notice in chapter three).

Such epistemic aspects of situations and events drop out of the question as Amnesty poses it: and yet they are crucial to answering it well. Again, a

9. Here I am drawing on my "Narratives of Responsibility and Agency."

commitment to maintaining objective detachment from the object of knowledge requires moral epistemologists to work with an imagined knowledge-and-subjectivity for which knowledge is achieved by a legislated purging of *imagination* and particularity; and subjectivity is uniform, yet rarely individuated. The worry is that imagination exercised by the knower would blur distinctions between knowledge and fantasy, and attention to particularity would paralyze inquiry by reducing its range to the merely anecdotal, incidental. (Recall also the bureaucratic skepticism Karen Messing encountered in seeking acknowledgment for her findings about the minutiae of women's workplace symptoms.) Affect, too, must be purged from the knower's rational processes, for it could only compromise objective clarity; and affect in those to be known would be chaotic, unstable, thus unknowable. Within these restrictions, the very idea of imaginative or affective *knowledge* becomes oxymoronic. Such assumptions block putative knowings prompted and informed by, or dependent upon, the very specific functioning of affect: of pain, pleasure, sorrow, passion, fear, commitment, enthusiasm, suffering, joy. Hence for orthodox epistemic subjects working within the Amnesty mandate, it is hard to know well enough to respond appropriately in situations that fall outside the limits of ordinary experiential expectations. For it is neither the self as onetime rights bearer nor the self as theoretically dispersed who pushes most urgently at the boundaries of received, objectivist knowledge, but the embodied, often injured subject, struggling to construct or reconstruct a livable way of being out of systemic oppression or out of trauma, grief, or despair. Its dispersal puts the affective-imaginative self-certainties of would-be (humanistic) knowers into question just when—as in Amnesty interventions—those putatively more "stable" selves encounter urgent demands to maintain a constancy that can allow them to know well enough to act responsibly, intelligently, effectively.

Despite more than three decades of feminist and postcolonial critique, at the beginning of the twenty-first century, idealized versions of a hybrid, depersonalized objectivism of Baconian, Cartesian, and positivistic lineage continue to exert a pull on regulative epistemic principles, even in theories committed to modifying or evading its reductive excesses.[10] That pull will not be resisted or countered merely by calling epistemology to account for being too abstract, scientistic, reductive, remote from ordinary epistemic lives; although that very project is well advanced in feminist and other postcolonial theories, the pull remains strong. Hence in this chapter I examine how these epistemic restrictions operate in places and circumstances where responsible knowing

10. For feminist critiques of this model, under the label *realism*, see E. Lloyd, "Feminism as Method"; and Barad, "Meeting the Universe Halfway."

makes a difference—often a vital difference—to people's lives, for the sake both of exposing certain obstacles produced by the trickle-down effects of an intransigent epistemic imaginary and of working within its interstices to disrupt and subvert it, for the orthodox epistemic subject is a plausible figure only within a reductively homogeneous everydayness represented as the experiential, circumstantial norm and masquerading as "the human condition." He does not travel well into situations where knowing people in complex, elaborated, and often extraordinary situations is the issue. There, it is not so easy for him to go on constructing his knowledge around unexamined assumptions that everyone is just like *him*, anyone can stand in as knower or known for anyone else, can "put himself in anyone else's shoes." The idea that circumstances and locations are interchangeable at least in those of their aspects worthy of epistemic scrutiny, so that their (contaminating) influence can be scraped away to afford access to an unreconstructed experiential immediacy, is simply implausible.

Contra such beliefs, I am advocating an *imaginative-interpretive* attentiveness to human and locational specificities and commonalities as essential for knowing people well enough to act responsibly and respectfully with them, toward them, or for them. Here again, as in my analysis in chapter three, the required sensitivity enjoins circumspect *negotiation* between subjects-to-be-known and putative knowers, in the interest of achieving reasonable understandings across experiences and situations far less knowable either instantaneously or from surface readings than simple observational givens are imagined to be. My hope is that such attentively sensitive engagement will contribute another piece to this project of reconfiguring epistemology and its "knowing subjects" by extracting epistemic projects from their long-standing complicity in sustaining antiecological, patriarchal, racialized, and other asymmetrical distributions of power and privilege. On this view, *imagination* as I have elaborated its implications here claims acknowledgment as a component of epistemic practices that is as rational as orthodox observational knowing and its multiples.

Paul Ricoeur raises the issue of imagination in his Amnesty lecture, "Self as *Ipse*," where he appeals to "the notion of *narrative* identity . . . [as] the indispensable link between the identity of a speaking and acting subject and that of an ethico-juridical subject."[11] Whatever its stability, veracity or contestability, and however contested the very idea of first-person privileged access has also become in the aftermath of the "deconstruction of the self," narrative identity is spatially and temporally situated in its own evolving specificity and socially located in its

---

11. Ricoeur, "Self as *Ipse*," 114 (emphasis added).

utterances connecting "an 'I' and a 'you.' "[12] Thus it is consonant with ecological thinking, particularly in the place it accords the bioregional narratives I mention in chapter one and their analogues. Because of narrative's proximity, likewise, to the descriptive methods of existential phenomenology, narrative identity can contribute to developing what Sonia Kruks, in a different register, refers to as "concepts of a subject that is neither reduced to pure freedom nor is the passive plaything of social and discursive forces."[13] Thus in response to Amnesty's question, Ricoeur proposes a revisioned, addressive-dialogic selfhood *enacted* in an ability to take present, and future, responsibility for its thoughts and deeds. This is a subject for which "*recognition* is constitutive of both the self and his/her other";[14] thus a subject open to first- and third-person narratives from which people often learn as much about themselves as about the other-as-narrator; and, perhaps most significantly, a subject not complete onto itself but one that requires interlocutors, listeners sensitive to the modalities and nuances of the tellings.

Carefully enacted, such a shift toward reciprocity and responsibility introduces a strategy for interrupting the orthodox conception of knowledgeable subjectivity, opening it out interpretively, imaginatively, into articulations that, in distancing themselves from monologic affirmations of rights and self-ownership, can begin to refuse suppressions of affect and specificity. But such refusals could not be mere add-ons to the already-imagined subject: properly incorporated, they might initiate a process whose potential would be radical in the reconfigurations it could set in motion. Grounding the project dialogically, *interpretively* as Ricoeur does, with appeals to imaginative variations on identity "enhanced by literature,"[15] suggests that self, subjectivity, and epistemic agency have to be radically renegotiated if imaginative knowing is to yield more than rehearsals of the ready-made scripts available in the hegemonic liberal social imaginary. On some readings, literature in the west, too, is associated with liberal democracies observant, in J. Hillis Miller's words, of "fundamental human rights or civil liberties"; and predictions of the end of literature, as "new media gradually replace the printed book,"[16] are as symptomatic of postliberal theory as announcements of the deconstruction of the liberal self (to which, according to Miller, literature since Foucault and Barthes also contributes). Thus, viable practices of enlisting narrative will have to cast their nets widely if they are to

---

12. Ibid., 111.
13. Kruks, *Retrieving Experience*, 18.
14. Ricoeur, "Self as *Ipse*," 119 (emphasis added).
15. Ibid., 115.
16. See Miller, *On Literature*, 3, 2.

avoid drawing the boundaries of responsible epistemic community in ways that restrict membership to populations of privilege defined by a breed of literacy that venerates a literature presumptively unfettered in its creative freedom and interpretation, and universal in its pertinence to *the* human condition. With this caveat, Ricoeur's appeal to narrative offers one plausible point of entry into ecological imagining.

In the next section I develop a critical response to these issues through a reading of Mark Johnson's *Moral Imagination.* My aim is to show how entrenched assumptions about the imagination, in the literary and social imaginary of the affluent liberal western world and the epistemic imaginary inherited from analytic philosophy, at once enable and confound attempts to rethink subjectivity and self-ownership. More specifically, here I am illustrating and amplifying my claims from earlier chapters to the effect that images, metaphors, imaginings, and a governing imaginary are more and other than mere rhetorical devices, superimposed upon or embellishing an otherwise flat-footedly literal language capable, without their help, of mapping the "outside world" congruently and with no leftovers. Responsible imagining is more and other than a simple stretching, an additive or variational extension of empirical seeing: indeed, imagination thus construed could not enable epistemic subjects to imagine rationally or know responsibly beyond a narrowly delineated "here." Paradoxically, as I have observed, acts of imagination themselves occur within an imaginary whose limits they may transgress, challenge, or destabilize, whose governing assumptions they may interrupt, but that nonetheless sets the conceptual frame—at least for now—and participates in constituting "the real" from, about, or within which imagining takes its point of departure, to articulate possibilities of comprehension, uptake, acknowledgment.

Ordinary Lives

In *Moral Imagination*, Mark Johnson develops a naturalized analysis of imagination at work in "ordinary" people's lives maintaining, with an appeal to cognitive science, that "we human beings are imaginative creatures, from our most mundane, automatic acts of perception all the way up to our most abstract conceptualization and reasoning."[17] Imagining, he claims, is integral to the "discriminations" that enable people to act "sensibly and *responsibly* toward others."[18] Referring to certain "prototypical" and "nonprototypical"

17. M. Johnson, *Moral Imagination*, ix.
18. Ibid., x (emphasis added).

conceptual structures that, according to experimental evidence, shape human reasoning across a range of situations, Johnson argues that imagination is no enemy of reason, for concepts and reasoning are "grounded in . . . bodily experience and . . . structured by various kinds of imaginative process." In his view, reason devoid of imagination lacks the conceptual-theoretical scope to go beyond simple, exemplary cases to "those that are either nonprototypical or completely novel."[19] Thus, consonant with claims I have been making throughout this book, Johnson deplores erasures of imagination and of the implications of embodiment from the governing conceptions of rationality in objectivist epistemologies and moral philosophies.

People interpret their lives through socially entrenched metaphors of "common moral understanding,"[20] Johnson argues, picking up a theme of his coauthored book *Metaphors We Live By*.[21] Such moral understanding evolves within a metaphorics, an open-ended, malleable system of metaphors and sedimented imaginings embodying a communal sense of how things are and framing moral perceptions and deliberations: a system somewhat analogous to an imaginary, then, in the sense I have evoked. Thus for Johnson, knowing emerges as an "imaginative exploration and transformation of experience" and not, he insists, as a "pigeonholing of cases under a set of fixed rules"[22] or descriptions: in consequence, the sheer plethora of "possible framings" for any situation enjoins modesty in claiming knowledge[23] and cautions against reductivism. Hence, as I have also suggested, good moral decisions depend in large part on the quality of the imaginings that shape and inform them. Nor, again, is imagination itself merely subjective: it is as communal as it is individual:[24] not, I think, just because of this communal sense to which Johnson appeals but also, and as significantly, because people talk to each other—an aspect of commonality too important to take simply as given, especially in view of the persistently monologic tone, and the presumed interiority, of so much epistemological discourse.

19. Ibid., 1, 3.
20. Ibid., 52.
21. Lakoff and Johnson, *Metaphors We Live By*.
22. *Moral Imagination*, 80.
23. Ibid., 12.
24. As I indicate in previous chapters, a system of communal imaginings is what Le Dœuff and Castoriadis, in different contexts, call "an imaginary"; see Le Dœuff, *Philosophical Imaginary*; idem, *Sex of Knowing*; and Castoriadis, "Radical Imagination." Johnson quotes Hilary Putnam, for whom Kant "is doing what he would have called 'philosophical anthropology,' or providing . . . *a moral image of the world*" (*Moral Imagination*, 65).

For Johnson, objectivists work with an "impoverished conception of reason . . . [and] an equally problematic correlative view of the self . . . [that] cannot account for . . . the moral identity of a person [as] an ongoing, culturally and historically situated, imaginative process of thought and action";[25] for how "we grope around for our identity, which is never a fixed or finished thing." What it knows and how it acts matters to this epistemic (and moral) subject, for the self is "at stake in moments of choice and deliberation," conceived as activities "of self-understanding, critical self-reflection, and self-formation."[26] Human beings, on this view, are both "*constituted* by sedimented cultural practices, institutions and meanings . . . and *constituting* beings who can . . . transform . . . structures of meaning and action."[27] Such constitutive activities manifest themselves (recalling Ricoeur) in "narrative unities"[28] that frame and reframe people's self-understandings: these epistemic subjects are storytellers about their lives.

Johnson goes a considerable distance toward contesting the caricatured activities (= passivities!) of orthodox epistemic subjects with which feminist and other postcolonial theorists of knowledge have long taken issue. His is an innovative analysis of the imaginings most readily available in the "normal" operative spaces of ordinary lives in western societies: spaces at once hospitable to "most people's" everyday experiences and sources of the conceptual frames, the common sense, and the imagery out of which they construct their sense of self, community, and world. Thus his work offers a corrective to the exclusions of imagination integral to postpositivist moral epistemologies, even as it suggests how theorists might fill some of the gaps in the experience-remote theories that call forth feminist and postcolonial critique. I have looked to Johnson's text as a resource for ecological thinking, cognizant of the significance of imagination in knowing and able to initiate a shift away from orthodox epistemologies of mastery; and this reading has been productive. Yet these several consonances highlight some equally significant dissonances between our positions, which I now address.

Johnson argues persuasively that the epistemic activities of a generic knower are as imaginative as they are conventionally rational. He locates his claims within ordinary lives, substantiating them with psychological evidence, to naturalize his conclusions. Thus again, the conceptual framing of his

25. Johnson, *Moral Imagination*, 126.
26. Ibid., 147, 148.
27. Ibid., 161.
28. Ibid., 154.

position places it close to my own engagement with a revisioned naturalism. Yet my hesitations about going more than part of the way with him are prompted by tacit assumptions throughout the text, whose effects are to represent the scope of his conclusions as much broader than the premises of the inquiry permit. An analogy with standard "S-knows-that-p" knowledge claims—"Sarah knows that the door is locked"—will begin to clarify the point. As I have argued elsewhere,[29] claims uttered in this rubric perform an exemplary function within circumscribed observational frames where perceptual evidence seems to warrant straightforward, one-off conclusions, and in uncontested multiples of such evidence-derived, empirically verifiable knowings. But, in fact, such empirical claims are uncontested only within that same narrow purview from which so many of these examples are drawn. Their epistemic pertinence diminishes in situations whose complexity differs in both kind and degree from anything potentially derivable from accumulations of such stripped-down claims; and their capacity to address the specificities of knowers, situations, and events disruptive of the settled frame in which such knowings pass as paradigmatic is equally hard to discern. In short, "S-knows-that-p" claims are representative, exemplary across a far narrower range than orthodox empiricist epistemologists tend to allow. Contrary to Johnson's assumptions, they are communal for/to only a certain select community of knowers who, even in Johnson's analysis, often come across as solitary individuals after all, sealed up within their own imaginings. Openings for deliberation or negotiation are not easy to discern.

Restrictions on the representative status of "ordinary lives" comparable to those that limit the scope of simple "S-knows-that-p" examples thus circumscribe Johnson's inquiry. His implicit assumptions about such lives show by contrast and omission that epistemic subjects could, in fact, be liberated from their rootedness in an unspecifiable "here" only by means of thoroughly revisionary social-political analyses, capable of contesting the conceptions of selfhood and self-ownership to which Barbara Johnson refers and by interrogating assumptions about the uniformity of lives and situations, which are not mentioned in her analysis. In the next sections I move in and out of Mark Johnson's text, showing how it contributes to reconfiguring the place of imagination in knowing, yet indicating where it sustains beliefs inimical to, and indeed often obstructive of, the development of politically effective successor epistemologies.

29. See my *Rhetorical Spaces*, chap. 2, "Taking Subjecting Into Account."

Contra Johnson, after All

Donna Haraway's observation that "knowledge from the point of view of the unmarked is truly fantastic, distorted, and so irrational"[30] catches some of the troubling aspects of Mark Johnson's position. We "imaginative creatures" appear in his text within an epistemic-ethical frame that, despite its initial promise, departs only minimally from orthodox, individualistic liberal thought. True, imagination as he analyzes it stretches ahead of and backward away from the imaginer: it is neither time-, place-, nor even body-bound; thus it seems to release the epistemic subject from his blinkered rootedness to one spot. Johnson heralds this potential release within a cognitive science frame—he naturalizes it, sometimes situates it ecologically, locates it within narrative structures. Because I have advocated similar-sounding moves, I thought to find examples of imaginative, ecologically mapped reconfigurations of knowledge and subjectivity in this text, continuous with, and informative for, the epistemological project that animates my investigations in this book. Yet even with so many of the ingredients in place, the mix does not quite work; and the reasons are instructive well beyond the scope of the discussion in *Moral Imagination.*

Especially telling among these reasons is one of the overarching metaphors "we" live by: "life is a journey," which Johnson explains thus:

> In our culture, living a life is conceived of as a massive purposeful
> activity made up of a huge number of intermediate actions directed
> toward various purposes. We are expected to have goals . . . and to
> formulate life plans that make it possible for us to attain [them]. . . .
> A PURPOSEFUL LIFE IS A JOURNEY is perhaps the dominant
> metaphor by which we structure our experience, understanding, and
> language concerning our ongoing life projects.[31]

But whose culture is this, and by which of its members is life thus conceived? Whose experience is he assuming? Who can be so clear about her/his purposes or hope to fulfill them? expect to formulate plans? have ongoing life projects? claim recognition for their validity? live so smoothly that they will easily go through? Even within "our" (North American) culture, their number has always been restricted to a small, privileged group; in the aftermath of the social

---

30. Haraway, "Situated Knowledges," 193.
31. Johnson, *Moral Imagination,* 39.

upheavals and the collapse of social support systems in the 1990s and world events of the early twenty-first century, even for large numbers of the affluent, disruptions have come more often to be the norm. The metaphor is race, class, gender, and able-bodied specific: according to my students, it is generation specific as well.[32] Plucked whole from the situations where it might indeed pertain, this metaphor as Johnson invokes it claims a scope and a pertinence beyond what its constrained particularity can allow, turning those circumstances into everywhere and nowhere while failing to acknowledge the epistemic effects of the spatially and temporally specific habitus and ethos of its crafting and enactment.

In short, Johnson's examples, drawn mainly, if tacitly, from the lives of right-thinking affluent white western men, perpetuate an illusion that rational imaginings and responsible knowings, "in general" or "as such," fit easily into the ready-made frame of "our" lives, presented in the text so as to sustain an assumed uniformity, transparency, and straightforward self-ownership.[33] The vanilla imaginings on which the argument depends tacitly allow it to bypass the necessity, urgent in feminist and postcolonial theory and practice, of imagining experiences, events, circumstances remote from that frame, and often unimaginable within it.[34] He takes "our shared" moral intuitions, thoughts, principles, even experiences for granted, in a benignly "evolving environment" to which "we" adapt in the course of life's journey. Thus his examples are caught within the confines of an imaginary for which everyone is similarly located on a level playing field, as merely one instance of a universally imagined sameness whose effects are to render bodily and situational differences (among others) not so different after all. Although his appeals to imagination in knowledge and morality seem to break through the seamlessness of a stark objectivism in many of the ways feminists and other Others have advocated, just below the surface, there are problems. Johnson succeeds quite well in imagining the familiar, less well in imagining the strange, where "strange" means alien to the life of an articulate white American man. Indeed this conceptual apparatus can neither make the familiar strange nor approach the strange except by making it familiar. In consequence, Johnson's epistemic and

32. For an analysis of the class and race specificity of life plans, see Walker, *Moral Understandings*, chap. 6: "Career Selves."

33. The main protagonist of Johnson's stories is the "innocent" white man Ross observes in stories of "victims" of affirmative action (*Just Stories*, xvii).

34. I use the adjective *vanilla* to capture the ordinariness of Johnson's imaginings, their failure to disturb or disrupt. It contrasts, though not conflictually, with Meyers's use of the term in "Emotion and Heterodox Moral Perception."

moral subject remains fixed in place after all, unable to see or imagine very far from there and—appearances to the contrary—"there" is no unmarked, innocent place. His imaginings remain imperceptibly rooted in a very particular here and now.

The person who inhabits this text, then, is implicitly male, and one of those very liberal "selves" whose deconstruction the Amnesty lecturers were asked to consider. Noting that "women have not been granted the same prototypical status as men with respect to moral personhood" and that "'phallocentric' and racist biases...pervade Western culture,"[35] Johnson proposes ways of imagining beyond the stratified, stereotyped assumptions that these recognitions record. Although it sounds like a tired old story, the practices of "we-saying" to which he appeals serve to keep the imaginative subject firmly, and unseeingly, in his place. References to an unidentified, universalizing "we," "us," and "our" are jarring in their unselfconscious frequency. Given what "we" can unquestioningly assume, think, expect, do, there can be little doubt that "we" are able-bodied adult educated affluent white American men and considerable doubt about the scope—even the imaginative scope—of the "we." In a sense this might not matter, for it could be read as evidence that Johnson's is indeed a *situated* position on imagination and knowledge. But only a casual reading of situatedness would suggest such a conclusion. Integral to Haraway's conception of *situated knowledges* is a requirement for knowers to learn how to acknowledge and take responsibility for the implications and effects of situation, to recognize the impossibility of an innocent positioning, while striving to achieve a politically-epistemically responsible one. Yet although Johnson contends that "our very prototypes are in dispute,"[36] he unquestioningly presents them as "ours"—everyone's—a locution that might be a mere slip of the pen were the "we" and "our" not so silently aggregated.

Prototypes, Johnson asserts, "*can* supply what we need to make intelligent moral decisions," via "principles of extension...from the central to the non-central members within a category."[37] To this end, he grants a pivotal place to "imaginative empathetic projection into the experience of other people," which he glosses as putting oneself "in the place of another."[38] Here is a

35. Johnson, *Moral Imagination*, 99. Interestingly, women must be "granted" it, whereas (some) men can simply assume it.

36. Ibid., 99.

37. Ibid., 190 (emphasis original).

38. Ibid., 199.

further point of potential intersection between feminist imaginings and Johnson's views. Feminists, too—and I among them—have debated the desirability and the dangers of empathy,[39] conceived not simply in its affective or moral modalities, but also for its epistemic effectiveness. At least in its benign articulations, empathy emerges from many such debates as *desirable* for enabling respectful engagement across the myriad differences that responsible knowings have to negotiate, thus for promoting a more-than-merely-instrumental social order. Yet empathy can also be *dangerous* in its potential for affirming the center's capacity to co-opt, appropriate, own the experiences and situations of Others precisely because it claims to know them so closely, and thus in its availability to being enlisted to serve the interests of the powerful. Such dangers are writ large, narratively, in Gillian Slovo's novel *Red Dust*, which recounts the story of a hearing near Port Elizabeth, before South Africa's Truth and Reconciliation Commission. Striking is the sense she conveys of how minutely the torturer knew his victim's vulnerabilities, how, because of that knowing, the torture was so much more effective than it might have been. Negotiations around affirmations of the power of empathy are always delicate, and often ambivalent.

Such dangers resurface, albeit less violently, in Johnson's assumption that "we" can "inhabit [other people's worlds] . . . in imagination, feelings, and expression"[40]—a multiply dangerous assumption. Among its most troubling aspects is the direction of the extensions he proposes: *from* the central *to* the noncentral members of a group or society. It is not easy to see how such a projection could do more than confirm and consolidate "our" prototypes: the ones that belong to those at the center. Nor does it appear that prototypes more readily available to—with greater explanatory power for—those at the margins will inform or reconfigure the intelligent and/or empathic decision-making of those at the center or interrupt the assuredness of their deliberative principles and processes: the extensions appear to be unidirectional.[41] The appeal to empathy is troubling also in the starkly individualistic conception of "the self," at work in the conviction that, with a little imaginative effort, anyone can put her/himself "in anyone else's shoes." In this regard, Marguerite La Caze offers persuasive arguments and examples to support her contention that this assumption

39. See Ferguson, *Feminist Case against Bureaucracy*, and my *Rhetorical Spaces*, chap. 6, "I Know Just How You Feel."

40. Johnson, *Moral Imagination*, 200.

41. This is the point I elaborate in chap. five, with reference to autonomous man as a regulative prototype.

is, in fact, "the fundamental characteristic of the analytic imaginary."[42] As she rightly suggests, imagining ourselves in another's place is more likely to identify "what *our* interests would be if we were in their position" than to identify *their* interests: she contends that there is "no reason to think that these interests would be the same."[43] Despite the effectiveness he claims for empathy in breaking the boundedness of self-certainty, then, Johnson remains caught within a liberal assumption that Nicola Lacey, too, aptly critiques: that "a single individual can 'get inside' the experiences of others, imagine what their lives might be, *without ever having actually to listen to anyone else.*"[44] Hard cases, harder than those Johnson adduces, expose the limitations of such easy imaginative extensions.

The hooker's tale, which Johnson evidently cites in order to unsettle the homogeneity of the "we," is one such case. Analyzing the story of a hooker trying to "reconstruct the narrative of her actual lived experience... [to] explain... herself and her actions from a *moral* standpoint,"[45] Johnson reads past textual evidence of a systemically embedded sex/gender system that shapes her story of how it is to be a woman in a sexist society, accustomed to supplying sexual favors in order to attract, hold a man. Glossing over its material-experiential specificity in the power-saturated politics of a gender order where she is commodified less as a "self" than as a (any) female body, he draws the hooker's tale into "our" narratives, to illustrate how "*we ordinary humans* understand, deliberate, and evaluate within... narrative contexts, even though we are seldom aware of this."[46] Thus again he evokes the idea that "we" are constituted by cultural practices more in the name of an assumed bodily, locational, and experiential sameness than in imaginative engagement with the radical differences that separate "us," especially when he and the (unnamed) hooker comprise the putative "us." Is she just like him? is he just like her? or do they, somehow, split the difference to meet in the middle? These are questions he does not ask. Despite his plea for a self-knowledge aware of its "limitations, and blind spots," differences reduce, both in his reading of the

42. La Caze, *Analytic Imaginary*, 89.
43. Ibid., 111. Citing the example of an advertising executive determining whether his advertisements are offensive to women by imagining how *he* would feel in the position of a woman viewing them, La Caze comments: "His test was designed to determine how women *should* respond... not how [they]... would or do respond" (112, emphasis original).
44. Lacey, *Unspeakable Subjects*, 65 (emphasis original). I discuss listening in more detail in the next section of this chapter.
45. Johnson, *Moral Imagination*, 154 (emphasis original).
46. Ibid., 160 (emphasis original).

hooker's tale—and in a briefer allusion to the "limited, situated freedom" of an (also unnamed, but presumably "generic") Afro-American woman in the 1950s American South—to differences that merely mask "our" (unquestioned) commonalities, to a freedom "we all possess."[47]

Representing human development as gradual change with "infrequent . . . moments of more radical and rapid transformations"[48] presupposes a stability of lives lived evenly from beginning to middle to end in predictable, reasonably safe, and manageable circumstances. Adaptability, and imaginative techniques for achieving it, assume processes within a frame, or along a designated road whose contours hold fast. Yet Johnson fails to consider how a frame *could* hold fast in conceptual (= prototype) crises—"gaps, disjunctions, reversals, fractures"[49]—which, in the ordinary lives of feminists and other Others, count more as the norm than the exception.[50] Lives lived within sustained oppression, fragmented in fractured processes, situated in circumstances of radical unsafety, cannot adapt so readily, cannot keep on "weaving together the threads"[51] any more than lives lived in the modalities of a pervasive cognitive dissonance that commonly, if variably, marks women's lives even in the affluent places in patriarchal societies. Nor, as feminists know well, are "our" narratives so indisputably "our own" as assumptions of narrative unity imply: throughout the history of western thought, women's capacity to know, and thus to own their experiences, has met with persistent, often paternalistic skepticism. "The power of fictional narrative to develop our moral sensitivity, our ability to make subtle discriminations, and our empathy for others"[52] may indeed—for some—offer a potential corrective to dislocated, depersonalized epistemologies. But it comes up against its own limitations when lives and/or events defy narrative elaboration beyond an unimaginative rootedness in one situation, oblivious to its own fixity; when neither literacy nor the capacity to articulate the issues can be assumed; or when tellers have no

47. Ibid., 187, 162.
48. Ibid., 109.
49. Ibid., 170.
50. James notes: "The self for whom psychological continuity is a possibility . . . has to be created through a series of interactions between the child, people around it, and the broader culture in which it lives" ("Feminism in the Philosophy of Mind," 37).
51. Ibid., 152. Reporting the difficulty of persuading female sex workers in Mozambique to insist on sex with a condom, for which they are paid much less than sex without, Nolen writes: "They say they don't care about the future": the important thing is to give their children something to eat today ("Safe-Sex Theatre a Tough Sell," A22). As I have observed, planning for the future, having a "life plan," is a luxury of the affluent.
52. Johnson, *Moral Imagination*, 197.

reason to believe anyone is listening. "We," whoever we are, delude ourselves if we imagine that such moments are merely extraordinary.

These recognitions shift the locus of epistemic negotiation to a different level, for stories, too, are products of situations and imaginaries: they neither speak for themselves nor attest without question to the accuracy of first-person privileged access to a core "owned self," speaking its experiences "truly." Johnson's smooth narratives of ordinary self-ownership expose the poverty of an imagination that merely extends out from positions at the center, thus failing in its monologic tellings to negotiate the reciprocity and recognition that, for ecologically conceived and lived subjectivities, are constitutive of the self and her/his other(s) and integral to the habitus and ethos of viable human lives.

Despite Johnson's contention that imagination is as communal as it is individual, his references to "a free play of the imagination" reinforce the impression that individual imagining is indeed unfettered, thus neither constrained nor even shaped by "the hegemonic imaginary" within which it takes place. Moreover, because he conceives of imagination as *belonging to* someone, it remains oddly individualized even through his affirmations of its communal, public character: its putative commonality fails to exceed the sum of its parts. On his own terms, such suggestions should be highly implausible. Here especially, the traditional liberal self has to yield space for thinking about *subjectivity*, enactment: a conceptual frame Barbara Johnson finds in a reconstructed Cartesianism. She observes: "While Descartes saw a *coincidence* of human thinking with human being, Lacan sees a *disjunction*...an illusion of the stable self [that] motivates a lifelong attempt to 'catch up' to the image." In a Foucauldian disciplinary society, she notes, this subject becomes "a function of what a given society defines as thinkable."[53]

Even with his innovative proposals, then, Mark Johnson remains within what is readily defined as thinkable in white, affluent regions of liberal societies. In consequence, the conceptual apparatus he works with affords scant directives for thinking beyond the limits of the social imaginary operative, and regulative, within such societies. Although he defies the restrictions that make "*rational* imaginings" merely oxymoronic, his imaginative knowers live, reason, and imagine within the self-certainties of late capitalism, (white) androcentrism, individualism, and the rational, transparent, bounded, and unified "self construed by the liberal tradition" (recalling the Amnesty phrase), within the uncontested rightness of the American dream, where everyone has a life

53. B. Johnson, *Freedom and Interpretation*, 6.

plan and the freedom to pursue it, where knowledge enables mastery over the external world and morality enables mastery over the self. These certainties underwrite and frame orthodox epistemologies with their impersonal, interchangeable objectivity and the moral theories whose appeal to autonomy, individual rights, and equality of opportunity naturalizes liberal-derived interpretations of freedom, human decency, and "the good life."

Exceeding the Thinkable

The complex of interlocking assumptions that presume comfortable human sameness and discount singular experiences at the limits of what a society defines as thinkable is held in place by the hegemonic, *instituted social imaginary* whose effects I have been tracing throughout this book. As I have noted, a social imaginary is distantly analogous to a Kuhnian paradigm or a Foucauldian episteme; but it is neither about normal science nor only about how knowledge is spread out before the knower. It is about systems of metaphorics and interlocking explanations within which people in specific historical periods and geographical-cultural situations make sense of their lives and enact their knowledge and subjectivities. Imaginaries, I have also noted, are self-reinforcing rather as self-fulfilling prophesies are. Ongoing successes within them, an undisturbed smoothness of "life's journey" that continually sustains the dream, consolidates their sense of rightness. In one structural feature, however, they resemble both paradigms and epistemes: pressures, destabilizations, ruptures, breaks—from above, within, or below—repeated explanatory stress, may become so insistent that the imaginary, ultimately, can no longer accommodate it in its seamlessly enveloping story. Clearly, the center can no longer hold: and this despite the tenacity of beliefs, at the core of the replicability and universalizability requirements integral to the epistemologies the orthodox epistemic subject silently inhabits, that the center *must* continue to hold. How, then, to dislodge it?

Consider how both the Amnesty Lectures and the writings in which Susan Brison develops a first-person philosophical analysis of a rape (*her* rape)[54] contest the stability of the dominant social imaginary and the limitations of what is thinkable within it, how they expose human *vulnerability* as integral to, constitutive of, ordinary lives and subjectivities, at least as fully as autonomy is

---

54. Brison, "Surviving Sexual Violence"; idem, "On the Personal as Philosophical"; idem, "Outliving Oneself"; and idem, *Aftermath.*

imagined to be.[55] These examples highlight the vexed nature, even within an intelligently imaginative conceptual apparatus, of claims to know responsibly from an unmarked, generic "here." They suggest that professional philosophy's professed unconcern with the specificities of subjectivity conceals how some specificities, in their urgency, draw its attention so sharply and self-protectively as to prompt philosophers to relegate certain kinds of events and testimonials to the category of the nonrational, the merely particular, to cast them as aberrant episodic disturbances and often to disqualify their tellers as reliable testifiers to the stories of "their own" lives.

In Brison's analyses of self and subjectivity in disarray, striving for viable cohesion in posttraumatic stress following sexual violence, the personal in its affective particularity is indeed as philosophical—as epistemological—as it is political in the better-known feminist sense. She tells this story of rape, prolonged trauma, and recovery frankly in the first person, recreating an ordinary daytime walk in the French countryside becoming the scene of a brutal rape, after which she was beaten and left for dead. In these narrative retellings, Brison refuses the comfortable option of distancing herself from the story in the interests of generality or objectivity, thus breaking a philosophical taboo that keeps the subject, as knower or as known, hovering silently in the wings, speaking dispassionately in the third person, as into a void. She addresses her readers, offers them "imaginative access to what is, for some, an unimaginable experience,"[56] asks them to *listen*, to try to imagine how an event that fractures prototypical imaginings of "ordinary lives" can disrupt a self in whatever assuredness of self-ownership it might avow. Her writings show that it is not only or even principally the deconstructions of postmodernity that fragment the presumed unity of this subject, but everyday events for which the polite liberal imagination rarely has adequate conceptual resources.

Indeed, and crucially, Brison reminds her readers of "the everydayness of sexual violence," a reminder that should dislodge the standard knowing subject from the certainties, built into the epistemic imaginary he inhabits, about the matter-of-course safety of ordinary lives, should unsettle the structures holding that imaginary together, should destabilize his faith in life as a journey, at whose way-stations and whose end people simply arrive in the fullness of time. Ironically, its very everydayness "leads many to think that male violence against women is *natural*." Yet—recalling the tenacity of

---

55. Bergoffen develops a provocative analysis of vulnerability as a modality at least as centrally operative in human lives as autonomy; see her "February 22, 2001."
56. Brison, "Surviving Sexual Violence." 5.

assumptions that the center must hold after all—Brison observes: "While most people take sexual violence for granted, they simultaneously manage to deny that it really exists."[57] As my discussion of naturalizing in chapter two indicates, such observations expose the artifactuality of "the natural" with its capacity to underwrite an unjust social order in which "we"—thus both victim(s)/survivor(s) and the many who think and deny in these ways—"live the cultural meanings prescribed for our bodies because of our sex... [and] live our bodies differently under... system[s] of oppression."[58] The observations highlight the persistent complacency of beliefs in the settled order and orderliness of a society so privileged as to make it possible for (some of) its citizens to imagine violence—and other "unfortunate events"—as mere blemishes on an otherwise unsullied social surface; they affirm the tenacity of the liberal model with the polite imaginings that comprise its standard repertoire. Such traumatic, albeit ordinary, events in women's lives count merely as extraordinary for a social imaginary nourished to uphold expectations of smooth journeying and to discredit evidence that life's journeys are commonly not so smooth by relegating it to the aberrant, to places where a woman has "asked for it," having failed to play by the rules. An ecology of incredulity maps the epistemic terrain surrounding such episodes, to sustain the dream of affluent, androcentered safety, all evidence to the contrary notwithstanding. Here, in an imperative register, situation truly *is a place to know*, as Debra Bergoffen shows with her analysis of the implications of the U.N. Hague war crimes tribunal's landmark move toward redefining rape as a crime against humanity. In effect, a new *epistemology* of rape had to be instituted, in which issues of consent and female sexual integrity came to displace violence as the sine qua non defining characteristics of rape as a crime. Convictions of Bosnian Serb soldiers for crimes against humanity, Bergoffen argues, show that "we cannot forget that human bodies are abused when their intentionalities, specifically the intentionalities of integrity, are violated."[59] In so dramatic a move away from equating "self integrity with the integrity of the unmarked autonomous self,"[60] the court initiates a conceptual breakthrough that could count as a small step toward denaturalizing male violence against women, toward developing a genealogical-ecological analysis of the violations it enacts.

57. Ibid., 7 (emphasis added).
58. I owe the turn of phrase to La Caze, *Analytic Imaginary*, 91.
59. Bergoffen, "February 22, 2001," 121.
60. Ibid., 127.

Brison's theme is "the disintegration of the self experienced by victims of violence";[61] "the undoing of the self" in the undermining "of its most fundamental assumptions about the world";[62] the severing, when trauma is of human origin, of "the sustaining connection between the self and the rest of humanity."[63] Analogously, Barbara Johnson notes: "Torture...becomes an interference with the tortured one's narrative self-determination,"[64] a fragmentation of narrative unity that sharply challenges the smoothness of life's journey. And, taking Brison's work as her point of departure for addressing certain effects of the deconstruction of the self in torture and trauma, Susan James observes: "Trauma victims do not just lose their memories of past events or actions. They lose the pattern of memory in which their expectations, emotions, skills, desires, and so on are rooted, so that loss of memory is, in these cases, part of a broader destruction of character."[65] When expectation and confidence are impossible—for instance, in the safety of life's journey or in its smaller, everyday activities and journeys—James observes, then psychological continuity in which, philosophically, personal identity is said to consist is impossibly difficult to assume or maintain. How, then, can Amnesty activists respond to the question about whose human rights they are defending?

Brison's writings chronicle the willed unknowings that too much particularity—and too much suffering—evokes within professional philosophy marked, as it is, by a "disciplinary bias against thinking about the personal"[66] and assured of its power to achieve the exclusions of corporeality and affect necessary to keep particularity off its agenda. Perhaps more disturbingly, she finds that secular listeners, too, tend to filter out experiential details too difficult to accommodate within the metaphors *they* live by, try to "explain the assault in ways that leave [their]...world view unscathed."[67] In short, orthodox epistemic subjects are trained to know only *instances* not particulars and to fit those instances into ready-made universals, generalities, however uneasy the fit may be.

Ironically, a different but related conundrum complicates the discussion at this juncture, for some of Amnesty's critics take it to task on this very issue—its detailed attention to particularity—arguing that concentration on particular

61. Brison, "Surviving Sexual Violence," 7.
62. Brison, "On the Personal as Philosophical," 38.
63. Brison, "Outliving Oneself," 14.
64. Johnson, *Freedom and Interpretation*, 12.
65. James, "Feminism in the Philosophy of Mind," 35.
66. Brison, "On the Personal as Philosophical," 38.
67. Brison, "Surviving Sexual Violence," 11.

victims blunts its effectiveness by allowing it to ignore the larger political-economic structures productive of victimization and suffering. With reference to the conceptual framing of my argument in this book, the charge seems to be that concentration on particularity would *truncate* ecological thinking rather than fostering it, as I have been maintaining it does. Thus in his lecture, Wayne Booth explores the vexed issue of uniqueness in an intellectual climate that withholds the honorific label knowledge from what it deems excessive particularity. Framing his inquiry around a puzzle about how to represent human violations as "fundamentally, *universally* wrong" in a world cognizant of "human variety and the elusive nature of the self,"[68] he worries that "Amnesty's program must be suspect if the victim's worth is to be found *only* in his or her individual uniqueness."[69] It is my sense, however, that the puzzle derives from a false dichotomy. True, an epistemological paradox runs through Brison's writings and the Amnesty questions, as it does through the larger, equally tangled epistemic issues they invoke. Knowing only generalities, instances, categories, knowing from a position centered within an uncontested moral-social imaginary, fails to equip epistemic subjects to imagine well enough to respond appropriately to the particularities of individual lives, hence to situational specificities and to sufferings whose pain is exacerbated by the impossibility of fitting them into "kinds" remote from the received conceptual frame or into kinds hitherto imagined or known. Yet attributions of radical particularity also risk relegating events and situations to a region beyond the boundaries of the commonable and the communicable, risk affirming an incommensurability that would, ultimately, be unspeakable and thence beyond intervention, both critical and practical. The tension admits of no easy dissolution, but it is, I think *the* productive (thus not *aporetic*) tension within which theorists of knowledge have to work, who are committed to thinking "locally and globally," for all the ambiguity and inconclusiveness such an exercise involves.

Resistance to particularity is more than just a policy for ensuring objectivity: it functions also to preserve the detached, presumptively disembodied, dislocation of epistemic subjects whose practices of dealing only with instances require from them neither response nor responsibility. Questions generated by events and subjectivities such as those I have been discussing undermine the self-certainty of the subject's vanishing act—into the shadows, into an allegedly ubiquitous "we." Thus an epistemology capable of engaging with particularity will unsettle the epistemic subject, require him *and now her* (for the generic self

68. Booth, "Mystery of the Social Self," 70 (emphasis added).
69. Ibid., 87 (emphasis added).

dissolves) to come out of the shadows, to engage in ways that put her/his subjectivity also on the line, and to assume responsibility for what and how he/she claims to know.

Yet a structural disanalogy between Brison's analyses and the Amnesty lectures has also to be taken into account: Brison tells her own story in the first person, from within the urgency of a unique specificity, whereas Amnesty *advocates for* its victims, in the third person, represents and argues for their particularity, most often without the option of addressing them in the second person, as "you," or of finding/making a space where they can speak for themselves without fear of dismissal or reprisal. Epistemologically, both forms of speaking have been fraught with difficulties: personal narratives for how the identity of teller and tale precludes the distance of dispassionate objectivity, and advocacy, which I have discussed in chapter five, for the imagined elusiveness of accurate representation, when personal involvement and the power of vested interest can produce analogous failures of distance. Thus despite their thematic contiguity, the two examples I have concentrated on demand subtly different analytic approaches and ask for different, if analogous, responses. These are just some of the difficulties within which epistemic subjects have to imagine and negotiate. For neither of these speakings (which is in each example explicitly *addressive*, hence no formal propositional monologue uttered into a void) is indifferent to the ears on which it falls; neither looks merely for detached assent to an indifferent truth; each seeks a second-person acknowledgment from and of (an)other(s) as a *you* so engaged as to make knowing possible. Nor must this acknowledgment be exclusively personal. Brison professes relief—epistemic relief I will call it—at professional *acknowledgment* from doctors and lawyers: a response with its counterpart in Amnesty's practices of seeking engagement with its subjects as specific people, also addressively, in its letter-writing campaigns. Each, albeit differently, looks to knowings that can become sensitively communal even in their explicit particularity, for the affirmations they, differently, seek.

What then to do? "We" may indeed be imaginative creatures, but prototypes and hegemonic imaginaries block responsible imaginings at least as frequently as they enable them. Booth resists the proffered alternative of framing the solution in the language of deconstruction, fearing that "the world's ubiquitous torturers will welcome the rumor that advanced thinkers in the most advanced nations find no solid reality in that victim who cringes and weeps before their dry eyes."[70] By contrast, Nicola Lacey notes how the

70. Ibid., 77.

liberal assumption of self-ownership in criminal law, with its focus on "an individualised notion of [sexual] consent" and its assumption of sexual autonomy "assumes the *mind* to be dominant and controlling, irrespective of material circumstances," leaving "no space for the articulation of the affective and corporeal dimensions of *certain* violations of autonomy."[71] These thoughts suggest that *both* subsumption under generalities *and* deconstruction into scattered specificities erase the self-as-knowable from epistemic agendas, analogously, if from opposite directions. The paradox admits of no easy resolution.

These processes of reclaiming particularity are complicated by the fact that, ironically, orthodox liberal-affluent epistemic subjects cannot bear—indeed, are rarely called upon to bear—too much truth. People in their ordinary lives, Brison notes, "are not taught to empathize with victims."[72] Nor, as habitual speakers of their knowledge claims as though into a void, are they trained in the *listening* essential to imaginative empathy. Yet the traumatized self in its fragility and vulnerability is often, Brison shows, "resilient enough to be reconstructed with the help of empathic others."[73] Empathy as she appeals to it, however, is no (Johnsonian) matter-of-course, self-assuredly putting oneself in the position of another, for in the encounters she envisages, the other can respond, confirm, or take issue with the interpretations proffered, can correct the would-be empathizer when/if she or he does not listen well enough or gets it wrong. Empathy thus construed is marked both by a "recognition of the distinctiveness of others and some acceptance of their claims"[74] and by a reciprocity that works toward a just measure of consonance between speaker and listener, where these places are more often interchangeable than they are fixed. As I suggest in chapter three, Kirsti Malterud offers a listening very like this to her patients, as does Karen Messing, as I indicate in chapter one, to the women whose symptoms she is investigating, though neither might be willing to call it empathy. In the circumstances Brison recounts, empathic subjects are responsible for knowings that are precisely *not* prototypical—not of generalities, but of particularities, specificities, whose very singularity pushes at the boundaries of the ready-made descriptions that "prototypical conceptual structures" (recall Johnson) make available.

---

71. Lacey, *Unspeakable Subjects*, 117 (first emphasis added). Lacey cites Brison's "Outliving Oneself" essay in her discussion of law's impotence to deal with the harms of rape.

72. Brison, "Surviving Sexual Violence," 11.

73. Brison, "Outliving Oneself," 12.

74. The words are La Caze's in *Analytic Imaginary*, 138.

This imaginative empathy, I suggest, is less about knowing than about *believing*, in a reconfigured sense of belief where the standard definition of knowledge as justified true belief undergoes a reversal.[75] Consider the locution, odd to an orthodox epistemologist's ears: "I always knew that X, but I did not believe it," where X could stand for the details and/or subjective effects, of rape, torture, trauma. For Brison, listening that starts from a palpable willingness to *believe* her, to enter into the story and become part of her interpretive community, her reality check, allows her to know her story, to own it, and to put her "self" together around it, if perhaps never in the unified way of the liberal tradition, with its promises of easy self-transparency and self-ownership. So long as she is caught within patterns of incredulity, her sense of reality and of self remain shattered and in suspense.

Amnesty, likewise, has to insist on the details of particularity because its members and activists have also to *believe* enough (which again is different from knowing enough) to exert engaged political pressure, to put themselves on the line in defiance of abusive practices, to convey a just sense of how, precisely, *those* specific practices abuse. Its project, too, is both individual in insisting on the full particularity of the known and not starkly individual in its appeals to commonality and social responsibility—not, then, so unrelievedly unique as its critics charge. It has to advocate well enough to enable activists to imagine fully enough to engage their participation—*and yet also*—as Brison, too, must, it has to call a society/government/political system/global order to account for holding open places where acts of violence against women/against political dissenters are simply about "how things are," condoned by a social imaginary that sustains harsh hierarchies of vulnerability and power. Ecologically speaking, responsible analyses of the situations I have been discussing call for a sensitively empathic listening committed to understanding "others' worlds" (to borrow Sonia Kruks's phrase),[76] to seeking out what one has to know in order to enter those worlds imaginatively, respectfully, with an intellectual-moral humility such as Rachel Carson enjoins in scientific inquiry and scientifically informed practice, to displace the hubris driving indiscriminate claims to "know just how you feel" and the crudeness of "one-size-fits-all" practices of intervention. The contrast is with philosophical practices of extracting those other "individuals" from the materiality of their situations, assuming them to be "just like us," and enacting the epistemic violence such

75. See my *Rhetorical Spaces*, chap. 3, "Incredulity," for a discussion of this reversal in a different context.

76. Kruks, *Retrieving Experience*, 172–75.

indiscriminate attributions of sameness entail. The issue (as it is in a different register in Kristin Shrader-Frechette's brief for a "'practical ecology' based primarily on case studies,"[77] which I discuss in chapter one) is about knowing that particularity is always insistently particular, *this* one whose experiences need to be imagined in their specificities, who asks an "us" to imagine how it is for a "you"; and at the same time and equally, it is part of/symptomatic of larger structures of power and privilege, listening and silencing (Kruks, too, urges careful, case-by-case, analyses of specific situations: analyses that are, at the same time, mindful of the limits of imagination). A victim/survivor is neither reducible to a symptom of a sick society nor knowable only as "a case, a statistic"; but she or he has to be understood that way as well, as situated within the habitus and ethos of a society where such violations can take place and are indeed sometimes the norm. Either way, knowers—epistemic subjects—have to emerge from the shadows, not only in their self-possession as thinkers and as interlocutors in a (possible) conversation, but as embodied subjects enacted in their knowings, whose subjectivity is in process around whatever corporeal and psychological stability it may achieve at its core, mobile in its positionings within and in relation to the people it has to know.

These examples contest the limits of imagination, and with it of coherent, monologic storytelling, stable epistemic assumptions, and the fixity of subject-object positions in knowings that matter more than knowing cups on tables. Just as significantly, they contest assumptions of a liberal, individualist self-ownership that contributes, also, to holding the orthodox epistemic imaginary in place. According to Booth, neither tortured nor torturer "is bounded by the skin that is being pricked or that is holding the electric prod. Both of them are 'societies,' both have experienced plot lines entailing world views that are now being shattered."[78] From positions scripted into ordinary "plot lines," knowing subjects cannot know the uniqueness, singularity, strangeness of those shatterings just by extrapolating or reaching out from where they are. Responsible epistemic practices have to move in an arc, not a linear path, along a trajectory of seeing and hearing, venturing to understand, that begins, somehow from *there*. María Lugones claims—albeit contentiously—such a potential for "world"-traveling,[79] where the engaged traveler is neither tourist nor anthropologist, aspiring merely to observe without participating or reassessing any of her/his entrenched beliefs. Her guiding assumption is that

77. Shrader-Frechette, "Ecology," 304–5.
78. Booth, "Mystery of the Social Self," 93.
79. Lugones, "Playfulness."

such empathic knowing can never be infallible or complete, yet it can sometimes be "good enough" to inform effective, transformative practice. It has to
be ever mindful of Deleuze's question, which I cite in chapter one: "How can a
being take another being into its world, but while preserving or respecting the
other's own relations and world?"[80] Like empathy less metaphorically conceived, it carries its own responsibilities and dangers, for in situations of
asymmetrical power and privilege, the more privileged—say, in the situations I
am discussing, the one(s) not raped or tortured—may indeed be able to offer
empathy as they attempt to enter the other's world, but they can also claim the
privilege of being able, at will, to return to their own, safer place. As Kruks
aptly cautions: "Too strong an identification with others permits us to deny
the responsibilities... *born of our own location.*"[81] Thus the epistemic stance I
am adopting enjoins skepticism about the possibility of understanding across
differences, though it amounts to a healthy skepticism, not to the despair
engendered by radical incommensurability. Things likely are less commensu-
rable than the unmarked "we"—represented here by Mark Johnson—have
blithely assumed. But neither is radical incommensurability a tenable position, given how often "we" demonstrably succeed in practice—albeit variably,
ambiguously, intermittently—in negotiating knowledgeably with one another,
across diverse situations and circumstances.

Nonetheless, framing these questions so that *cognition* (= *knowing*) functions as both the symptom and the cure, addressing them within an epistemological frame, comes with its own set of issues. The experience-and-affect
remote character of standard epistemologies, to which I have referred, prompts
Sandra Bartky, for example, to object to philosophers' conceiving "the resolution of the problem of difference... in largely cognitive terms"[82] and to argue,
persuasively, that cognition in its epistemological modes is impotent to engage
with the affective dimensions of lives situated outside the norms of epistemic
sameness. With respect to orthodox empiricist-positivist epistemology where
knowing amounts to "the mere acquisition of [more] knowledge(= more information)," her objections are well taken. In its place, Bartky advocates "a
knowing that transforms the self who knows, a knowing that brings into being
new sympathies, new affects as well as new cognitions and new forms of in-
tersubjectivity... in a word... a knowing that has a particular affective taste."[83]

---

80. Deleuze, *Spinoza*, 126.
81. Kruks, *Retrieving Experience*, 158 (emphasis added).
82. Bartky, "Sympathy and Solidarity," 178.
83. Ibid., 179.

Her point is well taken: it finds compelling affirmation in Jennifer Geddes's perceptive analysis of "useless knowledge," drawn from her reading of Charlotte Delbo's *Auschwitz and After*.[84] Geddes insists on a reader's responsibility to respect and preserve the gap between Delbo's "experience of extreme suffering and our ability to understand that experience." Yet in showing her readers what we do *not* know, Delbo, she suggests, "helps us unlearn what we have presumed to know or to be able to imagine . . . gives us a glimpse (a taste almost) of what we cannot really know." She urges would-be imaginers and empathizers to acknowledge that their/our knowledge will always be "partial and inadequate," to allow it "to be thoroughly interrogated by those who have another kind of knowledge of suffering, a 'useless knowledge' that haunts them." The listening thus enjoined, she suggests, can "lead us away from discourses of mastery"[85] to engage, sensitively, with the particularity of evil.

This injunction to learn how to live with the ambiguities of partial knowledge sits well with conceptions of ecological thinking as partial and incomplete, and not strictly cognitive in the attenuated sense Bartky resists, but for all that, effective within its limits. Yet listening is surprisingly unthought, undertheorized in epistemological analyses. The attuned conversations of close friends afford a more plausible everyday model than many of the situations I have discussed, although they translate only obliquely into asymmetrical relationships (such as those between Amnesty advocate and victim) as these contrast with the imagined—and sometimes realized—symmetry of friendships. Good listening is often as tactile, and visual, as it is auditory: thus neither disembodied nor closed to affect, and neither purely objective nor perfectly rational. It shelters and encloses without requiring the *literal* touch so invasive in relations of power asymmetry. Although, phenomenologically, it is a familiar part of many ordinary lives and its absence is easily perceptible, it resists conceptual analysis. In creating palpably safe discursive spaces, it invites and honors trust; and it opens the way for (reconfigured) modes of knowing, even as it departs from the accumulation-of-information or mastery senses of the term. In its "normative realist" aspect, it starts from a presumption of, and respect for, the integrity of tellers and listeners, although it may proceed to question and reinterpret both tellings and hearings in transformative interpretive processes such as Bartky advocates.

Narrative identities (recalling Ricoeur and thinking of Delbo) are as much about imaginers and listeners as about narrators, about conditions of

---

84. Geddes, "Banal Evil and Useless Knowledge."
85. Ibid., 113–14.

imaginative uptake and response, without which they could not escape the monologic mold of the cognition whose inadequacy Bartky deplores. In an evocative reading of Nawal El Saadawi's story of undergoing a clitoridectomy as a small child, Bartky writes that to have any idea of this experience "I must imagine . . . what it was for her to have *felt* this terror, this absolute incomprehension in the face of the cruelty of those she trusted." In this imagining, she observes, "I do not think of myself at all. Nor is my imagining really mine in any but the most trivial sense."[86] It is not, then, an imagining that claims an implausible degree of commonality. Such imaginings might be able to break the boundaries of self-certainty and to leave prototypes and self-ownership behind, not for the sake of incorporating more information, but in the affective transformations they initiate. Nor do they amount simply to letting the Other speak, "granting" the Other personhood or subjective status (recalling Mark Johnson), with the condescension, the arrogance, of self-satisfied rightness that such magnanimous lettings imply. The other is already speaking. It is a matter of listening, and not from here but from as close to there as responsible imaginings can go.

Conclusion?

The argument of this chapter is undeniably inconclusive. At most, it maps the promise and pitfalls of ecologically imaginative extensions of knowledge and epistemology, beyond immediately available observational evidence and assumed homogeneity. Rather than engaging principally with feminist writings on imagination—by Sabina Lovibond, Michèle Le Dœuff, Drucilla Cornell, or Susan Babbitt—it concentrates on Mark Johnson's analysis because its location close to the hegemonic mainstream confirms the tenacity of a social imaginary that needs to be interrogated, disrupted. It offers some cautionary tales, sets in motion a redirected line of reasoning, warns against premature conclusions. It pulls the discussion in the direction of epistemic responsibility, not just in order to expose inadequate or irresponsible epistemic practices but to gesture toward more responsible, negotiative, inductive engagement in epistemic projects.

Nonetheless, it is hard to avoid concluding on a note of pessimism that contrasts both with Mark Johnson's claims for the imagination and with an "ungrounded optimism" that Susan Mendus reads in Richard Rorty's equally self-assured praise for "the ability to think of people wildly different from

---

86. Bartky, "Sympathy and Solidarity," 192.

ourselves as included in the range of 'us.' "[87] The collapse of the welfare state in the affluent western world goes together with a breakdown of face-to-face local and more wide-ranging communication that is more about listening than about speaking: a crisis of listening in the age of sound bites. "We" are bombarded with information, pronouncements, analyses of how things are—yet even as there is more and more talk, there is less and less listening. Perhaps for me the problem is exacerbated by having lived in the arch-conservative Ontario of the late 1990s, when social support systems were disintegrating, and nobody was listening except to pick up bits and distort them to their own ends. To remain mindful of the problems a would-be responsible, imaginatively rational epistemic subject has to struggle with, it is salutary to read Mark Johnson—and Richard Rorty—against the background of Trinh T. Minh-ha's reminder: "On one plane, we, I, and he, may speak the same language and even act alike; yet, on the other, we stand miles apart, irreducibly foreign to each other."[88] The epistemic imperatives these meditations invoke count as reminders of how wary we, all of us, must be of assuming we can see very far from here.

---

87. Rorty, *Contingency, Irony, and Solidarity*, 192, cited in Mendus, "What of Soul Was Left," 58.

88. Trinh, *Woman, Native, Other*, 48.

To know what took place, summary is enough. To learn what happened requires
multiple points of address and analysis.

—*Toni Morrison, Race-ing Justice, En-Gendering Power*

7

PUBLIC KNOWLEDGE, PUBLIC TRUST:

Toward Democratic

Epistemic Practices

Captioned "Whistle Blower," the cover photograph of the 16 November 1998 issue of *Maclean's: Canada's Weekly Newsmagazine* features Dr. Nancy Olivieri, a hematologist at the University of Toronto and Toronto's Hospital for Sick Children (fig. 1). It names her principled breaking of a confidentiality agreement with a pharmaceutical company whose product she had been testing as the catalyst for "a debate over money and morality...raging through the medical world." The Olivieri case, which I read through diverse lenses in this chapter, exposes tangled issues peculiar to late-twentieth- and early-twenty-first-century politics of knowledge, which indeed require—and invite—multiple points of address and analysis. These issues figure among those I adumbrate in the introduction, about the preservation of public trust and the creation of responsible epistemic citizenship—concerns notably absent from putatively universal, a priori theories of knowledge and action. They show how knowledge claims advanced and substantiated even by the most authoritative of knowers—an

BRITISH COLUMBIA: Operation Salvage ● CENTRAL AMERICA: The Horrors of Mitch

CANADA'S   WEEKLY NEWSMAGAZINE

Maclean's

Whistle Blower

A top researcher warns that a drug she is testing could be dangerous. The drugmaker fights back. Now, a debate over money and morality is raging through the medical world.

Dr. Nancy Olivieri,
Hospital for
Sick Children

NOVEMBER 16, 1998 $3.95
46

6 20058 70001 3
http://www.macleans.ca

Figure 1. *Maclean's*, November 16, 1998. Photograph by Peter Bregg. Courtesy of *Maclean's*. Reprinted with permission.

eminent doctor and research scientist—are vulnerable to undermining by features of her social-political-ecological location. With respect to money, they generate questions about patronage in knowledge production and circulation, about open and closed research practices and communities, where openness can influence the availability or otherwise of funding and other infrastructural support. With respect to morality, they require reexamining relations of trust among producers of knowledge and reevaluating trustworthy approaches within epistemic communities, to "consumers" of the knowledge produced. In public deliberations prompted by the Olivieri case, both issues have tended to be addressed as matters of academic freedom in institutions of knowledge production and the societies that house and support them, and thence as requiring reconstructed science policies/knowledge policies and practices, capable of promoting habitable, democratic epistemic community. I will suggest, however, that academic freedom is just one of several matters of concern the case exposes. It opens a deliberative space for engaging with widespread, complex ecological issues generated by the politics of knowledge and public trust. Thus my intention in this chapter is to develop a multiply focused analysis in which I take "the Olivieri affair" as emblematic of late-twentieth- and early-twenty-first-century collisions between "money and truth."[1] I conduct the analysis, initially, by reading some gendered implications of the press coverage of the case, which further complicate the picture I have drawn of how an *instituted social imaginary* shapes public perceptions and evaluations of scientific-epistemic practice in medicine, science, and more secular knowledge domains. In the final sections of the chapter I show how questions about expertise, trust, and democratic epistemic practice relate to and are prompted by the particularities of this case.

Although "the sex of the knower" has received scant mention in the press coverage about Olivieri, a salient aspect of my purpose in reading the case ecologically is to examine the epistemological significance of its location not just within a corporate climate, but also within a sex-gender system, embedded in the culture of white western scientific research and practice and in the larger society.[2] Curiously in this instance, it is difficult, without endorsing a knee-jerk ideology bent on exposing blatant sexism in any equivocal or negative depiction of a woman's plight, to frame or even name the gender issue as operative within reports that maintain so audible a silence on the matter. Yet my proposal is that the hegemonic imaginary within which laboratory science

1. See Olivieri, "When Money and Truth Collide." Parts of this chapter draw on my "Images of Expertise."

2. I first posed this question in my essay "Is the Sex of the Knower Epistemologically Significant?" Chapter 1 of my *What Can She Know?* bears the same title, although the chapter does not replicate the original essay.

is practiced in the affluent western world colors this case "pink-for-girls," intentionally or otherwise producing a gender-inflected framing. Reading some of the imagery through a feminist lens and against the verbal silences that cloak the ambient sexual politics uncovers a set of gendered modalities that, in white western societies, routinely play into the politics of knowledge, responsibility, science, and expertise. With the silencing they condone and the forms of oppression they thus sustain, these issues, too, function as situational obstacles to the creation of habitable epistemic community. Their seeming effectiveness in shaping public perceptions of this case suggests productive analogies with other modalities of the politics of epistemic location and authority.

The *Maclean's* cover photo is striking in the way it positions its subject so as to glamorize, to sexualize her, positing a marked incongruity between her overt, professional self-presentation as a lab-coated doctor (albeit with stethoscope rakishly worn) and the tropes it mobilizes of the vamp, the defiant troublemaker, the woman who, as a whistle-blower, steps out of line to become as much a part of the problem as of its solution. Because such incongruities permeate the early press coverage, my reading of the case looks through a feminist lens at how the imagery installs *gender* as an analytic category[3] among the issues that invite address and analysis. One of my strategies, therefore, in attempting to understand what happened is to map samples of that coverage for how their positioning of events and protagonists highlights gender as an operative, if often silent, factor in the politics framing the case. These samples, I will suggest, expose a subtext to the *Maclean's* photograph and other visual and verbal representations, beneath the surface of the explicitly deployed rhetorical imagery. Both visually and verbally, the reports convey unspoken but legibly/audibly gendered messages that work, sometimes tacitly but also more overtly, to divert attention from and even to impugn Olivieri's scientific and medical credibility. Photographs are a peculiarly rich resource for thinking about gender for, by contrast with print, they cannot avoid displaying the players as embodied, thus sexed-gendered, beings; they cannot keep gender out of the picture. Thus the Olivieri photographs, like images more generally, work as much to generate meaning as to transmit it, nor does an image carry its meaning, preformed, from one venue to another. Its meaning depends as much on deployment and uptake as on its source: there is no uncontested

---

3. The concept of gender as an "analytic category" is due to Scott's *Gender and the Politics of History*, chap. 2, "Gender: A Useful Category of Historical Analysis." I follow Scott's definition of gender as both "a constitutive element of social relationships based on perceived differences between the sexes, and . . . a primary way of signifying relationships of power" (42).

"given" in the presentation. Hence, as I will show, the Olivieri photographs
lend themselves to multiple and often contradictory readings.

The Olivieri Affair

The broad outlines of the Olivieri affair[4] are as follows. In the *New England
Journal of Medicine* (*NEJM*) in 1994, Dr. Nancy Olivieri (then) of the Division
of Haematology/Oncology at Toronto's Hospital for Sick Children (HSC)
and professor of medicine at the University of Toronto, published a team-
authored article, "Survival in Medically Treated Patients with Homozygous
B-Thalassemia," reporting on "transfusion and iron-chelation therapy" (administered in a drug called deferiprone-L1) for the treatment of patients (mainly
children) with thalassemia major, a genetically transmitted condition of the
blood, prevalent around the Mediterranean, in the Middle East and Southeast
Asia, and in Canada among children of Chinese, Greek, and Italian parents.
Characterized by abnormalities in red blood cell production, thalassemia major
(also called Mediterranean anemia) results in oxygen depletion in the body and,
if untreated, can cause death within a few years. Growth failure, bone defor-
mities, enlarged liver and spleen, which begin to appear within the first year of
life, are some of its indications. Before deferiprone was available, patients had
required monthly blood transfusions, administered by connecting them for as
much as twelve hours a day to a drug infusion pump, a treatment whose effects
include a dangerous iron build-up. Because the procedure for clearing the iron
is so onerous, many patients opted out of treatment in their teenaged years, and
many died in their twenties. Thus 1993 press reports herald deferiprone as a
"revolutionary new treatment," promising "an entire new way to treat these
diseases" (= thalassemia and sickle-cell anemia),[5] citing testimony from parents relieved at the prospect of taking their children off the intravenous pump,
and children pleased with their newfound freedom.

Nonetheless, just a year after the first article appeared, Olivieri published
concerns about deferiprone's long-term effects, in response to emerging
evidence that, for some patients, it, too, could produce iron overload serious enough to cause heart, liver, and endocrine damage. In a 1995 letter to the
New England Journal of Medicine she cautions: "When new therapies are

---

4. Press reports tend to call it "the Olivieri case." Nancy Olivieri herself, in a public
lecture (September 2003), referred to "the Olivieri affair."
5. Quotations from Priest, "Sick Kids Doctor Finds Anemia Drug."

introduced, it is important to confirm promising initial findings... so that false hope and expectation on the part of patients with chronic disease can be avoided."[6] And in 1998, a second team-authored article concludes:

> Deferiprone is not an effective means of iron-chelation therapy in patients with thalassemia major and may be associated with worsening of hepatic fibrosis, even in patients whose hepatic iron concentrations have stabilized or decreased. After a mean of 4.6 years of deferiprone therapy, body iron burden was at concentrations associated with a greatly increased risk of cardiac disease and early death... in 7 of 18 patients (39%).[7]

For western scientists, philosophers of science, and an informed public alike, these events fit easily into received images of "normal science," following a standard trajectory from positive initial findings through cautionary warnings to (partial) refutation of a hypothesis in light of new evidence, with modifications of (putative) knowledge and treatment and/or withdrawal of the drug as its outcome. Yet in this instance the trajectory was blocked: what could and *should* have been a set of uncontroversial epistemic and ethical decisions devolved into a contest of wills and interests, generating the "debate over money and morality" announced in *Maclean's* cover story.

Deferiprone research had been generously financed by Apotex Inc, "one of Canada's most high-powered pharmaceutical firms";[8] in 1993 and again in 1995, Olivieri had signed confidentiality agreements prohibiting disclosure of information about the drug's trials without written permission from the company;[9] and Apotex was negotiating a large donation to the University of Toronto. Thus, making new evidence public, exposing the fallibility/corrigibility of the initial findings, cautioning parents and patients, withdrawing the drug from circulation, were not as straightforward as allegedly value-neutral empiricist epistemologies contend, according to which error suspected or exposed forces a reevaluation of knowledge claims, if it does not simply negate them. When, despite a warning from the Research Ethics Board (REB) at HSC, Olivieri insisted on modifying consent forms to warn patients of the dangers, Apotex

---

6. Olivieri, letter to the editor, *New England Journal of Medicine* 333.9 (1995): 1287–88.
7. Olivieri et al., "Long-Term Safety," 420–21.
8. Papp, "Firm Axes Outspoken Scientist's Research."
9. The 1993 contract with Apotex Inc., which Dr. Olivieri signed (with Dr. Gideon Koren), contained a "one-year, post-termination confidentiality clause"; the June 1995 contract that Dr. Olivieri signed "had a three-year, post-termination confidentiality clause" (Thompson, Baird, and Downie, *Olivieri Report*, 24–25).

threatened legal action, and both the hospital and the university refused to support her decision. Nonetheless, Olivieri publicly "defied the confidentiality clause and the company's threats to sue, arranged for her own legal counsel, informed her patients and the [hospital's] REB, informed the federal government's Health Protection Branch, reported her research at a medical conference"[10] and published the 1998 *NEJM* article. In consequence, she was dismissed from her position as head of the hospital's hemoglobinopathy program. Although subsequent collegial and public pressure forced a review of the case, and a settlement brokered by the Canadian Association of University Teachers (CAUT), with two of the world's other leading experts in blood disease testifying to Olivieri's scientific integrity and worldwide eminence, was instrumental in bringing about her early-1999 reinstatement, the story does not end there. Even a putative ending that Olivieri reports in October 2001 scarcely counts as a "resolution."[11] Nor is there any clear indication of justice having been done either for Olivieri and her supporters or in addressing the wider issues of "money and morality," academic freedom, corporate sponsorship, and public trust that permeate the case and its aftermath, with ongoing ripples spreading through western medical and scientific institutions. Indeed, taking the Olivieri case as their central example, David Nathan and David Weatherall observe in an October 2002 *NEJM* article that such things are still happening, although "they generally take milder and less public forms."[12]

Despite her 1999 reinstatement, the university was slow to restore Olivieri's research space, laboratory access, and lab assistants; for months she and her supporters were subjected to vicious email attacks and anonymous letters calling her supporters "pigs" and "unethical" and making damaging allegations about Olivieri's professional conduct. In a bizarre twist to the story, in January 2000 Dr. Gideon Koren, a colleague at the HSC, himself an eminent authority on blood disorders in children and highly respected for having established Motherrisk—a service that gathers evidence and dispenses advice to practitioners and lay people on risks to fetuses and children from drugs, chemicals, toxins ingested by their mothers—cosigner of the 1993 contract and a coauthor of the 1994 *NEJM* article, was exposed as the sender of the hate mail. The exposure surprised "a lot of people both inside and outside the hospital because of his stature and reputation

10. Valpy, "Salvage Group Tackles Sick Kids' Image Disaster," A9.
11. Olivieri, "Scientific Inquiry."
12. Nathan and Weatherall, "Academic Freedom in Clinical Research," 1370. See also Horton, "Dawn of McScience" (a review of Krimsky's *Science in the Private Interest*). The Olivieri case is discussed in both the article and the Krimsky text.

as a top scientist and caring doctor."[13] Meanwhile, in 2001, Apotex was still promoting Koren's "scientific opinions regarding its controversial drug"[14] and persevering in attempts to license the drug in the United Kingdom and Europe without the expertise—indeed over the protests—of Olivieri and of Dr. Gary Brittenham, who resigned his cochairmanship of the research team in Italy, following actions by Apotex, which left "less experienced and less principled investigators...[to] continue...a year-long study, not designed in the first place to examine efficacy,"[15] as Olivieri describes it. In 2004, Miriam Shuchman reports, doctors in the United Kingdom, Italy, India, and Taiwan were regarding L1 as a reasonable option for patients unwilling or unable to take the alternative, Desferal. According to Shuchman, L1 "owes its staying power to science."[16] But the question remains: does it?

The Scientific Imaginary

The claim that science—and thus medical science and technology—figures in the present-day western epistemic imaginary as the most objective, certain, and sophisticated knowledge humankind has achieved requires no argument to support it. Nor does the claim that expert scientific practitioners occupy positions of acknowledged epistemic authority, commonly stretching well beyond the boundaries of their specific domains of professional expertise. Merely prefacing a newspaper or television report with the words *science has proved* generates a public presumption in favor of taking the report seriously, accords it a credibility that frequently exceeds its evidential warrant, works to mask such agendas and vested interests as might underlie its presentation to the public eye. This same epistemic imaginary, with its adherence to an autonomy-of-knowledge credo, promotes a belief that scientific knowledge production takes place, appropriately, in enclosed, segregated laboratory settings—locations allegedly removed from the structures of power and privilege constitutive of all human institutions, practices, and societies—and in science itself as one such institution. Although self-critical work by scientists, and by philosophers and others in critical science studies, reveals this imaginary to be neither

---

13. Foss, "Sick Kids Doctor Breaks His Silence." Thanks to Dr. Sandy Macdonald for information about Dr. Koren.
14. Olivieri, "Scientific Inquiry."
15. Olivieri, "When Money and Truth Collide," 54.
16. Shuchman, *Drug Trial*, 363.

seamless nor impervious to critique, its tenacity in the public eye has not diminished to keep pace with these interventions. It sustains an imaginary of science (often cursorily essentialized) as self-contained and politically neutral—an imaginary within which members of an informed public judge and debate reported scientific "facts" and advance their own, derivative, claims to know.

As I have explained, a social imaginary is about often-implicit but nonetheless highly effective systems of meanings, metaphors, and interlocking explanations-expectations within which people, in specific time periods and geographical-cultural climates, enact their knowledge and subjectivities and articulate their self-understandings as knowers—as producers, perusers, critics, beneficiaries, and/or consumers of expert and everyday knowledge. An imaginary is as productive in generating and sustaining images, metaphors, and operative idea(l)s that underwrite patterns of epistemic legitimacy and credibility as it is in situating and evaluating practices of scientific inquiry. Imaginaries, I have also noted, are self-reinforcing rather as self-fulfilling prophesies are: although ongoing successes consolidate their sense of rightness, it takes more than a few counterexamples to unsettle them. Thus understood, a social imaginary carries within it the normative meanings, customs, expectations, assumptions, values, prohibitions, and permissions—the habitus and ethos—into which members of a society are nurtured from childhood, which they internalize, affirm, or contest and refuse, as they make sense of their place, options, possibilities and prohibitions, risks and responsibilities in a social and physical world, conceptions of whose "nature" and meaning are also instituted in these imaginary significations.

As I indicate in chapter one, this imaginary is social in the broadest sense: not only is it about principles of conduct, both epistemic and ethical, but it is about how such principles claim and maintain salience. It is about the scope and limits of human knowledge and its place in the social-political-material world; about the appropriate hierarchical ordering of institutions of knowledge production; about intellectual and moral subjectivity and agency; about social-political structures and the distribution of goods, privileges, power, and authority. In this complex sense, the social imaginary of mastery and instrumentality, animated, as we have seen, by an inflated individualism and born of the Industrial Revolution and late capitalism, extends across the ethos and habitus of an affluent western world where there seem to be no limits to human capacities for prediction, manipulation, and control—to possibilities of mastering this world's resources, be they animal (both human and nonhuman), vegetable, or mineral. Nor, apparently, is there any reason either to contest the rightness of "man's" claims to dominion over all the earth or to challenge the exclusionary scope of the putatively generic term *man*.

The operative public image of laboratory science in this imaginary—however incongruous it may be with "the facts"—is of an esoteric, authoritative inquiry, practiced by privileged, mainly white men in enclosed communities, sealed off from open public discourse by a language in which even the well-educated, literate, and privileged members of a nonscientific public cannot readily find their place. It effectively masks the human—thus fallible—provenance of scientific discoveries behind impersonal, passive locutions such as "it has been shown" or claims such as "the data show" or "science has proved," which erase the specificities, and thence the responsibilities, of human agency. The esoteric aura this discourse engenders creates a protected insularity for laboratory life, separating quests for knowledge itself from the social-political-ethical effects of its circulation and enactment, often dismissively labeled its "uses" that, in this rhetorical frame, are extraneous to science and epistemology proper. It underwrites a mystique of official secrecy in which a confidentiality agreement such as Nancy Olivieri signed would pass merely as a matter of course. Such rhetorical tropes may partially account for the efforts of Olivieri's detractors to contain her story by labeling it "a scientific controversy," situating it within procedures and rules that pose as self-justifying and thus impersonally apolitical (Olivieri observes: "Having created this fiction, they were able to express the desirability of 'not taking sides'").[17] The strategy echoes what Evelyn Fox Keller calls an "unspoken agreement that privilege[s] questions of truth over questions of consequences... [and] demarcat[es] the internal dynamics of science from its social and political influences"[18]—a strategy adept, even in these days of the "science wars," at protecting a laboratory "club culture"[19] from the public accountability regularly demanded of more secular forms of knowing. That such external factors would be operative in knowledge production is neither a surprise nor a sin; but in shielding them from view, an institution of knowledge production defies expectations of the transparency integral to public trust, thereby compromising its responsibly authoritative status.

The metaphor of the *hortus conclusus* in medieval painting—the walled garden, complete in itself, isolated from the outside world and protected from

17. Olivieri, "When Money and Truth Collide," 53, 59.
18. Keller, *Secrets of Life*, 84.
19. I owe these references to the "club culture" and "enclosed communities" of laboratory science to Hunter's *Critiques of Knowing*, 30, 104.

unwanted (unwonted?) intruders by the stone wall surrounding it[20]—conveys the flavor of how the laboratory figures in this imaginary. Michèle Le Dœuff, to whom (with Castoriadis) I am indebted in my thinking about epistemic and social imaginaries, invokes a related image in her conception of philosophy's islanded consciousness, elaborated from Kant's reference to the "territory of pure understanding" as "an island, enclosed by nature itself within unalterable limits."[21] Kant's first *Critique* endeavors to "prevent the understanding, which has at last applied itself to its proper, empirical employment, from wandering off elsewhere," leaving its rightful, island domain, Le Dœuff contends.[22] These rhetorical images prefigure the "enclosed communities" of present-day laboratory science, where whistle-blowers are bound to be vilified, pilloried, excommunicated from the ranks of those whose domain they threaten to unsettle. Residues of a chemistry-set imagery of the laboratory and of a tabula rasa theory of mind, yielding a picture of white-coated (thus pure white, politically innocent) practitioners engaged in solitary, value-, and theory-neutral quests for truth, still tacitly shape secular visions of scientific inquiry. They sustain an imaginary of scientific methodology and discovery as autonomous, internally justifying, and hence immune to the ethico-political critiques enunciated by feminists and other Others.

The Olivieri case challenges these aspects of scientific self-presentation head on. It exposes some of the strategies that institutional authorities employ to shore up cherished beliefs in scientific purity and isolation, as laboratory science has no choice but to emerge into public discourse to address matters of confidentiality in conflict with principles of informed consent. Moreover, as I will elaborate with regard to its implication with "the gender question," the case shows something of why medical science's social-ecological location as a *specifically populated* institution of knowledge production cannot be ignored.

No unequivocal conclusion about what took place is immediately forthcoming from the press coverage I have cited. Nor, despite Olivieri's having enlisted the authority of the CAUT in her defense, is it easy for members of a thoughtful public who have not been privy to its unreported aspects to judge wisely about what happened in this case, even after engaging "multiple points of address and analysis." For example, in a highly skeptical article in *MD*

---

20. Clark mentions the *hortus conclusus* in *Landscape into Art*, 24, 29.

21. Le Dœuff, *Philosophical Imaginary*, 8. The quotation is from Kant, *Critique of Pure Reason*, 257. See also Le Dœuff, *Sex of Knowing*, xvi: "I believe there is no intellectual activity that is not grounded in an imaginary."

22. Le Dœuff, *Philosophical Imaginary*, 10, 11.

Canada, editor David Dehaas disputes the credibility both of Olivieri's expressed concerns about deferiprone and of her allegations of dismissal, harassment, and other grievances; and he contests the plausibility of casting
academic freedom as a central issue in the case.[23] Emphasizing expressions of
incredulity vis-à-vis Olivieri's stance on the part of European researchers
who remain convinced of the drug's safety and effectiveness, and casting the
disagreements between Olivieri and Koren in a quite different light from the
CAUT report and the *NEJM* articles, Dehaas reads the case as an overblown
scientific controversy whose fervor is out of proportion to the facts of the
case. His piece complicates evaluating the case itself and the larger questions it
poses about credibility and public trust it: it cannot, for example, be concluded
that the pro-Olivieri side is right simply because it has generated *more* public
support, on a quasiconsensus reading of truth. And the Dehaas article's tone
of mockery, together with its flippant dismissal, compounds the difficulty
of evaluating "the facts" it reports, especially for a lay public trying to think
well both about the case and its larger ramifications.[24] Complicating the issues
still further, Shuchman's detailed documentation of the multiply contestable
details of "the scandal," from 1998 to 2005, confirms that there is more to be
told—that the jury is still out on the drug, its defenders, and its detractors.
These ongoing analyses attest at once, to the vital part that public disagreement
plays in keeping debate alive and open and to the complexity of the politics
of knowledge in a world where not even privileged and educated members of
the nonscientific public can easily acquire a level of scientific literacy adequate
to the task of enabling responsible readings of what people need to know
in order to pursue, and advocate for, conditions of viable epistemic cohabitability.

In the affluent twenty-first-century western world, public willingness to
trust what "science has proved" and, derivatively, to entrust people's lives and
well-being to medical science rests, if cautiously, on beliefs woven into the very
fabric of an instituted, entrenched scientific-epistemic imaginary. Its rhetorical
apparatus, in which the "science has proved" locution plays an emblematic
part, is structured around tacit assumptions that accredited practitioners will

23. Dehaas, "Much Ado about Nothing." Thanks to Dr. Sandy Macdonald for bringing
this article to my attention.
24. Dehaas writes, for example, "The public perception, gleaned from cursory news reports and some perhaps overly enthusiastic advocacy on the part of Dr. Olivieri's wider group of
supporters, is that she was restrained, reprimanded and ultimately fired by the hospital for
publishing her findings. But that's simply not so" (ibid., 29).

adhere to received research standards and submit their results to established procedures of critical review. Professional codes of conduct are designed to safeguard such confidence; and the value of testimony as a source of knowledge is routinely affirmed with reference to the credentials of the testifier. With knowledge remote from lay experience, accessible at first hand only to the initiated, giving or withholding trust rests on beliefs, widely nurtured in open democratic societies where free inquiry is said to flourish, that practitioners have conformed to the norms of "normal science" and the participation of patrons, sponsors, and institutional guarantors of projects carried out under their auspices fulfills the requirements of professional *epistemic and moral* responsibility. Public outrage in the media, the academy, and the wider world when violations of such assumptions are exposed shows how tightly they are wound into this web of social expectations.

Prior to the exposure of Apotex's role, the public credibility index of the deferiprone project was high, owing in part to the credentials of the research team, listed with their degrees—in effect, to confirm their conformity to these very norms—and reinforced by the articles' publication in the *New England Journal of Medicine* with its (erstwhile) proud policy of refusing to publish materials by authors whose research is sponsored by pharmaceutical companies or who are known to have other vested interests in its outcome. These are typical ingredients in maintaining public trust in research and in the responsible use of its products. Indeed, Olivieri's public credibility remained high, on the whole, throughout the unfolding of the case, because of her refusal to abide by the confidentiality clause, her commitment to her patients and to a cautious but careful reading of the evidence, her perseverance in making developments public despite high personal costs, her resistance to allowing "the profit motive [to take] precedence over scientific rigour" or to "lose [her] objectivity."[25] But she did not become the hero she might have been; and the dispute has been long and damaging. Even after the 2001 release of the CAUT's 540-page document, *The Olivieri Report*,[26] which (in her words) "vindicates" her and "set[s] the record straight" about the egregious attacks she and her supporters experienced, Olivieri remains pessimistic about prospects for resolving the larger issues of public responsibility and trust.[27]

25. The phrases are from Foss and Taylor, "Volatile Mix," A1, A4.
26. Thompson, Baird, and Downie, *Olivieri Report*.
27. Olivieri, "Scientific Inquiry."

The Gender Question?

Clearly, the mere fact of a high-profile *female* doctor as the main protagonist—
and in some reports the victim—is not sufficient to cast the events in the
Olivieri affair, unequivocally, as effects of gender politics. Despite, or more
likely because of, their often having been instrumental in forcing public inquiry
into conflict of interest and other unethical practices in medicine, science more
generally, and other public practices, whistle-blowers of any gender, race, class,
religion, ethnicity put themselves seriously at risk.[28] Yet since so much coverage
of this case focuses on Olivieri herself, rather than on the knowledge and/or its
misuses under investigation, it stands as a persuasive example of how even the
most authoritative practitioners' allegations of research misconduct are vulnerable to critique that enlists aspects of their social-ecological location. Thus in
my view, examining how Olivieri's female presence figures in and shapes public
understandings of what happened in this exposure of the research laboratory
and its inhabitants to scrutiny adds a vital dimension to projects of determining
why the events unfolded as they did, accompanied as they were by a media
chorus in which gender functioned as a recurrent, if secondary, *Leitmotiv*. In a
society where hierarchies of gendered power and privilege remain firmly in
place even after almost three decades of feminist research in epistemology, this
case raises crucial issues about the politics of representation, especially when the
press as a source of public knowledge is so active a participant in the unfolding,
positioning, and judging of what happened.

To a feminist eye, some early media reports point—if obliquely—to
gendered assumptions at the core of the attacks directed at Olivieri: First, in the
months leading up to her dismissal, the HSC publicly debunked—mocked—
Olivieri's claims that the administration was threatening to dismiss her; second, a CBC television documentary characterized by one of her strong supporters as full of "grave factual errors and innuendo," claimed that Olivieri was
"not only an incompetent scientist but carries responsibility for the suffering
and death of thousands of patients worldwide."[29] Third, a Toronto newspaper

28. See in this regard Faunce, "Healthcare Whistle-Blowing." Shuchman cites a 1998 U.S.
Office of Research Integrity analysis that concludes "that scientists who blow the whistle on
scientific misconduct are primarily males and nearly half hold senior appointments at their
institutions" (*Drug Trial*, 215).

29. Shafer, "Science Wars." That program, according to Dehaas, "was one of the few
media outlets to examine the other side of the dispute," contrasting "the hugely positive press
Dr. Olivieri had generated . . . with patients who had benefited from the drug" ("Much Ado
about Nothing," 30).

carried the heading "Firm axes outspoken scientist's research: Woman went public with concerns about drug's safety."[30] Fourth, a caller to *Maclean's* magazine from inside the hospital "accused her of stealing money from her research grant, treating her patients unethically, and sleeping with some of the scientists who looked favorably on her research findings," while another, with links to Apotex, "stubbornly referred to the trained medical specialist as 'Miss Oliveria.'"[31] And fifth, the pediatrician-in-chief at the HSC maintained that patient care would be unaffected by Olivieri's removal from the research program: she would "actually have more time to care for her patients."[32] Regardless of how the case is ultimately evaluated, these remarks expose a gendered subtext beneath the dominant readings. Discrediting a woman's take on events is a familiar ploy; just as, in the politics of discourse, "outspoken" is rarely a gender-neutral term;[33] nor is labeling her a "woman" who went public—not a doctor or scientist—a gender-neutral action. Attributing a woman's professional success to her having slept her way to the top is a common strategy in the politics of gender, as is casually "forgetting" her name and professional title; and announcing that her time would be better spent with her patients trivializes Olivieri's scientific stature, relegating her to a caring position where she will, assuredly, "be better off." In gendered divisions of labels and labor, these are familiar scripts for designating a woman's place in a man-made world and cautioning her should she fail to know that place.

Even these items are not enough to establish a pivotal role for gender in the politics of knowledge and ethics of inquiry operative here, for explicitly gendered comments are sufficiently rare in the early press coverage that skeptics can easily discount them as mere slips of the pen. But there are exceptions, so telling as to make the larger silences resoundingly audible: A reference to "the dysfunctional patriarchy in which she works—The Hospital for Sick Children" describes it as "a place where senior scientists are scolded like schoolgirls and their concerns ignored";[34] a feminist columnist quotes a male colleague and supporter of Olivieri at the University of Toronto saying: "If she were a six foot two male football player, her concerns for her patients' well-being would not have been treated this way."[35]

30. Papp, "Firm Axes Outspoken Scientist's Research."
31. O'Hara, "Whistle-Blower," 66.
32. Foss and Taylor, "Sick Kids Demotes Controversial MD," A12.
33. A subsequent article refers to scientists (apparently both female and male) who "have been outspoken in their support for Dr. Olivieri" (Foss and Mitrovica, "Sick Kids Battle Turns Bizarre"), but my point holds.
34. Valpy, "Science Friction," 28.
35. Landsberg, "U of T Should Back Demoted Doctor," A2.

And the HSC's CEO Michael Strofolino refers to her as "this poor little innocent researcher,"[36] a comment unlikely to be made of a man.

Striking as they are, these examples combine neither to support a focus on gender nor to single it out as an explanatory-causal factor, for male scientists face comparable sanctions from pharmaceutical sponsors and/or universities devoted to protecting their financial assets. To cite just three well-known examples, Dr. Arpad Pusztai of the University of Aberdeen found his contract terminated after he spoke out about the risks of genetically modified foods;[37] Dr. David Healy's offer of an appointment as clinical director of the University of Toronto's Centre for Addiction and Mental Health was revoked when he published concerns about increased suicide risks among patients taking antidepressants;[38] and Olivieri compares her experiences with threats directed at Dr. David Kern, formerly of Brown University, in response to concerns he expressed about interstitial lung disease in workers at the industrial plant Microfibers.[39] Nor are gender issues explicitly named in reports of the professional harassment directed at Dr. Ann Clark of the Plant Agriculture Department at the University of Guelph, following her opposition to the development and use of genetically modified seeds (although reading her situation through a feminist lens could yield quite a different interpretation).[40] Yet (partial) media silence notwithstanding, there is every reason to evaluate gender as an analytic category in analyzing this case, given a scientific-research climate where a sexualized politics of knowledge sustains hierarchies of credibility, epistemic authority and trust in ways detrimental to open, democratic epistemic negotiation.

Representations

Although the fact of a high-profile female doctor as protagonist—and sometime victim—cannot by itself catch the gendered tenor of events in the Olivieri affair, some photographs of the main players offer a way of rereading the silences around gender.[41] Their messages are as insistent, in the hegemonic scientific

---

36. O'Hara, "Whistle-Blower," 66.
37. See, e.g., Flynn and Gillard, "GM Food Scandal Puts Labour on Spot."
38. See Horton, "Dawn of McScience," 7; and Healy, "Conflicting Interests."
39. Olivieri, "When Money and Truth Collide," 58.
40. See Clark, "Academia in the Service of Industry."
41. In rereading the silences, I follow Davis, who remarked that no matter how she read the evidence, she could not discern clearly gendered implications. When a graduate student recalled her earlier insistence that gender is always an issue, if only for its invisibility, she reexamined the silences. See her *Gift in Sixteenth-Century France*, esp. 75–79.

imaginary, as the whistle-blower montage with which I open this chapter. Constrained by the very nature of the medium to represent these players as embodied, thus as gendered beings, photographs *display* gender at work in ways that the verbal imagery of the print medium cannot so explicitly achieve. Differently, but with effects continuous with those of the oblique verbal rhetoric I have cited, these photographs subtly shape, and work to complicate, public assessments of Olivieri's professional stature and the value of her testimony, in a society better equipped to read the more common, stock representations of disembodied, neutral expertise and authority kept in circulation by photographs that deemphasize the bodily specificities of (usually male) doctors and CEOs. Reading through the silences to how the early press coverage highlights Olivieri's gender while rarely naming it allows the gender question to surface in a different register, as the focus shifts to how Nancy Olivieri's public credibility— hence her trust*worthiness*—is unsettled, how it evolves into a contentious issue, in the politics and ethics of representation.

Figure 2 presents a typically feminine image of Olivieri's professional demeanor, showing her with a child, in a female-caring posture. In the larger montage from which this image is taken, the photo is placed together with head-and-shoulders images of four men in suits—two of them her detractors and two her champions (captioned "The men in the middle")—and a full-length photo of the (also suited) president of the HSC.[42] Contrasting sharply with the Olivieri photograph, the men stand against neutral backdrops that could be anywhere or nowhere. They are the dispassionate, neutral leading actors in the drama, exemplary autonomous men: men of reason, whose gendered positioning is itself neutralized, unmarked. She bends forward in a strikingly subordinate position, leaning toward her patient and the camera. The provocatively defiant image of the bad girl—captioned "Courage under Fire" (fig. 3)—recalls another set of stock of images, among which the taming of the shrew is a clear contender. Like the images in figures 4 and 5,[43] it provides an intriguing contrast with a press photograph of Dr. Gideon Koren in which, looking straight at the photographer, frankly, in a normal professional posture, he appears as the very image of the avuncular doctor, the man everyone can trust, a kindly, if misunderstood, physician who must be forgiven for his blunder because it was "the only way to express himself" against this out-of-control woman.[44] His

42. See *Toronto Globe and Mail*, 2 November 1998, A9.

43. The *Elm Street* article, where these frankly female-feminine poses appear, praises Olivieri's for her courage under fire. It is one of only a few pieces to refer to her consistently as a scientist.

44. See *Toronto Globe and Mail*, 7 January 2000, A2.

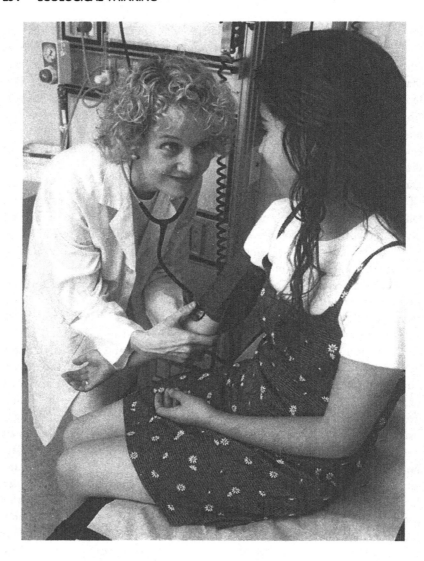

Figure 2. *Globe and Mail.* November 2, 1998. Photography by Tibor Kolley. Courtesy of *Globe and Mail.* Reprinted with permission.

body and clothing scarcely obtrude, leaving him to present himself as a thoughtful doctor who invites trust, a figure of appropriate professional detachment. Ironically, had he been depicted as the whistle-blower in a defiant pose such as Olivieri adopts, doing so might not have damaged his public

Figure 3. *Elm Street*, Holiday 1998. Photography by Derek Shapton, copyright © Derek Shapton. Reprinted with permission.

image or touched his credibility either way, if one is to credit the CAUT report. For even though male whistle-blowers, too, place themselves seriously at risk, a double standard was clearly operative in these events. For example, in 1999 the HSC made *public* allegations against "the quality of

Figure 4. *Elm Street*, Holiday 1998. Photography by Derek Shapton, copyright © Derek Shapton. Reprinted with permission.

Olivieri's work"; yet in that same year, despite forensic evidence produced by Olivieri and her colleagues, showing conclusively that Koren had been guilty of misconduct, the hospital's Board of Trustees "urged them 'not to take any unilateral steps which might damage the reputation of one of your

Figure 5. *Elm Street*, Holiday 1998. Photography by Derek Shapton, copyright © Derek Shapton. Reprinted with permission.

colleagues.'"[45] Surely Olivieri's professional stature might, similarly, have protected *her* reputation, contesting standard stereotypes and establishing their irrelevance. Yet the systemically gendered social-political climate generates strikingly asymmetrical readings of Koren's and Olivieri's actions. Viewed through the instituted social imaginary in a bioregion whose governing ethos holds stereotypes of masculinity, femininity, and science itself in place, Olivieri's credibility and trustworthiness have to be argued for, demonstrated, advocated with a degree of insistence that her professional stature should have rendered *hors de question*, while Koren's credibility persists unchallenged.

45. Thompson, Baird, and Downie, *Olivieri Report*, 396.

In ways such as these, ecological inquiry searches for, sleuths out, discerns factors specific to the place and the governing imaginary where knowledge is being negotiated, that contribute—however subtly and silently—to establishing or interrogating/destabilizing presumptions of trustworthiness, causally, temporally, and spatially distant though they may be from the matter at hand. (Compare Rachel Carson, who looked far afield for explanations, some as distant as the oriental home of the Japanese beetle, to determine what had happened where she was.) Images that focus attention on Olivieri's gender by sexualizing her public persona contribute, if at a subterranean level, to obscuring what, in the discourse of "normal science" should count as the main concern. They cast in doubt her scientific and medical expertise, in a research climate increasingly governed by practices that cannot help but skew expectations of scientific integrity when they place the pharmaceutical industry's gifts to the university, and its profits, above a quest for the reliable knowledge that has been science's long-imagined goal.

The *Elm Street* photos of Olivieri (figs. 3–5), like the *Maclean's* cover photo (fig. 1) admit of multiple "points of address and analysis": they can be read as self-consciously defiant, transgressing the scripts and expectations of docile, compliant white femininity, countering the negative social effects of the "blonde syndrome," to present a woman who has no need to downplay her femaleness in order to achieve professional distinction, who can be classy, good looking, assertive, *and* a rigorous research scientist. Olivieri is not without agency in their production: she authors herself, participates in crafting images of herself, acquiesces in the modes of address expected by *Elm Street*'s readers at that period in its publication history. She may have adopted such poses for just such purposes, by way of resisting those of the demure woman or the faceless professional. Indeed, Dehaas charges that Olivieri, together with a communications consultant, orchestrated this "highly successful 'media blitz'... that put [her]... on the cover of *Elm Street* and *Maclean's* magazines and made hers a household name synonymous with 'academic freedom.'"[46] Whether such effects figured in the planning process or are merely natural products of the hegemonic social imaginary, in both photos, the stance, the lip gloss, the earrings exploit an imagery overdetermined in spite of itself to take its point of reference from the entrenched disciplinary apparatus of gender politics—an imagery that requires Olivieri to navigate across a narrow range of options. She has to defy, evade, refuse, ignore, exploit, or reconfirm stereotypes, either of acquiescent or of out-of-control femininity.

---

46. Dehaas, "Much Ado about Nothing," 24.

Even the lab-coat image (fig. 4) is glamorized, flouted, trivialized, as is the fetching pose in figure 5, where Olivieri presents herself—or is represented—in the visual idiom of a fashion model or movie star, in her mock-assertive, come hither stance, posing as defiant, yet still unable to step outside the larger imaginary where such emphasis on her body works as readily to interrogate or mock her defiance as to celebrate it. Nor, despite the lab coat in figure 4, does she look, first and foremost, like a scientist or a doctor: she is a woman, and then—incidentally—a doctor.

Feminists of the second wave have asked whether science would be different if there were more women scientists, whether women would import "styles of reasoning"[47] or modes of inquiry capable of reconfiguring scientific practice in its process and products. In the first heady aftermath of Carol Gilligan's *In a Different Voice*, the essentialist imagery it generated, despite Gilligan's disclaimers, might have found in the Olivieri case an affirmative answer to the question, modeled on the exchange Gilligan constructs between Amy and Jake.[48] For a man (Jake), the Apotex contract would carry absolute, principled force, overriding all situational particularities. By contrast, Olivieri (as Amy) would respect the contract; yet her responsibilities to protect her patients, even from effects she had sworn not to disclose, would override its absolutism. Only by adhering to moral-epistemic principles respectful of circumstantial specificities could she ensure her ability to provide the adequately informed consent she required to prescribe the treatment. The press reports that highlight Olivieri's concern for her patients over her scientific authority are tacitly complicit in such a reading. But only a simplified, essentialized application of Gilligan's thesis could attribute overtly gendered styles of reasoning to the Olivieri story: an outcome that confirms the limits of this conceptual frame that was so plausible in the 1980s. Feminist ethico-political theory and epistemology have shifted from analyzing dislocated, dyadic relationships founded in stereotyped masculine and feminine styles toward addressing the intricacies of multiply situated knowledges and principles.

Yet it is instructive to read these displaced stereotypes and the photographs I have shown together with Londa Schiebinger's discussion of women scientists' efforts to achieve a credible professional image, both serious enough to present an authoritative demeanor and frank enough to avoid the dissembling that was one of the few options available to early women in western science.

47. The phrase is Hacking's in "Language, Truth, and Reason."
48. See Gilligan, *In a Different Voice*, 25–37.

Schiebinger's approach in her book *Has Feminism Changed Science?*[49] is at once more cautious and more wide-ranging than some previous feminist science writings (such as Keller's *Reflections on Gender and Science*),[50] assuming neither a hard-edged, dichotomous imagery of masculinity and femininity nor fixed, unified gendered scientific styles. Schiebinger examines structural-situational factors in the culture of science together with the substance of diverse scientific practices, to arrive at complex responses to her title question.

Analyzing an opposition between western images and ideals of science and femininity, Schiebinger traces its origins to the "privatization of the family and . . . professionalization of science" in the seventeenth and eighteenth centuries, when "the private, caring woman emerged as a foil to the public, rational man," and science "came to be seen as decidedly masculine" (hence Olivieri, by contrast, would be "better off caring for her patients"). As more and more women entered professional science, in the early twentieth century, the persistent effects of this opposition turned "shedding the trappings of 'femininity'" into one of the prices a woman had to pay to be taken seriously as a scientist.[51] At the beginning of the twenty-first century, Schiebinger suggests, both scientists and nonscientists still tend to see precise alignments between science and masculinity and to imagine science as naturally, appropriately populated by men.

So entrenched are residues of this history in the dominant social imaginary that it is scarcely surprising to find the Olivieri photographs delivering equivocal messages: they work both *toward* defying intransigent gender norms, undermining sedimented stereotypical imaginings, and *against* a measured representation of her as a scientist worthy of respect. It is a notorious double bind in patriarchal societies: women who flout the norms of femininity are rarely commended; women who conform to them are rarely taken seriously. Schiebinger recalls Martha Minow's "difference dilemma" according to which "calling attention to gender stereotypes can reinforce them and create friction where before there seemed to be none, but . . . ignoring gender differences can leave invisible power hierarchies in place."[52] Either way, the images insert a

---

49. Schiebinger, *Has Feminism Changed Science?* See also Creager, Lunbeck, and Schiebinger, *Feminism in Twentieth-Century Science*.

50. Keller, *Reflections on Gender and Science*.

51. Schiebinger, *Has Feminism Changed Science?* 69–70, 76. Schiebinger pursues her project of "understanding gender and other social aspects of science" in an investigation of "Europeans' efforts to globalize their understanding of nature" in her essay "Feminist History of Colonial Science," 234–35, which I read as ecological both in subject matter and in method.

52. Schiebinger, *Has Feminism Changed Science?* 68.

gendered dimension into the early stages of this controversy as it plays into an overactive rumor mill exploiting gossip about Olivieri's personal life and character ("she's known to have a flaming temper")[53] and representing her as a scapegoat just as often as she appears as an exemplary practitioner. They divert attention toward her person, thus away from her research as the appropriate locus of inquiry, and from larger, pressingly urgent ecological issues of institutional accountability and corporate complicity in circulating or suppressing putative truths that need to be open to deliberative evaluation. Thus they expose the irony of an official rhetoric that would construct the case as a "scientific controversy" in which the sex/gender, or any other personal attribute, of the scientist/knower would be insignificant.

Regardless of how the case is ultimately resolved, the images confirm that a high-profile "outspoken" woman scientist remains an anomaly in the dominant western scientific imaginary of the late twentieth and early twenty-first century, where everyday epistemic-moral discourse has no comfortable place for her. Nor could the standard conceptual frames have permitted gender to function analytically in the case's unfolding, unless by naming it simplistically to enlist the mere fact of one woman's extraordinary success, by entrenched criteria of "ordinariness," as evidence that the gender question has been resolved, ceased to be an issue, because women have "made it" even to the upper echelons of science. So long as they refrain from explicitly addressing the question in its multiple entanglements with power and privilege, explanatory-analytic accounts will remain too slender, the choices too stark. They reduce to two: *either* the affair generates a scientific controversy in which gender by definition is irrelevant; thus a new postfeminist era must be heralded, and one successful woman suffices to establish the point; *or* Nancy Olivieri is just being difficult, a "troublemaker,"[54] living proof, after all, that women cannot do science-by-the-rules; so it is easy to situate and contain her within a female/feminine domain, to downplay her expertise and blur the clarity of her professional profile. In other words, in this "imagined community"[55] forged around tacit understandings of what must and must not be said or shown in print—this community that coalesces around a set of common expectations and outrages to submit or admit Olivieri to a trial by media—it is nothing less

53. O'Hara, "Whistle-Blower," 66, spoken by a male caller who had not met Olivieri and offered no examples.

54. See Olivieri, "When Money and Truth Collide," 53. Shuchman quotes Janet Bickel, a U.S. expert on women in medicine, who "says that few academic women over forty escape being described as 'difficult' by their peers" (*Drug Trial*, 81).

55. I owe the phrase to Anderson, *Imagined Communities*.

Figure 6. CAUT Bulletin, v. 48, no. 9, November 2001. Photography by
Pat McGrath. Courtesy of *The Ottawa Citizen.* Reprinted with permission.

than disingenuous, a manifestation of false consciousness, to maintain silence
on the matter of gender when "everyone knows" how contentious a highly
successful female scientist is, with so visible a public profile. Hence the silences
amount to a studied avoidance, a public posturing of a would-be enlightened
postgender stance, enabled, in effect, by Olivieri's qualifications—her "bril-
liance" (in the word of one of her supporters). Yet when public opinion together
with the CAUT inquiry began, apparently, to vindicate her, the images shift:
Olivieri appears in frankly professional head-and-shoulders poses (figs. 6–7),
innocent, without dissembling, and with nothing to hide.

Had it been challenged, then, media neglect of the gender question might
have been excused with an argument that the very category is obsolescent,
beside the point, precisely because Olivieri—and others—have broken through
outmoded obstacles by doing what a woman must do to succeed in a world
shaped by male power: become twice as good as most men, and on male
territory. Thus, it would be ideologically excessive to raise the issue. But such a
response would show only that the entrenched social-conceptual imaginary is
not sensitively enough crafted to engage with gender's ongoing effects as an

Figure 7. CAUT Bulletin, v. 49, no. 1, January 2002. Photography by Wayne Hiebert. Courtesy of *The Ottawa Citizen*. Reprinted with permission.

oppressive mechanism—if more silently—even when a woman achieves eminence in a domain hitherto closed to members of her sex. The old tropes are right there, in the background: the gender stereotypes depicting and defending the legitimacy of a masculine, dispassionate, disinterested scientific expertise where a woman most easily finds her place when she assumes a feminine posture; and her defiance of the norms of femininity is readily invoked to cast her as hysterical, out of control. Such tropes, with variations, have been embedded in the western imaginary since the birth of experimental science in Britain from the work of Robert Boyle, for whom, Elizabeth Potter writes, the "new man of science [must] be a chaste, modest heterosexual who desires yet eschews a sexually dangerous yet chaste and modest woman."[56] Women could not be members of the British Royal Society, nor did they count among "those qualified to make knowledge by witnessing experiments and attesting to their validity."[57] There is scant evidence that these prohibitions have disappeared, even at the beginning of the twenty-first century.

Expertise, Credibility, and Trust

The questions about public credibility and epistemic responsibility generated by the Apotex sponsorship and complicated by the verbal and visual images I have recorded are entwined with larger questions about *trust* in knowledge and ethics. While it is not essentially—though it may be quintessentially— feminist to name public openness, answerability, and trust as central to an ethico-political analysis of inquiry or to social-material-ecological analyses of institutions of knowledge production, it is feminists who have moved the question "whose knowledge are we talking about?" to center stage in epistemology, where it occupies a conceptual space close to Schiebinger's question "has feminism changed science?" The epistemological question acquires a sharper edge when—as in the Olivieri case—it must open out to ask about the *provenance* and putative *ownership* of knowledge, prompted by the Apotex sponsorship and similar arrangements in an increasingly privatized research climate. It must investigate the sources of knowledge in practices more complex than direct, controlled observation and less available to straightforward verification-falsification, while examining genealogical, power/knowledge intrications to discern their effects. It must direct its attention to public access

56. Potter, *Gender and Boyle's Law of Gases*, 4.
57. Ibid., 16.

to knowledge, to determine how a lay population—patients, parents, relatives, and other caregivers—can "have" good enough knowledge to give adequately informed consent, when knowledge becomes a commodity whose purchasers and beneficiaries guard it zealously against unwanted challenges.

Images are integral to a society's ways of thinking about such questions; and the imagery of the *hortus conclusus*, the closed—therefore inaccessible—scientific community, is clearly still effective in these debates. Yet within that closely guarded space, the old chemistry-set/tabula rasa image of (male) scientists engaged in solitary, value-, and theory-neutral quests for truth has lost its plausibility, despite its tenacity in the public imagination.

In the new corporate research climate, public trust and epistemic responsibility, both individual and collective, are integral to and pressing within evaluations of scientific and other knowledge practices. This thought is not so new, even though questions about trust and trustworthiness were expunged from the epistemic imaginary when logical positivism heroically appeared on the scientific scene with a method heralded as capable of supplanting an allegedly unreliable, potentially subjective reliance on trust that, historically (according to Steven Shapin), had characterized both scientific and secular communities of inquiry, and not inevitably to their detriment.[58] As Apotex's policies and practices indicate, the emergence of new forms of patronage in present-day institutions of knowledge production confers a particular urgency upon issues of responsibility and trust. Yet they cannot adequately be addressed by condemning patronage unequivocally, either in scientific research or in other realms of inquiry and creativity: it has a long, often venerable history, even though neither its political innocence nor disinterested commitment to pure inquiry can be presumed before the fact. Contrary to the positivistic imaginary of scientific insulation from the circumstances of its making, in the early twenty-first century, the structures and effects of institutions and forms of patronage that underwrite and enable laboratory research and the circulation/application of scientific knowledge again—as in Shapin's reading of seventeenth-century England—count among conditions that make knowledge possible. Such conditions shape research findings, block or promote lines of inquiry, and regulate patterns of circulation and application. It would overstate the case to represent them, uniformly, as *determining* scientific knowledge as process or product, but understate it to gloss over their constitutive effects. Hence they demand investigation as integral to epistemological analysis and to the ecology and politics of

58. See Shapin, *Social History of Truth*, esp. chap. 1. See Shapiro, *Culture of Fact*, for a provocative reading of the history of factuality that contests many of Shapin's conclusions.

knowledge, for the structures of science as a public institution have under-gone such radical transformations since the Industrial Revolution and especially during the twentieth century as to reconfigure—reimagine—patterns of accountability and to redistribute epistemic, moral, and political responsibilities in ways that theorists of knowledge have still to think through. The persistence of intransigent gender, racial, class-, and ethnicity-based stereotypes, among others embedded in the everyday visual and verbal imagery of science and expertise, is just one reminder of how much remains to be done.

Prompted by these thoughts, I am adapting an insight of Cheshire Calhoun's to propose that, within the instituted social-epistemic imaginary, events like the Olivieri affair generate *abnormal contexts*. These, for Calhoun, "arise at the frontiers of moral knowledge...when a subgroup of society...makes advances in moral knowledge faster than they can be disseminated to and assimilated by the general public and subgroups at special moral risk."[59] Calling the events abnormal casts them neither as singular nor isolated: it shows how they disrupt the complacency of the presumed "normal," stretch the boundaries of fixed images and conceptual frames, multiply points of analysis. Olivieri's refusal to remain silent is by no means abnormal in the everyday discourse of knowledge and morality: in normal contexts it would be an obvious, straightforward choice. Its abnormality is more epistemic than moral, for the resilience of the hegemonic imaginary in sustaining a picture of normal science as a project of pure inquiry (all evidence to the contrary notwithstanding) deters the general public from assimilating exposures of scientific thralldom to the interests of its investors. It is difficult for a public, committed to imagining a direct correspondence between scientific-observational knowledge and independent "reality," to acknowledge the darker underside of scientific practice that the Olivieri case displays; it is not easy to assimilate the complexity of negotiations and often ruthless conflicts of interest integral to the production, validation, circulation, and now ownership of knowledge. My borrowing, then, extends Calhoun's insight into debates about the social-political location—temporal and spatial, demographic—of scientific knowledge, generated by thinking through these complexities. In my reading, these issues are the counterparts of Calhoun's "frontiers."

Questions about responsibility and trust arise at these frontiers. A renewed focus, in both feminist and nonfeminist writing, on "the role of trust in knowledge"[60] attests to their salience while reconfirming the ineluctable

---

59. Calhoun, "Responsibility and Reproach," 250.
60. See, e.g., Hardwig, "Role of Trust in Knowledge"; Barber, "Trust in Science"; and Scheman, "Epistemology Resuscitated."

situatedness, in Haraway's sense, of all inquiry. Situated knowers cannot perform the abdications of responsibility that orthodox positivism's value-neutral "god-trick" would allow, cannot, however persistently they may try, remove themselves from view as distinctively embodied, located epistemic agents. Nor is it possible, before the fact, to pronounce particularities of their embodiment or location irrelevant to their scientific practice. Abnormal moral contexts are, by definition, specifically inhabited and situated even though the knowledge production they foster will usually be more than locally valid.

In medicine throughout the affluent western world, trust, both epistemic and moral, is constitutive of practices of giving and seeking informed consent: trust in the knowledge underpinning such transactions (especially for the physician) having been responsibly sought, produced, and evaluated according to established criteria of scientific trustworthiness; trust that the information conveyed neither conceals nor mystifies that knowledge; trust in a commitment to establishing a reasonable openness and respect as a goal of physician-patient interactions. Physicians have also, judiciously, to know when to trust testimony conveyed in the professional literature and in collaborative practice. Because no practitioner can investigate everything, reconstruct every experiment for her/himself, responsible medical practice requires a just, reliable, and trust-presumptive, division of intellectual labor. Hence, speaking of Apotex's and others corporate efforts to suppress research findings, Dr. Miriam Kaufman comments, "if drug companies can control research...we're sunk as clinicians."[61] Nancy Olivieri could not seek appropriately informed consent from her patients or their parents as long as she observed the confidentiality agreement; thus it was impossible for her to invite their trust.

Perhaps paradoxically, feminists—and I among them—have argued that the "whose knowledge?" question confers a new salience upon appeals to *ad hominem*—in this case *ad feminam*—evidence.[62] So when "two of the world's other leading experts" testify to Olivieri's scientific eminence and professional integrity, their testimony enhances professional and public readiness to affirm her trustworthiness. Their (masculine) gender may enhance it still further. *My* defense of the plausibility of her cautionary findings would carry none of the presumptive knowledgeability imputed to the testimony of experts, whose credentials are cited to establish the credibility of their beliefs. Indeed, public presumptions in favor of believing in the truth or even the plausibility of knowledge claims are commonly generated, enhanced, or discredited by appeals to the credentials and

61. O'Hara, "Whistle-Blower," 67.
62. See my *Rhetorical Spaces,* 70–71.

character of the claimants, and reasonably so. Such appeals are strengthened or weakened by *ad hominem/ad feminam* images, both verbal and visual, that display modalities of conduct, character, and demeanor favorably or otherwise.

But such arguments lend themselves as readily to trust-destroying as to trust-enhancing purposes, as when media representations enter the *ad feminam* repertoire to deploy verbal and visual images whose effects are ambiguous as to whether they enhance or unsettle Olivieri's credibility. The contrast with Koren is again instructive: his depiction as a "top scientist and a caring doctor," is invoked to excuse his misconduct, thus to reestablish a credibility he might on some accounts be thought to have forfeited. Olivieri's *Elm Street* and *Maclean's* photos, by contrast, carry the potential to shift attention from her work's scientific merits to *her* unruliness. Such contrasts in imagery open out into other ways of asking the gender question even when the answer is equivocal; they approach it by circumnavigating standard propositional analysis and orthodox confirmation and/or falsification procedures to reveal the extent to which public credibility and trust emerge as artifacts of rhetoric and imagery.

Toward Democratic Epistemic Practices?

To continue our present course is to risk losing the one commodity which, for

physicians, universities and hospitals, should be viewed as beyond price: the

public trust.

—Nancy Olivieri, *Doctors for Research Integrity panel, Toronto, September 2003*

Questions posed by how corporate interests are served in pharmaceutical and other private research funding are about epistemic responsibility preserved, threatened, enhanced, compromised, even destroyed in reliance on commercial sponsorship at all levels, from the traditional contexts of discovery and justification, to circulation and practical deployment. They call urgently for democratic debate and collective rethinking of the very idea of trustworthy epistemic, scientific, and communicative practices.[63] Yet in the twentieth and early twenty-first centuries, as I have observed, trust has not ranked

---

63. Horton observes that societies need "a model of independent critical rationality for the proper conduct of democratic debate, judicial inquiry, and consumer protection" ("Dawn of McScience," 9).

unequivocally as an epistemic virtue or value. Nor, for epistemologists and philosophers of science who carry positivism's legacy forward, is its low epistemic status surprising. Autonomous, impartial knowledge seems to risk being destabilized beyond tenability when trust figures among necessary and sufficient conditions for knowledge in general. Hence, Shapin persuasively maintains, epistemologists have defined "legitimate knowledge" by "its rejection of trust": indeed, "trust and authority stand against the very idea of *science*"[64] as the putatively most reliable form of human knowledge. He exposes a curious paradox: "Knowledge is supposed to be the product of a sovereign individual confronting the world; reliance upon the views of others produces error. The very *distrust* which social theorists have identified as the most potent way of dissolving social order is said to be the most potent means of constructing our knowledge."[65] *Knowledge production*, on this account, is strangely anomalous among human practices: it is paradigmatically asocial, kept apart and isolated from the networks of social interdependence constitutive of viable human lives. According to Lynette Hunter: "Absolute objectivity, a fixed truth, value-free and neutral rationality . . . [comprise] a game that can be played by scientists and philosophers [only] so long as they remain isolated from society."[66] Introducing trust-related questions into rhetorical spaces thus delineated, thereby explicitly socializing epistemological inquiry, could scarcely fail to threaten disruption. Shapin contends, by contrast, that concerns with trust and trustworthiness were manifested, in early modern England, in the cooperation of "gentlemanly society" with the new "practice of empirical science" ("gentlewomen" were not judged equivalently trustworthy, nor were nonwhite, nonaffluent, nonheterosexual, non-Christian men). He sees the combination of a scientific method founded on individual epistemic self-reliance with an ethic for which the reliability of its gentleman practitioners could be taken on trust as providing a "local resolution of a pervasive problem about the grounds and adequacy of knowledge."[67] It took a sharp separation of the contexts of discovery and justification, instituted by the positivism of the Vienna Circle, to banish trust once more from the epistemic terrain.

64. Shapin, *Social History of Truth*, 16.
65. Ibid., 17 (emphasis added).
66. Hunter, *Critiques of Knowing*, 145.
67. Shapin, *Social History of Truth*, 42. Shapiro concurs on the centrality of trust, yet she argues for a different model, drawn from the legal arena: "The mere status of gentleman could hardly be decisive in the courtroom where one gentleman might well be contending against another and where witnesses of several classes might appear on both sides. I suggest that the scientific community adopted important elements of legal witnessing as constituent elements in the construction of the ideal scientific observer and reporter rather than relying on the courtier-aristocratic model" (*Culture of Fact*, 118).

As I propose in chapter two, in post-1969 naturalistic and social epistemology and at points where they intersect, a space opens for reintroducing
responsibility and trust into epistemic discourse, even though, in isolating the
laboratory from the rest of society to study it as a self-contained, self-justifying
unit, *Quinean* naturalism also distances itself from these issues. Ecological
naturalism, by contrast, and often making common cause with social epistemology, examines knowledge-making practices to expose the material, social-
political forces that conspire to foster or constrain inquiry.[68] Because of their
situational derivation, these analyses bring regulative epistemic principles into
closer ethological alignment with the diverse capacities and practices of real
knowers than Quine-line naturalism does, thereby beginning to close a gap
between theory and practice whose effects, I have observed, are often to keep an
instituted epistemic imaginary at a distance from the very knowledge epistemology purports to evaluate.

Recall John Hardwig's now-classic illustration of epistemic interdependence
in laboratory science, announced on the title page of a report of a physics experiment where ninety-nine "authors" are listed. He observes: "No one person
could have done the experiment . . . and many of the authors of an article like this
will not even know how a given number in the article was arrived at."[69] Analogously, with the division of intellectual labor in the Olivieri affair, it would be
impossible for every author listed for the 1998 *NEJM* article to repeat the experiment for her/himself. They have to *take on trust* a commitment of their coauthors
to responsible epistemic practice, in order to contribute knowledgeably to the
enterprise; and the case shows how fragile such trust can be. If knowing "is a
privileged state at all," Hardwig comments, "it is a privileged *social* state."[70]
Hence, I am affirming the *epistemological* significance of the structures—the situations, places, societies—that position some people as knowers and others not;
I am presenting the Olivieri affair as exemplary for developing an analysis at once
politically fraught and illustrative of the complexity of establishing the public
epistemic status and trustworthiness of knowers, and of scientific truths, in the
real world of empirical science, vested interest, power, and patronage.

Locating my discussion in a space where trust and epistemic responsibility are addressed and debated more publicly than in scholarly/professional

68. See in this regard Fuller, "Epistemology Radically Naturalized"; and my discussion in
chap. three above.

69. Hardwig, "Epistemic Dependence," 347. See also Latour and Woolgar's *Laboratory
Life* for a study of the ineluctably social character of knowledge making in a laboratory.

70. Hardwig, "Role of Trust in Knowledge," 697 (emphasis added). See also Barber,
"Trust in Science."

journals, I have enlisted newspaper reports and media imagery as sources, reading them as a midlevel locus/site of the making-public of knowledge, as a place in mass societies where a deliberative democratic public forum is often conducted.[71] They are commonly partisan, thus neither perfectly, objectively reliable; but neither are they always irresponsibly sensationalist, ideological. Public knowledge—albeit frequently contestable, merely putative knowledge—commonly derives from such sources and their analogues, where trust accumulates or diminishes, at least in part, according to judgments about the credibility of the testimonial claims of one or several report(s), and thus even of a particular reporter. As Hardwig's essay shows, it cannot be reserved for "knowledge-by-acquaintance," which, for classical empiricism, was the only knowledge in the world "so certain that no reasonable man could doubt it."[72]

In the Olivieri affair, responsibilities devolve across the epistemic and moral planes, as lines of confidentiality and trust become tangled in this head-on collision of "truths" and financial interest. Apotex's public responsibilities are both epistemic and moral: *epistemic* in the requirement to take new evidence seriously into account, following precepts assumed by a tacit "normative realism"; *moral* in the requirement to evaluate the impact for ordinary and professional human lives and for knowledge (hence not just for financial gain) of failing to do so. When such failures of responsibility are exposed, the fabric of epistemic reliance is torn. It is always more difficult to repair a fractured trust than to establish it initially.

In the individualistic language of *Epistemic Responsibility*, I advocate honesty and humility: "Honesty not to pretend to know what one does not know (and *knows* one does not) or to ignore its relevance; humility not to yield to temptations to suppress facts damning to one's theory."[73] These injunctions

---

71. My intention is not to contrast the press with scholarly/professional journals, implying that the journals are incontestably objective whereas media reports are not. Horton, for example, draws attention to sponsorship's role in determining which findings will be reported and how, charging medical journals with having become "an important but underrecognized obstacle to scientific truth-telling... information-laundering operations for the pharmaceutical industry" ("Dawn of McScience," 9). According to Miriam Shuchman the Nancy Olivieri case has had significant international repercussions. She notes, "In September of 2001, the editors of some of the world's leading medical journals (including the *Lancet*, the *New England Journal of Medicine, JAMA,* and the *British Medical Journal*) established a policy that they would not review or publish work by scientists whose sponsors prevented them from analyzing their data independently or publishing their work freely." *Drug Trial,* 359.

72. The phrase is from Russell, *Problems of Philosophy,* 1.

73. Code, *Epistemic Responsibility,* 137, where I cite Nozick's claim that "intellectual honesty demands that, occasionally at least, we go out of our way to confront strong arguments opposed to our view" (*Anarchy, State, and Utopia,* x).

translate, with modifications and refinements, into the socially-ecologically framed discourse of the present discussion. An informed public placing its trust in public knowledge tends, in western affluent societies, to expect such intellectual virtues to count, ex officio—so to speak—among the credentials of practicing scientists and other knowledge makers and for their patrons and sponsors, thus offsetting risks of epistemic imperialism and the oppressive effects of such putative knowings beyond the confines of the laboratory or other institution. Hence epistemic responsibility requirements are peculiarly stringent when it is mooted that the profit motive might take "precedence over scientific rigour" or "the researchers themselves [may] lose their objectivity,"[74] in consequence of these conflicts.

Apparently, Nancy Olivieri did not "lose her objectivity." Her cautionary 1995 letter to the editor of the *New England Journal of Medicine*, with its language of confirming findings, ensuring against false hope and expectation, tells in favor of maintaining public trust in her scientific responsibility, and many of the media assessments tend in this direction. Yet Dehaas's reading contests the very confirmations she has declared; and there is no easy resolution. Olivieri's responsibilities are analogous to those of Apotex, but they differ in her relationship to a wider scientific and secular public wondering how far to trust *her* knowledge as she reports on it publicly. They differ also in relation to the patients from whom she must, in good faith, ask informed consent, confident in her capacity to provide knowledge sufficiently sound and complete to inform that consent.

This discussion redirects the question "whose knowledge are we talking about?" toward larger matters of *democratic* epistemic-scientific practice: democratic in the sense of facilitating informed public participation in deliberating science and knowledge policies, fostering open debate, building bridges between accredited expertise and people reliant upon it across a range of specialized and everyday practices. It focuses on cultivating public sensitivity to the specificity of diverse social circumstances and positionings, in diverse habitats, and with acknowledged differences in habitus and ethos. My interest is in developing strategies and policies to address the ecological implications and effects of socializing and naturalizing epistemology in these ways, thus to locate inquiry in a community that bears—or shares—the burdens of epistemic responsibility. I think it is from similar interests that Ursula Franklin deplores the loss of moral literacy in an age of increasing technological literacy, and the rarity of public discussion about "the merits or problems of adopting a

74. Foss and Taylor, "Volatile Mix."

particular technology." Advocating public inquiry, open debate, she contends that "what the real world of technology needs more than anything else are citizens with a sense of humility,"[75] echoing Rachel Carson's plea for intellectual-moral humility in scientific inquiry and scientifically informed practice. Such democratic, participatory inquiry would engage critically and subversively with social arrangements that position citizens unequally in relation to sources of public knowledge, posing obstacles to democratic participation, and with patterns of informed consent and confidentiality as they inflect these larger issues.

It would be naive to imagine the mere act of locating epistemic practices within a social, communal frame as a straightforward solution, capable of redistributing burdens of justification or proof, enabling ready agreement and smooth epistemic negotiations. Situating knowledge socially and ecologically could not produce instant consensus within a community—nor is even the highest degree of consensus truth- or justice-guaranteeing. It could, as readily, close down interrogation and dissent: Apotex's silencing efforts are one pertinent example. Neither can the multiplicity of scientific micropractices be contained within a single communal vision—which could not, in any case, permit a sufficiently reflexive, self-critical relation to its own practices. Hence for Joseph Rouse, scientific practices have to become intelligible "within enacted narratives that constitute a developing field of knowledge, and they [= the practices] are important to the extent that they develop or transform those narratives."[76] In constructing such narratives, practices like those Haraway advocates in *Modest_Witness* suggest a productive model for democratic deliberation. As I note in chapter five, she writes of a Danish practice of "establishing panels of ordinary citizens, selected from pools of people who indicate an interest, but not professional expertise or a commercial or other organized stake, in an area of technology.... [They] hear testimony, cross-examine experts, read briefings, deliberate among themselves, and issue reports to a national press conference."[77] The debates generated in the Canadian press by the Olivieri case bear some informal resemblance to this process, as, more

75. Franklin, *Real World of Technology*, 69, 91.

76. Rouse, *Reconstructing Philosophy of Science*, 168–70.

77. Haraway, *Modest_Witness*, 95–97. Note that Haraway sees no automatic utopian promise in such panels. As Eckersley, for example, cautions in a different context, "simply ceding political and economic control (including environmental management powers) to existing local communities does not in itself provide any guarantees that those communities will exercise their powers in an ecologically responsible manner" ("Politics," 323). But their promise is nonetheless apparent.

formally, does Doctors for Research Integrity, "an independent, non-profit group that seeks to promote research integrity and academic freedom," established by Olivieri and her colleagues after the Olivieri vs. Apotex affair.[78] In societies where scientific-technological discourse remains largely inaccessible to a public comprised of people who have to make wise decisions about how, when, and why to confer or withhold trust, such debate could advance projects to establish properly deliberative democracy, whose citizens—when they can— have to assume some responsibility for interrogating the taken-for-granted status of institutions of knowledge production, even if only in gadfly questioning, in micropractices that demand accountability. Thus Calhoun observes, in a related context, "It is . . . the actions of engaged social critics and political actors—'moral gadflies,' who take potentially severe personal risks—that enable moral progress in a society."[79]

Enacting such responsibilities cannot be represented as a universal requirement, given the uneven social distribution of practical and structural access to sources of knowledge making and the contested relationship to patronage that twenty-first-century research scientists have often to maintain. But the present-day variation on the gentlemanly scientific culture Shapin details, which is as exclusive and exclusionary in its membership and esotericism as Shapin's society of gentlemen, has to be opened to social-political critique. In such cultures trust and credibility tend to attach less to putative truths than to their makers and promulgators; ordinary lay access to scientific facts is rarely unmediated, and practices of mediation, as with Apotex, are kept closed to scrutiny. When public knowledge can be crudely controlled by mechanisms such as Apotex's confidentiality clause, epistemic negotiations move uneasily across the power differentials whose structuring effects reinforce Rouse's doubts about the very possibility of community bearing the justificatory weight that some social epistemologists urge. Here, principled, informed critique has a vitally important part to play.

The issues are not simple. Patronage, which literally makes so much research and thus knowledge possible has long been in place, if not in the forms it takes in this era of multinational corporations and multimillion dollar funding. Shapin's gentlemen, like western laboratory scientists now, comprise a distinct, predominately male segment of civil society, privileged by class, race, and gender, even when such specificities go unmarked in the imagined naturalness of the social order and the presumed autonomy of scientific inquiry.

---

78. See their website www.doctorsintegrity.org/media/allmedia.htm.
79. Calhoun, *Setting the Moral Compass*, 17.

When patronage makes truth subservient to profit or ideology, the very possibility of evaluating knowledge and public trust collides head on with a power that simultaneously thwarts inquiry and, in a complex doubling back upon itself, immobilizes investigations of the very conditions of inquiry it is bent on examining.

The task, then, for philosophers and other citizens is to work through questions about collective responsibility and opportunities for critical intervention, in relation both to publicly and to privately funded institutions of knowledge production. Despite the notoriety of its conduct, Apotex is not solely answerable for the Olivieri affair: it is a symptom, not the disease. The social practices and institutions that make its funding style possible demand ongoing social-political intervention, committed to democratic, ecologically attuned epistemic-scientific process whose purposes include honoring the responsibilities capable of contributing to viable, habitable community. Analogously, although seeking informed consent was not possible so long as Nancy Olivieri observed the confidentiality—the nondisclosure—agreement (hence its centrality in prompting her to act), confidentiality requirements and their analogues are not the only obstacles to informed consent. The power-knowledge-privilege differential between doctor and patient is an equivalently complicating structural factor. Feminists have developed cogent analyses of the systemic politics of knowledge at work here, consequent upon women's and other Others' frequent silencing, mystification, and induced ignorance in their dealings with the medical profession. Susan Sherwin, for example, writes of some physicians' persistent allegiance to a paternalist model that, despite feminist and other activist pressures, requires only "minimal standards of informed consent."[80] Lucy Candib remarks on the legalistic tenor of informed consent language, observing that it is rarely intelligible to the point of giving patients "a clear idea of risks, benefits, side effects, and alternatives to tests or treatment"; often its purpose reduces to relieving "the hospital or doctor of the charge of battery . . . it does not constitute *informed* consent."[81] Thus conceived, it scarcely attests to a physician's wish for good relationships with her/his patients.

Feminist philosophers have been among the most persistent interrogators of beliefs that consent can count as informed before the fact, that patients can know well enough what they are to consenting to; nor is it easy for a physician to ascertain how much/how well a patient knows, given that one effect of the power-privilege differential is to produce wariness, for patients, of the humiliation that can follow seeming not to know. This issue, in a different register, is also about money and morality. With respect to money, it is about public health policy reluctance to allow for the (billable) time it takes to insure well-informed consent; with respect to morality, it is about the mutual responsibilities of doctor and patient to work together to the point where consent is as informed as it can be. Here again, advocacy is instrumental in making knowledge possible—concerted advocacy to funding agencies about the time that "good enough" explanations take, where the threshold of "enough" must not be set too low. It is equally about education. Virginia Warren, for example, urges patients and physicians to work together—democratically— to develop an educational model that could facilitate properly, responsibly informed consent.[82] Her recommendation extends beyond the borders of the medical world to represent many of the issues I have addressed in this book as educational issues. Such a model would, at minimum, have to take situational specificities and circumstances seriously, as integral to, not extraneous details to, medical and other epistemic practices. It would work toward developing safeguards against universal, impartial one-size-fits-all formulas, thereby endeavoring to set right an irresponsible epistemic neglect, so irresponsible and at the same time so culturally entrenched as to be beyond simple reform within the received social imaginary.[83] As I have urged throughout this book, it would require nothing less than a Copernican revolution in knowledge.

In medical knowledge, as in other modes of knowing I have examined, I am suggesting that the conceptual apparatuses of mainstream epistemology, of natural and social epistemology, and of epistemic responsibility, need to be reconfigured, often collaboratively, reciprocally. Detractors might contend that an old-style empiricism could have addressed the Olivieri situation perfectly well. But my argument has been that the goal of disentangling knowledge production from the effects of its social-institutional situation, to submit it to unmediated justification or falsification procedures, is so remote from the habitus and ethos of actual epistemic practices and institutions of knowledge production as no longer to merit respect. Evaluative projects have to be situated close to and engage sensitively with the particularities of real, natural-social knowledge; and public assessments of responsibility have to be conducted on a deliberative-democratic model constructed out of a commitment to eschew imperialistic pronouncements from on high, while cultivating sensitivity to the requirements that emerge from acknowledged human diversity. Negotiation is

---

82. Warren, "Feminist Directions in Medical Ethics," 38–40.
83. Thanks to Peta Bowden for suggesting this way of formulating the matter.

integral to such deliberations, in knowledge-making practices and policies engaged by numerous participants, incorporating multiple points of view, diverse locations and situations, resisting too-early closure, aware that there can be few once-and-for-all, or once-and-for-everyone/everywhere solutions, yet that often people have to proceed with the best available explanation, have simply to act.

My readings of the Olivieri affair in this chapter have, admittedly, posed more questions than they answer. Answering them, I have suggested, requires negotiations more cognizant of the detail of human lives and locations than the stripped-down examples that orthodox epistemology serves up as paradigmatic. Institutions of inquiry are not populated by the faceless, disembodied knowers who figure in the positivist imaginary, but by diversely gendered, classed, raced, abled, aged practitioners whose embodied specificities and material-cultural situatedness cannot be disregarded. Although issues such as these rarely figure in academic epistemology, feminists and other Others are in the business of crafting conceptual tools to enable theorists and practitioners to see their pertinence to the politics of knowledge. Recall my chapter three discussion of Haraway's brief for a vision not found but made, for a seeing that requires *learning* to see what is ordinarily invisible, to see from below, from the margins, and—self-critically—from the center.

In such inquiry, evaluations and justificatory practices will be more nuanced, less certain, more multifaceted than philosophers of science and epistemologists have hoped; but directing attention to metaphors, images, styles of reasoning for which the instituted scientific-epistemic imaginary has no place makes for a more ambiguous but richer, more ecologically informed and informative analysis than truncated summary accounts can provide. Ecologically grounded, gender-sensitive analyses enlarge the scope of inquiry while media imagery adds layers of complexity to gender itself as an analytic category, refining and expanding its explanatory scope. The result may not be a never-ending story, but premature closure—a too-easy dismissal of the part gender and other Otherings play in the politics of knowledge—risks truncating explanatory approaches capable of making all the difference.

Just as medical doctors ought not be so scientific that they neglect advocacy for

their patients, so also ecologists ought not be so scientific that they neglect advocacy

for the planet. . . . In the presence of uncertain, underdetermined, untestable

ecological science, ethical advocacy (for all that ecology studies) is the only way to

preserve the very things we wish to study.

—Kristin Shrader-Frechette, "Ecology"

CONCLUSION

Ecological thinking, I have shown, examines the contributions of epistemic and ethico-political practices to producing habitats where people can live well together and respectfully with and in the physical/natural world:[1] it initiates a refocusing that decenters philosophical inquiry, moves it toward learning to see horizontal patterns and interconnections of diverse, multiply complex epistemological terrains. Within this renewed instituting imaginary, both epistemological and ethico-political inquiry require conceptual/geographical remappings sensitive to detail and diversity, resistant to the hasty translation from situation to situation by which deductive (= vertical) reasoning from overarching premise, principle, or governing law to conclusions systematically deduced and applied often claims solitary dominion over all the earth.

The discourses of mastery with which I have engaged throughout this book enlist ready-made, easy-to-apply categories to sum up and contain items and events in the personal, social, and physical-natural world within neatly manageable arrays of "kinds." Ecological thinking, by contrast, is more sensitively

---

1. See my references to Raymond Williams in chap. one.

respectful of differences and thence resistant to the desire for unity propelling these practices toward neat solutions designed to assemble the confusion of the human and natural world into maximally homogeneous patterns. As the examples I have discussed show, such epistemic control rationalizes extrapolating from the situations, symptoms, needs, and goals of the powerful into diagnoses and policy decisions enacted upon people who must, if they are sufficiently enlightened, want to be just like them. These enactments do not, in my analysis, count as advocacy in the productive, responsibly enabling sense I have discussed in chapter five, but as one of *its* perversions. Ecological thinking, in its commitment to complexity, urges attention to detail, to minutiae, to what precisely—however apparently small—distinguishes this patient, this welfare recipient from that, this practice, this locality from that, as Rachel Carson would distinguish this plant, this species from that, Lucy Candib this heart patient from that, all the while acknowledging and respecting their commonalities, where pertinent. It endeavors to interpret the meaning of differences and commonalities, even when they appear in the form of minor deviations from an artifactual norm; studies how they promote or thwart possibilities of knowing responsibly and living well; works to articulate appropriate guidelines for interventions appropriate to population and place. Ecological thinking thus resists practices, common in science-venerating cultures, of superimposing a grid upon events, experiences, and situations, tucking in the bits that spill over the edges, letting putative aberrations drop through the cracks. It combines careful readings of evidence characteristic of empiricism in its creative, deliberative versions with investigations that locate events, experiences, symptoms, social issues, problems within wider patterns of power and privilege, oppression and victimization, scarcity and plenty, joy and sorrow. It is prepared where necessary to negotiate long and carefully before reaching a conclusion, to wait an extra season or two, to resist premature closure, and to set high standards for the understanding that responsible action requires, yet to act on the best available explanation when definitive conclusions are elusive. It is, and it promotes, thoughtful practice.

As I observe in chapter one, being-in-the-world guided by ecological thinking differs radically from the masterful way of autonomous man who, in assuming he can be master of all he surveys, allows surveying to substitute for engaged participation, and mastery to suppress diversity for the sake of instrumental simplicity. For Verena Conley (following Michel de Certeau) ecological thinking is "*a way of inhabiting the world*," "a social and natural concern aimed at measuring habitability."[2] These *structural* features inform ecological

---

2. Conley, *Ecopolitics*, 110, 114 (emphasis original).

thinking through and through. I have also discussed some of their sources in feminist and postcolonial theory: ecofeminism is a principal source, as are deep ecology and the Green movement. All are contested and contestable positions, neither politically innocent nor able single-handedly to remake the world. All contain the seeds of "perversions" as inimical to habitability and ideal cohabitation as the philosophy of rights, as capable of sowing renewed subjections as autonomy in its hyperbolized modes. Yet their intellectual-activist promise justifies the risks involved in drawing judiciously upon them, even within the frame of a principled refusal to endorse the alignment—indeed, the identification—in some ecofeminist writings of an essential "woman" with an equally essential "Nature," which threatens to reconfirm the biological determinism that has kept women "in their place" in autonomy-venerating societies.

Often, ecological thinking works in concert with reasoning that traces evidential analogies and disanalogies horizontally, from situation to situation—"transversally," as Conley puts it, "making a link between ecosystems that international capitalism seeks to polarize and ecological issues that pertain to local cultures."[3] Cognizant of the force of disanalogy, practitioners of analogical reasoning are wary of practices of universalizing conclusions and solutions, evident in institutional dismissals of syndrome X, of local environmental damage, or of specifically detailed workplace harms. Analogical reasoning, at its most effective, is interpretive, deliberative, collaboratively negotiated, more inductive than deductive, more modestly conjectural than arrogantly conclusive, but not thereby lacking the courage of its convictions. While it has been discredited as subjective, particularist, and situational, and thus contrasted unfavorably with objective and universal modes of reasoning, it is often more carefully attuned to situated empirical evidence and thus more responsible *to* its subject matter than conventionally respectable deductive-nomological reasoning can be.[4] It meshes well with Kristin Shrader-Frechette's characterization of the ambiguities and indeterminacy endemic to ecological science that I discuss in chapter one. Nor, in my rendition, is analogical thinking exclusively horizontal, for it derives its understandings also from genealogical (longitudinal) analyses of the power that permeates and legitimates the currently hegemonic, instituted social imaginary.

Ecological thinking finds its point of departure in the—natural—dependence of knowledge production on interactive negotiations such as the

---

3. Ibid., 110.
4. For an analysis of analogy's dubious epistemic status, see Wylie, "Reaction against Analogy."

advocacy practices I have sketched in chapter five. It draws critically on empirical evidence to assess how survival, in specific situations for specific populations, could be ensured and enhanced, not just quantitatively but qualitatively. As my reading of the Olivieri case indicates, it is wary of the tendency of power-infused racial/gender/class stereotypes and essentialized conceptions of science and nature to become self-fulfilling and self-perpetuating. Yet if work within it is to avoid replicating the exclusions endemic to traditional epistemologies, its advocacy practices and negotiations have to be engaged out of the vigilant monitoring on which transformative social movements always depend to preserve their fragile gains and to counter threats of renewed oppressions. In such epistemically responsible, sensitive negotiations, hyperbolized autonomy yields to a fuller recognition of the guiding powers of *integrity*, a principle less individualistically based, more at home on this spread-out landscape. While refusing to romanticize nature, ecological thinking assumes an integrity and an agency in many natural processes and considers biodiversity worthy of respect if not of such fanatical preservation as principled refusals to swat a mosquito, inoculate against diphtheria, or restrain a dangerous offender might display.

For Cornelius Castoriadis, as I have noted, genealogies of the *creation* of the "individual" complete with his needs, within the dominant imaginary, expose its contingency and the interests it tacitly serves, thereby generating possibilities for turning it against itself by utilizing that same scientific, technological, and social-psychological knowledge to reconstruct human relations to the social and natural world.[5] The ecological movement thus becomes a resource for addressing the "political problems of the reconstruction of autonomous society" and acting accordingly.

In developing the conception of ecological naturalism that informs this book I have claimed a debt to Kristin Shrader-Frechette's work on the philosophy of ecological science and have cited her claim (with E. D. McCoy) that ecological science needs "epistemological and ethical analyses as well."[6] I have taken these claims as a point of entry for introducing questions of epistemic responsibility into ecological thinking about the politics of knowledge complicit in producing and sustaining demonstrably unjust social-epistemic orders

---

5. Here Castoriadis is referring to technology, but his argument permits this expansion. He writes: "The transformation of present technology . . . will have to seize part of what exists at present as technology and utilise it to create another technology" ("From Ecology to Autonomy," 20).

6. Shrader-Frechette and McCoy, *Method in Ecology*, 86.

and for its capacity to promote better ways. Shrader-Frechette engages explicitly and in impressive detail with these concerns in her 2002 book, *Environmental Justice*, where, on my reading, she shows something very like ecological naturalism at work in an argument firmly grounded in particular ecological situations yet translatable, if not without remainder, into other locations across the epistemic terrain.

In an analysis directed toward establishing the need—and indeed the civic responsibility—for "advocacy on behalf of people victimized by environmental injustice,"[7] Shrader-Frechette demonstrates the effectiveness of the " 'practical ecology' based primarily on case studies, natural history, and rules of thumb" she argues for in her earlier writings.[8] To this end she produces detailed studies of environmental harms in bioregions as diverse as cancer alley in Louisiana, nuclear waste disposal on Mescalero Apache lands, and Shell Oil's policies in Nigeria. None of these studies are superficial, none aim to aggregate bioregional differences into a unified, overarching analysis; each pays careful attention to the minutiae of place and situation and to environmental harms inflicted on specific populations and locations. The analyses are epistemically-politically-ecologically informed and savvy: they draw analogies from place to place without losing sight of disanalogies, and they are as careful in assessing the benefits of projects, industries, developments located there as they are in assessing the risks and harms. Aware of the power structures that silence individual voices, Shrader-Frechette, is attentive, also, to the unequal distribution of harms in their impact in the lives of African American, indigenous and Third World populations, and skeptical about what passes as informed consent when mining is to occur, pesticides to be applied, or waste to be incinerated or dumped.

Prohibitions against paternalism, which figure prominently in the imaginary that spawns autonomous individualism, are commonly invoked to justify an imagined but often unrealizable capacity for fully informed consent by people and populations whose ecological situation and circumstances—whose habitus and ethos—afford scant access to the knowledge upon which appropriately informed consent must depend.[9] Theirs is a systemically disenfranchised epistemic situation, thus not one of individual culpability or failure in epistemic autonomy, all appeals to logical possibility notwithstanding. *Sapere aude!* would amount merely to a whimsical supererogatory injunction for

---

7. Shrader-Frechette, *Environmental Justice*, 3.
8. Shrader-Frechette, "Ecology," 304–5.
9. See, e.g., Shrader-Frechette, *Environmental Justice*, 122.

the people most deeply affected, in many of the circumstances Shrader-Frechette details. Similar observations, with situation- and biography-appropriate variations, pertain to the women for whose workplace health Karen Messing advocates, to many of the patients Kirsti Malterud and Lucy Candib treat, to the victims for whom Amnesty advocates, to survivors of sexual assault less able to speak for themselves and claim credibility than Susan Brison is, and to patients and their parents needing trustworthy advice from Nancy Olivieri. These are some of the notable points of congruence between Shrader-Frechette's position and mine.

Shrader-Frechette constructs a powerful case for the value and indeed the necessity of advocacy—Environmental Justice Advocacy—that takes into account the dangers, and the potential accusations, of acting merely on behalf of special interests that plague advocacy projects, even as she insists, rightly I believe, that without advocacy the kinds of knowledge, protest, negotiation, and radical change on which environmental justice has to depend simply are not possible. She reminds her readers of how, in the middle of the twentieth century, vested interests suppressed the truth about pesticide policy, commenting, "One reason so many people violently attacked the largely accurate work of Rachel Carson . . . was that many of the leading scientists of the day had financial ties to the pesticide industry."[10] Her analysis calls for exposing and evaluating such ties, in whatever local form they take, and for civic action by, for, and on behalf of vulnerable people. It reminds her readers that we are all of us vulnerable and, as ecological citizens, called upon to engage where we can, to promote possibilities and places for forms of cohabitability committed to respecting and nurturing rather than exploiting that vulnerability in its diverse forms.

My project in this book has drawn both literally and metaphorically on ecology as a way of repositioning epistemological inquiry in both its traditionally epistemic and its ethico-political dimensions, in an effort to identify how some founding epistemological assumptions make it difficult to see the ecological issues clearly. Thus I have endeavored to clarify how entrenched ways of thinking about knowledge can obscure some of these vital issues. The point of my inquiry has been less to counterpose new and old models with the goal of having one of them emerge victorious than to uncover the social imaginary that has claimed ascendancy, to show how it can be challenged and enriched to make different ways of thinking possible. In the early twenty-first century, it can no longer be assumed that all species and variations of

10. Ibid., 187.

knowledge are spread out on a single plane, awaiting observation, classification, or ordering. Those of "us" who think about knowledge are faced with determining how to bring together and to move back and forth between different ways of organizing knowledge that may appear mutually incompatible, to engage in methodological pluralism. I have proposed (literal) ecology, together with the instituting imaginary it could generate, as a model for showing how apparently impossible communications across incompatible orderings could function. So long as knowledge is conceived on a top-down, aloof, and interchangeable spectator model, certain kinds of knowing are indeed possible, many of which have been remarkably effective in informing certain actions, practices, policies, values. But my guiding thought has been that knowledge thus pursued and claimed performs a kind of epistemic violence, even as it informs some practices quite well. The thought recalls Foucault's comment in "The Discourse on Language" about how every discipline, hence every way of knowing, "repulses a whole teratology of learning"[11] and in so doing attests to the effects of a pervasive social imaginary, in generating and legitimating a putatively comprehensive picture of human being, complete with its ways of thinking of and being in the world, and of attributing rights, entitlements, expectations—all of which follow as a matter of course. This is the picture on which ecological thinking refuses any longer to focus: its turning away allows it to turn its intelligence and its best energies toward bringing about the revolution in philosophy I announce in the introduction to this book.

---

11. Foucault, "Discourse on Language," 223.

Bibliography

Abram, David. *The Spell of the Sensuous: Perception and Language in a More-than-Human World.* New York: Pantheon, 1996.

Abrams, Frederick R. "Patient Advocate or Secret Agent?" *Journal of the American Medical Association* 256.13 (1986): 1784–85.

Addelson, Kathryn Pyne. "Knowers/Doers and Their Moral Problems." In Alcoff and Potter, *Feminist Epistemologies.*

Alcoff, Linda Martín. *Real Knowing: New Versions of the Coherence Theory.* Ithaca: Cornell University Press, 1996.

Alcoff, Linda Martín, and Elizabeth Potter, eds. *Feminist Epistemologies.* New York: Routledge, 1993.

American Medical Association Council on Ethical and Judicial Affairs. "Ethical Issues in Managed Care." *Journal of the American Medical Association* 273.4 (1995): 330–55.

Anderson, Benedict. *Imagined Communities: Reflections in the Origin and Spread of Nationalism.* London: Verso, 1983.

Antony, Louise. "Naturalized Epistemology, Morality, and the Real World." In Campbell and Hunter, *Moral Epistemology Naturalized.*

————. "Quine as Feminist: The Radical Import of Naturalized Epistemology." In Antony and Witt, *A Mind of One's Own.*

————. "Sisters, Please, I'd Rather Do it Myself: A Defense of Individualism in Feminist Epistemology." *Philosophical Topics* 23.2 (1995): 59–94.

Antony, Louise, and Charlotte Witt, eds. *A Mind of One's Own.* Boulder, CO: Westview, 1993.

Ayer, A. J. *Language, Truth, and Logic.* London: Gallancz, 1936.

Babbitt, Susan. "Feminism and Objective Interests." In Alcoff and Potter, *Feminist Epistemologies.*

Baier, Annette. *Moral Prejudices: Essays on Ethics.* Cambridge: Harvard University Press, 1995.

————. *Postures of the Mind: Essays on Mind and Morals.* Minneapolis: University of Minnesota Press, 1985.

Baker, Jeannie. *The Story of Rosy Dock.* New York: Greenwillow, 1995.

Barad, Karen. "Meeting the Universe Halfway: Realism and Social Constructivism without Contradiction." In Nelson and Nelson, *Feminism, Science, and the Philosophy of Science.*

————. "Posthumanist Performativity: Toward an Understanding of How Matter Comes to Matter." *Signs: Journal of Women in Western Culture and Society* 28.3 (2003): 801–31.

Barber, Bernard. "Trust in Science." *Minerva* 25.1–2 (1987): 123–34.

Bar On, Bat-Ami, and Ann Ferguson, eds. *Daring to Be Good: Essays in Feminist Ethico-Politics.* New York: Routledge, 1998.

Bartky, Sandra. "Sympathy and Solidarity: On a Tightrope with Scheler." In Meyers, *Feminists Rethink the Self.*

Baudrillard, Jean. *Simulations.* Translated by Paul Foss, Paul Patton, and Philip Beitchman. New York: Semiotext(e), 1983.

Bergoffen, Debra. "February 22, 2001: Toward a Politics of the Vulnerable Body." *Hypatia: A Journal of Feminist Philosophy* 18.1 (Winter 2003): 116–34.

Bermúdez, Jose Luis, Anthony Marcel, and Naomi Elan, eds. *The Body and the Self.* Cambridge: MIT Press, 1995.

Bernal, Ellen. "The Nurse as Patient Advocate." *Hastings Center Report* 22.4 (1992): 18–23.

Biehl, Janet. *Rethinking Ecofeminist Politics.* Boston: South End, 1991.

Birke, Linda. *Feminism and the Biological Body.* Edinburgh: Edinburgh University Press, 1999.

————. *Women, Feminism, and Biology.* Brighton: Harvester, 1986.

Birke, Linda, and Ruth Hubbard, eds. *Reinventing Biology: Respect for Life and the Creation of Knowledge.* Bloomington: Indiana University Press, 1995.

Bohm, David. "Postmodern Science and a Postmodern World." In Merchant, *Ecology.*

Booth, Wayne. "Individualism and the Mystery of the Social Self; or, Does Amnesty Have a Leg to Stand on?" In Johnson, *Freedom and Interpretation.*

Bourdieu, Pierre. *The Logic of Practice*. Translated by Richard Nice. Stanford: Stanford University Press, 1990.

Bowden, Peta. *Caring: Gender Sensitive Ethics*. London: Routledge, 1997.

Brison, Susan J. *Aftermath: Violence and the Remaking of a Self*. Princeton: Princeton University Press, 2002.

———. "On the Personal as Philosophical." *APA Newsletter on Feminism and Philosophy* 95.1 (1995): 37–40.

———. "Outliving Oneself: Trauma, Memory, and Personal Identity." In Meyers, *Feminists Rethink the Self*.

———. "Surviving Sexual Violence: A Philosophical Perspective." *Journal of Social Philosophy* 24.1 (1993): 5–22.

Bruner, Jerome. *Acts of Meaning*. Cambridge. Harvard University Press, 1990.

Buck-Morss, Susan. "Socio-Economic Bias in Piaget's Work and Its Implications for Cross-Culture Studies." *Human Development* 18 (1975): 35–49.

Burgess, Ann Wolpert. *Rape and Sexual Assault*, vol. 2. New York: Garland, 1988.

Burman, Erica. *Deconstructing Developmental Psychology*. London: Routledge, 1994.

Burt, Sandra, and Lorraine Code. *Changing Methods: Feminists Transforming Practice*. Peterborough, ON/Orchard Park, NY: Broadview, 1995.

Butterworth, George. "An Ecological Perspective on the Origins of Self." In Bermúdez, Marcel, and Elan, *The Body and the Self*.

Cafaro, Phil. "Rachel Carson's Environmental Ethics." *Reflections: Newsletter of the Program for Ethics, Science, and the Environment* (Department of Philosophy, Oregon State University) 9.2 (May 2002): 17–21.

Calhoun, Cheshire. "Responsibility and Reproach." In *Feminism and Political Theory*, edited by Cass R. Sunstein. Chicago: University of Chicago Press, 1990.

———, ed. *Setting the Moral Compass: Essays by Women Philosophers*. New York: Oxford University Press, 2004.

Callahan, Daniel. "Autonomy: A Moral Good, Not a Moral Obsession." *Hastings Center Report* 14 (Oct. 1984): 38–42.

Callebaut, Werner. *Taking the Naturalistic Turn; or, How Real Philosophy of Science Is Done*. Chicago: University of Chicago Press, 1993.

Campbell, Kirsten. "The Promise of Feminist Reflexivities: Developing Donna Haraway's Project for Feminist Science Studies." *Hypatia: A Journal of Feminist Philosophy* 19.1 (2004): 162–82.

Campbell, Richmond. *Illusions of Paradox: Feminist Epistemology Naturalized*. Lanham, MD: Rowman & Littlefield, 1998.

Campbell, Richmond, and Bruce Hunter, eds. *Moral Epistemology Naturalized*. *Canadian Journal of Philosophy* Supplement 26. Calgary: University of Calgary Press, 2001.

Candib, Lucy. *Medicine and the Family: A Feminist Perspective*. New York: Basic Books, 1995.

Card, Claudia. *The Unnatural Lottery: Character and Moral Luck*. Philadelphia: Temple University Press, 1996.

Carey, Susan. "The Origin and Evolution of Everyday Concepts." In Giere, *Cognitive Models of Science.*

Carnap, Rudolph. "Autobiography." In P. Schilpp. *The Philosophy of Rudolph Carnap.* LaSalle, IN: Open Court, 1963.

Carson, Rachel. "Biological Sciences." In *Good Reading.* New York: American Library, 1956.

——. *The Edge of the Sea.* Boston: Houghton Mifflin, 1955.

——. *Silent Spring.* Boston: Houghton Mifflin, 1962.

Castoriadis, Cornelius. "From Ecology to Autonomy." *Thesis Eleven* 3 (1981).

——. *The Imaginary Institution of Society.* Translated by Kathleen Blamey. Cambridge: MIT Press, 1998.

——. *Philosophy, Politics, Autonomy: Essays in Political Philosophy.* Edited by David Ames. New York: Oxford University Press, 1991.

——. "Radical Imagination and the Social Instituting Imaginary." In *Rethinking Imagination: Culture and Creativity,* edited by Gillian Robinson and John Rundell. London: Routledge, 1994.

Cheney, Jim. "Postmodern Environmental Ethics: Ethics as Bioregional Narrative." *Environmental Ethics* 11, 2 (1989): 117–34.

Chodorow, Nancy. *The Reproduction of Mothering: Psychoanalysis and the Sociology of Gender.* Berkeley: University of California Press, 1978.

Cixous, Hélène. "We Who Are Free, Are We Free?" In Johnson, *Freedom and Interpretation.*

Clark, E. Ann. "Academia in the Service of Industry: The Ag Biotech Model." In Turk, *The Corporate Campus.*

Clark, Kenneth. *Landscape into Art.* Middlesex, UK: Penguin, 1949.

Coady, C. A. J. *Testimony.* Oxford: Clarendon, 1992.

——. "Testimony and Observation." *American Philosophical Quarterly* 10 (1973): 149–55.

Code, Lorraine. *Epistemic Responsibility.* Hanover, NH: University Press of New England, 1987.

——, ed. *Feminist Interpretations of Hans-Georg Gadamer.* University Park: Penn State University Press, 2003.

——. "How Do We Know? Questions of Method in Feminist Practice." In Burt and Code, *Changing Methods.*

——. "How to Think Globally: Stretching the Limits of Imagination." *Hypatia: A Journal of Feminist Philosophy* 13.2 (1998): 73–85.

——. "Images of Expertise: Women, Science, and the Politics of Representation." In *Figuring It Out: Visual Languages of Gender in Science,* edited by Ann B. Shteir and Bernard Lightman. Albany, NY: SUNY Press, 2006.

——. "Is the Sex of the Knower Epistemologically Significant?" *Metaphilosophy* 12.3–4 (July–October 1981). Reprinted with a 1986 Postscript in *Applying Philosophy,* edited by Terence Bynum and William Vitek. New York: Metaphilosophy Foundation, 1988.

————. "Naming, Naturalizing, Normalizing: The Child as Fact and Artifact." In Miller and Scholnick, *Toward a Feminist Developmental Psychology*.

————. "Narratives of Responsibility and Agency: Reading Margaret Walker's *Moral Understandings*." *Hypatia: A Journal of Feminist Philosophy* 17.1 (Winter 2002): 156–73.

————. "The Perversion of Autonomy and the Subjection of Women: Discourses of Social Advocacy at Century's End." In *Relational Autonomy*, edited by Catriona Mackenzie and Natalie Stoljar. New York: Oxford University Press, 2000.

————. "Rational Imaginings, Responsible Knowings: How Far Can You See from Here?" In Tuana and Morgen, *Engendering Rationalities*.

————. *Rhetorical Spaces: Essays on (Gendered) Locations*. New York: Routledge, 1995.

————. "Statements of Fact: Whose? Where? When?" In Campbell and Hunter, *Moral Epistemology Naturalized*.

————. *What Can She Know? Feminist Theory and the Construction of Knowledge*. Ithaca: Cornell University Press, 1991.

————. "What Is Natural about Epistemology Naturalized?" *American Philosophical Quarterly* 33.1 (Jan. 1996): 1–22.

Cole, M., J. Gay, J. Glick, and D. W. Sharp, eds. *The Cultural Context of Learning and Thinking*. New York: Basic Books, 1971.

Collingwood, R. G. *An Essay on Metaphysics*. Oxford: Oxford University Press, 1939.

Conley, Verena Andermatt. *Ecopolitics: The Environment in Poststructuralist Thought*. London: Routledge, 1997.

Cornell, Drucilla. *Beyond Accommodation: Ethical Feminism, Deconstruction, and the Law*. New York: Routledge, 1991.

Crawford, M., and Jeanne Marecek. "Psychology Reconstructs the Female: 1968–1988." *Psychology of Women Quarterly* 13 (1989): 147–65.

Creager, Angela N., Elizabeth Lunbeck, and Londa Schiebinger, eds. *Feminism in Twentieth-Century Science, Technology, and Medicine*. Chicago: University of Chicago Press, 2001.

Cuomo, Chris J. *Feminism and Ecological Communities: An Ethic of Flourishing*. London: Routledge, 1998.

Curtin, Deane. *Chinnagounder's Challenge: The Question of Ecological Citizenship*. Bloomington: Indiana University Press, 1999.

Danto, Arthur. "Naturalism." In *The Encyclopedia of Philosophy*, edited by Paul Edwards. New York: Macmillan, 1967.

Davion, Victoria. "Listening to Women's Voices: Rape, Epistemic Privilege, and Objectivity." In Bar On and Ferguson, *Daring to Be Good*.

Davis, Natalie Zemon. *The Gift in Sixteenth-Century France*. Madison: University of Wisconsin Press, 2000.

D'Eaubonne, Françoise. *Le féminisme ou la mort*. Paris: Horay, 1974.

————. "The Time for Ecofeminism." Translated by Ruth Hottell. In Merchant, *Ecology*.

Dehaas, David. "Much Ado about Nothing." *MD Canada: Matters for the Medical Mind* 1.2 (May–June 2003): 19–30.

Deleuze, Gilles. *Spinoza: Practical Philosophy*. Translated by Robert Hurley. San Francisco: City Lights, 1988.

Deleuze, Gilles, and Felix Guattari. *A Thousand Plateaus: Capitalism and Schizophrenia*. Translated by B. Massumi. Minneapolis: University of Minnesota Press, 1987.

———. *What Is Philosophy?* Translated by Graham Burchell and Hugh Tomlinson. London: Verso, 1994.

Deutscher, Penelope. *Yielding Gender: Feminism, Deconstruction, and the History of Philosophy*. London: Routledge, 1997.

Devall, Bill. "The Deep Ecology Movement." *Natural Resources Journal* 20 (April 1980): 299–322.

Diamond, Irene, and Gloria Feman Orenstein, eds. *Reweaving the World: The Emergence of Ecofeminism*. San Francisco: Sierra Club, 1990.

Downes, Stephen. "Socializing Naturalized Philosophy of Science." *Philosophy of Science* 60 (1993): 453–68.

Duran, Jane. *Philosophies of Science/Feminist Theories*. Boulder, CO: Westview, 1998.

———. *Toward a Feminist Epistemology*. Savage, MD: Rowman & Littlefield, 1990.

Eckersley, Robin. "Politics." In Jamieson, *A Companion to Environmental Philosophy*.

Ehrlich, Susan. *Representing Rape: Language and Sexual Consent*. London: Routledge, 2001.

Engels, Friedrich. *Dialectics of Nature* (excerpts). In Merchant, *Ecology*.

Falmagne, Rachel Joffe. "Positionality and Thought: On the Gendered Foundations of Thought, Culture, and Development." In Miller and Scholnick, *Towards a Feminist Developmental Psychology*.

Faunce, Thomas. "Developing and Teaching the Virtue-Ethics Foundations of Healthcare Whistle-Blowing." *Monash Bioethics Review* 23.4 (2004): 40–55.

Fausto-Sterling, Anne. *Myths of Gender: Biological Theories about Women and Men*. New York: Basic Books, 1985.

Ferguson, Kathy. *The Feminist Case against Bureaucracy*. Philadelphia: Temple University Press, 1984.

Ferrell, Robyn. "Richard Rorty and the Poet's Utopia." In *Cartographies: Poststructuralism and the Mapping of Bodies and Spaces*, edited by Rosalyn Diprose and Robyn Ferrell. Sydney: Allen & Unwin, 1991.

Ferry, Luc. *The New Ecological Order*. Translated by Carol Volk. Chicago: University of Chicago Press, 1995.

Flax, Jane. "Displacing Women: Toward an Ethics of Multiplicity." In Bar On and Ferguson, *Daring to Be Good*.

Flynn, Laurie, and Michael Sean Gillard. "GM Food Scandal Puts Labour on Spot." *Guardian Weekly*, 21 February 1999.

Foss, Krista. "Sick Kids Doctor Breaks His Silence." *Toronto Globe and Mail*, 7 January 2000, A2.

Foss, Krista, and Andrew Mitrovica. "Sick Kids Battle Turns Bizarre." *Toronto Globe and Mail*, 21 December 1999.

Foss, Krista, and Paul Taylor. "Sick Kids Demotes Controversial MD." *Toronto Globe and Mail*, 8 January 1999, A12.

———. "Volatile Mix Meant Trouble at Sick Kids." *Toronto Globe and Mail*, 22 August 1998, A1, A4.

Foucault, Michel. "The Discourse on Language." Translated by Rupert Swyer. Appendix to *The Archeology of Knowledge*. New York: Pantheon, 1972.

———. "Nietzsche, Genealogy, History." In *Language, Counter-Memory, Practice: Selected Essays and Interviews by Michel Foucault*. Edited by Donald F. Bouchard. Translated by Donald F. Bouchard and Sherry Simon. Ithaca: Cornell University Press, 1977.

———. *Power/Knowledge: Selected Interviews and Other Writings, 1972–77*. Edited by Colin Gordon. New York: Pantheon, 1980.

———. "What Is Enlightenment?" Translated by Catherine Porter. In *The Foucault Reader*, edited by Paul Rabinow. New York: Pantheon, 1984.

Franklin, Ursula. *The Real World of Technology*. Toronto: Anansi, 1992.

Fricker, Elizabeth. "The Epistemology of Testimony." *Aristotelian Society Supplementary Volume*, 1987.

Fricker, Miranda. "Feminism in Epistemology: Pluralism without Postmodernism." In Fricker and Hornsby, *The Cambridge Companion to Feminism in Philosophy*.

Fricker, Miranda, and Jennifer Hornsby, eds. *The Cambridge Companion to Feminism in Philosophy*. Cambridge: Cambridge University Press, 2000.

Frye, Marilyn. "The Possibility of Feminist Theory." In *Women, Knowledge, and Reality: Explorations in Feminist Philosophy*, edited by Ann Garry and Marilyn Pearsall. New York: Routledge, 1996.

Fuchs, Stephan. "The New Wars of Truth: Conflicts over Science Studies as Differential Modes of Observation." *Social Science Information* 35.2 (1996): 307–26.

Fuller, Steve. "Epistemology Radically Naturalized: Recovering the Normative, the Experimental, and the Social." In Giere, *Cognitive Models of Science*.

Gadamer, Hans-Georg. *The Enigma of Health: The Art of Healing in a Scientific Age*. Translated by Jason Gaiger and Nicholas Walker. Stanford: Stanford University Press, 1996.

———. "The Problem of Historical Consciousness." In Rabinow and Sullivan, *Interpretive Social Science*.

Gatens, Moira. "Through a Spinozist Lens: Ethology, Difference, Power." In *Deleuze: A Critical Reader*, edited by Paul Patton. Oxford: Blackwell, 1996.

Gaylin, Willard, and Bruce Jennings. *The Perversion of Autonomy: The Proper Use of Freedom and Constraints in a Liberal Society*. New York: Free Press, 1996.

Geddes, Jennifer L. "Banal Evil and Useless Knowledge: Hannah Arendt and Charlotte Delbo on Evil after the Holocaust." *Hypatia: A Journal of Feminist Philosophy* 18.1 (2003): 104–15.

Gee, Henry. "Force of Nature." *Guardian Weekly*, 26 April 2001, 23.

Giere, Ronald N., ed. *Cognitive Models of Science*. Minneapolis: University of Minnesota Press, 1992.

Gilligan, Carol. *In a Different Voice: Psychological Theory and Women's Development*. Cambridge: Harvard University Press, 1982.

Glendenning, Victoria. *Electricity*. London: Random, 1995.

Goldfarb, W. "Effects of Psychological Deprivation in Infancy and Subsequent Stimulation." *American Journal of Psychology* 103 (1945): 113–17.

Goldman, Alvin. "Epistemic Folkways and Scientific Epistemology." In Kornblith, *Naturalizing Epistemology*.

———. *Epistemology and Cognition*. Cambridge: Harvard University Press, 1986.

Gopnik, Alison. "Developing the Idea of Intentionality: Children's Theories of Mind." *Canadian Journal of Philosophy* 20.1 (March 1990): 89–114.

Gopnik, Alison, and Andrew Meltzoff. *Words, Thoughts, and Theories*. Cambridge: MIT Press, 1997.

Gordon, Linda. *Pitied But Not Entitled: Single Mothers and the History of Welfare, 1890–1935*. New York: Free Press, 1994.

Gotanda, Neil. "Tales of Two Judges." In *The House That Race Built*, edited by Wahneema Lubiano. New York: Vintage, 1997.

Graycar, Regina. "The Gender of Judgments: An Introduction." In *Public and Private: Feminist Legal Debates*, edited by Margaret Thornton. Melbourne: Oxford University Press, 1995.

Griffin, Susan. *Woman and Nature: The Roaring inside Her*. New York: Harper & Row, 1978.

Griffiths, Morwenna, and Margaret Whitford, eds. *Feminist Perspectives in Philosophy*. Bloomington: Indiana University Press, 1988.

Hacking, Ian. "Language, Truth, and Reason." In *Rationality and Relativism*, edited by Martin Hollis and Steven Lukes. Cambridge: MIT Press, 1982.

Hamlyn, D. W. "Logical and Psychological Aspects of Learning." In Peters, *The Concept of Education*.

Haraway, Donna J. *Modest_Witness@Second_Millennium.Female_Man©_Meets_OncoMouse^{TM}: Feminism and Technoscience*. New York: Routledge, 1997.

———. "Otherworldly Conversations, Terran Topics, Local Terms." In Shiva and Moser, *Biopolitics*.

———. *Primate Visions: Gender, Race, and Nature in the World of Modern Science*. New York: Routledge, 1989.

———. *Simians, Cyborgs, and Women: The Reinvention of Nature*. New York: Routledge, 1991.

Harding, Sandra. "Rethinking Standpoint Epistemology: What Is 'Strong Objectivity'?" In Alcoff and Potter, *Feminist Epistemologies*.

Hardwig, John. "Epistemic Dependence." *Journal of Philosophy* 82.5 (1985): 335–49.

———. "The Role of Trust in Knowledge." *Journal of Philosophy* 88.12 (1991): 693–708.

Hartsock, Nancy. "The Feminist Standpoint: Developing the Ground for a Specifically Feminist Historical Materialism." In *Discovering Reality*, edited by Sandra Harding and Merrill Hintinkka. Dordrecht: Reidel, 1983.

Harvard Women's Health Watch 1.6 (Feb. 1984).

Hayden, Patrick. "Gilles Deleuze and Naturalism: A Convergence with Ecological Theory and Practice." *Environmental Ethics* 19 (Summer 1997): 185–204.

Healy, David. "Conflicting Interests: The Evolution of an Issue." *Monash Bioethics Review* 23.4 (2004): 8–18.

Henig, Robin Marantz. "Kind Hearts and Coronaries." *Toronto Globe and Mail*, 20 November 1993, D8.

Henriques, Julian, Wendy Hollway, Cathy Urwin, Couze Venn, and Valerie Walkerdine, eds. *Changing the Subject: Psychology, Social Regulation, and Subjectivity*. London: Methuen, 1984.

Herb, Alice. "The Hospital-Based Attorney as Patient Advocate." *Hastings Center Report* 25.2 (1995): 13–19.

Hiley, David R. *Philosophy in Question: Essays on a Pyrrhonian Theme*. Chicago: University of Chicago Press, 1988.

Hiley, David R., James F. Bohman, and Richard Shusterman, eds. *The Interpretive Turn: Philosophy, Science, Culture*. Ithaca: Cornell University Press, 1991.

Hollway, Wendy. *Subjectivity and Method in Psychology: Gender, Meaning, and Science*. London: Sage, 1989.

Honneth, Axel. *The Fragmented World of the Social: Essays in Social and Political Philosophy*. Edited by Charles W. Wright. Albany: SUNY Press, 1995.

———. *The Struggle for Recognition: The Moral Grammar of Social Conflicts*. Translated by Joel Anderson. Cambridge: MIT Press, 1995.

hooks, bell. *Bone Black: Memories of Girlhood*. New York: Holt, 1996.

Horkheimer, Max, and Theodor Adorno. "The Concept of Enlightenment." In Merchant, *Ecology*.

Horton, Richard." The Dawn of McScience." *New York Review of Books* 51.4 (March 2004): 7–9.

Hubbard, Ruth. *The Politics of Women's Biology*. New Brunswick: Rutgers University Press, 1990.

———. "Science, Facts, and Feminism." *Hypatia: A Journal of Feminist Philosophy* 3 (1988): 5–17.

Hubbard, Ruth, Mary Sue Henifin, and Barbara Fried, eds. *Biological Woman: The Convenient Myth*. Cambridge, MA: Schenkman, 1982.

Hull, David. "How to Get beyond the Purely Descriptive." In Callebaut, *Taking the Naturalistic Turn*.

Hunter, Lynette. *Critiques of Knowing: Situated Textualities in Science, Computing, and the Arts*. London: Routledge, 1999.

James, Susan. "Feminism in the Philosophy of Mind: The Question of Personal Identity." In Fricker and Hornsby, *The Cambridge Companion to Feminism in Philosophy*.

Jamieson, Dale, ed. *A Companion to Environmental Philosophy.* Oxford: Blackwell, 2001.

Jecker, Nancy S. "Integrating Medical Ethics with Normative Theory: Patient Advocacy and Social Responsibility." *Theoretical Medicine* 11.2 (1999): 125–39.

Johnson, Barbara, ed. *Freedom and Interpretation: The Oxford Amnesty Lectures 1992.* New York: Basic Books, 1993.

Johnson, Mark. *Moral Imagination: Implications of Cognitive Science for Ethics.* Chicago: University of Chicago Press, 1993.

Kant, Immanuel. "An Answer to the Question: 'What Is Enlightenment?'" In *Kant's Political Writings,* edited by Hans Reiss. Cambridge: Cambridge University Press, 1970.

———. *Critique of Pure Reason.* Translated by Norman Kemp Smith. London: Macmillan, 1970.

Keller, David, and Frank Golley, eds. *The Philosophy of Ecology: From Science to Synthesis.* Athens: University of Georgia Press, 2000.

Keller, Evelyn Fox. *Reflections on Gender and Science.* New Haven: Yale University Press, 1985.

———. *Secrets of Life, Secrets of Death: Essays on Language, Gender, and Science.* New York: Routledge, 1992.

Kim, Jaegwon. "What Is Naturalized Epistemology?" In Kornblith, *Naturalizing Epistemology.*

Kingsland, Sharon. *Modeling Nature: Episodes in the History of Population Ecology.* 2nd edition. Chicago: University of Chicago Press, 1995.

Kirkman, Robert. "Why Ecology Cannot Be All Things to All People: The 'Adaptive Radiation' of Scientific Concepts." *Environmental Ethics* 18 (Winter 1997): 375–90.

Kornblith, Hilary. "Epistemic Normativity," *Synthèse* 94 (1993), 357–76.

———. *Inductive Inference and Its Natural Ground: An Essay in Naturalistic Epistemology.* Cambridge: MIT Press, 1993.

———. "The Laws of Thought." *Philosophy and Phenomenological Research* 52.4 (Dec. 1992): 895–911.

———. "Naturalism: Both Metaphysical and Epistemological." In *Midwest Studies in Philosophy XIX,* edited by Peter French, Theodore E. Uehling, and Howard Wettstein. Notre Dame: University of Notre Dame Press, 1994.

———. "The Naturalistic Project in Epistemology: A Progress Report." Unpublished American Philosophical Association Pacific Division paper, 1990.

———, ed. *Naturalizing Epistemology.* 2nd edition. Cambridge: MIT Press, 1994.

Koss, Mary. "Hidden Rape: Sexual Aggression and Victimization in a National Sample in Higher Education." In Burgess, *Rape and Sexual Assault.*

Krimsky, Sheldon. *Science in the Private Interest: Has the Lure of Profits Corrupted Biomedical Research?* Lanham, MD: Rowman & Littlefield, 2003.

Kroll, Gary. "Ecology as a Subversive Subject." *Reflections: Newsletter of the Program for Ethics, Science, and the Environment* (Department of Philosophy, Oregon State University) 9.2 (May 2002): 11.

Kruks, Sonia. *Retrieving Experience: Subjectivity and Recognition in Feminist Politics.* Ithaca: Cornell University Press, 2001.

———. "Simone de Beauvoir: Teaching Sartre about Freedom." In *Feminist Interpretations of Simone de Beauvoir,* edited by Margaret Simon. University Park: University of Pennsylvania Press, 1995.

Kuhn, Thomas. *The Structure of Scientific Revolutions.* 2nd edition. Chicago: University of Chicago Press, 1970.

La Caze, Marguerite. *The Analytic Imaginary.* Ithaca: Cornell University Press, 2002.

Lacey, Nicola. *Unspeakable Subjects: Feminist Essays in Legal and Social Theory.* Oxford: Hart Publishing, 1998.

Lakoff, George, and Mark Johnson. *Metaphors We Live By.* Chicago: University of Chicago Press, 1990.

Landsberg, Michele. "U of T Should Back Demoted Doctor." *Toronto Sunday Star,* 17 January 1999, A2.

Latour, Bruno. "Irreduction." In Callebaut, *Taking the Naturalistic Turn.*

———. *The Politics of Nature: How to Bring the Sciences into Democracy.* Translated by Catherine Porter. Cambridge: Harvard University Press, 2004.

Latour, Bruno, and Steve Woolgar. *Laboratory Life: The Social Construction of Scientific Facts.* Princeton: Princeton University Press, 1986.

Lear, Linda J. *Rachel Carson: Witness for Nature.* London: Penguin, 1977.

———. "Rachel Carson's Silent Spring." *Reflections: Newsletter of the Program for Ethics, Science, and the Environment* (Department of Philosophy, Oregon State University) 9.2 (May 2002).

Le Dœuff, Michèle. *The Philosophical Imaginary.* Translated by Colin Gordon. Stanford: Stanford University Press, 1989.

———. *The Sex of Knowing.* Translated by Kathryn Hamer and Lorraine Code. New York: Routledge, 2003.

Leiss, William. "The Domination of Nature. In Merchant, *Ecology.*

Lemmens, Trudo. "Confronting the Conflict of Interest Crisis in Medical Research." *Monash Bioethics Review* 23.4 (2004): 19–40.

Lennon, Kathleen, and Margaret Whitford, eds. *Knowing the Difference: Feminist Perspectives in Epistemology.* London: Routledge, 1994.

Levins, Richard, and Richard C. Lewontin. "Dialectics and Reductionism in Ecology." In Keller and Golley, *The Philosophy of Ecology.*

Lewontin, Richard. *Biology as Ideology.* New York: HarperCollins, 1992.

———. "The Interpenetration of Environment and Organism." Keynote Address at the conference "Taking Nature Seriously." Eugene, OR, February 2001.

Lloyd, Elisabeth. "Feminism as Method: What Feminists Get That Philosophers Don't." *Philosophical Topics* 23.2 (1995): 189–220.

Lloyd, Genevieve. *The Man of Reason: "Male" and "Female" in Western Philosophy.* 1984. 2nd edition. London: Routledge, 1993.

Longino, Helen. *The Fate of Knowledge.* Princeton: Princeton University Press, 2002.

———. *Science as Social Knowledge.* Princeton: Princeton University Press, 1990.

Lovibond, Sabina. "The End of Morality?" In Lennon and Whitford, *Knowing the Difference.*

———. "Feminism and Postmodernism." *New Left Review* 178 (Nov.–Dec. 1989): 5–28.

———. *Realism and Imagination in Ethics.* Minneapolis: University of Minnesota Press, 1986.

Lugones, María C. "On the Logic of Pluralist Feminism." In *Feminist Ethics,* edited by Claudia Card. Lawrence: University Press of Kansas, 1991.

———. "Playfulness, 'World'-Traveling, and Loving Perception." *Hypatia: A Journal of Feminist Philosophy* 2.2 (1987): 3–21.

Maffie, James. "Recent Work on Naturalized Epistemology." *American Philosophical Quarterly* 27.4 (1990): 281–93.

———. "Towards an Anthropology of Epistemology." *Philosophical Forum* 26.3 (1995): 218–41.

———. "What Is Social about Social Epistemics?" *Social Epistemology* 5.2 (1991): 101–10.

Malterud, Kirsti. "The Art and Science of Clinical Knowledge: Evidence beyond Measures and Numbers." *Lancet* 358 (2001): 397–400.

———. "The Legitimacy of Clinical Knowledge: Towards a Medical Epistemology Embracing the Art of Medicine." *Theoretical Medicine* 16 (1995): 183–98.

———. "Strategies for Empowering Women's Voices in the Medical Culture. *Health Care for Women International* 14 (1993): 365–73.

———. "Symptoms as a Source of Medical Knowledge: Understanding Medically Unexplained Disorders in Women." *Family Medicine* 32 (2000): 417–25.

———. "Women's Undefined Disorders: A Challenge for Clinical Communication." *Family Practice* 9 (1992): 299–303.

Malterud, Kirsti, Lucy Candib, and Lorraine Code. "Responsible and Responsive Knowing in Medical Diagnosis: The Medical Gaze Revisited." *NORA: Nordic Journal of Women's Studies* 1.12 (2004): 8–19.

Malterud, Kirsti, and Hanne Hollnagel. "The Magic Influence of Classification Systems in Clinical Practice." *Scandinavian Journal of Primary Health Care* 15 (1997): 5–6.

Marecek, Joanne. "Psychology and Feminism: Can This Relationship Be Saved?" In *Feminisms in the Academy,* edited by Domna C. Stanton and Abigail Stewart. Ann Arbor: University of Michigan Press, 1995.

Markman, Ellen. "Natural Kinds." In Kornblith, *Naturalizing Epistemology.*

Marks, Elaine, and Isabelle de Courtivron, eds. *New French Feminisms.* Amherst: University of Massachusetts Press, 1980.

Mathews, Freya. "Deep Ecology." In Jamieson, *A Companion to Environmental Philosophy.*

Mathews, Freya. "Ecofeminism and Deep Ecology." In Merchant, *Ecology.*

May, William. "On Ethics and Advocacy." *Journal of the American Medical Association* 256.13 (1986): 1786–87.

Mendus, Susan. "'What of Soul Was Left, I Wonder': The Narrative Self in Political Philosophy." In *Literature and the Political Imagination*, edited by John Horton and Andrea Baumeister. New York: Routledge, 1996.

Merchant, Carolyn, ed. *Ecology*. Atlantic Highlands, NJ: Humanities Press, 1994.

———. *The Death of Nature: Women, Ecology, and the Scientific Revolution*. New York: Harper & Row, 1980.

Messing, Karen. "Don't Use a Wrench to Peel Potatoes: Biological Science Constructed on Male Model Systems Is a Risk to Women Workers' Health." In Burt and Code, *Changing Methods*.

———. *One-Eyed Science: Occupational Health and Women Workers*. Philadelphia: Temple University Press, 1998.

Meyers, Diana Tietjens. "Emotion and Heterodox Moral Perception: An Essay in Moral Social Psychology." In Meyers, *Feminists Rethink the Self*.

———, ed. *Feminists Rethink the Self*. Boulder, CO: Westview, 1997.

Mill, John Stuart. *On the Subjection of Women*. 1869. In John Stuart Mill and Harriet Taylor Mill. *Essays on Sex Equality*. Edited by Alice Rossi. Chicago: University of Chicago Press, 1970.

Miller, J. Hillis. *On Literature*. London: Routledge, 2002.

Miller, Patricia H., and Ellin K. Scholnick, eds. *Toward a Feminist Developmental Psychology*. New York: Routledge, 2000.

Mills, Charles. *The Racial Contract*. Ithaca: Cornell University Press, 1998.

Minow, Martha. *Making All the Difference; Inclusion, Exclusion, and the American Law*. Ithaca: Cornell University Press, 1990.

Monk, Ray. *Ludwig Wittgenstein: The Duty of Genius*. London: Jonathan Cape, 1990.

Morrison, Toni. *Beloved*. New York: Knopf, 1988.

———, ed. *Race-ing Justice, En-Gendering Power: Essays on Anita Hill, Clarence Thomas, and the Construction of Social Reality*. New York: Pantheon, 1992.

Naess, Arne. "The Deep Ecological Movement: Some Philosophical Aspects." *Philosophical Inquiry* 8 (1986): 10–31.

Nagel, Thomas. *Mortal Questions*. Cambridge: Cambridge University Press, 1979.

Nathan, David G., and David J. Weatherall. "Academic Freedom in Clinical Research." *New England Journal of Medicine* 347.17 (2002): 1368–70.

Nelson, Katherine, Sarah Henseler, and Daniela Plesa. "Entering a Community of Minds: 'Theory of Mind' from a Feminist Standpoint." In Miller and Scholnick, *Towards a Feminist Developmental Psychology*.

Nelson, Lynn Hankinson. "Epistemological Communities." In Alcoff and Potter, *Feminist Epistemologies*.

———. "A Feminist Naturalized Philosophy of Science." *Synthese* 104.3 (1995): 399–421.

———. *Who Knows: From Quine to a Feminist Empiricism*. Philadelphia: Temple University Press, 1990.

Nelson, Lynn Hankinson, and Jack Nelson, eds. *Feminism, Science, and the Philosophy of Science*. Dordrecht: Reidel, 1996.

————, eds. *Feminist Interpretations of W. V. O. Quine*. University Park: Penn State University Press, 2003.

Nolen, Stephanie. "Safe-Sex Theatre a Tough Sell." *Toronto Globe and Mail*, 11 November 2003, A22

Novick, Peter. *That Noble Dream: The "Objectivity Question" and the American Historical Profession*. Cambridge: Cambridge University Press, 1988.

Nozick, Robert. *Anarchy, State, and Utopia*. New York: Basic Books, 1974.

Nye, Andrea. "Saying What It Is: Predicate Logic and Natural Kinds." In *Representing Reason: Feminist Theory and Formal Logic*, edited by Rachel Joffe Falmagne and Marjorie Hass. Lanham, MD: Rowman & Littlefield, 2002.

O'Connor, Peg. "Moving to New Boroughs: Transforming the World by Inventing Language Games." In Scheman and O'Connor, *Feminist Interpretations of Ludwig Wittgenstein*.

O'Hara, Jane. "Whistle-Blower." *Maclean's*, 16 November 1998.

Olivieri, Nancy. "Scientific Inquiry: The Fight's Just Starting." *Toronto Globe and Mail*, 31 October 2001, A17.

————. "When Money and Truth Collide." In Turk, *The Corporate Campus*.

Olivieri, Nancy, Gary M. Brittenham, Christine E. McLaren, Douglas M. Templeton, Ross G. Cameron, Robert A. McClelland, Alastair D. Burt, and Kenneth A. Fleming. "Long-Term Safety and Effectiveness of Iron-Chelation Therapy with Deferiprone for Thalassemia Major." *New England Journal of Medicine* 339.7 (1998): 417–23.

O'Neill, Onora. "Paternalism and Partial Autonomy." *Journal of Medical Ethics* 10 (1984): 173–78.

Papp, Leslie. "Firm Axes Outspoken Scientist's Research: Woman Went Public with Concerns about Drug's Safety." *Toronto Star*, 26 January 1997, A2.

Pearson, Keith Ansell. "Viroid Life: On Machines, Technics, and Evolution." In *Deleuze and Philosophy: The Difference Engineer*, edited by Keith Ansell Pearson. London: Routledge, 1997.

Peters, R. S., ed. *The Concept of Education*. London: Routledge & Kegan Paul, 1973.

Piaget, Jean. *Insights and Illusions of Philosophy*. Translated by Wolfe Mays. New York: Meridian, 1971.

————. *The Language and Thought of the Child*. Translated by Marjorie Warden. London: Routledge & Kegan Paul, 1926.

Plant, Judith, ed. *Healing the Wounds: The Promise of Ecofeminism*. Philadelphia: New Society, 1989.

Plumwood, Val. *Feminism and the Mastery of Nature*. London: Routledge, 1993.

Poovey, Mary. *A History of the Modern Fact: Problems of Knowledge in the Sciences of Wealth and Society*. Chicago: University of Chicago Press, 1998.

Potter, Elizabeth. *Gender and Boyle's Law of Gases*. Bloomington: Indiana University Press, 2001.

————. "Gender and Epistemic Negotiation." In Alcoff and Potter, *Feminist Epistemologies*.

Preston, Christopher J. *Grounding Knowledge: Environmental Philosophy, Epistemology, and Place.* Athens: University of Georgia Press, 2003.

Price, H. H. *Perception.* London: Methuen, 1933.

Priest, Lisa. "Sick Kids Doctor Finds Anemia Drug." *Toronto Star,* 14 January 1993, A3.

Quine, W. V. O. "Natural Kinds." In Kornblith, *Naturalizing Epistemology.*

———. *Ontological Relativity and Other Essays.* New York: Columbia University Press, 1969.

Rabinow, Paul, and William M. Sullivan, eds. *Interpretive Social Science: A Second Look.* Berkeley: University of California Press, 1987.

Raglon, Rebecca. "Rachel Carson and Her Legacy." In *Natural Eloquence: Women Reinscribe Science,* edited by Barbara T. Gates and Ann B. Shteir. Madison: University of Wisconsin Press, 1997.

Rawls, John. *A Theory of Justice.* Cambridge: Harvard University Press, 1971.

Ricoeur, Paul. "Self as *Ipse.*" In Johnson, *Freedom and Interpretation.*

Rorty, Richard. *Contingency, Irony, and Solidarity.* Cambridge: Cambridge University Press, 1989.

Rosenberg, Leo T. "Delaying Approval of a Critical Drug." *Journal of Medical Humanities* 15.4 (1994): 243–50.

Ross, Thomas. *Just Stories: How the Law Embodies Racism and Bias.* Boston: Beacon, 1996.

Rouse, Joseph. "Barad's Feminist Naturalism." *Hypatia: A Journal of Feminist Philosophy* 19.4 (2004): 142–61.

———. *Reconstructing Philosophy of Science: How to Understand Its Practices Philosophically.* Ithaca: Cornell University Press, 1996.

Russell, Bertrand. *The Problems of Philosophy.* Oxford: Oxford University Press, 1912.

Sandilands, Catriona. "Environmental Science." In *Encyclopedia of Feminist Theories,* edited by Lorraine Code. London: Routledge, 2000.

———. "From Natural Identity to Radical Democracy." *Environmental Ethics* (Spring 1995): 75–91.

Sayers, Janet. *Biological Politics.* London: Tavistock, 1982.

Scarry, Elaine. *The Body in Pain: The Making and Unmaking of the World.* Oxford: Oxford University Press, 1985.

Scheman, Naomi. "Epistemology Resuscitated: Objectivity as Trustworthiness." In Tuana and Morgen, *Engendering Rationalities.*

Scheman, Naomi, and Peg O'Connor, eds. *Feminist Interpretations of Ludwig Wittgenstein.* University Park: University of Pennsylvania Press, 2002.

Scheppele, Kim Lane. "Just the Facts Ma'am: Sexualized Violence, Evidentiary Habits, and the Revision of Truth." *New York Law School Law Review* 37.1–2 (1992): 123–72.

Schiebinger, Londa. "Feminist History of Colonial Science." *Hypatia: A Journal of Feminist Philosophy* 19.1 (2004): 233–54.

———. *Has Feminism Changed Science?* Cambridge: Harvard University Press, 1999.

Schmitt, Richard. *Beyond Separateness: The Social Nature of Human Beings—Their Autonomy, Knowledge, and Power.* Boulder, CO: Westview, 1995.

Scott, Joan Wallach. *Gender and the Politics of History.* New York: Columbia University Press, 1988.

Sellars, Wilfrid. "Does Empirical Knowledge Have a Foundation?" In *Empirical Knowledge,* edited by R. M. Chisholm and R. J. Schwarz. Englewood Cliffs, NJ: Prentice Hall, 1973.

Seller, Anne. "Realism versus Relativism: Towards a Politically Adequate Epistemology." In Griffiths and Whitford, *Feminist Perspectives in Philosophy.*

Shafer, Arthur. "Science Wars: Olivieri under Media Folly." *Toronto Star,* 10 April 2000.

Shapin, Steven. *A Social History of Truth: Civility and Science in Seventeenth-Century England.* Chicago: University of Chicago Press, 1994.

Shapiro, Barbara J. *A Culture of Fact: England, 1550–1720.* Ithaca: Cornell University Press, 2000.

Sherwin, Susan. *No Longer Patient: Feminist Ethics and Health Care.* Philadelphia: Temple University Press, 1992.

Shiva, Vandana. "Biotechnological Development and the Conservation of Biodiversity." In Shiva and Moser, *Biopolitics.*

———. *Staying Alive: Women, Ecology, and Development.* London: Zed, 1989.

———. *Tomorrow's Biodiversity.* New York: Thames & Hudson, 2000.

Shiva, Vandana, and Ingunn Moser, eds. *Biopolitics: A Feminist and Ecological Reader on Biotechnology.* London: Zed, 1995.

Shrader-Frechette, Kristin. "Ecology." In Jamieson, *A Companion to Environmental Philosophy.*

———. *Environmental Justice: Creating Equality, Reclaiming Democracy.* New York: Oxford University Press, 2002.

Shrader-Frechette, Kristin, and E. D. McCoy. *Method in Ecology: Strategies for Conservation.* Cambridge: Cambridge University Press, 1993.

Shuchman, Miriam. *The Drug Trial: Nancy Olivieri and the Scandal That Rocked the Hospital for Sick Children.* Toronto: Random House Canada, 2005.

Slovo, Gillian. *Red Dust.* London: Virago, 2000.

Smart, Carol. *Feminism and the Power of Law.* London: Routledge, 1989.

Solomon, Miriam. "Social Empiricism." *Nous* 28 (1994): 325–43.

Sommers, Christina Hoff. *Who Stole Feminism?* New York: Simon & Schuster, 1994.

Sorell, Tom. *Scientism: Philosophy and the Infatuation with Science.* London: Routledge, 1991.

Stanley, Liz, and Sue Wise. *Breaking Out: Feminist Consciousness and Feminist Research.* London: Routledge & Kegan Paul, 1988.

Stich, Steven. "Could Man Be an Irrational Animal? Some Notes on the Epistemology of Rationality." In Kornblith, *Naturalizing Epistemology.*

Strong, David. "Disclosive Discourse, Ecology, and Technology." *Environmental Ethics* 16 (Spring 1994): 89–102.

Stump, David. "Naturalized Philosophy of Science with a Plurality of Methods." *Philosophy of Science* 59 (1992): 456–60.

Sturgeon, Noël. *Ecofeminist Natures: Race, Gender, Feminist Theory, and Political Action.* New York: Routledge, 1997.

Tanesini, Alexandra. *An Introduction to Feminist Epistemologies.* Oxford: Blackwell, 1999.

Theis, Charlotte. "Ethical Issues: A Nursing Perspective." *New England Journal of Medicine* 315.19 (1986): 1222–24.

Thompson, John, Patricia Baird, and Jocelyn Downie. *The Olivieri Report: The Complete Text of the Independent Inquiry Commissioned by the Canadian Association of University Teachers.* Toronto: Lorimer, 2001.

Tiles, Mary, and Jim Tiles. *Introduction to Historical Epistemology: The Authority of Knowledge.* Oxford: Blackwell, 1993.

Trinh, T. Minh-ha. *Woman, Native, Other: Writing Postcoloniality and Feminism.* Bloomington: Indiana University Press, 1989.

Tuana, Nancy, and Sandra S. Morgen, eds. *Engendering Rationalities.* Albany: SUNY Press, 2001.

Turk, James L., ed. *The Corporate Campus: Commercialization and the Dangers to Canada's Colleges and Universities.* Toronto: Lorimer, 2000.

Unger, Peter. *Ignorance: A Case for Scepticism.* Oxford: Clarendon, 1975.

Urwin, Cathy. "Power Relations and the Emergence of Language." In Henriques et al., *Changing the Subject.*

Valpy, Michael. "Salvage Group Tackles Sick Kids' Image Disaster." *Toronto Globe and Mail,* 2 November 1998, A1, A9.

———. "Science Friction." *Elm Street* 3.3 (1998): 28.

Venn, Couze. "The Subject of Psychology." In Henriques et al., *Changing the Subject.*

Vygotsky, L. S. *Mind in Society.* Cambridge: Harvard University Press, 1978.

———. *Thought and Language.* Cambridge: MIT Press, 1962.

Walker, Margaret. *Moral Contexts.* Lanham, MD: Rowman & Littlefield, 2003.

———. *Moral Understandings: A Feminist Study of Ethics.* New York: Routledge, 1998.

Walkerdine, Valerie. "Developmental Psychology and Child-Centred Pedagogy: The Insertion of Piaget into Early Education." In Henriques et al., *Changing the Subject.*

———. *The Mastery of Reason: Cognitive Development and the Production of Rationality.* London: Routledge, 1988.

Warren, Karen. *Ecofeminist Philosophy: A Western Perspective on What It Is and Why It Matters.* New York: Rowman & Littlefield, 2000.

———, ed. *Ecological Feminism.* Special issue of *Hypatia: A Journal of Feminist Philosophy* 6.1 (1991).

Warren, Virginia. "Feminist Directions in Medical Ethics." In *Feminist Perspectives in Medical Ethics,* edited by Helen Bequaert Holmes and Laura M. Purdy. Bloomington: Indiana University Press, 1992.

Weisstein, Naomi. "Psychology Constructs the Female." In *Woman in Sexist Society*, edited by Vivian Gornick and Barbara K. Moran. New York: Basic Books, 1971.

Welch-Ross, Melissa K. "A Feminist Perspective on the Development of Self-Knowledge." In Miller and Scholnick, *Toward a Feminist Developmental Psychology*.

Wendell, Susan. *The Rejected Body: Feminist Philosophical Reflections on Disability*. New York: Routledge, 1996.

West, Cornel. *Race Matters*. New York: Vintage, 1994.

Willett, Cynthia. *Maternal Ethics and Other Slave Moralities*. New York: Routledge, 1995.

Williams, Patricia J. *The Alchemy of Race and Rights: Diary of a Law Professor*. Cambridge: Harvard University Press, 1991.

———. *The Rooster's Egg: On the Persistence of Prejudice*. Cambridge: Harvard University Press, 1995.

———. *Seeing a Color-Blind Future: The Paradox of Race*. New York: Noonday, 1997.

Williams, Raymond. *Keywords: A Vocabulary of Culture and Society*. 2nd edition. London: HarperCollins, 1983.

Wittgenstein, Ludwig. *On Certainty*. Edited by G. E. M. Anscombe and G. H. von Wright. Translated by Denis Paul and G. E. M. Anscombe. Oxford: Blackwell, 1968.

———. *Philosophical Investigations*. Translated by G. E. M. Anscombe. Oxford: Blackwell, 1968.

Wong, James. "Adventures in Socio-Historical Meta-Epistemology: The Idea of the Normal Child." *Explorations in Knowledge* 14 (1996): 1–24.

Wylie, Alison. "The Reaction against Analogy." *Advances in Archaeological Method and Theory* 8 (1985): 63–111.

Zimmerman, Michael. *Contesting Earth's Future: Radical Ecology and Postmodernity*. Berkeley: University of California Press, 1994.

Index

domination, 15
  in the name of mastery, 197
  See also mastery
Duran, Jane, 74
Dutch elm disease, 46, 48

Eckersley, Robin, 273n.77
ecofeminism, 14n.17, 16–18, 281
  (*see also* feminism and politics of
    ecology)
ecological naturalism, 22, 67–69, 88–89,
    90–94, 125–28, 282–83
  and responsibilities, 100
  ecological naturalism, 22, 67–69,
    88–89, 90–94, 125–28, 282–83
  and responsibilities, 100
  (*see also* epistemic responsibility)
ecological science, 89
ecological subject, 5, 128
  embodied, situated, and
    interdependent, 91
ecological thinking, 3, 7–9, 279–81
  in Carson, 36–48
  causality in, 87
  contrasted with laboratory empiricism,
    41–42
  as counterstrategy to imaginaries of
    mastery, 13, 20–21, 29, 32, 33–34,
    50–51
  Deleuze and, 28
  and epistemic responsibility, 62
  ethico-political potential of, 197
  and feminism, 13–19
  imagination in, 215
  and judicial notice, 111–12
  and knowing other people, 61
  methodological pluralism in, 199, 285
  negotiation in, 281
  and occupational health, 55
  and politics of advocacy, 196–200
  and presumptions of trustworthiness,
    258
  primacy of content in, 102
  and principles of ideal cohabitation,
    19, 24, 28
  productive tension with discourses of
    autonomy and individualism, 38

reconciling advocacy and autonomy,
    170–71
  and strong objectivity, 61–62
  wary of holism, 67
ecology, 25–26, 89, 284–85
  deep, 281
  and environmental movements, 66
  equivocal scientific status of, 64, 65
  "hard" vs. "soft," 42
  of incredulity, 226
  instability of, 7
  instituting imaginary of, 285
  language of, 4
  language of, as epistemic tool, vi–vii
    (*see also* ecological thinking)
  literal and metaphoric, 51
  and multiculturalism, 16
  politics of, and feminism, 13–21
    (*see also* ecofeminism)
  social, and colonialism, 16
  and theoretical pluralism, 65
  as a "weak" science, 22–23
ecology movement, transformative
    possibilities of, 125
economic man, rational, 169
ecosystems, nature of, 6
Edge of the Sea, the (Carson), 36–37
efficiency and profit, 53
electricity, 34–35
El Saadawi, Nawal, 235
embodiment
  epistemic, 131
  See also body
empathy, 48, 220
  imaginative, 231
  liberal assumptions in, 221
  as non-prototypical knowing, 230–31
  with victims, 230
  and "world-traveling," 232–33
empiricism
  feminist critical, 98
  negotiated, 23, 108, 111, 119, 144
  negotiating, 100
energy
  alternative sources of, 35
  production of, and imaginary of
    mastery, 34

responsibility
  advocacy as antithetical to, 175–76
  in citizenship, 200, 237
  in cohabitation, 156, 170
  epistemic (*see* epistemic responsibility)
  in epistemic practice, 194
  in imagining, 206–207
  in inquiry, 160
  of knowers, 210–11
  moral and epistemic, professional, 249
  and reciprocity, 212
"retreat into autobiography," 190–91
rhetoric
  and advocacy, 174, 175–76
  of mastery, 35
  of romanticized nature, 4
  of "the natural," 77
  trope of insular laboratory, 246
rhetorical spaces, 8
Ricoeur, Paul, 204n.6, 211–12, 215, 234
rights
  discourse of, 202–204, 204nn.5–6
  literature privileging, 212
Rorty, Richard, 6, 235, 236
Rouse, Joseph, 273, 274
Rousseau, Jean-Jacques, 136
Rushton, Philippe, 83, 150n.51
Russell, Bertrand, 145

sameness, *see* difference; similarity
same-sex parents, 152
Sandilands, Catriona, 20, 38
sapere aude, 167. 180, 183, 195
Sartre, Jean-Paul, Kruks's analysis of, 121–22, 122n.53, 124–25
Scarry, Elaine, 186, 190, 192
Schiebinger, Londa, 259–260, 260n.51
Schuchman, Miriam, 244, 247
science
  "normal," 63, 189, 242
  orthodox, 43
  positivist-empiricist, 68
"science has proved..." knowledge claims, 244, 246, 248
scientificity, 57
  Carson and, 63
  See also scientism

scientism, 8, 116, 143, 171–72
  of the analytic imaginary, 86n.73
  in developmental psychology, 144
  in naturalism, 86
  in Quinean naturalism, 141–42
  reductive, 72
secrecy, in laboratory science, 246
  See also mystification, medical
self
  as disembodied fictive creature, 203
  humanistic, rights-bearing, 201
  knowledge of another, 205–206
    (*see also* knowledge: of other persons)
  as property, 202
    (*see also* self-ownership)
  as standardized epistemic subject, 207–208
  western, 166
"Self as *Ipse*" (Ricoeur), 204n.6, 211–12
self-mastery, 166
self-or-subjectivity dyad, 202, 204
self-ownership, 166
  liberal legal assumption of, 230
  See also self: as property
Seller, Anne, 174, 187
sense-data, women's, trust in, 190
sensorimotor activity, knowledge grounded in, 131
sex-gender system, in scientific research and practice, 239
sexual abuse, history of, and undefined disorders, 114
sexual assault
  survivors of, and credibility of testimony, 284
  trials, 107, 108–109
sexual consent, 230
sexualizing of imagery, in Olivieri affair, 258
sexual violence, everydayness of, 225–26
sex workers, Mozambique, 222n.51
Shapin, Steven, 265, 269, 274
Shapiro, Barbara J., 269n.67
Sherwin, Susan, 275
Shiva, Vandana, 10, 11, 47, 60

symptoms, medical
  credibility of, 185–86
  as evidence, 112–115
  of pain, 188–89
  reports of, discredited as truth
    manipulation, 174n.25
  testimony about, 54–55
syndrome X, 113, 188, 189n.56, 193,
    194, 281

taxonomy not an end in itself, 50
technology, transformation of, 282n.5
testimony, 23, 172–74
  about medical symptoms, 112, 174n.25
  at core of advocacy, 175
  in ecological science, 43
  epistemic respectability of, in
    perception and memory, 172–73
  in Carson's work, 43, 52
  in Messing's occupational health
    studies, 58–59
  situated, 172
  as source of evidence, 51–52
text, and context, 5
thalassemia major (Mediterranean
    anemia), 241
"theory theory," 142, 157
thinkable, the, 223, 224
three bears story, 146–47, 155–56, 178
torture, 227, 229–30
  boundary-shattering, 232
  and empathy, 220
toxicity-producing practices, 194
toxic solvents, 84
train cleaners, and gender differences, 54
transfer payments, 182
  See also social welfare
transparency, and public trust, 246
trust, v
  and ad hominem/feminam arguments,
    267–268
  and advocacy, 190–196
  and credibility, in scientific research,
    264
  epistemic equivocality of, 268–69
  and healthy skepticism, vii
  in medicine, 191–92, 267–68

politics of, 190
presumption of, 191
public, 24, 237, 246, 265
relations of, among producers of
    knowledge, 239
required in advocacy, 176
trustworthiness, gendered, 257
truth
  and money, collision of, 239
  as "truth to," 7
  and virtue, separation of, 69n.22
  (see also epistemic responsibility)

"Unbearable Autonomy of Being, the"
    (Williams), 181
"undefined disorders," 112–16
unity-of-knowledge/unity-of-science
    assumption, 17
  in standard theories of knowledge,
    68
"unnatural lottery," 182, 200
Unnatural Lottery, the (Card), 168
Urwin, Cathy, 139, 147, 155, 156

validity, external vs. internal, 90n.80
values vs. facts, 177
Venn, Couze, 81
victimization, and undefined disorders,
    114
Vienna Circle, 269
"view from nowhere," 118, 119, 133,
    172n.19
  in developmental psychology, 159
  See also "god-trick"
virtue and truth, separation of, 69n.22
  see also epistemic responsibility
vision, in Haraway, 118–20
voluntarism, epistemic-doxastic, vi
vulnerability, 224, 231
Vygotsky, L. S., 131, 137

Walker, Margaret, 169, 173–74
Walkerdine, Valerie, 23, 129, 133, 137
  critiques Piagetian theory, 139–40
  on invented "natural" childhood,
    149–50
  on natural child, 141

Made in the USA
Columbia, SC
24 February 2018